I0818992

Further Praise for *The Almighty Dollar*

"The history of the dollar is longer and more interesting than people realize. Brendan Greeley, in *The Almighty Dollar,* provides the ideal guide to understanding the world's most important currency."

—TYLER COWEN,
New York Times bestselling author of
The Great Stagnation and *Average Is Over*

"Despite being a brilliant and surprisingly fun read, in writing a history of the dollar Greeley inadvertently gives us a new history of money. His key insight is that money is not some kind of magical barter-replacement device or a ring of confidence. Rather, it's a product. If it's a good and useful one, people use it. When it stops being that, they shift. Seen this way, the history and the future of the dollar stand far less assured than many assume."

—MARK BLYTH,
author of *Inflation: A Guide for Users and Losers*

"Greeley's splendid quest, from Saxon mines to stable coins, makes an epic story vividly accessible. Brimming with startling details, this is also serious financial history with a conclusion ripe for our unsettled times: Rulers and borders come and go, but the dollar has outlasted our illusions of sovereignty and control."

—EVAN OSNOS,
New York Times bestselling author of
The Haves and Have-Yachts

"Brendan Greeley's *The Almighty Dollar* is a grand tour-de-force about the origins and longevity of our monetary system. Come for the sweeping—and accessible—history of the dollar and the faith people have put in it. Stay for the delightful cameos from the Saxon miners searching for Joachimsthaler, Maryland bills of credit, Hawarden scrip, and Andrew Brimmer's quest to get the Federal Reserve to allocate credit."

—WILLIAM D. COHAN,
New York Times bestselling author of
Power Failure and *The Last Tycoons*

"For more than a century, the dollar and the United States have seemed inseparable. Now, with almost uncanny timing, comes Brendan Greeley's book to show that the dollar's dominance long predates that of the United States and may well outlive it. From Saxons investing in Bohemian silver in the 1510s to the Midland Bank of Manchester inventing the eurodollar in the 1950s, by way of Toledo (Spain), China,

New Orleans, and Iowa, Greeley insists both on the varied ways in which dollars (be they coins, bills, or electronic signals) have been made and the investments that gave them meaning and value. This is a reporter's book of detailed, engaging stories and a historian's book—telling a tale that is stranger, longer, and richer with significance than any economist's fable."

—REBECCA SPANG,
author of *Stuff and Money in the Time of the French Revolution*

"This is a mesmerizing and fascinating book, breathtakingly researched and spectacularly written, that connects the big story of the dollar—and indeed of other currencies—to the actual experiences of very ordinary people whose lives are transformed, and often wrecked, by money."

—HAROLD JAMES,
author of *Seven Crashes* and *The End of Globalization*

"*The Almighty Dollar* asks us to rethink our fundamental assumptions about how money works. With curiosity, good humor, and a keen eye for human stories, Greeley guides us from centuries-old silver mines to the ongoing machinations of the Federal Reserve Board. Myths about economic sovereignty and objective monetary policy give way to a clear-eyed understanding of a global dollar that has always benefited some at the expense of others. Greeley's expertise as both historian and financial journalist makes this a captivating and insightful read."

—SETH ROCKMAN,
author of *Plantation Goods: A Material History of American Slavery*

"There has never been a better time to understand the U.S. dollar, its strengths, its weaknesses, its history, and, more important, its profound role in not just American but global finance. Brendan Greeley has done us all a service with this terrific, erudite, breathtaking story of the Almighty U.S. Dollar, which, I now know thanks to his scholarship, came well before the United States itself! Whizzing from Bohemia of the Middle Ages right up to today's multitrillion-dollar eurodollar market, Greeley weaves a fascinating narrative, populated by extraordinary innovators, leading us to a revolutionary conclusion that challenges many of the assumptions monetary economists make about how the modern monetary economy actually works. For insiders and interested laymen, *The Almighty Dollar* is a must for anyone who wants to understand the dollar in today's world."

—DAVID McWILLIAMS,
#1 international bestselling author of *The History of Money: A Story of Humanity*

The Almighty Dollar

The Almighty Dollar

500 YEARS OF THE WORLD'S MOST POWERFUL MONEY

Brendan Greeley

CROWN
CURRENCY
New York

CROWN CURRENCY
An imprint of the Crown Publishing Group
A division of Penguin Random House LLC
1745 Broadway
New York, NY 10019
crownpublishing.com
penguinrandomhouse.com

Illustrations courtesy of Evan Applegate

Dollar paper background on pages iii, 1, and 153: Shutterstock / Ruslan Lytvyn

Library of Congress Cataloging-in-Publication Data is on file with the publisher.

ISBN 978-0-593-13888-5
Ebook ISBN 978-0-593-13889-2

Editor: Kevin Doughten
Editorial assistant: Jessica Jean Scott
Production editors: Christine Tanigawa and Craig Adams
Text designer: Aubrey Khan
Production: Christopher Andrus
Proofreaders: Chris Jerome, Deborah Bader, Chuck Thompson, Pam Rehm
Indexer: J S Editorial, LLC
Publicist: Gwyneth Stansfield
Marketer: Mason Eng

Manufactured in the United States of America

1st Printing

First Edition

The authorized representative in the EU for product safety and compliance is Penguin Random House Ireland, Morrison Chambers, 32 Nassau Street, Dublin D02 YH68, Ireland, https://eu-contact.penguin.ie.

FOR

Clyde, Delphia, Luke, Phebe

AND ESPECIALLY

for Beth

GONZALO

When every grief is entertain'd that's offer'd,
Comes to the entertainer—

SEBASTIAN

A dollar.

GONZALO

Dolour comes to him, indeed: you
have spoken truer than you purposed.

—William Shakespeare, *The Tempest,*
written more than 160 years before
the founding of the United States

Contents

Part I

The Silver Dollar

Introduction

THE UNITED STATES DID NOT INVENT THE DOLLAR

Robert Henwood probably died an unspectacular death. His name appeared in a brief notice in the *Maryland Gazette* on November 25, 1773. Anne Catharine Green, the *Gazette*'s publisher, liked to share lurid details when she could—killed by lightning, capsized in the Chesapeake Bay, murdered by a servant, a Christmas Eve gunshot from a drunken son. But when Robert Henwood died, Green wrote only that he had left behind a wife and five young children.

He didn't leave much else. Henwood had worked as a carpenter in Anne Arundel County, near the province's capital of Annapolis. His most valuable possessions were his two beds: one with two pillows, one with a bedstead. We know this from a probate record filed with the province, a list of all the stuff that was left to count when the head of a household died. Henwood had his beds and not much else: a bag of tools, a tin sugar box, four chamber pots, four teaspoons.

The record also lists Henwood's rights and credits: money he was owed and money he owed. He died with debts to the county sheriff and to Wallace, Davidson & Johnson, a partnership that imported manufactured goods from London. And at the top of the record is a note from John Campbell and Francis Fairbrother, the two men who appraised Henwood's estate. They signed the record on February 25, 1774, and wrote that they had completed their work in a currency they called "dollars at 6/ shilling Each."

In dollars.

I have developed an affection for Robert Henwood. I grew up in Annapolis, and I'm raising a family not far from where Henwood raised his. But there's nothing remarkable about his life. He was a tradesman in a colonial American port city. When he died, though, the two men who summed up all his worldly goods left behind one small clue in a much bigger story: The dollar is both older and more powerful than the United States. The dollar came first.

Histories of the dollar tend to start in America's colonial era, moving quickly through the American Revolution to the story of a new country and its new currency. These histories explain that there was a coin in circulation in the colonies called the Spanish milled dollar, with a name that came from the German, *Taler.* That's all true, but it's a description, not an explanation. Why was Spanish silver in a British province? Why did British colonists call a Spanish coin by its German name? The answers to those questions led to this book. What came before the American Revolution is just as important as what's come since. The biography of the dollar is not the biography of America. The dollar has its own story.

As a young, weak country, America adopted the dollar because it had no choice. Silver dollars were already the dominant form of money for international trade, and foreign silver dollars were current in America and even recognized by the federal government as money until the 1850s. We can't even begin to talk about a single currency—the U.S. bank dollar—until after the dislocations of massive new gold finds in California and then the Civil War. At its birth, the United States was not sovereign over its own money. America did not invent the dollar.

Before I started this book, I was a journalist, covering the Federal Reserve for *Bloomberg Businessweek* and the *Financial Times.* In the United States, the banks of the Federal Reserve System are responsible for making sure that dollars work—for you and me, for little community banks and big Wall Street banks, and, though the Fed doesn't like to talk about it, for banks and investors abroad. It was my job to understand what money was in America. I was a dollar correspondent.

When you work in a newsroom, you are taught to loathe theory. Your job as a journalist is to find facts and then confirm them with more facts. Emails to an editor will often come back with the reply "Interesting if true." This is a good approach, and it's one of the reasons I love newsrooms. Whether we know it or not, though, we all look at the world through theories. You do not run a test every night to make sure your socks will fall in the hamper when you drop them. You have a theory that they will fall, and they do.

To cover the Federal Reserve, I spent a lot of time talking to macroeconomists, who make predictions by plugging data into models. Those models seem like machines, but they rest on theories. I learned how to speak economist, which meant that I started to accept the explanatory power of those theories on money the same way I accept the explanatory power of gravity on socks. I started this book to answer a question: Why do dollars sit somewhere at the bottom of almost every financial transaction in the world, even as I type today, in the chaotic late summer of 2025? How did America's money become so powerful? At first I used the tools of a Fed reporter: theories about money I had learned from macroeconomists.

They are not great theories. "Wrong" is a hurtful word, but what economists had taught me about money couldn't explain why two appraisers in colonial Maryland thought in dollars before the American Revolution. And so I realized with some despair that to tell a useful story about the dollar, I would have to find simple ways to talk about theories of money.

The absolute intellectual dominance of economists in public life means that we all at one point learned the same basic story. Money started as a commodity, an object like a hunk of metal or a special shell. It was easier to trade than a cow. It had value because it was rare. A piece of paper came to represent the metal. Then the metal went away and the paper still had value. Now money is a social convention we call *fiat,* Latin for "let it be done." The state decrees money, and it exists. If this is still your preferred history, you're likely to think that money is inherently commercial and private, and that politicians need to be restrained; they will always be tempted to manufacture too much fiat money, and destroy it through inflation. Historians sometimes call this the metallist story of money. It starts with gold and silver.

In the decade since the global financial crisis, we've seen a reanimation of other theories as well. Anthropologists, sociologists, and historians now tend to argue that money started as credit, a record of something one person owed another. It could be recorded on a clay tablet, or as a notch on a stick, or just as a verbal commitment. In this history, money is inherently social and political, and has become a creature of the state and its laws. It was *always* fiat, from the very beginning. Historians think of this broadly as the chartalist story of money; *charta* is Latin for "ticket," a token the government spends on wars and bread, then collects back again as taxes.

Origin stories are almost always instructions for the present. If money began as a hard commodity, then that's what it should be again, and humans will need to adjust. If money began as a handshake agreement, then we should again approach it with more flexibility, bending money around human needs. I find the argument between metallists and chartalists frustrating. It's unwinnable. In almost any historical market, anywhere, you can find several different kinds of money working together, and evidence of both long-standing commercial habits *and* government interventions, of hard pieces of metal *and* agreements on credit. So let me start with a proposition: *There is no one true essence of money*. There is no point to claiming, as some people do, that a coin is just a special kind of credit. Or that credit is just a record of a coin owed in the future. What matters is how different kinds of money work together.

The metallist and chartalist stories of money also treat the actual production of the money itself as a secondary concern. We use the word "creation" to describe this production, but that word makes money sound like a kind of transubstantiation. When the market or the state says the right words—FIAT!—money happens. But I have stood in a Federal Reserve cash warehouse in front of a German-made bill-counting machine the size of a VW bus, and I have dropped to the bottom of a silver mine in Czechia and looked at five-hundred-year-old chisel marks. I have driven around North Dakota in the middle of a pandemic in a pickup truck with a loan officer at a community bank who had to figure out how to get forgivable loans—free dollars—to bartenders, mechanics, and hairdressers. I can tell you that money is not created. It's not a miracle. It's not fiat. Governments do not poof money into existence. Money is manufactured. Someone needs a certain kind of money, to buy something specific. Someone else has to produce that money, often for a profit and always for a reason. The details matter.

To understand the dollar, then, I have found it helpful to try to figure out what people thought they were doing with their own dollars, at the time. Who could manufacture dollars? Who did manufacture dollars? Why? Who needed dollars? What kind? For what? Histories of money often seem a little condescending, arguing that people in the past didn't yet understand what they were doing, and so money had to be fixed with better ideas over time. Or perhaps people made a terrible mistake at some point, deviating from the ideal. The problem with this approach is that people in the past were often astonishingly thoughtful about money, and knew exactly what they were doing and why. I don't mean philosophers. I mean merchants, tradespeople, bureaucrats, diarists.

Public discussions about how reliable, valuable, and plentiful money should be were sophisticated and often angry, and to read the pages of the *Maryland Gazette* now sometimes feels like reading a research newsletter from a Wall Street analyst. Exchange rates, money stock, discounting bills on London, different assets in different denominations—these are ideas that today only financiers have to deal with. You definitely know more about physics or medicine than Anne Catharine Green, the publisher of the *Gazette*. But you probably know less about money.

THERE ARE DIFFERENT DOLLARS FOR DIFFERENT PURPOSES

I started working on this book in 2019. By the time it's printed, it will be 2026. Part of that delay came out of a frustrated realization that I had already built a basic framework for understanding money, even though I couldn't see it when I started. I had to completely dismantle that framework, then reassemble a new one that fit the story I was finding. In 2019, I was a financial journalist. By the fall of 2021, I had started a PhD in financial history, and I had begun to read the work of a few historians who took the production of money seriously.

Crawling through footnotes, I found the work of Carlo Cipolla, an Italian medievalist who in 1956 published a slim book, *Money, Prices, and Civilization in the Mediterranean World,* which drew distinctions between *moneta grossa*—big money—for long-distance trade and the petty or little money for local retail. At a conference someone urged me to read Akinobu Kuroda at the University of Tokyo, who described how big and small moneys could circulate separately in the same markets, paying for completely different things without an obvious exchange rate. Perry Mehrling at Boston University pointed me toward the way bankers think about money, as assets and liabilities on a ledger—bankers know better than anyone how money works. And I read Rebecca Spang's *Stuff and Money in the Time of the French Revolution,* in which she focused on the barrelhead details of how people bought things, and argued that any woman buying bread at a market knew as much about money as Adam Smith or David Hume. I found this insight so profound I emailed her and forced her to be my friend.

These historians led me to a language of money that had been lost to most of us. We now speak of the dollar as if it were a single thing. It's not. There is no such thing as *the* dollar. American banks pay each other in reserves held at the Fed. If you don't know what this is, it's because you can't hold it or use it. Most dollars in the United States are held as deposits at commercial banks. If you don't have access to a bank account, you can't use those dollars, either. Traders in financial markets rely so heavily on Treasurys—bonds from the federal government—that they refer to them as dollar cash. You might own a Treasury, but you would never think of it as cash. Economists have come to see all these different kinds of financial instruments as fungible. Increase one, and it works its way through the whole system. But all these different kinds of dollars don't always trade cleanly and logically with each other. Not all dollars are the same.

Before about a hundred years ago, everyone would have understood the differences between big and little money, and no one would have assumed that they were fungible. In the nineteenth-century American Midwest, settlers from the Appalachian south distinguished between the "filthy lucre" of full-weight silver dollars and large-denomination bills, on the one hand, and the "shillings and bits" of small coins and cut silver. Rebecca Spang points out that the poor in eighteenth-century Paris relied on *menue monnaie*—little money, small coins of a mix of copper and silver. In the seventeenth-century Dutch Republic, coins that circulated locally were *standpenningen,* and large coins for trade were *negotiepenningen.* Investors at the sixteenth-century silver mine at Joachimsthal in Bohemia had to ship in silver pennies to pay their own miners, and referred to the pennies as *pagament*—from the Italian *pagamento,* or payment money.

Histories of money tend to focus on the *substance* of money. But sitting right there in the archives staring out at us is a constant, furious argument over money and class. Merchants and the wealthy needed what Carlo Cipolla called big money. Shopkeepers and day laborers needed little money. So let me offer you a second proposition: *Whom money is for is every bit as important as what it's made of.* In every place, in every time, there are different markets, using different kinds of money. The political fight between big and little money was just as fierce as—if not fiercer than—the fight between metal and paper. In general, the big money wins. The kinds of money useful to long-distance merchants are the kinds that get made, at high quality, in sufficient quantity. Small money for small purchases is often an afterthought, and people will scramble locally to make their own. The dollar is no different. Its history, too, has been one of big and little dollars in tension with each other, produced inside systems that remain imperfect today.

Historians often remind each other to treat the past like a foreign country. The past may seem alien and weird, but people have always had their own logic about the world, an internally consistent way of making sense of things. In this book you will read a record of my attempt to learn that older language about money, one that profoundly changed the way I think about how money works today. I hope to walk you through what I learned, through the lives of actual human beings making decisions. And I hope to show you your own framework for money and—as gently as possible—ask you to rattle it a bit, to see whether it holds up.

REAL AND IMAGINARY MONEY IN COLONIAL AMERICA

In eighteenth-century Annapolis, any shopkeeper would have thought in terms of real and imaginary money. These words weren't value judgments. Real money wasn't any better than imaginary money. Rather, each had its proper use, described in detail in textbooks at the time. Real money was a coin in the hand or sometimes even a printed note. It wasn't the substance of real money that was important, but its function: You could hand it to a stranger, and your relationship was over. The transaction had cleared. It was done. Imaginary money sat as book credits on a ledger, a record of a debt. Colonial ledgers show customers canceling out their debts over time; a shop would hand over goods in return for some coins or even a day's labor six months later. Or a customer could go to a tavern and, as if they were making a transfer at a bank, say that someone else was going to take care of their tab. To pay with imaginary money implied some kind of ongoing relationship. The tavern keeper had to know where to find you.

In the small port town of Annapolis, book credits were an efficient way to trade with neighbors. The merchants themselves marked up credits in their own books. When they did that, they manufactured their own imaginary money for local use. But the credits didn't all cancel perfectly, and in particular a death would create a rush of account clearing. This was the purpose of Robert Henwood's probate record. His debts don't mean he was improvident. The rights and credits in his probate were a public record of imaginary money. He was part of the local economy, and it was time to settle up with some kind of real money—coins or bills.

Often heirs would publish advertisements, urging anyone with credits or debts with the deceased to come close out their accounts. Anne Catharine Green had lost her own husband, Jonas, in 1767. When he died, he had been holding on to a lot of imaginary money, the book credit he had kept for his customers as a printer. To move things along, Anne Catharine threatened to publish in the *Gazette* the names of the twelve hundred people with unpaid balances on her husband's books.

Imaginary money works only if everyone counts it the same way, using the same units. Economists call this a money of account. In finance they call it a denomination. Anne Catharine Green and Robert Henwood would have thought of it as a currency. We tend to think of currencies now as something the state decides: The United States says you have to pay in dollars, and so in the United States you pay in dollars. But in the eighteenth century a currency was more like a set of local customs. Travelers would return from somewhere with a description of what was current—what passed as real money, and the rates at which it converted into imaginary money. Think of a currency like a tradition. It's difficult to make up a new one out of nothing, but they do vary from place to place, and change over time.

In the eighteenth century, the English counted money in pounds, shillings, and pence. Like much of continental Europe, they had inherited that system from the Carolingian Empire of the early Middle Ages, which in turn relied on cultural memories of coins like the *denarius* and *solidus* that had moved across the borders of the Roman Empire. Imaginary money wasn't always paired precisely with real money, though. In the Carolingian system, there were 12 pence in a shilling, and 20 shillings in a pound. But until the twelfth century, the only actual coins were silver pennies. Imaginary moneys tend to endure. Coins of different weights and fineness jingled promiscuously across political borders, but the basic accounting system of imaginary money—12 and 20—remained intact, both in Britain and on the Continent.

Until the dollar.

I didn't find Robert Henwood on my own. In the late 1960s, Alice Hanson Jones, an economic historian, dug up almost a thousand probate records from county courthouses to create a full picture of economic life in the American colonies for one year, 1774. She noted that each colony kept its records in its own imaginary money. Pennsylvania shillings, for example, or Massachusetts shillings—the old Carolingian system, adapted for local use. In Maryland, however, Jones noticed that a few records were recorded in dollars. I looked through her data for the first mention of a dollar, and it just happened to be on Henwood's probate record. That document offers a single, identifiable moment when we can watch two Englishmen decide to stop counting in shillings—money we can trace all the way back to the Roman solidus—and start counting in dollars.

John Campbell and Francis Fairbrother, like everyone else in the world at the time, would have thought of the dollar as real money—a big silver coin. There were several different kinds of dollar coins in circulation in the colonies, but all of them were copies of copies of a coin first minted in 1520 in the mountains of northern Bohemia, in what is now Czechia, in St. Joachim's Valley—in German, St. Joachimsthal. The coins were called *Joachimsthaler,* and eventually just *Taler*. In the first half of this book, we'll follow those big silver coins, copy by copy, from sixteenth-century Bohemia to Robert Henwood's probate record in provincial Maryland.

Those first taler from the 1520s were pure, well made, and plentiful. They had been incredibly useful for trade up through the Baltic Sea and to the east. Like an invasive species, they ripped up currencies as they passed, changing habits that were centuries old. Copies appeared in Sweden, Denmark, the city-states of Hamburg and Lübeck. By 1611, Shakespeare could throw a pun on the word "dollar" into *The Tempest* with no explanation at all, even though there were no dollars in the English currency of pounds, shillings, and pence. To a groundling at the Globe Theatre, a dollar was obviously a coin from the Low Countries that paid for English cloth. These connections aren't linguistic. They're monetary. It wasn't a word that traveled from a Bohemian valley to the Globe Theatre to provincial Maryland. It was a kind of money.

By the time Robert Henwood died, as much time had already passed since the production of those first taler in Joachimsthal as has passed since. Alexander Hamilton—that Alexander Hamilton—called it the "ancient dollar." By the eighteenth century, the American colonies were just a backwater in an established, flowing, global trade system based on big silver dollars. Dollars fetched up in America by accident, sometimes dropped off by literal pirates of the Caribbean. Or they passed through, on their way to somewhere more important.

There were *leeuwendaalders* from the Dutch Republic: "lion dollars," for the lion on the coin's face. They were also sometimes called Dutch dollars, or dog dollars. The lion, particularly when the coin was rubbed down with use, looked like a dog, sitting back on its hindquarters, begging for a scrap. Dog dollars came in through New York and Pennsylvania, mostly at the end of the seventeenth century and the beginning of the eighteenth.

From the Spanish crown's mines in modern-day Mexico, Bolivia, and Peru came the *real de a ocho*—a silver coin worth 8 reales, or a piece of eight. The real de a ocho had been shoehorned into an older Castilian currency system, but it was copied directly from the taler that had been so successful in northern Europe. American colonists considered dog dollars and reales de a ocho to be different members of the same category and happily called both the same thing: dollars. Sometimes Spanish dollars were referred to by their mint—Seville dollars, or Mexico dollars, for example. Rough pieces hacked from a silver bar and stamped at the silver mine in Potosí in modern-day Bolivia were sometimes called cobs.

All these kinds of dollars had slightly different weights and values, and colonial legislation on money made clear distinctions among them. In their letters and account books, colonists were less precise. If we pay attention to how people used the word "dollar" at the time, then we can say there was a broader understanding of what a dollar was: It was one of any number of silver coins of roughly the same size and weight, all copies of copies of that first joachimsthaler. By the mid-eighteenth century, Spain's Bourbon kings had added precise milling to the edge of the coins, and by the time Robert Henwood died, a colonist who said "dollar" probably meant what had become a global standard: the Spanish milled dollar.

These coins were so important in Asian markets that even today currencies still carry their name. The Japanese *yen* and Chinese *yuan* still both come from the word "round," a reference to the old Spanish dollars. The Malaysian *ringgit* comes from a word for "jagged," a reference to the milling. The Hong Kong dollar and the Canadian dollar don't take their name from the U.S. dollar. Both currencies were originally tied to that same silver coin.

In the 1760s, the Spanish milled dollar had been so important as money in Maryland that the province had produced America's first paper dollars. Jonas Green had printed them, in a shop behind a brick-and-shingle house he rented with Anne Catharine that still stands on Charles Street in Annapolis. The first Maryland paper dollars featured a precise engraved reproduction of two Spanish milled dollars. The engravings made clear what financiers today would call a peg: It tied Maryland's paper dollar to the value of the Spanish dollar, at a fixed rate. Silver Spanish milled dollars and paper Maryland dollars were real money—tangible, physical assets that literally passed from hand to hand. But the province's imaginary money—credits and debts kept on a ledger—was still counted in currencies of pounds, shillings, and pence.

Currencies, plural. There were different economies within Maryland, each with its own currency. A planter with land and enslaved people would have sold hogsheads of dried tobacco for bills of exchange—a kind of check that could only be presented for cash in London. These bills were drawn up in pounds and shillings sterling, the tightly controlled domestic currency of Britain. A planter might use a bill of exchange as real money to pay another planter for land, but it wouldn't work for a meal at a tavern. Parliament, however, had not cared to share with its colonists the mints, bank charters, and careful administration that made the sterling system work at home. And so Americans had taken that old Carolingian imaginary money of pounds, shillings, and pence and built their own traditions around them.

The province of Maryland kept its own records in a completely different currency it called current money. The silver Spanish milled dollar was so ubiquitous that Americans expressed exchange rates among different currencies in terms of dollars. In sterling, one dollar was 4 shillings, 6 pence. In current Maryland money, a dollar was 6 shillings. Economic historians will sometimes look back and turn this into a direct conversion rate, sterling to current Maryland. But that's not how merchants recorded it at the time. All currencies were quoted relative to the silver dollar. Here are two parts of the same empire, counting imaginary money in a type of real money that came from somewhere else entirely. Spain's Bourbon kings did not have a policy of pushing the dollar into English colonies, but dollar trade had its own rules. Emperors do not command money the same way they command armies.

When Robert Henwood died, John Campbell and Francis Fairbrother counted up all the beds and teaspoons, then wrote them down the way it made sense—in Maryland's provincial currency of "dollars at 6/ shilling Each." They put the dollar first. In eighteenth-century America, well before independence, Britain's currency of sterling was just for buying stuff from London. Dollars were what mattered. They were already the standard. Imaginary money is stubborn. It's a habit of mind. But right there in the probate record, we can watch a habit change, from shillings to dollars. Campbell and Fairbrother were not revolutionaries, declaring a sovereign new state and a sovereign new money. They were just two guys doing a job, trying to figure out how to count. They decided the milled silver dollar from Spain's empire was the best way to do it.

THE UNITED STATES IS NOT SOVEREIGN OVER ITS DOLLAR

Economists have a delightful phrase for things they all agree on but don't completely understand. They call it hand-waving. We all literally hand wave in our own lives. It's the dismissive motion you use when you get to the part of your story that's too hard to explain, and probably not worth the trouble. It's a gesture of futility, but also camaraderie. When you hand wave, you are sparing the listener the pain of hearing you talk about something you don't completely understand. As a journalist, I often listened to economists and central bankers talk about "monetary sovereignty"—the power a state has to control its own currency. This sounds like a serious idea for serious people, but it's actually just handwaving. The economists who study money assume that the state is sovereign, but that sovereignty is poorly defined and impossible to measure. There is a different tradition, however, that sees monetary sovereignty as the exception, sustained imperfectly and only with great effort. Money is still today a frantic, unending, global competition, with different assets wandering across borders to serve as money without any regard to sovereignty at all.

We owe much of the way we think about dominant, global currencies to the economist Robert Mundell. His work on exchange rates won him a Nobel Prize in 1999 and provided the theoretical arguments in favor of a common currency for the European Union. Mundell, looking back at the history of dominant currencies, saw them as a product of empire. His theory rests on sovereignty: All moneys start domestic, and some become international. If an empire was politically stable, minted reliable coins, and favored trade, its coins would start to become current beyond its own borders.

But there was no empire pushing those first joachimsthaler coins into the world. They weren't even part of the domestic monetary standard in Bohemia. Even the mines didn't keep their own books in taler. A legal gray area meant that Saxon investors could collect their mine dividends as large coins made to a Saxon standard, and those coins poured up into the Baltic, so useful for trade that they changed every place they touched. Spain, too, never adopted the real de a ocho as a domestic standard. The retail trade in Iberian Spain was priced in *maravedís,* a small coin of mixed copper and silver. Loans to the Spanish crown from Genoa were priced in *ducats*. Even the silver mines at Potosí initially kept their books in *peso corriente,* a local accounting currency worth less than a real de a ocho.

The dollar did not start inside an empire and then spread beyond. From the very beginning, it became current all over the world for two reasons. First, it was useful. Merchants in Russia and particularly China, who had been dealing with larger blocks of silver, found the coins easier to work with. Second, there were a lot of them—endless hulls, ringing with dollars, sailing everywhere, well before and well after the foundation of the United States. The dollar was a global currency first.

It's not even clear that strong, global currencies are good for the empires that are nominally in charge of them. By the eighteenth century, Spain had learned how to administer its silver mines—minting reales de a ocho at a predictable quality, moving them among its American viceroyalties as payroll for the empire, shipping them back to the Crown's creditors in Europe. But the success of the silver dollar and the growth of an imperial court economy in the city of Madrid had also shut down manufacturing and dragged down economic growth in the Spanish kingdom of Castile, the heartland of the empire.

In the second half of this book we'll return to the United States, to follow a shift in how people used dollars and thought about them. In the early years of the American republic, a dollar was still that old silver coin from the Spanish Empire. By the end of the nineteenth century, a dollar had become a piece of paper or a deposit, both sitting on the balance sheet of an American bank. That system is now so vast and stable that people all over the world want to hold their cash in dollars, if possible as deposits in American banks. Wall Street tries to meet that demand by turning almost any asset into a dollar deposit, but there are far more dollars in the world now than America can hold. Banks abroad create their own dollars, on their own balance sheets, without any explicit permission from the United States. These foreign-made dollars can seem like impossible beasts, and we'll spend a whole chapter making them as simple as possible. Think of them for now as offshore copies, just as the silver Spanish milled dollar was a copy of the original silver joachimsthaler.

Histories of money—both metallist *and* chartalist—tend to describe that transition from silver to banks as a rupture. Metallists see the end of metal-backed money and the beginning of fiat, money that stays aloft on its own. Chartalists see a missed opportunity, where princes and parliaments had power over mints and money and then handed that power over to the banks. I will not offer you either of these histories. We'll walk through changes in the dollar, but I have found that the continuities are just as important. Silver and credit worked as part of the same system for centuries before the banks took over. Just like mints, banks are a product of slow changes in habits and laws over time. Some things about the old silver dollars are still true today in Annapolis, where I sit now as I type. Some kinds of dollars are still manufactured for merchants and the wealthy, some for daily purchases of meat and bread.

In America's bank dollars, for example, we can still hear an echo of imperial Spain. The strong dollar is good for Wall Street. But just as was true for Spain, it's not clear that the prestige and power of a strong global currency does that much good for American manufacturing towns that have collapsed because it no longer pays to export. A strong dollar doesn't help young graduates trying to buy a house, discovering that everyone in the world is fighting to hold assets—like houses—denominated in dollars. It has been historically difficult for any state to maintain a single currency for everyone, and the same strong dollar doesn't work equally well for everyone in America.

Once I abandoned the idea of monetary sovereignty, I found myself looking for a protagonist. If not an empire, who made the dollar powerful? I'm now stuck with an uncomfortable idea: The dollar itself is in charge. Of course, this is nonsense. It was people who made laws and traded with each other on ships. It was people who manufactured dollars, and I will try to make it clear who some of these people were, and what kinds of dollars they produced. But a strong, useful currency has its own power over the people who use it. It doesn't always need an empire.

When I started work on this book, my mother went through my grandfather's papers, looking for what she insisted was a colonial Maryland paper dollar. That was impossible, I told her. It had to have been a Maryland shilling. They were far more numerous, in circulation for far longer. But, of course, my mother was right. Sitting on my grandfather's desk for my entire childhood, taped between two small panes of glass, had been one of the most historically important dollars—one of those first American paper dollars, printed in 1774 by Anne Catharine Green, redeemable in London in silver, gold, or sterling bills of exchange. The dollar has started to seem to me like a puckish demigod, prodding and dragging people wherever it wishes. I have tried to resist the temptation to turn the dollar itself into a character. I have not completely succeeded.

If you are already familiar with financial history, you will open this book looking for things that aren't there. I won't spend a lot of time on Alexander Hamilton's financial plan, or the Civil War paper greenbacks, or the creation of the Federal Reserve, or even the way Richard Nixon ended gold convertibility in 1971. These were all political decisions. Each had some impact on how people produced and used dollars, which I will explain when necessary. But just as important as the political decisions were the often slow changes in *habits:* the way most people manufactured dollars, used them, and thought about them.

Early in my research on this book, I visited a friend in Germany and told him what I was working on. He produced an archive from his childhood, a collection of paperback Disney comics. In German translation, when Uncle Scrooge McDuck dove into his vault, he dove into a pool of taler—the old silver coins from St. Joachimsthal. As late as the early 1980s, a five-century-old *idea* of a dollar still had cultural meaning. There is an academic movement now that argues money is a creature of law. Certainly laws matter. But money is also a creature of habits, carried out in private mints, private banks, and private lives. These habits are as resistant to laws as they are shaped by them, and shifts in how the dollar worked often began far away from the centers of political power.

The history of the dollar moves across borders and oceans. It follows a path that kings and presidents found difficult to bend. No country, no kingdom, has ever held complete sovereignty over the dollar, not even the United States, not even today. This is not a story about the Federal

Reserve, or the U.S. Treasury, or even the United States of America. It is a story about the dollar, the world's most powerful money. The document at the end of Robert Henwood's life is one small point where we can look back and watch the dollar do to America what it's done all over the world, for five centuries. America didn't invent the dollar. America succumbed to the dollar.

1

A Big Silver Coin from Bohemia

St. Joachimsthal, 1518

THE PARTY AT THE BIRTH OF THE DOLLAR

On the Feast of Epiphany in January 1518, silver miners in the town of Konradsgrün in the mountains of northern Bohemia threw a party. Things got out of hand. By the end of the night, they had lit their empty beer kegs on fire, hauled them up on their shoulders, and run with them down the street, screaming and singing.

We know exactly where they ran, because at the time Konradsgrün had only one street. Every single one of the town's three thousand inhabitants had arrived within the previous two years. They lived in about four hundred shacks, perched on a hillside too steep to walk without switchbacks, overlooking a valley narrow enough for a crossbow bolt to reach the other side. The street ran from a chapel, north along the mountain, to a small green—the *Grün* from the town's name. At the start of the sixteenth century, the Ore Mountains that divided Bohemia and Saxony were still socked in with virgin forest. In the town's first few years, bears would sometimes still trot over the green.

It's possible that the miners set the kegs on fire at the end of the night because they'd run out of beer. At the time, Konradsgrün didn't yet have a license for its own brewery, and beer had to be hauled in from Schlackenwerth, a town about an hour's walk away. Schlackenwerth was also the seat of Stephan Schlick, a minor Bohemian nobleman who had claimed the earth around the brand-new mines. The land wasn't his to claim. He shared the title of count with several other members of his extended family; they all had a claim to the same land. But Stephan Schlick had just brazenly decided he should be lord of the valley, then started acting as if he were.

We do have a good idea of what the party in January 1518 was about. I have found two mentions of the event. One says only that a new captain of the mountain, Heinrich von Könneritz, was "festively installed" on the Feast of Epiphany in 1518. The other describes a christening party, to give the town a new name.

The party marked a temporary victory for the miners in a long fight with Schlick. His title as lord was questionable to begin with, but he was also just bad at it. In the summer of 1517, the miners at Konradsgrün had downed tools over work conditions and threatened to walk out of the valley. Schlick had agreed to a list of demands, among them a requirement to pay the miners with higher-quality silver coins. The miners had also demanded that they give the town a new name of their choosing. The morning after the party, the miners woke up, hungover and likely singed, in a town called St. Joachimsthal—the Valley of Saint Joachim. The silver coins that came out of the valley would become known as joachimsthaler, and then simply thaler or taler.

By the early 1530s, the kingdom of Sweden would begin producing a big silver coin called a *jockumsdaler,* and the kingdom of Denmark would mint a *Jochemdaler,* both copies of the same big silver coins that came out of St. Joachimsthal and both named for the town itself, the start of a centuries-long process of copies of copies of copies of the same silver coin. Today the U.S. Mint still makes a coin it calls a silver dollar, with almost the exact same dimensions as the ones that came out of the mint at Joachimsthal. If you were ever given a silver dollar as a child for your birthday, you held in your little palm a direct descendant of that christening party in the mountains in Bohemia in 1518.

The mining town of St. Joachimsthal often shows up in histories of the dollar as the origin of the name itself. Over time the German word taler became, in English, "dollar." But those histories suggest that what happened at the actual mine in the valley is now irrelevant. They argue that a domestic currency simply became international: Count Schlick had so much silver that the coins of his own realm spread beyond his own borders. But nothing in that sentence about Schlick is really true. Stephan was only one of several Counts Schlick, an ambitious huckster without a clear claim on anything in the valley. In the sixteenth century, St. Joachimsthal was the single most productive silver mine in Europe, but it wasn't completely out of proportion with the other mines. The big silver joachimsthaler coins that came out of the valley were never meant as local currency. They were far more useful for trade across the Baltic than they were for making payments in a tiny corner of Bohemia.

Stephan Schlick never even wanted to make coins. He just wanted to buy silver cheaply in a place that called him lord, then sell it as silver bars at a profit to bankers in Nuremberg. But his scheme fell apart. By the 1520s, other Bohemian lords and even his own family caught up with Stephan Schlick and forced him to start minting the coins that eventually became the world's currency. We now think of coins as just money, but in a silver-producing kingdom like Bohemia a mint was also a form of control, a way to count all the silver, stamp it, and tax it. During his short life Schlick was also constantly at the mercy of his miners, who walked out of the mines several times because they couldn't get paid in the same good silver they were pulling out of the ground. That is, the man who set in motion the money we now call the dollar didn't even make reliable money for the people who lived in his valley. The joachimsthaler wasn't Stephan Schlick's money, or even Bohemia's money. The dollar was an accident.

The Feast of Epiphany in that one valley in northern Bohemia in 1518—with the flaming beer keg runs from the chapel to the green—marked the beginning of what we today call the dollar. It also marked only a temporary peace in the fight over whose dollar it would be. I have on my desk a copy in silver of one of those first joachimsthaler coins.

When I drop it, it doesn't jingle. It clanks. It has heft. It's a coin for lords and merchants; it's not the kind of thing a carpenter would hand over to pay for a loaf of bread. That world with its clanking, physical coins is not so different from our own, with its banks and credit cards and storefronts for check cashing. Today some kinds of dollars work for the wealthy, for investors, and for people who ship goods from one continent to another. Some kinds of dollars work for everyone else. Stephan Schlick had a hard time making the right mix of silver bars and big and little coins to make everyone happy: his miners, the investors at his mines, his bankers, and the other lords of Bohemia. That problem never went away. It's still with us now.

A SILVER FIND IN THE FOREST

Until 1512, Konradsgrün had been a ruin, a collection of abandoned houses and a forge on the valley floor, with trees growing up through the frames. That year two men walked up from the valley floor, began to dig, and discovered something so overwhelming that they covered their holes back up with slag and immediately left. One of the men was local, from Schlackenwerth—Stephan Schlick's home county, the place where the beer kegs came from for that party. The other came from a silver-mining town in Saxony, and probably had some understanding of mining law. The two might have been able to establish a legal claim to the mine and sell the silver they'd found, but together they weren't able to get past any of the basic hurdles of silver mining. Silver under the ground doesn't automatically become silver in your hand. Even in the sixteenth century, someone had to pay for skilled miners and huge machines to dig up ore, refine it into silver on the surface, and sell it into an international market. There's no silver without investors to pay for silver mining. And what investors wanted determined where the silver went.

In 1515, Stephan Schlick was taking the baths at Karlsbad, about a three-hour walk from the mouth of the valley, when he heard about what the two men had found. By the next spring, he had invited a small group of investors from Saxon mines south for a visit. They met with Schlick at Karlsbad, where he dressed them up as a hunting party and rode with them up the valley floor to check out the slag heap. Schlick's visitors began production immediately. By the last two quarters of 1516, they were pulling ore out of the ground and refining it into silver.

Joachimsthal is now called Jáchymov, in what is now Czechia. Karlsbad is still a spa town, but also now goes by its Czech name, Karlovy Vary. Both lie in what used to be called the Sudetenland, the part of Czechia that was majority German until the end of World War II; the names all changed after the war, when the Germans were forced to leave. In the summer of 2019, I spent a week in Karlovy Vary in the office of Jan Nedvěd, a historian at the city's regional museum, reading through a collection of the histories of Joachimsthal, watched by Jan's two dogs and his poster of the American punk band Fugazi.

Map by Evan Applegate.

The most comprehensive histories of Joachimsthal come from the 1930s, part of a broader attempt to record and teach the region's German heritage. They're filled with fun details, but they're also a little suspect. They treat Stephan Schlick as what we might today call a heroic entrepreneur: a German-speaking nobleman with connections to Saxony, stamping St. Joachimsthal out of nothing, and with it the taler and the dollar. It was a useful story when there were political reasons to confirm that parts of what was then Czechoslovakia should, in fact, be Germany. These are the histories that gave us the traditional story about Stephan Schlick and the taler. In the last decade, however, Petr Vorel, a historian at the University of Pardubice in Czechia, has been working on a less flattering story, one where Schlick is more desperate than cunning.

Medieval and early modern European kings were not omnipotent. They did not automatically own all the silver that came out of the ground. In the early sixteenth century, Bohemia had a weak king, with strong cities and regional lords. Private silver miners in the kingdom kept most of what they dug up and refined, and had to give only an eighth of their final product in silver to the king. Bohemian kings were constantly in debt to their own regional lords, borrowing with a promise to repay with silver due in the future from private miners.

The regional lords were skeptical of any king's promise, and made sure they collected on royal debts by forcing Bohemian mines to send all their silver as bars to a single Bohemian mint near the rich silver mines of Kutná Hora, just east of Prague. The mint allowed the king to collect his tax. And it allowed the Czech lords to track silver production and collect what the king owed them. Manufacturing money has always been a carefully guarded privilege, an act of power with consequences for both the wealthy and ordinary citizens. Medieval minting was no different. That single mint at Kutná Hora gave the king control over the silver, and the nobles control over the king.

The Schlick family was new money, elevated to nobility early in the fifteenth century with the fortunes of a clever German-speaking son of a burgher who became chancellor to the Bohemian king. By the time Stephan was born in Schlackenwerth in 1487, the family held the estates around Konradsgrün, but they never got along with the Czech-speaking aristocracy in Bohemia, who had always seen them as illegitimate. Stephan was twenty-eight in 1515, when he heard rumors about the silver strike in Konradsgrün. His father had died that year, and although Stephan was the eldest of his brothers, he hadn't inherited all the Schlick estates, or even all the estates around Schlackenwerth. That land was held in its entirety by the extended Schlick family, divided under an internal agreement.

What Stephan Schlick did after hearing about the silver was breathtakingly illegal. He brought foreign investors to a slag heap he didn't own, to pay for mining expertise he didn't have and to produce a product—silver in ingots, smuggled out of the kingdom—that was expressly prohibited under Bohemian law. When Schlick first took his investors up the valley, he dressed them as a hunting party to hide his intentions from the Bohemian king, the Czech-speaking regional lords, and even his own cousins. It worked for about a year.

FIRST, SCHLICK BORROWED FROM BANKERS

Stephan Schlick brought two different kinds of capital to the valley, which would send silver in two different directions. He started by taking out a personal loan. Just as was true of the Bohemian king, Schlick didn't own all the silver. As self-declared lord, all he had was the monopoly right to purchase silver at below-market prices from private miners in the valley. He could then sell that same silver again at a profit. But even that required what financiers now call liquidity. As lord on the mountain, Schlick had to have some kind of cash on hand to buy the silver, manage the flow of payments for miners and investors, and pay a few key local mining administrators.

Just like the king of Bohemia, though, Schlick could borrow against the income his monopoly would give him in the future. In 1516, the same year he took his guests from Saxony up the valley to encourage them to start mining, Schlick signed an agreement with Hans Nützel, a banker from Augsburg. Nützel fronted Schlick 34,000 in a currency called the *Rhine florin*. In addition to paying back the loan, Schlick had to sell all of his silver to Nützel. The next year, this agreement followed Nützel when he moved to the German banking capital of Nuremberg, to work with the banker Jakob Welser. To start with, then, all of the silver from the valley moved west to Nuremberg, as bars.

To understand the kind of pressure that loan put on Schlick, we need to understand exactly what a Rhine florin was. From the ninth to the twelfth century, money in what we would today call western Europe was simple. There was only one kind of precious metal: silver, mostly from Goslar and then Freiberg, in what is today Germany. And there was only one coin: the silver penny. Remember that in colonial America people distinguished between the real money of coins in hand and the imaginary money of marks on a ledger, which needed to be recorded in some big, important, commonly accepted money of account. This was true in medieval Europe, too. The pound, a literal pound weight of silver, was the money of account. The silver pennies were anchored in an accounting structure that survived in Great Britain until the twentieth century: 12 pennies in a shilling, 20 shillings in a pound. But there were no shilling or pound coins. These were just ideas, units for imaginary money on the books of merchants and lenders.

The system used different names in different places—*pfennig, schilling,* and *pfund* in the German-speaking states, or denarius, solidus, and *lira* on the Italian peninsula. But the basic units were the same everywhere. The pennies, pfennig, and *denarii* from different states were cosmopolitan and promiscuous. Regions that accepted the same coins didn't always overlap cleanly with political borders. Some rulers took a cut to accept taxes in foreign coins, and peasants and merchants had to learn how to "discount" different pennies—to accept them as payment at less than face value. Contracts didn't just specify costs by the penny; they had to name the specific penny they were referring to.

In the thirteenth century, new silver was discovered at Kutná Hora, and local rulers started directing their mints to fill out the rest of the old system. The mints issued larger silver coins in the value of a shilling—*groats,* or *groschen,* or *grossi,* worth 12 pennies. Around the same time, merchants in the Italian republics figured out how to get gold from the other side of the Sahara Desert, and mints in Florence and Venice began issuing gold florins and ducats. Originally these high-value gold coins were anchored in the old system, too. In Florence, the florin was designed to be worth 1 lira—it was a gold pound coin. It was stable, the Florentines traded with everyone, and the florin earned a rare promotion: from real money to imaginary money. Around the Continent, the florin became the money of account, replacing the pound as a reference for bookkeepers.

The Rhine florin was a copy of the Florentine florin, minted by a small group of German princes and dukes along the Rhine River. Like most of the rest of the Continent, these rulers didn't have any gold of their own, but they could stop barges on their way down the Rhine and demand tolls in gold. By Stephan Schlick's time, the Rhine florin had become smaller and less pure than the florin from Italy, but served as a local accounting standard in the German-speaking patchwork of the Holy Roman Empire and among the powerful bankers of Augsburg and Nuremberg.

Just 1 Rhine florin could buy a lot. The year Schlick took out his loan, a pound of bacon in nearby Saxony was 1 groschen. A day's wages for the best-paid carpenters were 3 groschen. At the time, there were 21 Saxon groschen to 1 Rhine florin. So a single florin was worth seven days of well-paid work, or twenty-one pounds of bacon.

Stephan Schlick started his lordship in the valley with personal debts of 34,000 Rhine florins. He immediately put some of it into a defensive castle on the ridge. He couldn't just act like a lord; he had to look like one. Schlick spent the next ten years until his death trying to outrun that first loan, under constant pressure to get bars of silver west to Nuremberg. He continued to borrow to the end of his life. More than a decade later his brothers still owed 40,000 Rhine florins to Nützel and

Welser in Nuremberg. And even that first personal loan didn't get any mining started. Schlick had some cash, but he still didn't know what he was doing. Silver mining was arduous, technical, and expensive. The miners, the expertise, and even more capital were over the ridge to the north, among the Saxons.

THEN SCHLICK BROUGHT IN MINERS AND INVESTORS FROM LEIPZIG

For that first quiet trip to the valley in 1516, Schlick had invited guests from Annaberg, a mine in Saxony. They were likely investors in a *Gewerk,* an early type of joint-stock company. The structure of these companies had been developed in the German mountains in the fourteenth century to pay for the increasing up-front capital costs of mining. The deeper into the mountain you dig, the more you need to build expensive structures in the earth to support the mine, and on the surface to get the ore out. Saxony had seen its own silver boom in the second half of the fifteenth century, and Leipzig had developed an active market for mine shares. Investors in a Leipzig *Gewerk* had specific expectations from a mine. Every shareholder paid in before the digging started. Every quarter, they either paid in more to keep the dig going or got a payout in proportion to the shares they owned.

By Stephan Schlick's time, shares in Saxon mines had started paying out as large, pure silver coins, each worth 1 gold Rhine florin. The ore came up and then was immediately refined and minted on-site to pay investors. Just as in Bohemia, the mints were there to control the silver, to make sure all the investors got paid and that none of the ore got lost in the woods on its way down the mountain. The coins weren't meant to be money. They were quarterly dividends, called colloquially by the names of the mines. *Annaberger,* for example, were dividend coins from the silver mines at Annaberg—Saint Anne's Mountain. Twice a year, at market time in Leipzig, dividend coins poured in from the mines. Then investors passed them out of Saxony altogether, in exchange for wheat from Poland or leather and tar from Russia. The market for mining shares in Leipzig was what you would today call deep and liquid. There were a lot of shares, and a lot of people with the capital and the connections to buy and sell them.

This system was so successful that, in 1500, Saxony had rearranged its entire currency system around it. At the top was a Saxon silver florin, identical to the dividend coins from the mines, and worth the same as a gold Rhine florin. The goal wasn't to create better money for local transactions; it was to simplify the accounting around the mine profits. Leipzig merchants bought shares in mines, but so did nobles and even the Dukes of Saxony. Likely all three were part of that first Saxon joint-stock company, invited over the mountains by Stephan Schlick to start mining in the valley.

In 1516, Saxon miners working for that joint-stock company began bringing silver out of the ground Schlick had claimed, and refining it on the surface. There was no mint yet; the purpose of a mint at a mine is to legally control the silver, and none of this was in any way legal. Instead, Stephan Schlick paid for bars of silver from the valley using imported coins he had borrowed from Nuremberg, then shipped those bars from St. Joachimsthal west, back to Nuremberg, to start paying down his loan. It was a terrible business for Schlick, but he wanted to be a powerful silver lord like the Dukes of Saxony, and this was his only way to get started. He wasn't himself even an investor in any of the mining companies. All he got was a slim profit from his dubious right to buy the silver that came out of the mines.

Schlick must have known that the only way he could possibly pay back those loans was by dramatically expanding production. In July 1516, right around the time the mining started, he wrote to Heinrich von Könneritz, the captain of the mountain at Annaberg. It was a powerful position. Under Saxon mining law, a captain managed the local lord's interests on the mountain, keeping peace with the miners and controlling the bursar, who paid out both investor dividends and miner salaries.

Schlick wanted to know whether any more Saxon companies might be interested in the valley. Von Könneritz arrived in person six days later and found the mountain already so crammed with miners there was nowhere to sleep. He spent the night in a watchhouse at the head of a passage into the mountain. We no longer have his memoirs, but we do know that he noted on that trip that there was enough water and wood to build industrial mines in the valley and start digging up an industrial amount of silver.

THE MINERS REVOLT

Today it's only fifteen minutes north by car from Karlovy Vary—the spa town where Stephan Schlick first received his investors—to Jáchymov. A fire in 1873 destroyed all the valley's half-timbered houses from the sixteenth century, and what remains are several rows of Renaissance stone mansions, built for investors in the 1520s and 1530s. To support the weight of the stone, they're wider at the basement than the roof, with columns framing wooden doorways wide enough for a horse. You can still walk along what is now Mincovní Street—Mint Street—where they ran drunk in 1518.

The Pinc family lives in number 33. Martin, an architecture professor, commutes to the Czech Technical University in Prague during the week. Milana remains in Jáchymov and raises the children, ten of them. Inside the door is a line of eighteen downhill and fourteen cross-country ski boots. The Pincs moved to Jáchymov in 1996. The house was empty when they arrived. After World War II, the town's German speakers were sent to Germany, and the repopulation took decades. For a time, Milana says, Romani had squatted in the house. When the Pincs moved in, 33 Mincovní was in such disrepair that snowdrifts remained in some rooms through July.

Shortly after they arrived, Milana and Martin were hosting a friend, a geologist. He heard drips of water coming from behind a brick wall that faced into the mountain, and so the three found a hammer, began pulling out bricks, and discovered a cavern. Wide enough at the mouth for all of them to stand abreast, it narrowed to the size of a single crouching person, then ran three hundred feet into the mountain. Standing just inside the cavern now, Milana points to a blue-gray vein of ore, still in the wall, wet with a dew that seeps everywhere out of the mountain. "It was a surprise to us," she says. "Our private silver mine." It is one of the oldest in Jáchymov, dating back to 1517.

Rotted splinters show where a wooden drain used to run. The passage is now lit with Christmas lights; when the kids were little, Milana used to send them into the mountain to look for a chest she had filled with plastic coins. There's a doormat where you can clean the mine off your feet before stepping back into the house. Next to the passage is a ten-by-ten-foot stone room. The Pincs use it as a wine cellar; it keeps cold, Milana says.

In 1517, this room would have been all there was to the house. Silver ore was passed from inside the mountain through a small hole into the room, where it was stored under protection. Milana shows me where one wall is fortified with an embrasure for an archer, who would have looked directly out onto the street. In his first night in the valley, von Könneritz would have slept in a watchhouse exactly like it.

It was easy to find silver in that first year in Konradsgrün. You could get lucky if you just stood on the side of the mountain—as someone once did in what is now the Pincs' ground floor—and started banging with a hammer and an iron. The widest part of the mine, where the Christmas lights are now, is an adit, a horizontal passage into the side of a mountain that lets people in and gets ore and water out. It's where a joint-stock company would have paid for miners to get started; where it narrows is where they found a seam of silver, and the passage began to pay out dividends. The very first adit in 1516 hit silver within two yards at Joachimsthal. Miners at the time were astonished that they could produce silver by daylight.

That first year, the Saxon investors brought their own miners, who came for two reasons. First, no one in Bohemia yet had the power or inclination to enforce the kingdom's mining laws in Konradsgrün. The

Saxon miners could increase their wages by sometimes working two eight-hour shifts in a single day, a privilege of the chaos of the valley that they weren't allowed at home. Second and far better, on their own time they could prospect. According to stories collected by the pastor Johannes Mathesius decades later, veins of silver ran in the forest under the grass and between the tree roots. There was still room all over the mountain for new claims. You could start with nothing, book a claim, and get rich in Konradsgrün. In those early years, miners in the valley were both workers and entrepreneurs: They would dig for the joint-stock companies *and* prospect for themselves. Some miners worked their own claims with small groups. Some sold their claims immediately to a company.

It was this opportunity, the ability to stake a silver claim in the wilderness of the Bohemian side of the mountain, that provoked among the Saxons on the other side a *Berggeschrei,* literally a scream in the mountains—a silver rush. Those histories of the valley from the 1930s all use the same word to describe the growth: "American"—growth so rapid that the only comparisons were the exotic legends of Chicago and New York. In 1516 there were 1,050 people in the valley. By the next year that had doubled, to 2,170. A popular Saxon couplet from the early sixteenth century offered unconditional advice: *Ins Tal, ins Tal, mit Mutter mit All*—"To the valley, to the valley, with Mother, with everything."

Within a year, more than two thousand people had walked over a mountain and through a forest to live ten to a shack and dig two shifts a day. Some were getting rich. There were no clear laws. Saxon investors were tearing down trees and throwing up stamping huts to break up the ore, melting huts to turn it into silver, and sawmills to build everything and keep the furnaces going. The holes in the side of the valley had started to spit out silver, but both above and below the surface the rules were unclear and poorly enforced, and in 1517 the miners walked off the job for the first time.

Strikes in the valley always came in the summer. On July 13, 1517, the miners put down their tools, declared that they were leaving for Buchholz, a mine on the other side of the mountain in Saxony, and settled in just outside the valley "like a great flock of ravens," where they waited for negotiators. On August 3, Schlick, desperate to get the miners back underground, hosted a conference in Schlackenwerth. Von Könneritz presided; he clearly by this time had decided he had an interest in the valley. The miners were represented by a Saxon *Knappschaft,* a kind of union for each mine, and several mountain officials from Saxony came as well.

Even Saxon investors and Saxon miners weren't enough to turn the valley into a functioning industrial site. Mining is complicated and dangerous and usually takes place in the middle of nowhere; it doesn't work unless everyone agrees to a common set of laws. The conference decided that the Bohemian mining law was no longer working; Schlick had already grossly violated it by sending silver straight to Nuremberg, and it was likely poorly enforced at worksites as well. Schlick agreed instead to take up the Saxon mining law that was already in place in Annaberg, where the investors and the miners had already worked together.

The new law assured the miners that the new shafts and passages in the wilderness in Bohemia would work exactly like the ones back home, making it easier for more of them to pour over the ridge into the valley. It also gave confidence to joint-stock investors, who knew that when they paid into the new mines, they were taking on the exact same financial risks they already understood. The miners also got something else out of the negotiations: They renamed the valley, marrying their old mine in Saxony to the new one on the other side of the mountains in Bohemia. Saint Joachim was Saint Anne's husband—the father of Mary, mother of Jesus.

The agreements that followed the strike in 1517 made it possible to get even more silver out of the ground. And more silver headed north out of the valley, to Leipzig, where Saxon mining investors traded their shares and sold their silver. Schlick was still frantically shipping silver west in bars, to Nuremberg, but his importance in the valley had already been eclipsed. He wasn't necessary anymore for any of it to work. After the strike, the valley had essentially become a Saxon colony.

That fall, Schlick's captain died, and he offered the job to von Könneritz, who accepted. It was an odd decision for von Könneritz, who already worked for George the Bearded, Duke of Saxony—he would eventually become a diplomat court adviser to the duchy—and had a home with six children and his wife, Barbara, on the other side of the mountain. By going to work for Schlick, a Bohemian nobody with a tenuous claim to the valley, von Könneritz was endorsing him. The new hire sent a signal to Saxon investors in Leipzig—the same way that a young, growing company today will hire an experienced CEO to project stability.

As with the rest of the changes, it's unlikely that Schlick would have installed the miners' old captain from Annaberg without their consent, particularly as he continued to negotiate the details of the new mining law through early 1518. Which is probably why the miners threw that party for von Könneritz in January, running drunk with flaming beer kegs through what is today Milana Pinc's first-floor pottery studio.

There aren't a lot of documents left from the early years in the valley. The whole thing was supposed to be a secret. But we do have the new laws that came out of the strike, and it's possible to read in those laws what was important to the miners. After the strike, they no longer had to pay their shift leaders directly for food and lodging, at exploitative prices. They were guaranteed that they could double their pay by putting in a second shift; the joint-stock investors hated the second shift, since it was less productive than the first.

The miners were also worried about not just how much they were paid but *how* they were paid. We think about money in terms of quantity now, but the miners were worried about quality. The bursar on the mountain who worked directly for Schlick hadn't been paying the silver miners on time, in pennies of the same high-quality silver that was leaving the valley in bars. The law from 1518 stated that miners should be paid in good silver pennies "and no other." A strike today would ask for more money. In St. Joachimsthal in the sixteenth century, the miners asked for *better* money.

NO SMALL MONEY IN THE VALLEY

In 1953, Carlo Cipolla gave five lectures at the University of Cincinnati. Three years later he published them as a slim book, *Money, Prices, and Civilization in the Mediterranean World.* In his lectures, he pointed out that smaller coins had a higher brassage; they were more expensive, per unit of value, to manufacture. Every coin had to be hammered, literally banged out on top of a stump. The cost for that skilled labor was the same for every coin, which meant it took more bangs on more small coins to create the same value. For the people who mined, stamped, and sold coins, there was a massive difference between petty coins for daily transactions—small money—and what Cipolla called *moneta grossa*—big money—the high-value coins for merchants and the wealthy.

The gold florins and Rhine florins were big money, what Cipolla called the "dollars of the Middle Ages." Big-money coins, he argued, tended to have two properties. First, there was always one coin that was more eagerly accepted across kingdoms and republics, and carried more prestige. Second, most of the other big-money coins tended to be a "more or less faithful copy" of the dominant coin. The florin was consistent, well made, pure, and accepted north and south across the Alps. The Rhine florin began as a more or less faithful copy of the florin.

Kings, dukes, and princes usually didn't mint their own money. Far more often, they licensed private mints to do it for them, and the mints expected to run a profit. For the mints, the brassage was lower on big money; big coins cost less to make, per unit of value. Given a choice, mints preferred to make big-money coins, because they were more profitable. This caused what Cipolla called "the big problem of the petty coins," one of the more consistent complaints in monetary history: How do you get the mints to make enough low-value coins for small transactions? For mints, the business of stamping bigger coins was profitable and mostly unproblematic. When rulers demanded petty coins, mints would often make up for slim profit margins by lowering the silver content. We're used to talking about good, pure money or bad, impure money, but often an impure petty coin was a perfectly acceptable compromise. A merchant paying for long-distance trade had a need for pure gold florins and an incentive to test them. A carpenter paying for bread had neither the means nor the incentive to test the copper-silver mix of a penny, and was more likely to tolerate something less than pure—within reason.

Stephan Schlick was supplying the valley with bad pennies, mixed with so much copper that miners didn't find them reasonable. In 1517 the valley was already one of the most productive silver mines in Europe, but it was a bad place to get paid in good silver groats and pennies, which was particularly galling when high-quality silver bars were leaving the valley for Nuremberg. Schlick didn't want to run a mint; he just wanted to buy and sell silver, as much of it as possible, to get his slim cut. But he still had to get coins from somewhere.

To start with, investors in the Saxon joint-stock companies expected to split up their dividends every quarter in full-value, big-money Rhine florins, an accounting exercise that ran through Schlick's own bursar on the mountain. These coins likely came from Nuremberg as part of the money Schlick's bankers advanced him against his silver monopoly. The miners, too, expected smaller coins for their shift work. New miners arrived in the valley all the time, and numbers swelled every spring, when it was easier to get over the ridge. The demand for coins in the valley was constantly growing, and Schlick had consistent difficulties getting enough of them.

Stephan Schlick just wanted to be the lord of a silver mine. But in claiming it, he became the lord of a valley, one that, because it was still hiding from Bohemian law, wasn't supplied by coins from Bohemia's mint at Kutná Hora. This meant he couldn't just mine silver. He also had to manage the supply of large and small coins in a remote location, a challenge central banks now have entire departments to figure out. It's still difficult today to move physical money around the world; the more people who need payments in different denominations, the harder the logistics get. The lack of regular payment in high-quality coins was a common complaint among all miners at the time, but the ones who worked in the valley had an extra problem: Stephan Schlick wasn't very liquid. He couldn't be bothered to keep enough petty coins on hand to pay everyone all the time.

Schlick had to pay big-money coins to build his castle and pay his bursar and captain. Then he had to pay big-money coins to the joint-stock companies for their bars of silver, or else the mine would stop growing. The miners were last in line. Small-money coins were a nightmare for rulers. Manufacture too many by adulterating them and you could face a revolt. Produce too few of them and you could face a revolt. Stephan Schlick neglected to import enough good pennies and groats to pay his miners, and they walked out on him.

IMPORTANT PEOPLE FORCED SCHLICK TO START MINTING COINS

In August 1518, less than a year after the Joachimsthal miners' revolt, prospectors began furiously entering their claims into a new *Bergbuch*—literally a book of the mountain, a record of claims on silver in specific locations in the valley. We no longer have the book itself; it showed up in a rare-book store in the 1930s, then disappeared into the private collection of a museum worker in the 1960s. In the library at the regional museum in Karlovy Vary, however, there's a slim, saddle-stitched record written from the claims book by a genealogist, looking for proof of Saxon names in Bohemian St. Joachimsthal.

The claims weren't entered in any chronological order at first, meaning that St. Joachimsthal was catching up from not having any records at all. Hans Dickmichel from Annaberg, for example, said he had been working a silver claim for three months, but had lost his papers. The claim was booked anyway. Dickmichel had been one of the negotiators after the strike; perhaps his own claim had been one of his conditions. You could get rich in Joachimsthal.

It's likely there's no record of claims before the summer of 1518 because Schlick wanted to keep them secret. But powerful people on both sides of the border already knew what was happening in the valley. On September 3, there's an entry for a claim in the *Bergbuch* by Henry IV, Duke of Saxony, George the Bearded's little brother. One of the first claims, on July 8, went to the master of Bohemia's state mint at Kutná Hora. As the town grew—and with it the potential to create real revenue from silver mining—Schlick found himself constantly negotiating with all the people he'd been hiding from when he first rode up to the valley from Karlsbad.

In June 1518, Schlick's uncles, the lords of Hasslau, asserted their own rights to the valley. They had inherited land near his and, through the family, had an equal claim to the silver. After what Schlick described later in a letter as a "gathering of honorable men," he bought his uncles off with 2,000 Rhine florins and four shares in his original joint-stock company. By the end of 1518, Stephan's own brothers were part of an active market in claims on new silver mines and shares in the valley's joint-stock companies. The pace of new claims accelerated, and after that first rush they were time-stamped down to the hour, with a verified site visit for each. St. Joachimsthal's miners founded their own Knappschaft that year as well. In 1519, there were 598 new single holders working their own claims and 44 new joint-stock companies working a claim together. The next year, 395 more single holders emerged, and 61 more companies. By 1520, there were almost five thousand people living in the valley.

That year Schlick's uncles also decided they were no longer happy with the arrangement among honorable men and reopened negotiations. One of the uncles, Nicholas, held up a shipment of silver bars to Nuremberg, while the two from Hasslau blocked all transport to the valley—no food or coins in, no silver out. Stephan had no way to pay his bankers, his investors, or his miners. He had to settle. The two Saxon dukes, George and Henry, brokered a deal that required Stephan to offer the rest of his family a cut of the whole operation: a seventh of his already slim income from the entire valley.

In 1520, Stephan Schlick even found his own bankers working around him; that year Jakob Welser began investing directly in a joint-stock company, as did another group from Nuremberg. The histories from the 1930s describe Schlick as a titan, but he was never anything more than the nominal lord of the valley. He always wanted more silver coming out of the ground, because he needed to buy it and pass it on to his bankers to pay down his debt. But there's only one record of a Schlick hut—an actual mining operation owned by a member of the Schlick family—in the town's history. If we describe Stephan Schlick as an entrepreneur, we have to add that he franchised out the valley early, for a small and dwindling cut. And this whole time, he hadn't yet figured a way around the basic flaw in Joachimsthal's ownership structure: Under Bohemian law, everything in the valley was still illegal.

Petr Vorel believes that the Holy Roman Emperor Maximilian I at first encouraged the king of Bohemia to ignore both the Saxons arriving from the north and the silver bars leaving to the west. The king was only ten years old in 1516, a dauphin under the protection of the emperor, who in turn owed money to the same Nuremberg bankers who had staked Stephan Schlick. But in 1519, Maximilian and the young Bohemian king, Louis Jagiello, had been forced to notice what was happening in the valley. The Bohemian regional lords, who had never liked the upstart Schlick family to begin with, realized that all the new silver mines in the valley might be another way to get the Bohemian crown to pay them back. They already controlled the king by forcing the kingdom's silver through the one mint at Kutná Hora. The silver from Joachimsthal was outside that system. It would have to be brought in.

On January 9, 1520, Bohemia's lords ruled that all the silver in the valley had to be turned into coins before it left. Bohemia's king could claim his share, and then the estate lords would take their repayment from him as coins, right there in Joachimsthal. The king approved the

Saxon mining law on Bohemian soil to keep the silver flowing for everyone, but Stephan Schlick couldn't quietly send his ingots to Nuremberg anymore. Heinrich von Könneritz remained the captain at Joachimsthal and became the master of a brand-new mint in the valley as well. It was the position with the greatest authority—the man trusted to make sure everyone got paid. And in 1520 a brand-new mint in the valley struck the first joachimsthaler coins—the first silver dollars. Just like the *Annaberger* coins from the silver mines at Annaberg on the other side of the border, they were meant at first as dividend payments for the Saxon investors. That year, a little over 136,600 silver coins, each worth a full Saxon florin, left the valley for the silver markets in Leipzig. You could say it was a victory for Stephan Schlick; all the people with power finally recognized his claim to the valley. But it was also a year that put him in his place. All the people with real power finally started getting their cut.

THE DOLLAR WAS BIG MONEY

I met Petr Vorel at the University of Pardubice, an hour east of Prague. I had some difficulty getting into his building; the guard did not speak English and was hostile to the suggestion that he and I might try communicating in German. When I found Vorel in his office, he was waiting with a stack of books and papers, and a surprise: He had borrowed from a museum collection a real, honest-to-God, 1520 silver coin from the mint at St. Joachimsthal. He handed it to me, right there in his office: the first dollar. I flipped it over in my hand and then watched it nervously; it rattled on the table as we looked through his papers. There are about a hundred of these left in public collections in Czechia, he says, maybe the same number in Germany and Austria. I have been to coin museums in Germany, and I can assure you: They do not let you touch their five-hundred-year-old silver.

The coin itself is an exquisite compromise, a product of that year's negotiations. Heads for the coin is the lion of Louis Jagiello, king of Bohemia, a nod to the Crown and the Czech lords behind it. For the tails the Schlicks were allowed to put their coat of arms on a shield, and even snuck "Stephan Schlick and brothers" in abbreviated Latin onto the legend. Behind the shield stood Saint Joachim.

Different artisans at the mint in the early 1520s created their own dies to stamp out the joachimsthaler. One Saint Joachim is wise, trimmed, upright. He carries his cloak. One is almost young, with clear eyes. On one coin, the father of Mary is broader-shouldered and defiant. But on that first 1520 joachimsthaler—the coin Vorel casually handed me in his office—Saint Joachim is old, sorrowful, his beard long. He wears his cloak, and leans against the Schlicks' shield for support. It's an odd image to put on a coin. It's not the proud patron saint of any kingdom, but Vorel points out that those first joachimsthaler coins were never meant to be local money, either in Bohemia or in Saxony. They were dividend coins, tied to the mine, not the land, minted to the Saxon standards to be worth exactly 1 gold Rhine florin.

The first joachimsthaler from 1520, showing Saint Joachim and Stephan Schlick's coat of arms. (Image from the Staatlichen Museen zu Berlin.)

In the same way that Saxons had called the dividend coins from Annaberg Annaberger, they began referring to the new coins as joachimsthaler. The coins had one purpose: to pay out pure silver to investors in the joint-stock companies and to the Czech lords who wanted to recover their loans to the king of Bohemia. The new silver coins minted right at the mine replaced Schlick's system, where he brought in coins from Nuremberg to pay investors. The Saxon investors wanted the exact same system they had in Saxony, and they got it. The new silver joachimsthaler were never local money. They were designed expressly for export north to Leipzig. The reason there are so few of these first coins left in Czechia, where they're from, is that they all immediately left the valley—and soon thereafter the continent of Europe—to be melted down and used as money somewhere else.

The agreement to make coins obliged the mint in St. Joachimsthal to produce Bohemian groats, too, to pay the miners. The joachimsthaler were an export, but the groats would have been currency, for local payments. But groats weren't in the interest of anyone expecting a return from the valley, and so von Könneritz just didn't bother minting them. Both the mint at the mines in Saxony and the centralized mint at Kutná Hora in Bohemia had always had to produce small money to satisfy peasants and small merchants. But Vorel points out that the valley was a legal exception. It was located in Bohemia but had snuck around its obligation to produce Bohemian pennies or groats. It used Saxon law, but because it wasn't *in* Saxony, it didn't have to make Saxon small money either. The people who controlled what was becoming the richest silver mine in Europe didn't have to bother with minting silver pennies or silver groats. Both then and now, there's no profit in small money, and Joachimsthal was its own little place, perched in a borderland, set up by accident to produce an unprecedented gusher of *moneta grossa*—big, pure silver coins.

The decision in 1520 to make the mines legal and mint the dividend coins right there in Joachimsthal also made it easier to pull investment from German merchants and nobility in through the city of Leipzig. All the valley's most important social and economic ties ran north, over the ridge. In 1521, Stephan Schlick even married Margarete, daughter of Hans Pflug von Rabenstein, one of that first small group of Saxon investors who had visited the valley disguised as a hunting party. That year joint-stock companies earned 127,452 silver joachimsthaler, and the town sent invitations out to German and Czech trading and banking cities for a three-day shooting festival—both an actual shooting contest and a massive party. Henry IV, the Duke of Saxony listed in that first claims book in 1518, came down for the event, as did Hans Pflug von Rabenstein, Schlick's Saxon father-in-law. Schlick and von Könneritz ordered new robes with cloth from London, and paid for a herald from Augsburg to narrate the day for them in song. Almost three hundred shooters competed for a prize of 1,000 Rhine florins, supplied by Stephan Schlick, and then everyone returned to the brand-new city hall and got hammered.

Philipp Robinson Rössner, a monetary historian from the University of Manchester, has referred to the silver mines on either side of that ridge as a "Silicon Valley"—a fluid network of capital and experts, constantly rearranging themselves in joint-stock companies, hopeful that their next investment would produce a miracle. In the language of Silicon Valley—particularly for anyone who covered that particular valley in the heady, guilt-free years of the early 2010s—the shooting festival represents a familiar event. Joachimsthal had a product. The founder had been demoted to a harmless, symbolic position. The CEO was in place, early investors were already being rewarded, and regulatory approval had been locked down. The city was ready for another round of investors, and so it threw an impressive party. That party is always, *always* an indicator that the founders have gotten ahead of themselves.

WORK AT THE SILVER FACE WAS DANGEROUS

The elevator down the shaft of the Svornost mine at Jáchymov travels at three meters per second. It holds eight bodies at a time, in a two-story car: one cage, stacked on another cage, hurtling into the earth. I packed into the bottom cage with Jiri Pihera, who had worked at the mine for twenty years, and Jan from the regional museum at Karlovy Vary. The mine is not normally open to visitors, and so Jan's twelve-year-old stepson was with us, with several of Jan's colleagues in the cage above us. Jiri casually propped open the cage as we descended, calling out the levels as they skimmed past. He spoke in an inconsistent mix of German, English, and Czech, but what he really liked to do was grab my notebook and draw diagrams, labeled with chemical elements. As we dropped, he drew a straight line down, marking each depth with a century as we passed it.

The oldest passages lie near the surface; in general, mines got deeper as tools improved and there was more capital to pay for them. Jiri labeled the top levels "16th century," but to get there we had to walk through a passage blasted out of the schist with machines, wide enough for two buses to pass each other. This part of Svornost was well known to the CIA in the twentieth century. The early miners at Joachimsthal left clumps of useless ore in slag heaps that turned out to be made of uranium. The Curies did some of their work using ore from the valley. Jan has written a grim history of the political prisoners that Czechoslovakia used as slave labor to mine uranium in Svornost in the 1950s. Piled casually against the schist wall were sections of rusting six-inch steel pipes. I asked Jiri what the pipes were for, and he said something in Czech to Jan. "The pipes are radioactive," said Jan, "so they have to stay below the surface." Another 150 meters down this passage was an intersection. Right and left ran crooked, claustrophobic tunnels just wide enough for two miners to pass each other, standing face-to-face. This is where the sixteenth century begins.

A lot of what we know about mining at the time comes from St. Joachimsthal. In 1527 a man who later took the pen name Georgius Agricola arrived in the valley to serve as the town doctor. He spent all his free time either reading the classical sources on mining and metallurgy, or up at the mine talking to the foremen. He became a scholar, well known in his own time to the major figures of the Reformation, and an adviser to the duchy of Saxony. In 1550, Agricola finished *De re metallica,* a twelve-volume collection that for at least the next two hundred years served as a standard industrial reference. The book is known to an English-speaking audience through a translation in 1912 by a married couple, both Stanford-trained geologists, named Herbert and Lou Hoover—the future president and first lady of the United States. The Hoovers worked nights and weekends for several years while Herbert was a full-time mining consultant and investor in London. They reveal their enthusiasm to us in their footnotes, with page-long digressions on cobalt, for example, or the history of mining law.

De re metallica lays out in detail just how much capital it took to get ore out of the ground, with woodcuts of great wheels: some that pulled water and ore up the shafts, some that stamped the ore on the surface to separate metal from rock. Sometimes in the woodcuts it's a stream turning the axle; sometimes it's a capstan, hitched to horses that turn in a circle under a cupola; sometimes it's two men, bearded and wearing peaked miners' hoods, walking endlessly up battens nailed to the inside of a wheel.

By the early 1520s, joint-stock companies from all the financial centers of the Holy Roman Empire had begun to invest in Joachimsthal—not just Leipzig and Nuremberg, but Augsburg and Cologne as well. Sometimes thousands of Rhine florins in a mine could yield nothing. Or the mine could fill with water, a problem investors could fix with more capital: more pumps, more wheels, more horses. Two cities started growing at Joachimsthal: one down into the valley floor, and one straight into the mountain. By the middle of the sixteenth century, seventy-three passages had yielded silver. The shafts and passages and

A—Toothed drum which is on the upright axle. B—Horizontal axle. C—Drum which is made of rundles. D—Wheel near it. E—Drum made of hubs. F—Brake. G—Oscillating beam. H—Short beam. I—Hook.

Sixteenth-century woodcut from Georgius Agricola's *De re metallica*, showing a horse-drawn capstan for hauling ore out of a mine. (Image from Project Gutenberg.)

adits were named in the same ways they had been in Saxony—piously, after saints, and more profanely, after people, animals, and inside jokes. At Joachimsthal the first major adit to clear water from the mines was named Barbara—same as the wife of Heinrich von Könneritz, captain of the mountain.

When Jiri took us from the uranium mine into the sixteenth century, we entered a passage called Seagull. Water ran down the floor of the passage, six inches deep. Agricola recommended that miners wear high rawhide boots to protect the sinews of the feet from the water, and avoid poor health in old age. The miners believed in demons that could bring about a quick and brutal death underground, and Agricola recorded a long list of ways to die—falls, suffocation in stagnant air, drowning in pools of water.

To get silver ore out of the face at the end of a passage, a miner would hold a sharpened iron bar with one hand and swing at it with a short-handled sledgehammer. The work moved forward at an inch a day, Jiri says. Miners would follow each seam carefully to avoid wasting any effort. In Seagull, I could still see scars in the rock where the iron dug in. The passages reached overhead, often at a crooked angle, as high as you could swing a hammer. A miner would climb down the shaft with a basket of eight irons, and dull them at the rate of one per hour. Imagine swinging a short-handled sledgehammer above your head into rock for eight hours, and you can see why investors hated the double shifts. Two shifts didn't produce double the amount of silver ore; no one can do that for sixteen hours. Sometimes during the second shift a miner would fall asleep at the silver face.

The Schlicks had never found an enduring agreement with the people who climbed down and up those ladders. In 1521, the same year Stephan Schlick ordered clothes from London and hired a herald to record his shooting festival, six men were arrested in Joachimsthal for planning a revolt, and an anonymous writer published a satirical pamphlet, "A Beautiful Poem on the Remarkable Mine at St. Joachimsthal," with a list of complaints: The bursar held back, and paid with "bad pennies."

The miners had nothing to eat but "a dry crust of bread." Schlick and his brothers knew, the poem claimed, and didn't do anything.

In 1522, the dividends that came north to Leipzig from St. Joachimsthal dipped to 90,000 joachimsthaler, from 127,000 the year before. The next year they stayed relatively low, at 110,000. It could have been an infectious disease that caused the drop in production; a "great dying" had rippled through the crowded wooden huts packed up the side of the valley in the winter of 1521. But it also became clear at the end of 1522 that Stephan Schlick had lost control of payments on his own mountain. Peter Hettersberger, the bursar in Joachimsthal who was responsible for paying out both dividends and wages, had been pocketing both, and was discovered to have embezzled 36,000 joachimsthaler—a third of the profits from the entire valley that year. The miners walked off the job again. To get them back to work, Stephan Schlick likely had to make good on at least some of the losses out of his own pocket.

Schlick found a new bursar. It didn't work. The problem in the valley wasn't just a self-dealing official. The bursar's office was always short of coins for payment, because the Schlicks themselves wanted it that way. Ultimately the family was so burdened with debts that they came to an agreement with their creditors to collect payment directly from the bursar's office. In 1525, dividends out of the valley collapsed again, this time to 71,000 joachimsthaler. Schlick couldn't keep the silver flowing, because this time there was a real revolt.

A REVOLT IN JOACHIMSTHAL

The valley's special status after 1520 as an exception to the law ensured that its mint produced only big, uniform, reliably pure silver coins. No silver bars to pay bankers. No pennies or groats for local transactions. Just big money, for investors. But that alone didn't turn the joachimsthaler into the dollar, the coin that was already universal less than a hundred years later, when Shakespeare mentioned it. Money is a product, and the process that manufactures it matters. Before anyone can rely on it, the supply has to *be* reliable. In 1525, Stephan Schlick had silver, capital, labor, and even a mint, but that wasn't enough to create a *moneta grossa,* copied all over Europe and eventually the world. For that, the supply of coins out of the valley needed to become more predictable for investors, and for the merchants they did business with in Leipzig and Nuremberg. So long as the Schlicks were in debt and remained nominally in charge, they either wouldn't or couldn't keep the bursar liquid enough to make payments on time.

On May 20, 1525, three thousand miners sacked the new city hall and took the mayor with them up to the mines. Previously, they had simply stopped working and left the city as a sign they were ready to negotiate. This time, they broke into Heinrich von Könneritz's house and tore up everything—letters, records, claims. Von Könneritz and the Schlicks fled to Schlackenwerth. The miners went house to house in Joachimsthal, asking everyone to either join them or leave. They took Schlick's new castle atop the valley, marched all the way to the border of Saxony, ripped up the customs house, blocked passage over the ridge, then sat down and sent word to von Könneritz that they were ready to talk.

In Schlackenwerth, Schlick had pulled together twenty-five hundred men and was ready to ride back up the valley and respond with force. He was talked into a negotiation instead. The three thousand miners sent a list of demands on May 25, and on July 4 a familiar constellation sat down to negotiate: Schlick's father-in-law, Hans Pflug von Rabenstein; several large shareholders; representatives from the brotherhoods in Annaberg and the mining town of Freiberg; and the Joachimsthal miners.

That May there had been an uprising in nearby Thuringia, what we now know as the Peasants' War. There has been some argument among historians about whether the revolt at Joachimsthal was inspired by the one in Thuringia, but the miners in the valley had a clear set of demands that were particular to their own booming mine. The smaller shareholders, many of whom were miners themselves, accused the Schlicks of smuggling uncoined silver to Nuremberg, even as the bursar's office still wasn't liquid enough to pay dividends on time, every quarter. The miners still wanted to end the truck system that forced them to buy food from their own foremen. They still wanted a guarantee that they could work two shifts in a day and get paid for the hour it took to get down to the silver face. And Schlick had still never fixed the problem of bad pennies in the valley; once again, the miners demanded regular pay in good coin. Nine years after that first revolt, investors and laborers in the town where the silver joachimsthaler came from still couldn't get paid in pure silver.

By July 7, Schlick had agreed to another brand-new set of laws for the city. To get the mines going again after a month and a half without work, Schlick allowed two shifts and ended the truck system. He also had to agree to pay out dividends to investors on time, something he was already supposed to be doing, "in large joachimsthaler coin"—coins made right there, at the mint in the valley. He promised to pay wages in good "white" Bohemian pennies. For the next two years, a third of all wages would be paid in pennies from the Joachimsthal mint as well. After that, half.

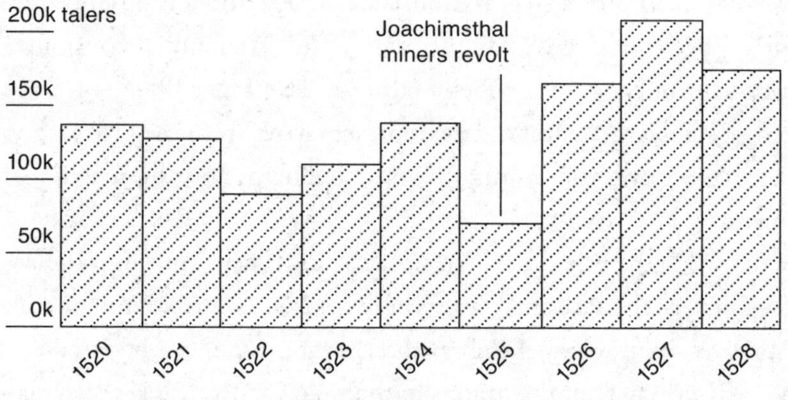

Graph by Evan Applegate.
(Data courtesy of Petr Vorel.)

The next year, 1526, Schlick's bursar in the valley paid out dividends worth 166,000 large joachimsthaler coins. Stephan Schlick couldn't produce a reliable supply of joachimsthaler until the actual town of St. Joachimsthal had clear, enforceable laws that served both investors and miners. The big silver coins had been moving into the Baltic trade through Leipzig for five years, but the supply of them didn't become reliable until everyone got paid with the same good silver. Before the joachimsthaler could become money, though, Stephan Schlick disappeared.

STEPHAN SCHLICK DIED INGLORIOUSLY, AND IT DIDN'T MATTER

Georgius Agricola, the scholar who learned about mines from the foremen in St. Joachimsthal, published his first work, *Bermannus,* in 1530. It's written as a conversation with a thinly fictionalized version of the miner Lorenz Bermann that takes place in St. Joachimsthal in 1527, the year more than 200,000 big silver joachimsthaler left the valley. Desiderius Erasmus, the Dutch humanist and biblical scholar, wrote the introduction; von Könneritz, the valley's worldly captain, had passed the book along through his sons, whom he had sent to study with Erasmus in Rotterdam. Agricola, in turn, dedicated the work to von Könneritz.

Two doctors run into Bermann at the market, where the green had been. Bermann points to the mountains, where the forest has been stripped bare to feed the mines. The wild animals are gone, and the creek down the valley floor has been diverted. They remark that the new houses make the town feel like Prague, or Bologna; by that year there were fifteen thousand people in Joachimsthal. They begin a walk up out of the valley to where the shafts had been sunk into the ridge, right where I met Jiri at the minehead at Svornost. In *Bermannus,* the three men marvel at a massive, horse-drawn windlass at the top of a shaft, protected by a shingled cupola.

They talk of the passages they pass as they walk, like the one cut straight into the valley wall in the Pincs' basement. They note that the Hettersberg passage, still named for the bursar who got run out of town, had paid dividends of 75 Rhine florins a share in the third quarter of 1519. One passage was called Bacchus; it paid so well that shareholders could afford wine from Crete. The name came from Bartholomäus Bach, Joachimsthal's town secretary after 1522; it was his documents that had been destroyed in 1525. The name is ironic, the men agree, because Bach doesn't drink, and made his own friends a gift of printed books of poetry when his dividends came.

The three mourn some friends. Heinrich von Schlick, one of Stephan's younger brothers, has just died of a plague he caught on a field campaign against an Ottoman army. And they remember Stephan Schlick, who "chose to stand and fight" the Ottomans at the Battle of Mohács the previous August, "rather than save himself through flight." The Battle of Mohács had been a disaster for the heavy medieval cavalry of the Bohemian and Hungarian nobility, including Louis Jagiello, king of Bohemia, who fell from his horse into a branch of the Danube and drowned in his armor.

Stephan Schlick's body was not found on the field. Whether he stood or fled, he never returned to St. Joachimsthal. Johannes Mathesius, the preacher who in the 1530s collected stories from the early years in the valley, said that Schlick was captured and taken to an Ottoman prison. Two men traveled from the valley all the way to Constantinople to attempt to buy his freedom, carrying both silver and chunks of ore that were supposed to cure the plague. They discovered only that Schlick might have been sold as a slave, to Armenia. His surviving brothers couldn't come to an agreement over who owned the valley, but it wouldn't have mattered if they had. Von Könneritz remained captain. The horses continued to walk in a circle around the windlass. The silver came up and got hammered into coins. In 1528, the valley paid out 175,000 joachimsthaler in dividends.

That same year the new Habsburg king of Bohemia, Ferdinand, decided he didn't need any of the Schlicks at all, took full control of the mint, and removed their crest and even Saint Joachim from the joachimsthaler. Ferdinand had the power to do what Stephan Schlick had always wanted to: avoid the costs of minting coins by selling 70–80 percent of the valley's silver as bars straight to the Fuggers in Augsburg, with whom he had debts of his own. Mindful of the need to keep paying dividends to investors, the new king continued to mint the rest of the silver as joachimsthaler, stamped not to his own Bohemian standards but still to the Saxon joint-stock investor standard of the value of a full Rhine florin. The joachimsthaler continued to move north over the ridge to Leipzig, but the coins with the old saint, taking up the full volume of the silver that came out of the valley, lasted only eight years. Between 1520 and 1528, according to records of coin tests in Leipzig, likely just over 2 million joachimsthaler in total came out of the valley.

After his disappearance, Stephan Schlick's widow, Margarete, had a special joachimsthaler struck to honor her husband. It's the only image we have of Schlick made by his contemporaries. He is not in his field gear, fighting at Mohács; he's dressed like a merchant. His ruffed collar sits high, his hat rakish, lips pursed, beard trimmed over a strong chin.

The men chatting about mines in *Bermannus* do not linger on what has happened to the Schlicks. They watch a man named Colmann go by and note that he is headed to meet with stockholders to buy some shares. They laugh that until now Colmann has been quietly unlucky with his investments in Joachimsthal. As they laugh, they casually drop in a word that is familiar to all of them: "taler." What had been referred to in the agreements after the uprising in 1525 as "large joachimsthaler coin" had become, in a conversation among friends, "our taler"—our dollar.

In the regional archives at Karlovy Vary, under the disapproving watch of a Czech archivist, you can still read through Bartholomäus Bach's handwritten records—begun in 1526, after the miners destroyed the town's papers. The archives have three leather-bound books, dotted with ink spills, that run through 1533. All the transactions recorded in

Joachimsthal for the entire seven years are entered in only one money of account: the Rhine florin. The taler wasn't yet the money of account in St. Joachimsthal, even more than a decade after the first dig. But by 1527 it had become a word there, a shorthand for the more than 208,000 big silver coins that left the valley that year.

After Jiri returned us to the surface at Svornost, I told Jan I was going to take some more time in town, and that I would meet him back in Karlovy Vary later. The houses in Jáchymov are still mostly as the Pincs found theirs in the 1990s—empty, crumbling. The Czech government has laid new asphalt in the last year on the road up over the ridge to the German state of Saxony, though, and there are new paving stones on the sidewalks. I walked down the valley floor for no reason other than that it was a beautiful evening and noticed, on the facade of Square of the Republic number 8, a historical marker.

It was Stephan Schlick's house.

The house was empty. A courtyard behind it, visible from the stairs up the valley wall, had been reclaimed by trees. At some point in the last century someone had plastered over the facade, but the plaster had flaked to reveal the flat, stacked schist underneath. The window arches had been bricked in to support modern frames, but even those windows were gone, replaced with fiberboard or sheet metal. The great Renaissance doorway was chipped, the latch secured with only a splinter of wood. I pulled it out, and the door to Stephan Schlick's house swung open.

It is not the largest house in town. Where the Pincs live is far more impressive. Schlick built this house in 1520, the year his uncles held up his silver shipments to get a better deal. He lived in it for only five years. According to the historical marker, it's the only house in Joachimsthal with well-preserved joisted ceilings, though the vaults in the entry hall appeared to be about to collapse in places. A two-liter soda bottle sat on the floor in a room that looked out over the valley.

A stone circular staircase led up to a second floor. I didn't take it. No one knew I was there, and I wasn't confident the joists in the rooms were in any better shape than the vaults at the entrance. I slipped out, replaced the splinter of wood in the latch, and drove back to Karlovy Vary to meet Jan for a beer. Everyone else in the bar was convinced I was a CIA operative, snooping around the mine. I told Jan the Schlick house was empty, and he said that a lot of property in Joachimsthal and Karlovy Vary belonged to rich Russians who never visit. Then I admitted to him that I had snuck in for a look. "It's probably okay," he said. "I think the gypsies are all gone now."

THE JOACHIMSTHALER BECOMES THE BALTIC TALER

In August 1963, Christian Kasbohm, an agronomist at a state farm in what was then East Germany, was working with a group of farmers in the town of Glave, about forty miles south of Rostock on the Baltic Sea. They gave him a silver coin, one of several that had been kicked up out of a field by a horse-drawn seed drill. The coin was meant to be a present for Kasbohm's father, but he showed it to the Blaschkes, a married couple who both worked at a local museum. Within hours, the Blaschkes were in Glave, where the farmers said there were more coins and, after some hesitation, led the couple to the field where they'd found them.

The Blaschkes were running out of daylight, but they squared off a small area and began digging. They found the shards of a clay drinking jar, 2 gold ducats, and 165 silver taler. Within days they had expanded the dig to five square yards of the field. Some children in Glave had admitted that they, too, had found some coins. More were found in homes around town.

By the end of the next year's potato harvest, the Blaschkes had unearthed 234 taler, from sixty different mints—in the Netherlands, Denmark, Poland, the German Hanseatic cities, and kingdoms from all over the overlapping lands of the Habsburgs and the Holy Roman Empire. The earliest came from 1546, struck in Öttingen, near Nuremberg. There were taler from several places dated 1629, but none later. The jar, the Blaschkes decided, had been buried in haste by someone who never made it out of the Thirty Years' War.

A 1537 taler from the German city of Lübeck, one of the early copies of the joachimsthaler. (Image from the Staatlichen Museen zu Berlin.)

The couple eventually published an exhaustive catalog of what came out of the potato field in Glave; from the entire find, they identified only 7 taler from the mint masters at Joachimsthal in Bohemia. Only 12 of them come from Saxony. The rest are faithful copies—big silver coins of a consistent value, just like the ones that came out of the valley.

In just over a hundred years, the joachimsthaler had acquired prestige. It had inspired its own faithful copies and become what we would today call a trade currency or a vehicle currency—a way to move a lot of value over long distances. Whoever buried 234 of them in a ceramic jar definitely thought of them as a "reserve currency"—a way to store value. Just like the Florentine florin or the Rhine florin, the coin called the joachimsthaler had become an idea called the taler; it had become *moneta grossa*.

Many of the traditional explanations for how money becomes big money are easy to see with the joachimsthaler. Because it was originally meant as a silver dividend, to be sent straight to the markets at Leipzig for testing and export, the taler was remarkably stable. The coin flowed into the city's open, deep capital markets and out through established northern trade routes. The big silver coin had stability, openness, and trade. But it didn't satisfy the last of the traditional conditions for becoming big money: It wasn't part of the domestic currency of any empire. The coins were minted in an area of Bohemia that followed Saxon mining law, to standards set by George and Henry, the Dukes of Saxony. Both Bohemia and the duchy of Saxony were part of the Holy Roman Empire of the German Nation, a loose and ungovernable confederation run in theory at the time by the Habsburgs, but in practice by no one.

The taler didn't become a coin of the Holy Roman Empire until 1566. Over four decades and several empire-wide conferences on money, Saxony promoted the taler but wasn't powerful enough to force the Habsburgs to accept it. The Habsburgs, in turn, wanted to make their own preferred currency system universal but weren't powerful enough to make the taler go away. During this impasse taler continued to pass merrily from hand to hand, through Leipzig and out into the world.

At the beginning of the sixteenth century, there were two main trading routes that ran past the silver mountains of central Europe. The Via Imperii ran north to south, from Stettin on the Baltic Sea down over the Brenner Pass to Florence and Venice. The Via Regia ran west to east, from Santiago de Compostela up through Frankfurt, or Antwerp through Cologne, and then on to Kiev or Moscow. Both contained bits of Roman road that had been expanded and connected during the Holy Roman Empire. Before Stephan Schlick, dukes and kings with silver in central Europe could get advances from German banking houses in Augsburg and Nuremberg. In 1486, for example, Sigismund, a Habsburg Archduke of Tyrol who constantly owed money to the Fuggers in Augsburg, began minting large silver coins worth a florin, something like the joachimsthaler. But after only two years of production he sold his silver rights to the Fuggers. They took their shipments in bars and moved the silver as they always had: south along the Via Imperii, over the Brenner Pass to Italy, and then on to Alexandria for cotton, silk, and spices.

Joachimsthal was different: a Bohemian town with Saxon miners, Saxon investors, and Saxon law. All those joachimsthaler coins left the valley, and instead of going west to Augsburg or Nuremberg, they went north over the ridge to pay Saxon investors in Leipzig, right at the spot where the Via Regia and the Via Imperii met. During Saxony's silver boom at the end of the fifteenth century, Leipzig had already become a center of finance, too. In 1471, only about three merchants in the city earned more than 10,000 Rhine florins a year in income—enough to be taxed. By 1506, there were fifty. As the silver market grew in Leipzig, traders and bankers began to arrive from the financial centers of Nuremberg and Cologne and request citizenship. The Dukes of Saxony used Leipzig's scheduled market days to pay their officials, pay interest on their debts, and buy imported luxury goods.

All this meant that as the coins from Joachimsthal began to arrive at volume, they moved out through Leipzig's existing trade routes: east through Poland to Kiev, to buy furs, leather, and wax; or north, through Lübeck and across the Baltic to Riga, for the same products. Or they moved west to the Low Countries, to buy cloth. By the end of the sixteenth century, though, even that western trade still ultimately sent the silver east, as the Dutch began to trade up through the Baltic as well. All that silver that bought furs in Riga or Kiev, in turn, continued south and east over the Black Sea for all the same luxury goods the Venetians were getting through the Mediterranean. An English traveler who passed through Russia to Persia at the end of the sixteenth century noted "an incredible summe" of what he called "Dutch dolers," which were used to pay for bolts of silk cloth. As the taler moved out of Leipzig, for the first time, large amounts of silver were moving north and east through the Baltic as high-quality coins, rather than bars.

A series of political accidents turned the silver under Joachimsthal into a flood of high-quality coins. They didn't grow as the currency system of an empire. They gained acceptance because there were a ton of them, and they were a great product. There was a huge and growing demand for silver outside Europe, and joachimsthaler were a useful way to verify and count silver as it left. Wherever they passed on their way out of the Continent—Sweden, Denmark, the Netherlands—they became money.

The flow of actual cash is hard to track—even today—so to follow the spread of the joachimsthaler, we're left with mentions of the coin in accounting documents. A list compiled by Bavaria's coin museum in Munich has a mention of *Daler* showing already in 1526 in Wernigerode, just northwest of Leipzig. In 1527, there's a mention of *Joachimer* in Kleve, on the present-day border with the Netherlands. And in 1529, a merchant in the port city of Hamburg recorded *Jochim Daler.* In Marinus van Reymerswaele's *The Money Changer and His Wife,* painted in the Dutch province of Zeeland in 1539, the poor money changer is oblivious to the charms of his wife, focused instead on the scale in his hand and a pile of coins on a table. In the pile, van Reymerswaele placed several precisely re-created joachimsthaler. By the end of the 1540s, accountants in both Augsburg and Hamburg—at the time these were opposite ends of the empire—had agreed on just plain taler, or Thaller.

Within decades, the joachimsthaler was widely accepted in a circle to the north and west of Leipzig, as well as a southern commercial center, Augsburg, with commercial ties to the valley. And the coin was no longer novel; it had acquired a common name, taler. Over the same period, the coin began to inspire what Carlo Cipolla called "more or less faithful copies." In 1534, the kingdom of Sweden and Finland, which controlled trade into Russia, began to mint jockumsdaler. The kingdom kept its own domestic currency system, adding the new coins for international trade only. Denmark, which controlled the trade through the Baltic at Helsingør, began stamping its own jochemdaler in 1537.

Münster, a German city near the Dutch border, began making taler in 1535. The port cities of Lübeck and Bremen followed in 1537 and 1541. None of these cities had their own supplies of silver; they were buying silver and making taler, because people farther east with furs and leather to sell had come to expect to be paid that way. By 1551, just three decades after the first coins were minted at Joachimsthal, the Holy

Silver joachimsthaler coins in a 1539 painting from Marinus van Reymerswaele, *The Money Changer and His Wife.* (Image from the Museo del Prado.)

Roman Empire produced a complete inventory of coins during one of its conferences on money. Of 130 different silver coins from seventy-six different regional authorities, 64 were some kind of taler.

This is the map we can read from that jar of coins someone buried in Glave in 1629. No empire conquered the kingdoms of Denmark and Poland, the Hanseatic cities of Hamburg and Lübeck, or the Dutch Republic, then forced them all to use the dollar. They chose it, one by one.

The stories we tell about powerful moneys almost always start with sovereignty. An empire has its own money. As the empire grows in power, so does the money. But the hapless Stephan Schlick wasn't an emperor or a king; he wasn't even really a count. He never had control of his miners, his investors, or his bankers. The silver wasn't his, and neither were the joachimsthaler coins. We can't look to the qualities of Schlick or his empire to understand the spread of the taler; he had few qualities and no empire. What we're left with is the qualities and the power of the coin itself.

Money is a product, and it's only as good as it is useful. Miners, investors, Bohemian lords, Saxon dukes, Stephan Schlick, and his cousins all fought each other for a decade over rules at the St. Joachimsthal mines. But they came to an accidental agreement over the purpose of the mint. It wasn't there to create money to spend in the valley. It was there to create a steady supply of lots of big, silver coins, useful for investors and merchants. Joachimsthaler were from the very beginning the perfect big money, inspiring more or less faithful copies wherever they passed. Once the dollar left the valley, it had its own power. It was anyone's coin.

2

The Spanish Dollar and the Collapse of Toledo

Toledo, 1620

CASTILE HAD SILVER. WHAT WENT WRONG?

Approach Toledo on the highway from Madrid and you can already see the city's most important and vexing feature: It sits on a hill, one so obviously defendable that it was already occupied by the Celts when the Romans arrived twenty-three hundred years ago. You can now park where the Roman circus used to be, then invade on a string of escalators. At the top, you will find streets so narrow you have to step into a doorway to let anything as large as a Mercedes sedan pass. You will also find a small army of construction cranes. Investors in Toledo are converting medieval homes to vacation rentals.

In December 2019, I visited the Archivo Histórico Provincial on Toledo's Calle Trinidad. On arrival I was shown straight down, past two stories of shelves dug into the hill. At the bottom Carlos Flores Varela, director of the archive, offered a civilized coffee and, unconcerned that my translator had not yet arrived, began speaking at pace. He pulled out an accordion envelope and produced from it a four-hundred-year-old document—several sheets of printed paper, folded and cut to the dimensions of a paperback. I held it, briefly, and then Carlos whisked it back to the protection of its envelope. Because he is an archivist, Carlos had prepared for me a photocopy, labeled in pencil with the date of the original: August 23, 1620.

When mining began in the valley in Bohemia, what we think of today as the country of Spain was just a group of kingdoms allied by marriage. Toledo had been by medieval standards an industrial city, exporting cloth and steel all over Europe. Medieval Iberian kingdoms didn't have capital cities the way we think of them now, but up on its hill Toledo was the spiritual and political center of Castile, the largest and most powerful of the kingdoms on the Iberian Peninsula.

Charles V, Philip II, and Philip III, the father, son, and grandson who held the Castilian crown in the sixteenth and early seventeenth centuries, had been blessed with two gifts. First, they were Habsburgs. The family had married its way into land all over Europe. Second, Castile had claimed some of North America and most of Central and South America, and with them a little bit of gold and a lot of silver. The volume of silver coming out of the Americas was wildly out of scale with anything Europe had ever seen. At their peak in the 1530s, European mines produced about eleven thousand kilograms of silver a year. By the 1550s, American mines had reached fourteen thousand kilograms. By the 1580s, that had more than doubled, to thirty-four thousand. A vast imperial apparatus served a single purpose: move silver out of the ground, down the mountains, and out across the Atlantic to Europe, or across the Pacific to China, all so the Habsburg kings of Castile could take their cut.

By law, the kings had the exclusive right to operate any mines underneath their pieces of the earth. But a hole in a mountain on the other side of an ocean is a difficult thing to manage, and so the Habsburgs let private speculators stake claims and run the mines, pushing that silver into existing markets. In return, speculators had to pay the *quinto*—a tax of a fifth of all that silver—to the Spanish crown. By the second half of the sixteenth century silver fleets arrived in Seville every year, and the Habsburgs treated their *quinto* on that silver the same way Stephan

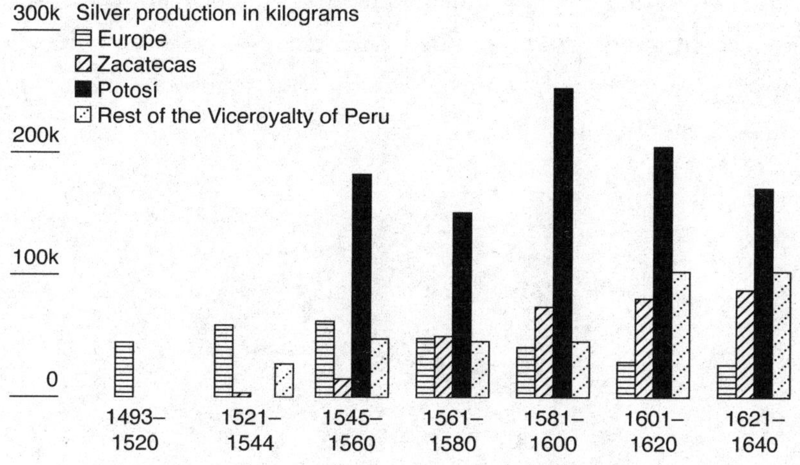

Graph by Evan Applegate. (Data from Adolf Soetbeer, *Edelmetall-Produktion und Wertverhältnisse Zwischen Gold und Silber seit der Entdeckung Amerika's bis zur Gegenwart.*)

Schlick had treated his monopoly right to buy at St. Joachimsthal. They went to bankers and borrowed against the future.

All this new silver ultimately took on a familiar form. The Habsburgs coined their silver at almost the same weight, size, and purity as the joachimsthaler. By the middle of the sixteenth century, merchants in Leipzig, Hamburg, Antwerp, Amsterdam, and even Florence and Genoa had come to expect their silver in taler, and the Habsburgs tweaked Castile's monetary system so they could coin silver in something so much like a taler that in northern Europe it was immediately recognized as one. In 1581 we get the first English mention of a "Philippes doler," for Philip II. The dollar coins that would eventually begin to circulate in England's American colonies came not from Saxony or Bohemia but from mines and mints in what are today Bolivia, Peru, and Mexico.

The Habsburgs commanded a new empire, but they weren't in charge of Europe's silver markets, and so they minted more or less faithful copies of the old joachimsthaler. Then they eclipsed the investors at

St. Joachimsthal as the world's dominant supplier of silver dollars. It was silver Spanish dollars that would end up in England's colonies in North America, by then always stamped with the two pillars of Hercules, draped with S-shaped banners and the old Habsburg motto, *plus ultra*—farther beyond.

A silver Spanish milled dollar from the eighteenth century, similar to the ones circulating in colonial America. (Image from the Staatlichen Museen zu Berlin.)

In the sixteenth and seventeenth centuries, war was the Habsburgs' single largest expense. The *quinto* allowed Philip II to send armadas to win at the Battle of Lepanto against the Ottoman Empire in 1571, then lose in the English Channel against England and the weather in 1588. Silver sustained a brutal, decades-long war to hold Habsburg possessions in what are today Belgium and the Netherlands. The *quinto* also paid to run new viceroyalties in Central and South America, and for regular subsidies to outposts like Havana to protect and sustain the fleets on their way to Seville. Silver made the Spanish Empire possible and served as its unifying purpose. By the beginning of the seventeenth century, war and expansion had turned Castile from a kingdom into a heartland—both the center and the origin of something larger called Spain.

Castilians also looked around their own cities at home and saw an economic and demographic catastrophe. In 1500, per capita GDP in the kingdoms of Spain had been just below that of the Netherlands. By 1600, however, economic growth in the Netherlands had taken off, leaving Spain far behind. From 1530 to 1591, population more than doubled in Castile, growing more than in almost any other part of Spain. But between 1591 and 1700, population shrank by a fifth in the same region, even as it continued to grow almost everywhere else on the peninsula. Spain's empire had been good for the Habsburgs. It had been bad for Castile. It had been terrible for Toledo.

The city had been a prize of late-antique and medieval invasions for a millennium—the Visigoths, the Moors, the Christian kings of the reconquest. It had its own archbishop. It was the home of the Inquisition, and a frequent host to the *Cortes,* a meeting of Castilian cities. In 1535, Charles V had taken the city's Alcázar, a medieval fort, and turned it into a palace. But Toledo isn't laid out for the spectacles of an imperial capital. In the sixteenth century, it was crowded and overbuilt, hemmed in by nature and surrounded by walls. And so in 1561, Philip II started building a brand-new imperial capital in the small town of Madrid. For a while, the hilltop continued to grow. In 1597, Toledo was still bigger than Madrid. Twenty years later, however, Toledo had lost three-quarters of its population. In 1602, there were 1,000 baptisms in Toledo. By 1622, that had dropped to 640. Imagine that within two decades almost half the children of your city have disappeared. It would feel like the end of the world.

Toledo had a strong intellectual community of church and civil leaders who were proud of the university and even met at regular poetry contests. They were bewildered by depopulation, and spent so much time and ink trying to explain it we can now identify a Toledo School, a philosophy to explain how an industrial city dies. The document Carlos showed me over coffee at the archives came from that community. Addressed to the king from the University of Toledo, it opens with a simple plea: Manufactured goods should not leave Spain, and foreign-made goods should not enter. We have documents like this today. It's an open letter from a trade group, begging for tariffs. The letter would have been passed around in Madrid, at a special council that Philip III had called to figure out an answer to the question that had consumed the kingdom: We have so much silver. What went wrong? Toledo's answer, grounded in the self-interest of its merchants, was to flip the question on its head. The city hadn't collapsed despite all those silver dollars. It had collapsed because of them.

SANCHO DE MONCADA, A PHILOSOPHER FOR MERCHANTS

After a pleasant and mostly incomprehensible coffee with Carlos, I was joined at the archives by María Victoria Guadamillas Gómez and Francisco José Aranda Pérez, both from the University of Castilla–La Mancha. María Victoria teaches in the English Department, and had offered to translate. Francisco José is a historian and came to the archives to tell me about Sancho de Moncada, the man who wrote that open letter to Philip III.

The Moncadas, a family of merchants and priests, were *conversos viejos;* they had converted from Judaism in the 1380s. As Francisco José points out, though, more than two hundred years later, old convert families would still be looking over their shoulders, and a position in the church was a good way to stay unimpeachable. Sancho de Moncada, born in 1580, had a chair in theology at the University of Toledo. But his grandfather had been a silk merchant, and his uncle continued in the family business. The Moncadas were registered at San Nicolás de Bari, a parish full of wealthy converso merchants. The church is just a short walk from Toledo's Zocodover, the city's center of trade since antiquity—the word comes from Arabic, for "market of the beasts." Moncada's family in business gave him a practical understanding of how money worked. He cared about what mattered to his family: making things, and selling them.

Moncada wanted the kingdom's universities to teach what we would today call political economy, the study of markets and the state together. I asked whether he had invented the discipline. María Victoria quickly shook her head no, lest I get the wrong impression. Francisco José paused, then waved his hands to indicate maybe. "Más o menos," he said. More or less. Moncada was the first practical economist, he explained. The first in modern times. Sancho de Moncada was a bit of a crank. He encouraged the king to expel the Roma from Spain, calling them whores and wolves. His prescription to fix the cities of Castile—ban imports of manufactured goods and exports of raw materials—would have been as unworkable in seventeenth-century Spain as it has been for twenty-first-century America. But he was a careful observer of what had happened to Toledo.

In the early seventeenth century, Castilians descended into what one historian called an "orgy of national introspection." Men called *arbitristas* recorded their suggestions for projects, or *arbitrios,* documents like the one that Carlos had pulled from his archive. These projects would be familiar to any policy journalist in any national capital today. The king needed to cut spending. He needed to reform the tax system, reduce the tax burden on Castile, and encourage more contributions from the rest of the empire. He needed to halt the depopulation of Castile and bring in immigrants. He needed to improve infrastructure, irrigate fields, and clear rivers for boat traffic.

Miguel de Cervantes, who was injured on one of Philip II's ships at the Battle of Lepanto, used the *arbitristas* for sport. In one of his novellas, an *arbitrista* proposed that everyone fast for one day a week and send what they save to Madrid so the king could pay off his debts. Even Don Quixote had his own *arbitrio,* to gather all the knights of Spain and find one to fight the Turks. Cervantes, like many Castilians, saw the *arbitristas* as the kinds of men who offer a single answer to all the problems of the world. But they were just tilting at a question we're still after now: The Habsburgs were rich. Why did Castile become poor?

There are two traditional explanations for what went wrong in Castile. One is institutional: The Habsburgs were too focused on war abroad and absolute control at home. The other explanation is monetary: Waves of silver poured into the kingdom, raising the price of everything as they crested. Moncada, born into a family of merchants and cloth manufacturers who had watched their own industries collapse in Toledo, offered an explanation that was both monetary and institutional. He believed that the silver had changed Castile. The kingdom used to make things, but then it stopped.

Moncada produced only one book, *The Political Restoration of Spain,* a companion to the arguments in his open letter. It was written with only one audience in mind: the king in Madrid, a man known to have had limited capacity for deep reflection. Moncada's book has never been translated into English. I found him through a single quotation in an academic article, where he wrote that France, Flanders, Genoa, and Venice had all become wealthy through industry, while Spain had agriculture and silver fleets, but no industry. I went to Toledo to understand Moncada's argument. We often take it for granted that producing dollars, the world's dominant currency, is a blessing. Writing in Toledo, a fading industrial town on top of a hill in Castile, Sancho de Moncada saw the Habsburgs' silver as a curse.

The poverty of Spain, Moncada wrote, came from the discovery of the Americas. It would have been a conquest of immortal glory had it only served to spread the gospel and left all the metal in the ground. Moncada didn't say that the Habsburg kings had misused their *quinto*. He said they'd be better off without the silver mines, period. To start with, almost none of that silver had ever made it into Spain. "It is well known that there is more gold and silver with your majesty's stamp in any kingdom of any region than there is currency in Spain," Moncada wrote. "In June 1618 it was recorded that within the walls of a single city in Italy there were 18 million of your majesty's coins. . . . China alone, they say, takes more than 4 million of your Majesty's coins a year."

Meanwhile, he continued, republics that had no silver of their own had become rich through industry and trade. But trade had collapsed in the cities of Spain—Burgos, Medina, Seville, and Moncada's home of Toledo. "The prosperity that is usually the life of other kingdoms is the death of Spain," he wrote. Silver wasn't even a Castilian industry. Foreigners ran the silver trade, and they treated Castilians like *indios,* according to Moncada: They took out silver and raw materials, and in return brought trinkets. The kingdom had one great product—the silver dollar—and it had destroyed everything else.

BEFORE THE SILVER, TOLEDO MADE THINGS

We tend to use words like "manufacturing" and "industry" for later centuries, but in the first part of the sixteenth century Toledo already had pieces of what we would recognize today as a manufacturing hub. Sitting at the provincial archives, I asked Francisco José what Toledo had made. He puffed his cheeks out and exhaled—the international sign for "Where do I begin?"—and then he and Carlos talked over each other trying to list it all.

Merchants in Toledo brought in silk thread north from Valencia and Murcia on the Mediterranean coast, then wove silk cloth with it. Wool came in from Burgos and Segovia and was turned into cloth as well. Linen came in from Flanders, to be finished into robes and reexported. Cloth merchants like the Moncada family shipped raw wool and finished silks, woolens, and linens from Toledo out to Lisbon, Flanders, and Genoa. Almonds came from Alicante and in Toledo became marzipan. Iron came from as far away as Italy and became swords that were sold all over Europe. All of this was run under a medieval guild system, which provided training in the trades and decided who got to participate. There were no factories in the sense that we would think of them now, just people in their own homes, pulling in raw materials and making things with them. Francisco José and Carlos laughed as they talked over each other. Families were packed in with apprentices and animals, they explained, all hemmed in behind the city's walls, all on top of the hill together. It was tight.

A couple of things had to go right for these industries to grow in Toledo. Manufacturing and in particular cloth production required fresh water; the Tagus River wraps around Toledo on its way to Portugal. The city sat along a trade route that connected it to the medieval trade fairs at Medina del Campo—and through them, all of Europe. Toledan merchants were tied to commercial networks all over the peninsula, particularly in the silk-spinning areas along the Mediterranean coast. The hilltop was secure, too. It held a lot of capital. Francisco José explained that Castilian nobles and clergy had incomes from agriculture in the surrounding area, which they would keep safe at the city's convents. He gestured over my shoulder. Right here, he said, the Convento de San Pedro Mártir—steps away from the archives, now part of the university—offered loans and took in what we would think of today as deposits. It was a common practice in medieval and early modern Spain. Merchants in Toledo would have at different times both lent to and borrowed from the nuns.

Sancho de Moncada grew up inside this system. As a child, he lived with his grandfather, a merchant active in the city's cloth guild who had learned the trade from his own father. The Moncadas bought raw silk in Granada, then sold it to spinners and weavers in Toledo, who in turn made velvet and taffeta cloth to sell in cities around Castile and at the fair in Medina del Campo. Like other merchants in the city, Moncada's grandfather sold raw materials on credit, to be paid back with finished goods. When he died in 1588, he had credit with most of his spinners and weavers.

In his *arbitrio,* Moncada pointed out that even in 1620 products from Castile still had a reputation for quality: Steel blades, like the ones made in Toledo. Cloth from Segovia. The problem was cost. Foreign goods were cheaper, no one from abroad bought Castilian knives or cloaks or stockings anymore, and Castile's cities were closing their workshops and losing their skilled workers. Countries still try today to build industrial areas from scratch, but it's difficult to create an industry on purpose. It takes decades and sometimes centuries of learning and passing on skills, building relationships with suppliers and investors. Think of the cloth and steel production in Toledo like a hillside of vineyards—a millennium old, specialized for soil and climate, tended by experts who had learned from their own families. Right before the conquest of the Americas, Toledo had already had everything in place. It had been an industrial city through Sancho de Moncada's childhood. Then, suddenly, it wasn't.

What had changed was empire. In the middle of the sixteenth century the Crown had created several new viceroyalties, territories that covered what are now Mexico, Texas, Florida, the Caribbean, all of Central America, and much of South America. The viceroyalties were Castilian in theory—they answered to whoever held the Castilian crown—but the rapid colonization of Castilian territories in the Americas gave Toledo what economists would now call a shock. An economic shock is inherently neither positive nor negative. It just changes things. Suddenly. A lot.

THE CHINA SILVER SINK

A metallist would say there was a lot of silver in the Americas, and so it became a lot of money. Done. But process matters. You can't just push money out into the world, even silver, and hope it works. It needs a destination, what economic historians sometimes call a sink. For money to have value, somebody somewhere has to want it; you won't accept something as payment unless you know you can pass it on to the next person. Moncada understood the details of how silver moved, which is why he explained to the king that foreigners took silver from Spain because it was more valuable elsewhere, the same way His Majesty took copper from Germany. The entire global trading system of the sixteenth century hung on one simple fact: Silver was much, much more valuable in China than it was in Europe. China was the sink for the world's silver.

When they look at trade, economists prefer to make a clear distinction between goods and money. In the most basic model, two countries swap goods. Wool goes one way, porcelain goes the other, and trade is balanced. If the porcelain is worth more than the wool, the wool country has a trade deficit, and has to make up the difference with a surplus of payments. In this model, the *type* of payment is irrelevant; it's all just money. But the type of money was relevant to the merchants of southern China. Over the last two decades, two economic historians, Dennis Flynn and Arturo Giráldez, have been arguing that the economists' traditional descriptions of trade balances and money can't capture what happened to Spain's silver. Just like Sancho de Moncada, Flynn and Giráldez point out that silver was in such high demand in China that it wasn't payment. It was a product. It was the only thing anyone else had that Chinese merchants wanted. Trade *was* balanced. Silk and porcelain went one way. Silver went the other.

In the sixteenth century, silver was far more valuable in the port cities of southern China than it was anywhere else in the world. Around 1500, it would have taken six pounds of silver to buy a single pound of gold in China. In Europe, that same pound of gold would have cost twelve pounds of silver. Any sixteenth-century merchant in Mexico City, Seville, Lisbon, or Antwerp would have known as an incontestable truth that the best thing to do with silver was to get it to someone who could get it to China.

Demand for silver in China had reached a peak right as the mines in the Americas began to produce for the Habsburgs. Since the third century BC, China's emperors had maintained a complex and effective system of bronze coins. In the thirteenth century, however, that system began to break down. Three different dynasties introduced paper currencies but didn't always ensure they'd convert at reliable rates to the bronze coins, or even do all the administrative work to keep producing the coins. By the early fifteenth century the value of the paper money had collapsed, and the Ming dynasty started accepting taxes in silver at a premium, to pull something of value into the treasury. Merchants in commercial centers still made their own bronze coins as small money, but fist-sized weighed lumps of silver called *tael* became big money, a reliable store of value that a merchant could hand over for a larger purchase.

Smugglers brought silver in from Japan to pay for silks, and by the early sixteenth century the Portuguese had started moving silver from Japan into China as well. This encouraged a cycle of reliance on silver, then demand for more of it, turning China into what Dennis Flynn and Arturo Giráldez call a silver sink. In 1621 a Portuguese merchant looking back on his career in Asia wrote that silver "wanders throughout all the world in its peregrinations before flocking to China, where it remains, as if at its natural center." No matter where silver came from, it was headed eventually to China.

That's likely what happened to the first silver that came out of Joachimsthal. Already in the 1490s, far more silver left the continent of Europe than stayed. Some of the Saxon silver went north into the Baltic; some went on the land routes south to Venice. Silver investors in Leipzig and bankers in Augsburg and Nuremberg also sold some silver west through the Low Countries, and after about 1500 this became the dominant route. The Portuguese had connected a string of trading forts around the Cape of Good Hope to Malacca, but to trade for spices, they needed silver, which they began to buy at volume from German silver agents in Antwerp.

In 1517, the year mining began at St. Joachimsthal, already a third of the silver leaving Lisbon for the cape was *alemão*—German. That year the Welsers, the bankers who had staked Stephan Schlick in the valley, sent more silver from Antwerp on the Portuguese route to the east than almost any other seller. All the major banking families in Augsburg and Nuremberg supplied the Portuguese, a source so important that German agents exporting silver through Antwerp paid no import duties on silver when it arrived in Lisbon. By at least 1525 the Leipzig joint-stock companies had also started selling to Portugal, which meant that the silver would have started to arrive in Antwerp both as bars and as the big silver joachimsthaler coins paid to the investors as dividends. Martin Luther, who grew up in a Saxon mining region, complained a century before Sancho de Moncada that Germans were wasting their silver on spices from Portugal, and that the path through Frankfurt to Antwerp was a "gold and silver sink, through which everything that springs and grows, is minted or coined here, flows out of the German lands."

All the other routes out of Europe eventually connected with China as well. Over the course of the sixteenth century, Dutch trade moved silver north around Denmark and then east through the Baltic to Russian traders in what are now Estonia, Latvia, and Poland. In turn, that silver passed through cities in what is now Uzbekistan to pay for caravan goods from India and China. The Russians opened routes to the Caspian Sea and took Baltic silver down to Persia, where they competed with the silver coming over land through the Balkans and Turkey. When silver moved south from central Europe, it left Venice for Aleppo in what is now Syria, then continued east from there. Each transaction followed that same trade, always east.

In Toledo in 1620, Sancho de Moncada already knew how silver moved. And he was right about what had happened to the silver from the Americas: Almost none of it had stayed in Castile. In 2011 a group of chemists at several universities in France compared silver, copper, and lead isotopes in European and American coins and determined that for the entire sixteenth century no American silver made it into Castile's domestic coins. A path had already been cleared to the other side of the world. The silver in the Americas would not become money in Castile. It would be an export, one that sank inexorably in the direction of China.

THE PIECE OF EIGHT, A FAITHFUL COPY OF THE JOACHIMSTHALER

In 1521, immediately after the fall of the Aztec Empire, Castilians began mining silver around what is now Mexico City; Hernán Cortés himself was an investor in twenty mines. But Castile remained on the edge of the silver market for about two decades. Between 1531 and 1535, for example, just over five thousand kilograms of silver came in through Seville. Over the same period, Joachimsthal alone still produced more than three times that amount.

Some of that silver from Mexico belonged to Charles V, as his *quinto*—his right as king to a fifth of it. A Habsburg born in what is now Belgium and grandson of the Holy Roman Emperor Maximilian I, Charles had inherited his family's patchwork of kingdoms, including Castile. He had not inherited the title of Holy Roman emperor, however; that he would have to earn. When an emperor died, seven electors including three bishops, a Duke of Saxony, and the king of Bohemia all voted on a new one. Charles became emperor by bribing the electors, and paid for the bribes by borrowing from the Fuggers and the Welsers, the same German banking families that were active in the Saxon and Bohemian silver markets. Charles guaranteed those loans with future tax revenues out of Castile, but he would pay them back in American silver.

By the early 1530s Charles had silver coming in from plunder and some mining, and it had become apparent that more would follow. He had figured out how to channel everything going to and coming from the Americas through a single point, the *Casa de Contratación* in Seville—the House of Trade. But silver only has value when someone wants it and you can get it to them. Charles had debts with the same German bankers who had lent to Stephan Schlick, and so he had to move his silver through Antwerp into the same flow that was already heading toward China. And as countinghouses in northern Europe began increasingly to recognize and rely on the joachimsthaler and all its copies, Charles V had reason to turn his silver into something that looked like a taler, even though the Saxon system of silver-mining dividends had nothing to do with the money of Castile.

The Iberian Peninsula had remained outside the Carolingian system of pennies, shillings, and pounds that the rest of the Continent had adopted. At the bottom of the Iberian system was the maravedi, a petty coin made of vellon, a brittle alloy of a little silver and a lot of copper that turned black with use. In 1501 in Toledo, you could buy a pound of nails for 9 maravedis, and a quart of olive oil for 12. Thirty-four maravedis also got you one silver real. The name comes from the word for royal—a coin made in the mint of a Christian king during the reconquest. In theory, the silver real was supposed to work for medium-sized purchases, the same way the silver shillings and groats did on the rest of the Continent. But anything a normal person might buy, like nails or olive oil, was priced in maravedis.

Just as with the Italian city-states, a big gold coin sat on top of Castile's money—the *excelente de Granada,* named to honor the Christian conquest of the Iberian Peninsula. It was a faithful copy of the Venetian ducat, a recognition that the ducat was the most important big money of the Mediterranean economy. Castile minted only a few gold excelentes, and these tended to leave the peninsula to pay for imports. And when the Castilian king borrowed from abroad, he borrowed in ducats; no contracts ever referred to the excelente.

We should resist thinking of ducats, reales, and maravedis like dollars, quarters, and cents. They weren't just different ways of making change within the same system. Each kind of money had a completely different purpose. In sixteenth- and seventeenth-century Castile, you could in theory trade 375 vellon maravedis for 1 gold excelente. In practice, though, these two currencies had almost nothing to do with each other. Gold ducats and excelentes were real and imaginary money for long-distance trade and loans; the copper-silver maravedi was real and imaginary money for local trade. They were different currencies, each with its own distinct job.

You can read this entire history on the wall of the Museum of the Royal Mint in Madrid. It starts with the maravedis, originally minted in gold during the centuries of Al-Andalus. Then, over time, the maravedis get smaller; once they're made out of vellon, they turn black as they start to include more copper. The silver real shows up with the Christian kings of the medieval *Reconquista,* along with some half and quarter reales. Then, from the mint in Seville and dated only to the reign of Charles V in Castile, the first big silver coin shows up. It's a real de a ocho—a piece of eight.

We now think of the piece of eight as the Spanish dollar, the most important coin for global trade through the end of the nineteenth century. The first mention of the piece of eight comes in a decree from 1537, authorizing the brand-new mint in Mexico City to make 2-, 4-, and 8-real silver coins. The real de a ocho is a numismatic accident. If you take one silver real and multiply it by eight, you get a large coin with 25.2 grams of fine silver—about 2 grams shy of a joachimsthaler. These were Castilian coins in theory, and seem to fit neatly into a domestic system. In practice, they were just copies of the joachimsthaler, like the ones all over northern Europe. Charles V wasn't interested in adding to Castile's money supply. He was trying to figure out how to sell his share of the silver from conquest and mining in the new viceroyalties in the Americas. The piece of eight put Habsburg symbols on American silver, but in weight, size, and fineness it was a more or less faithful copy of the joachimsthaler.

José Maria Pérez García, curator of the museum at the Royal Mint, says the real de a ocho was Spain's recognition of a new monetary reality: In Nuremberg, Augsburg, and Antwerp, where Charles's bankers did their business, the taler was a powerful coin. On the walls of that museum in Madrid, you can see centuries of big silver pieces of eight. But you'll also continue to see the same old system in Castile—cracked black vellon maravedis, small silver 1- and 2-real pieces. The Habsburgs continued to borrow in ducats from abroad, and the Castilians continued to pay for food and rent at home in maravedis. The silver real de a ocho—the Spanish milled dollar still familiar two hundred years later to colonists in British North America—was never meant to be money for Castile. Just like the joachimsthaler, it was an export from the very beginning. Even the Holy Roman emperor had to move his silver across the desk of that money changer in Antwerp painted in 1539, joylessly adding up all those big silver coins from Bohemia.

Markets in the Holy Roman Empire were also going through a series of changes in the early sixteenth century, pitting the old gold Rhine florin against the new silver joachimsthaler. As the Portuguese built out their ocean trade, the routes through the Mediterranean and Venice became less important, which made passage on the Rhine through Europe less important, too. This, in turn, sent fewer barges down the Rhine to pay tolls in gold, which put stress on the mints that made the gold Rhine florin, the old unit of account. At the same time, other mints around the empire weren't always careful with their silver copies of the joachimsthaler, which meant that merchants everywhere took coins from Joachimsthal and Saxony, with their reliable 27.1 grams of fine silver, at a premium. What had been a stable system for counting and paying was breaking up, and parts of the empire began to ask Charles to intervene and force the entire Holy Roman Empire to adopt a common currency.

Charles was never able to pull this off; the historian Oliver Volckart has documented decades of unsuccessful attempts. Mountain duchies with silver mines fought against bishoprics along the Rhine that could take in tolls in gold. Princes who wanted to pay back their loans in silver fought against the merchants who had lent to them in gold. The silver mountain lords of Saxony and Bohemia fought against almost everyone else, who wanted them to accept a common coin with less fine silver in it. The mountain lords who had silver didn't compromise, because they didn't have to. There was high demand for their full-weight joachimsthaler among merchants all over the empire and up into the Baltic, and it was difficult for any bishop or prince to compel merchants to stop using a coin that had become useful.

People who follow the modern oil market will sometimes talk about the swing barrel. Lots of people in lots of countries can drill for oil, but there are a few who can drill cheaply, at high volume. It's these few that control the production and price of oil all over the world. For the last few decades of the twentieth century, anyone drilling in the Kingdom of Saudi Arabia had among the lowest production costs for oil in the world; they could basically suck crude out of the ground with a straw. Whoever was in charge of Saudi Arabia ran the swing barrel, and had some control over global production. In the early twenty-first century, American fracking companies in North Dakota and West Texas began producing cheap crude at high volume. Whoever ran those companies could suddenly produce more cheap oil than the Saudi royal family, and so control of the swing barrel moved, from the Kingdom of Saudi Arabia to investors in U.S. oil companies.

Within the Holy Roman Empire in the early sixteenth century, the Saxons in Joachimsthal had the swing dollar. The commercial structure of the valley was designed to do one thing only: crank out a lot of big, consistent, silver coins at the Saxon standard. This, in turn, was perfect for two groups of people: the investors in the valley's mines and all the merchants around the Continent moving silver abroad. It didn't matter who wanted to hold on to the old system of gold Rhine florins, or who wanted a more flexible system of underweight copies of the joachimsthaler. In the early sixteenth century the old long-distance trade system of gold ducats and Rhine florins was weakening in northern Europe, in ways that princes and even the emperor couldn't fix. The taler were replacing everything else.

SPAIN TAKES THE SWING DOLLAR

In the 1540s, silver finds in the Americas opened mining areas that over the next four centuries would produce 80 percent of the global output of silver: Zacatecas in what is now Mexico, parts of what is now Peru, and Potosí in what is now Bolivia. Just as in St. Joachimsthal, however, silver in the ground doesn't mean anything unless there's a way to dig it up, refine it, and get it to the people who can use it. It had been hard enough in the valley to move an existing system of Saxon investors and miners over the mountains and into Bohemia. In the Americas, the Habsburgs had to build an almost completely new system on the other side of the ocean. What historians often refer to as a flood of silver didn't really start until the 1570s, when the Crown became more brutally efficient at getting silver out of the ground.

In Zacatecas, the mining technology came from Saxony and Bohemia. German miners settled in Sultepec near Mexico City in 1536 and began building the same smelting furnaces and stamp mills they knew from home. It's possible this became a place from which new technology spread to the rest of the viceroyalty; centuries later, miners in Mexico still used tools identical to what the Saxons had used at St. Joachimsthal, and the public library in Zacatecas still has a sixteenth-century printing of *De re metallica,* Agricola's twelve-volume encyclopedia on mining technology, annotated by a local engineer in the seventeenth century. The labor wasn't German, though. In the 1530s and 1540s, most of the actual digging was done by natives from nearby *encomiendas,* a kind of feudal estate awarded to soldiers of the conquest.

Just like in St. Joachimsthal, once the miners moved past the rich lodes near the surface, the mining demanded more capital, and the refining became more difficult. And the mountains of central Mexico aren't like the ones in northern Bohemia. There wasn't a lot of running water, so miners relied on mules to power the stamping mills. Miners in Mexico also frequently lacked wood to fire the smelting furnaces; miners in St. Joachimsthal had by then already stripped the forest to the valley floor. In the early 1550s, local officials in Zacatecas made the king aware of a crisis: Food and fuel at the mines had become too expensive. Reforms of the encomienda system made it harder to force natives to work for free. Enslaved Africans had been brought in to work the smelting furnaces, but they, too, were expensive. Silver yields were dropping, because mining had already become a bad business.

At Potosí the challenge was even more difficult. The mountain itself was a plume of igneous rock that had welled up and plugged its own hole. The formation of the Andes had pushed the plume up to thirteen thousand feet, while fractures had allowed water to dissolve and then concentrate the silver, leaving veins near the surface as the plume weathered and oxidized to a rusty red. Just as had been true in St. Joachimsthal, in the middle of the sixteenth century at Potosí you could find silver standing on the side of the mountain. But the mountain was high and windswept, with some water and no wood.

Under the growing empire of the Habsburgs, only a *minero*—a Spaniard with a claim—could use the law to hold and defend the right to mine silver. But for the first quarter century of mining at Potosí, *mineros* relied on mostly Native technology and an Incan social class called *yanaconas,* who answered directly to the sovereign and had the liberty to move for work. Digging mostly in open pits with Basque iron tools, yanacona miners would buy the ore they found from the Castilians who held the claims. Then they'd sell it to other specialized yanacona who ground the ore under huge stones by hand and smelted the way they always had, in cylindrical clay stoves. Dung burned in the bottom of the stove, and wind blew through vents in the cylinder to stoke the fire. Mining in the early decades at Potosí wasn't entirely fair for the yanacona, but it wasn't entirely exploitative, either. Potosí quickly ran out of easy claims at the top of the plume, though, and the ore beneath required more refining than the old yanacona stoves could handle. Just like the mines in New Spain, silver yields at Potosí dropped. They got too far below the surface, and it became hard to make a profit.

In the early 1550s, Bartolomé de Medina, a cloth merchant from Seville, had a midlife crisis, decided that he would solve the smelting problem, and began teaching himself metallurgy. A German merchant suggested he try amalgamation, a process described for refining gold in *De re metallica:* grind the ore to a powder; then mix it with mercury and brine until the mercury creates an amalgam with the gold. Burn the mercury off, and what's left is just gold. Medina figured out how to make the process work for silver and joined the German miners in Sultepec, where he applied to the viceroyalty for a patent and found German engineers to build mills to grind the ore. By the early 1560s, Medina's amalgamation process had been adopted by the rest of New Spain—what is now Mexico. By 1572, amalgamation had reached Potosí.

Amalgamation was a shock to silver production, particularly on Potosí. The Castilian crown had a monopoly on the mercury that came from Huancavelica, in what is now Peru. The viceroyalty of Peru built aqueducts for waterpower, and *mineros* began dragging logs up to Potosí to build drainage and stamping mills modeled on the ones in *De re metallica*. The clay stoves disappeared, and the yanaconas were pushed out of the skilled, technical process of refining and out of a share in the profits from the mine. The only scarce resource left was human bodies to climb down ladders and bring up ore, and so both viceroyalties came up with their own forced labor system.

In New Spain, *mineros* paid for some labor, but a system called the *repartimiento* also forced villagers from around each mine down the shafts every week. Over time, however, people began to migrate to the mines on their own for paid work, and Zacatecas began to look like Saxony and St. Joachimsthal: Skilled local workers earned a wage and had a small share in profits. Because the margins were lower in New Spain, *mineros* persuaded the Crown to lower taxes as well; instead of a fifth of output, at Zacatecas they paid the king only a tenth.

The *mita* system at Potosí, however, was far more vast, destructive, and enduring. Starting in 1574, every year more than ten thousand Native Andeans—one out of every seven adult men in an area that stretched all the way to Cuzco—were marched up the mountain to work. One week in three, they worked unpaid; the other two weeks they could hire themselves out. The mita was cheaper than slavery, because the Andeans weren't considered property; when they fell down a ladder, another *mitayo* stepped in, and there was no loss of capital. In 1585, Luis Capoche, a *minero,* wrote that the dead were brought down from the mountain every day. Others arrived at the base with cracked skulls or broken legs. The workers at the stamp mills had the worst job, out in the cold, their eyes and mouths full of dust. "This fierce beast," wrote Capoche, "swallows them alive."

Potosí could have developed the way Zacatecas did—slowly building a local core of well-paid, skilled miners. The viceroyalty didn't need the mita to produce silver at Potosí; they needed the mita to produce *a lot* of silver, cheaply and quickly. During the 1570s, production at Zacatecas in New Spain recovered modestly, but production in the viceroyalty of Peru more than tripled. At its peak, from 1591 to 1595, Potosí produced 192,000 kilograms of finished silver, almost four times the entire peak output from every mine in central Europe put together. And at Potosí, the profit margins were so high that *mineros* always paid the full fifth to the Crown. Potosí became known as the *cerro rico,* the rich mountain. But the mountain wasn't rich because there was a lot of silver in it. It was rich because there were a lot of people in it, working in an incredibly dangerous environment, with little or no pay. Potosí was not a geographic accident. It was a political decision.

As Castile's mines in the Americas began to produce silver at volumes that outstripped anything imagined at St. Joachimsthal, the old negotiations over how to coin that silver in Europe began to change as well. In 1556 Charles V abdicated all his crowns and retired to a monastery in the province of Extremadura in Spain. Charles's son, Philip II, inherited several crowns, including the crown of Castile—and with it the viceroyalties in the Americas. Charles's brother, Ferdinand I, was elected Holy Roman emperor. Ferdinand understood German princes and was a more patient negotiator than Charles. But he also had leverage that Charles had never enjoyed. The new silver from Zacatecas and Potosí stripped power from the Saxon dukes and their silver investors. They couldn't dictate terms anymore, because they weren't the ones producing all the cheap silver.

The Saxons lost, but the dollar won. The powerful bishoprics along the Rhine had preferred their gold Rhine florin, but finally accepted that they couldn't make the taler go away. Big silver coins were too useful, and merchants liked them too much. And so in 1566 the silver taler from mines in central Europe became an official part of the empire's monetary system, blessed as a *Reichstaler,* or imperial dollar. Even though the Holy Roman Empire and Castile were no longer ruled by the same emperor, the new reichstaler contained 25.2 grams of fine silver, just like the Castilian real de a ocho. Ferdinand and his empire were bowing to reality. In the 1540s, Castilian mints in Burgos, Segovia, Seville, and Toledo had all started minting pieces of eight at volume. Thomas Gresham, an English merchant and a sharp observer of how money worked, wrote that by 1553 all long-distance trade through Antwerp was already conducted in silver reales; he meant reales de a ocho, Spanish dollars. Even before the peak silver years at Potosí of the mita, Castile's answer to the joachimsthaler already had power far beyond what Philip controlled.

The reichstaler became the new trade standard in northern Europe. The Dutch minted *rijksdaalder* for export only, outside their domestic currency system. The Danes minted *rigsdaler*. The Swedes minted *riksdaler.* In English, these came to be known collectively as rix-dollar, all trading at the same value as the real de a ocho. And in 1571, the Saxons finally dropped the silver content of their own taler to 25.1 grams, just under the reichstaler. Then they added an apple to the design of their taler, a sign of the Holy Roman Empire, proof that even the Saxons had succumbed to the power of American silver.

Remember that in the 1520s and 1530s, the Saxons at St. Joachimsthal still held the swing dollar. They produced big silver coins faster, cheaper, and at higher quality than anywhere else, which meant their coins set the standard. Castile's piece of eight began in 1535 as one of many copies of the joachimsthaler. By the 1550s, though, St. Joachimsthal's advantage had evaporated. Castile was beginning to think of itself as the center of a Spanish empire, and it held the swing dollar. It had power to control money in places it had no armies.

It wasn't just Spanish silver moving out from Seville into global trade. Increasingly, it was Spanish dollars. Thousands of pieces of eight were found in a Portuguese shipwreck from 1585 off the coast of Mozambique. In 1589, Genoa banned foreign coins from domestic circulation—except pieces of eight. By the 1590s, more than half of the silver coming ashore in Seville to the House of Trade immediately moved literally next door to the mint to become reales de a ocho. That decade Dutch merchants were already reckoning the silver trade up from Seville in *stukken van achten*—pieces of eight. Over the next two decades, Spanish dollars show up around the Netherlands in several hoards—jars or boxes of coins buried for safekeeping that accidentally stayed safe for centuries. Records in Venice show that between 1610 and 1614 almost 2 million of various kinds of dollars left for the Levant; 84 percent of them were Castilian pieces of eight. In 1614 the Dutch exported 600,000 pieces of eight to Aleppo. Around the same time, Ottoman sources started to distinguish between *gurus*—groats, or large silver coins—and Spanish gurus. Thousands of pieces of eight have been recovered from two Dutch East India Company ships that sank in the 1620s, one near England and one off the coast of western Australia. More pieces of eight from the 1630s appear in hoards from Venice and what is now Kenya, and in a spectacular find of 4,600 Spanish silver coins in an old market in Moscow.

Pieces of eight were moving east to China, through central Asia, and around Africa. But in the 1570s, right as the viceroyalty of Peru was turning Potosí into a productive inferno, Spanish dollars started moving west, too, straight across the Pacific. Dennis Flynn and Arturo Giráldez date the beginning of globalization to 1571, when Philip II established a trading colony in Manila and merchants in New Spain began the Manila trade. Galleons carried silver from Acapulco to the Philippines, west with the trade winds. They returned with silk and porcelain in an often deadly slog up and across the North Pacific and down the California coast. No stops in Antwerp, Lisbon, Venice, or Moscow. No middlemen. There is some argument still about the volume of silver that moved across the Pacific, but isotope analysis of English coins from the sixteenth century found silver from only Zacatecas and central Europe. Everything from Potosí likely went straight to Manila.

At first, this silver would have moved across the Pacific as bars. It's possible that's what Chinese merchants in Manila preferred; they were already used to their own silver tael, the lumps of silver valued by weight. But the local economies at Potosí and Zacatecas needed coins. Silver moved from *mineros* to refiners, then through silver merchants to the viceroyalty to be assayed, weighed, and taxed by the Crown. At each step, someone had to get paid, and what had been true in Saxony and Bohemia was true in the Americas: The big silver coins were there to make sure everyone got a cut. Charles V had already established a royal mint in Mexico City in 1535, and in 1572 Philip II approved a mint right on the mountain at Potosí. But for the first two centuries of their existence, the mints in the Americas didn't produce perfect, rounded dollars like the Seville pieces of eight or the rix-dollar. They didn't need to. At first, the mints in the American viceroyalties were just there to make sure all the silver got taxed, and so they made cobs—rough divots, hacked off a silver bar and then weighed and stamped.

Remember that in the sixteenth and seventeenth centuries the only sensible thing you could do with silver was sell it in the direction of China, and so the cobs from Mexico City and Potosí started moving west across the Pacific, too. By the 1640s we can find proof of that movement in hoards. In 1644, someone buried a black earthenware pot in Anhai, near the port city of Quanzhou in what is now the People's Republic of China. In the pot were 10 cobs from the mint at Mexico City. In 1647, someone in the nearby town of Guanqiao buried a pot with silver bars and forty-two coins—cobs stamped in Mexico City and this time also in Potosí.

By the time Sancho de Moncada sat down in Toledo to write to the king in 1620, this whole system of mining, minting, and shipping silver was already in place. When Moncada wrote that His Majesty's silver was in Italy and China, he already understood at least the rough outlines of what we now know to be true. Silver shipped as bars and cobs from Zacatecas in what is now Mexico to Castile's House of Trade in Seville, where it became pieces of eight and moved on to Genoa, Antwerp, and Lisbon. Silver shipped as bars and cobs from Potosí to Manila, where it moved on to the ports of southern China. In the 1530s the joachimsthaler had moved from Bohemia west through Antwerp and up into the Baltic, becoming money as it passed. By the 1620s the Spanish dollar was passing through the hands of merchants all over the world.

THE INDUSTRIAL COLLAPSE OF EL GRECO'S TOLEDO

In the spring of 1577 a thirty-six-year-old Greek painter named Domenikos Theotokopoulos traveled to Castile, looking for work. Born on the island of Crete, he had trained in Venice, then opened a studio in Rome. In Castile there was money for luxuries around the court of King Philip II, but Domenikos's one painting for the court did not please the king. A commission for the cathedral in Toledo took the painter south and up the hill, where he found more work, moved in with a woman, had a son, and stayed. We know Domenikos Theotokopoulos today as El Greco—the Greek. But that name came later, an invention by the impressionists who rediscovered him in the late nineteenth century. He signed his own paintings with his full name in Greek letters, but Toledo's clergy and merchants knew him as El Dominico, or Dominico Greco. He seldom left the city, and in his own lifetime was barely known outside it.

At the archives in Toledo, Francisco José said that Dominico Greco lived through the city's swan song, its last great moment at the close of the sixteenth century. Greco liked intellectuals and had his own library of classics in Latin and Greek. He painted portraits of gentlemen, a physician, a cardinal—the same small group of elite Toledans who would worry about the city's collapse. The best-known scholar of Sancho de Moncada's work even believes that Greco's *Portrait of a Young Scholar* shows Moncada as a university student. The painter was not removed from his subjects, and in fact developed a reputation in Toledo for suing them. But he was also part of their community, as concerned as they were about the rise of an imperial capital in Madrid and its effect on ancient Toledo up on its hill.

We can read this concern in Dominico Greco's *View of Toledo,* one of the world's best-known landscapes. Greco's Toledo looms in the painting, ragged on its hill. A thunderhead rolls in behind, and through a tear in the clouds a last bit of sunlight falls on the cathedral and the fortified palace of the Alcázar. The way we interpret that painting now is a consequence of the time when it was made famous, after the wife of an American sugar baron bought it in 1909. Spain was by then already a failed empire, a place where adventurous Americans came to buy paintings on the cheap and gawk at peasants. That made *View of Toledo* an omen, one last look before everything went black. F. Scott Fitzgerald, who likely saw the painting at an exhibition in New York in 1920, used it in *The Great Gatsby* as a metaphor for grotesque excess.

In his own lifetime, though, Dominico Greco was not an old master from a failed empire. He was a commercially successful artist who settled in Toledo because it was a good place to sell portraits and altar panels. Two historians, Jonathan Brown and Richard Kagan, have proposed that we look at the painting the way Greco himself might have seen it. In 1595 a group of powerful Toledans wrote to Philip II, by then an old man, and asked him to leave his capital in Madrid and bring his court back up to the top of the hill. Brown and Kagan think the painting was part of this effort, commissioned to show Toledo for what its merchants and clergy still believed it could be: the spiritual, political, and *industrial* heart of a powerful kingdom.

Dominico Greco took the cathedral and Alcázar palace and rearranged them to show the seats of Castile's spiritual and earthly power in the same view. Then he placed some tiny white figures on the riverbank, just below the center of the painting. Art historians have puzzled over those figures, but Brown and Kagan argue that anyone at the time would have known that they're textile workers. They've walked down to

El Greco, *View of Toledo.* (Image from the Metropolitan Museum of Art.)

the river to wash and beat cloth before bringing it back up to the city to be dyed. *View of Toledo* wasn't an omen. It was an advertisement. It's the way the city saw itself, at close to its absolute peak of production. Toledo was a capital for the Crown, the church, *and* the merchant. The thunderhead isn't rolling in. It's rolling away.

There was no manufacturing in the Americas, and so as Potosí and Zacatecas boomed in the middle of the sixteenth century, Castile began shipping out through Seville everything the new viceroyalties needed, in particular Toledo's specialties: weapons and cloth. Toledo expanded production to meet the demand, and people followed that growth up the hill. In 1528 there were twenty-nine thousand people living in Toledo. By 1561, that had almost doubled, to fifty-six thousand. The city's cloth merchants also started contracting out piecework to villages around the city to meet the demand; in 1572 about twenty corporations near the Zocodover market alone manufactured rope, saddles, linen towels, clothing, silks, and hats. And the merchants raised prices. Already at a *Cortes* in 1548—the meeting of the kingdom's urban leaders—there had been complaints about the quality and price of domestic cloth, and a suggestion that if clothing was needed in the new viceroyalties, perhaps they should make it there.

What we know about prices in early modern Spain we owe to Earl and Gladys Hamilton. In 1926, the Hamiltons left the United States for Spain on a ship with their six-week-old daughter. Together they spent the next six years, and by Earl's calculations more than thirty thousand hours, sorting through local archives in more than a hundred towns, including the financial accounts of the Tavera Hospital in Toledo. They produced an astonishing record of local prices, sorted by region, of everything—almonds, beef, conger eel, hens, nails, alphabetically all the way down to wine. In 1552 the Hospital de Tavera paid 77 maravedis for a hen. In 1577, when Dominico Greco took his first commission in Toledo, a hen already cost 85 maravedis. In 1597 it was 112 maravedis. Even as places like Toledo boomed, they got dramatically more expensive to live in, quickly enough that it was disorienting at the time.

Earl already had a theory to explain the inflation before he even got on the boat. He was part of a group of economists who wanted to add rigor to the quantity theory of money—the idea that prices are always and everywhere tied to the *amount* of money sloshing around, and how quickly it sloshes. To quantity theorists, more money almost always means more inflation. Quantity theory isn't dominant among macroeconomists now, but it does have a hold on the popular imagination about money. When someone says that the United States today is printing dollars, they're worried about quantity theory: There will be too many dollars, each dollar will become less valuable, and prices will rise.

In Spain, Hamilton found exactly what he went looking for: The silver had come in through Seville, "pouring in a mammoth stream," and then became silver reales and silver-copper maravedis. He assumed that silver pooled in Castile as coins, drove up prices, then spilled over the edge of the peninsula into the rest of Europe. The price data Earl and Gladys Hamilton collected in the 1920s is still valuable today, and in his book Earl produced an argument so powerful anyone writing about the economics of imperial Spain still has to reckon with it.

Hamilton was thorough, but he was also fixated on what was in his own time a modern explanation for inflation. Even though he read Castilian writers from the sixteenth and seventeenth centuries—including Sancho de Moncada—he was puzzled that they failed to see what was clear to him, that silver coming in through Seville caused inflation in Castile. It was clear to the Castilian writers actually watching it happen, though, that very little of that silver actually stayed in the kingdom. There were constant complaints of a lack of silver at the trade fairs on the Iberian Peninsula, and Thomas Gresham, the English merchant, was shocked in 1554 at how little gold and silver were in Castile. Something else had to have gone wrong.

Already in the middle of the sixteenth century, clerics in Castile were wrestling with how trade with the new viceroyalties had changed the kingdom. Tomás de Mercado, a Dominican friar born in what is now Mexico, had spent time as a lecturer at the university in Salamanca, then took a royal appointment to the House of Trade in Seville, where the silver arrived. Mercado understood the details of credit and trade and in 1569 wrote a manual for merchants on how to both prosper and hold on to their souls.

Mercado, who was in constant contact with merchants in Flanders, knew that silver was always more in demand in Antwerp than in Seville, which meant that it drained quickly through the hands of Seville's bankers after coming ashore, headed for Antwerp or Genoa. The flow of silver through Seville made things more expensive, he argued, in part because the regular arrivals of the fleet made it easy to borrow against silver that was on its way, and buying a lot of things on easy credit has the same effect as buying with hard silver. Mercado also described what we'd today call demand-pull inflation; when everybody wants something, it becomes more expensive. He explained how haggling in Seville to buy cloth to ship to the Americas bid up prices all the way back to weavers in Segovia and Toledo. And it wasn't just cloth. It was wine, oil, wheat, leather, swords.

Castile was going through a demand shock: Everything it made and used at home was suddenly needed on the other side of the ocean. On its face, a demand shock seems like a good thing, but that depends on how an economy responds. Every industry has a capacity, the ability to make a certain number of products every year. Prices rise when demand outpaces capacity. Sometimes high prices cure themselves. As something gets more expensive, more people want to sell it, and so they invest in new production—they expand capacity. But more capacity is tricky. You have to find people, train them, house them, feed them. Within a couple of decades, Toledo's industries, centuries old, had to grow. Quickly. Behind walls. On the top of a hill. Controlled by guilds.

You could describe inflation in Castile as a silver problem or a credit problem, but it was also a capacity problem: People in the Americas wanted to buy more than Toledo could make. Traditionally, the city had sold its cloth and steel north, through the fairs at Medina del Campo, then to the rest of Europe. Demand from the Americas shifted that trade south, out through Seville and across the Atlantic into an annual fair at Veracruz, on the Gulf of Mexico. Toledo started competing with cheaper foreign manufacturers who sold through foreign merchants in Seville, and by the middle of the sixteenth century Toledan merchants like Moncada's grandfather and uncle had started meeting demand by raising prices and lowering quality. The Habsburgs didn't care about making cloth in Toledo. They cared about their *quinto* from the silver in Potosí. Whatever it took to keep their share of silver coming ashore at Seville to pay the Crown's debts, that's what the Habsburgs wanted, regardless of how expensive things got in Castile.

For a time, this all worked fine for Toledo. The city's population peaked in 1597 at eighty thousand people—comparable to the total number of people living in Toledo today, on and off the hill. Things didn't break in Castile until about 1590. Before that, wages were rising and people were moving into towns to work in manufacturing. After 1590, people started leaving towns for the fields, and wages dropped again. The Hamiltons' price data shows that inflation rose sharply in the 1590s, then flattened out after 1600. Contracts at the Zocodover market with surrounding villages for wool and silk weaving disappeared, and Toledo's old commercial parishes lost almost all the households that registered as craftsmen or weavers.

Dominico Greco's painting of Toledo did not lure the king back up the hill. Philip II died in 1598, in the magnificent palace he had built at El Escorial. His son Philip III continued to build out the new capital in Madrid. *View of Toledo* never sold; it was still in Dominico Greco's workshop when he died in 1614. And by 1600, tax revenues from wool and linen production in Toledo finally started to fall. Looking back from 1620, Sancho de Moncada described the kingdom as an old but vigorous man who had a sudden accident and was buried within days. The Habsburgs had created a system in Castile and the Americas entirely dedicated to manufacturing the world's most valuable money—the silver Spanish dollar. To Castilians, this seemed as if it might work, right until the moment it didn't.

In the archives in Toledo, Francisco José told me that Dominico Greco came to a city that was powerful, then spent his life serving a city that was vanishing. In 1607, Greco took a contract to paint altar panels for a chapel at the Church of San Vicente Mártir—Sancho de Moncada's mother's parish. The chapel had been funded by a woman from Toledo who had become rich in the Americas. There was still wealth in Toledo to pay for paintings. But it had become what Francisco José calls an ecclesiastical city. Of the themes in *View of Toledo*—the Crown, the church, and the weavers by the river—only the church was left.

In the El Greco rooms of the Prado in Madrid, you can now see a portrait of Jerónimo de Ceballos—head cocked, eyebrows raised. Greco painted it in 1613, the year before he died. Ceballos, a lawyer and a member of the *ayuntimiento,* was friends with both Dominico Greco and Sancho de Moncada. In 1620, he wrote that the "streets of Toledo were deserted, industry was ruined, and homes were shuttered and closed." When Moncada took his *arbitrio* to Madrid, it had become clear that centuries of manufacturing experience in Toledo had evaporated. There was no more capacity to produce.

MANUFACTURING IN TOLEDO COLLAPSED BECAUSE OF DUTCH DISEASE

Sancho de Moncada probably handed a copy of his manuscript to the king in 1619, the year before he had it printed. Philip III was a pious man, and Moncada the lobbyist knew his audience. In the first discourse of his *arbitrio,* he offers the story from Proverbs of the virtuous wife. She is "intelligent in business, and a good negotiator," he writes. She buys wool and flax; she works the spindle and distaff with her own hands; she sells cloth to the merchant. Moncada's argument was that Spain does it all wrong. It sells wool abroad, buys back the cloth, and will soon be naked.

Moncada describes a Castile that had lost its ability to make things. Quoting figures he knew from his own contacts in business, he notes for the king that half of the price of silk was in the manufacturing—even more for wool, linens, and iron. Almost all the value of paper came from manufacturing. Then he lists, item for item, the value of everything the kingdom was importing: linen, silks, canvas, lace, paper, cottons. Castile even imported poorly made swords, he said, which was inconvenient when one actually needed a good sword. The kingdom imported books, too, and printing had suffered what Moncada called the same barbarism as the rest of the industries: There was no one left who knew how to do it.

Theories about why the Castilian economy collapsed are as old as the collapse. Already in the 1640s, an English traveler to the kingdom blamed poverty and depopulation on the Inquisition, "a bad religion," wars, "the multitude of Whores," poor soil, and "the wretched laziness of the people, very like the Welsh and the Irish, walking slowly and always cumbred with a great Cloke and a long Sword." Spanish historians in the nineteenth century called this the black legend—a version of Spain held back by defects of character.

There's a gentler, more recent version of the black legend, where the Habsburgs just made bad decisions. Castile's kings spent too much of their wealth on wars all over Europe, and not enough encouraging economic growth at home. Or they had too much power, and the wealthy were never given the right incentives to invest in new industries. These explanations aren't wrong, but they fail to wrestle with what Sancho de Moncada reported from Toledo. It can't just be that the Habsburgs were too distracted or powerful to create new industries, because there had already been manufacturing in Spain *before* the Habsburgs. Toledo didn't fail to industrialize. It deindustrialized.

In 1983, two economists from Australia offered a different way to think about why Toledo had lost capacity, one that takes account of the industrial Toledo Moncada had known. Peter Forsyth and Stephen

Nicholas were both familiar with new work on economies rich in natural resources. Perhaps, they suggested, Spain's silver had given Castile what economists call Dutch Disease.

In the early 1970s, the Netherlands had begun exploiting natural gas fields just off its coast in the North Sea. By the end of the decade, economists had noticed a shift in what the country made. At the time, the Netherlands had its own currency: the *guilder*. To buy the gas, people outside the country needed to buy guilders, and so the value of the guilder rose. A strong currency is good if you want to travel or import things from other countries. But it's bad if you want to export your own products abroad; nothing changes about what you make, but to foreigners it becomes more expensive.

At the same time, the Dutch government taxed the production in the natural gas fields and began spending that revenue on social programs and benefits for government employees. This raised wages. After that, any company in the Netherlands that wanted to export anything other than natural gas was getting squeezed at both ends: Skilled labor was more expensive, and the strong guilder made it hard to raise prices. Paradoxically, the great natural gift of the offshore gas fields became a burden. Unemployment started creeping up. In the 1950s, the country had been a net exporter of clothing and shoes; by the 1970s, it became a net importer of both. In 1977, *The Economist* named this paradox the "Dutch Disease."

Since then, economists have added to a list of what can happen when a country gets a windfall and starts to suffer Dutch Disease. Powerful groups can argue for favors like lower taxes that the government can suddenly afford, increasing corruption and inequality. Dutch Disease can discourage countries from making workers more productive through education. Once industrial skills are lost, they're lost forever. There is no blood test to diagnose Dutch Disease. It's a bit like monetary sovereignty; it's hard to definitively say whether a country has it or not. But it does offer a way to think about a sudden shock of income from a single export. If we take what Sancho de Moncada said at face value—the silver wasn't money, it was a harvest, and it was already all in Genoa and China—then we can start to think of Spain's silver dollars the way we would a gusher of oil. What did the export of silver bars and pieces of eight from Seville do to weavers in Castile?

In a paper published in 2005 Mauricio Drelichman, an economic historian at the University of British Columbia, took the Hamiltons' detailed price data to show how it was Toledo's specialized products—leather, iron, and cloth—that became more expensive, giving way to cheaper imports, exactly what you would expect for a country suffering from Dutch Disease. He called Castile's silver-driven collapse "the curse of Moctezuma." More recently, Drelichman and several other economists have argued that Castile suffered first from Dutch Disease, then from what economists call the institutional resource curse: Sudden wealth can make governments *worse.* The wealth increases the value of political patronage, as seeking favors becomes a better investment than making things and selling them. And politicians are more likely to buy off powerful interests than negotiate with them. Nobles and the church were exempt from taxes in Castile, and the *quinto* of silver dollars prevented the Habsburgs from ever having to renegotiate that bargain.

In the first half of the sixteenth century, the cities of Castile were the only real sources of tax revenue for Charles V. He was the Holy Roman emperor, but he had to go to the *Cortes* to beg merchants in cities to pay taxes, his only regular source of income. When silver started arriving at volume with the fleets at Seville every October in the 1540s, the Habsburgs' *quinto* gave them a brand-new source of revenue. They didn't always have to beg the *Cortes* for money anymore, and started to worry less about making sure places like Toledo were still healthy enough to pay taxes. The Moncada family in Toledo had been part of a system of investment and production that ultimately served the Crown. Then the Habsburgs didn't need that system anymore, and let it wither.

The Habsburg purse wasn't like a household budget, where the king took in taxes and silver, then spent on his priorities. The Habsburgs didn't use their income to buy things. They used it to pay interest on debt for things they had already bought, and to keep rolling that debt over. The Castilian crown borrowed in two ways. The *asientos* were short-term contracts, mostly with banking families in Genoa. Philip II's income came in dribbles of black vellon maravedis from taxes in Castile, and in a yearly flood of silver dollars from the fleets that arrived in Seville. The asientos allowed the Genoese bankers to turn irregular income into regular payments all over Europe; think of the Genoese as providing Philip with payroll services.

About 40 percent of these payments from Genoa went to the Spanish Netherlands as *escudos,* a silver coin worth 10 reales that the Army of Flanders preferred as pay. Another 40 percent went to Castile, to pay all of Philip's expenses in maravedis. The last 20 percent stayed in Italy, to build fleets. Median interest on the *asientos* was 13 percent, normal for loans to a sovereign at the time. Philip paid the bankers back in pieces of eight minted in Seville and shipped to Genoa in special crates built to carry 2,500 silver Spanish dollars apiece. Philip stopped payment on the *asientos* several times during his reign, but the Genoese were rational lenders: None of the banking families lost money on Philip over the long run. The asientos were a reliable machine that moved dollars to Genoa, in return for funding Philip's court in Castile and his wars all over Europe.

The *asientos* were only a small part of Philip's overall debt, though. Over the course of his reign, he took a medieval form of borrowing, the *juro,* and professionalized it, expanded it, and completely changed the way wealthy Castilians invested. A *juro* is an annuity—a grant of a little bit of money, every year, for life. In medieval Europe, kings had handed them out as favors. Philip II put them up for sale. At first, he placed them privately with nobles and religious orders. Then the Crown organized auctions and finally just placed them through Genoese bankers. Philip II's *juros* paid about 7 percent, and he never defaulted on them. The *juros* traded on a secondary market like cash and became one of the most stable and sought-after investments in Europe. In 1560, Philip had

19 million ducats of outstanding *juros* and paid just under 30 percent of his yearly revenues in interest on them. By the 1590s, that had grown to an inflation-adjusted 68 million ducats in *juros,* which took almost 50 percent of the king's revenue to service.

The dollar didn't just change what Castilians made. It changed how they invested. Think about the nuns at the Convent of San Pedro Mártir in Toledo, stashing away savings in the building that's now a part of the University of Castilla–La Mancha. Before the *quinto,* this is how capital worked in Castile. Landowners took in rents. They deposited them at the convent. To earn a return, those savings went as short-term loans to merchants, to expand the industries in Toledo like silk weaving and sword making.

As Philip II continued to sell *juros,* wealthy Castilians and religious orders, who in the past had financed merchants like the Moncada family, didn't have to find a way to earn a return on their wealth. They handed it over to the king for a guaranteed 7 percent. There are few investments this reliably good anywhere in the world today. Over the sixteenth and early seventeenth centuries, the Habsburgs sold *juros,* then turned around and spent what they borrowed on palaces and the court.

Those *juros* also made taxes less crucial. The Habsburgs had constantly bickered with the cities of Castile over taxes, and in the early years of Charles V's reign the cities had even revolted, refusing to pay tribute to a new king from Flanders. Powerful Toledo had been the last holdout. But even in revolt, Charles V and the cities in the kingdom ultimately shared an interest: They both needed the cities to be as successful as possible. After the yearly *quinto* started coming in, those interests diverged. It just wasn't as important to Philip II that the cities of Castile thrive. He could let their industries fail and their populations disappear. By 1620, there were 20,000 people in Toledo, but 180,000 in Madrid. The new capital didn't manufacture anything. Madrid was the Habsburg company town, where Spaniards with influence went to beg for something from the king's purse.

Moncada's solution to Castile's industrial collapse was to ban imports of manufactured goods. This is what we'd today call import substitution—cut off imports, and domestic producers will figure out how to fill the void. This is hard to do, and usually more destructive than it is helpful. Once factories close, institutional knowledge disappears; people forget how to do their old jobs, and it gets harder each year to help them figure it out again. Sancho de Moncada is often dismissed as a mercantilist, or a bullionist—fixated on exporting manufactured goods, then hoarding the silver that comes in to pay for them. But he was trying to fix the way capital worked in Castile. To create new manufacturing capacity, someone would have to invest to build it, and he hoped that the convents would play that role again. But the people with wealth weren't investing in manufacturing or trade anymore, he explained, because they had a better, safer investment: the king himself.

THE DOLLAR CAME TWICE FOR TOLEDO

It's hard to find evidence of the Moncada family in Toledo now. Sancho de Moncada spent the rest of his life in Madrid, though he always signed his letters with his title at the university in Toledo. There had been a Calle de Moncada in the sixteenth century; it has been renamed. The house where Moncada lived with his grandfather has become a school. Sancho de Moncada's grandfather had made one attempt at a memorial, shortly before he died. In 1585, he donated 3,400 maravedis to the Church of San Nicolás de Bari for the Chapel of Our Lady of the Conception. A chapel was a sign of wealth, a way to guarantee you and your family a burial at the parish.

San Nicolás de Bari dates to 1125, shortly after the first Christian king took the city. It's easy to walk right past the church. It has been built into the hill, and to get to the pews, you have to walk down a couple of stone steps. When I visited San Nicolás, a few tourists were sitting in the pews, but it was close to the 12:30 Mass, and older Spaniards began to join them. In the twentieth century, San Nicolás incorporated the parish of San Vicente, and inherited the panels that Dominico Greco had painted for a chapel in the parish church. But the panels are gone now, displayed a few blocks away, in the Museo de Santa Cruz on the other side of the Zocodover.

The Moncadas' chapel at San Nicolás de Bari is gone now, too. In the church, I waited awkwardly outside the sacristy for the priest to notice me. I asked in pidgin Spanish whether he knew anything about the chapel for the Moncada family. He was kind and invited me in, but the name meant nothing to him. He showed me some pamphlets about the history of the parish, and we sat down and attempted to understand them together. Then, right at 12:30, he excused himself, pulled on his stole and chasuble, put a CD on the parish PA, and walked out to the altar. The tourists in the pews quietly gathered their things, leaving behind just the older Toledans.

Poking around for something to do that night, I found the International, a bar with a bookstore: heaven. Inside a man was reading poetry in Spanish from his phone. I ordered a drink, asked about credit cards, was told it would have to be cash, dug in my pocket for my last 7 euros, placed them on the bar, and said I would drink as much as that would buy.

Javier sitting next to me told me he'd moved to Toledo for a job painting murals at the Alcázar, but had started painting scenes for movies—most recently *Terminator 6,* which had filmed just outside Toledo. He told me with Netflix, which had opened a studio in Madrid, anyone with experience in television in Castile could have a job. He lived up in the old city, on top of the hill. Juan, who poured me a generous 7 euros' worth of wine, had lived in Toledo for forty-three years. He told me everything had changed. I asked what had changed and when, and he said, simply, Airbnb. There used to be fifty thousand people in old-town Toledo, he said; now there were ten thousand. Many doorbells in Toledo had no names, just numbers, a sure sign that the names turned over every week.

The Spanish Empire was for three centuries the world's most

dominant producer of both silver and silver dollars. It was Spain's silver pieces of eight that would wash up in England's American colonies, connecting the valley of St. Joachimsthal and its taler to the United States and its dollars. Pieces of eight built Spain's empire. But it's possible now to still see the damage they did, leaving Toledo preserved as it was before the silver—a cramped medieval city that never got to be a part of what we think of now as the Industrial Revolution. The dollar came twice for Toledo. Once, when the silver in the sixteenth century made it too expensive to make anything up on the hill and prevented the king from ever having to care about the city again. Then again at the beginning of the twenty-first century, as American tech firms used the global demand for any kind of dollar assets to issue shares and expand everywhere, including Spain. One of Netflix's most popular series that year, *Money Heist,* was set in a fictional version of the Casa de la Moneda in Madrid, the same building where you can read the history of Castilian money on the museum wall.

By 1620, the Habsburgs' silver dollars had built Madrid and hollowed out Toledo. By 2019, Airbnb, an American company wallowing in the privilege of issuing shares in American dollars, had hollowed out Toledo again, swapping in tourists for residents. We think of a flood of money as a good thing—how could it be bad for anyone to have more dollars? But money that comes in doesn't always go to everyone equally. Some things become easier. Some things, harder.

3

The First American Dollar

Annapolis, 1764

THE COLONIAL GOVERNOR OF MARYLAND WAS DESPERATE TO PRODUCE MONEY

In the last week of August 1764, Horatio Sharpe hurried two letters on a packet across the Chesapeake Bay to get them on a ship about to depart for England. Sharpe was the governor of the Province of Maryland. One letter went to his boss—Frederick Calvert, the sixth and final Lord Baltimore, the province's lord proprietor. The other letter went to Lord Baltimore's uncle and secretary, Cecilius Calvert. Sharpe, who had been a captain in a regiment of marines in the West Indies, was forty-six years old. He had already been governor in Maryland for more than a decade, and in both letters knew his audience exactly. He was supplicating, strategic, and a little annoyed. Sharpe was under pressure to produce for Maryland something that would function as money.

He didn't need to create wealth; there was plenty of that in Maryland. In the middle of the eighteenth century, about a third of the people in the province were enslaved; most worked tobacco fields along the tidewater. An enslaved adult could produce about fifteen hundred pounds of tobacco a year, at a return to the planter of 5 percent. Sharpe was instead dealing with an acute version of a problem that England's colonists on the Atlantic coast had almost always complained about: a lack of small money. There just weren't enough physical coins or bills to make it possible for one colonist to buy something from another.

It's hard for Americans now to grasp how unimportant the North American colonies were to the rest of the world, and even to Britain. There were no silver or gold mines in colonial America and no urgency from Parliament or the Crown to let the colonies have mints or supply them with coins. Money is difficult to control across an entire empire; Maryland, like the other colonies, didn't share a currency with England. Provincial officials in Annapolis, tobacco plantation owners in the south of the province, and wheat farmers in its north all had to string together their own loose system of foreign coins and the older English habits of handwritten notes and credit on store ledgers.

The way Americans used money also shows how important the silver dollars from Spain were in North America, as early as the seventeenth century. Marylanders, like the rest of the colonists, kept their own accounts in local versions of the old Carolingian system of pounds, shillings, and pence. But they all knew to the penny the value of their own local currencies in dollars, because Spanish silver dollars were the coins most likely to actually cross their palms. Just as silver dollars had become the standard of trade through Antwerp by the end of the sixteenth century, by the late seventeenth century they had become the common standard of the Atlantic economy, too.

Sharpe's two letters mark the beginning of a negotiation within Maryland and across the Atlantic to produce the first American dollars—printed slips of paper that replicated the value of the same silver Spanish pieces of eight that had been moving around the world since the middle of the sixteenth century, themselves copies of the first silver joachimsthaler. The dollar didn't start with the United States; it came ashore in England's North American colonies. The dollar had to *become* American, a long process that accelerated when Horatio Sharpe sent those two letters to London.

Maryland printed its dollars almost a decade before the American

Revolution. It was a colonial governor—a loyal Englishman and faithful servant to Lord Baltimore—who fought to make those printed dollars possible. Horatio Sharpe wasn't a revolutionary. He just needed a way to produce something that would work as money in the province without alarming Lord Baltimore or Parliament or the Board of Trade and Plantations in London. Those printed Maryland dollars weren't an act of sovereignty or a declaration of monetary freedom. They were a desperate colonial work-around. They were an accident.

NEVER ENOUGH COINS, BUT DOLLARS EVERYWHERE

Colonists up and down the North American Atlantic coast had a consistent complaint: There were never enough coins, and what coins they had were mostly Spanish, moving from Spain's American viceroyalties with trade through the Caribbean. In Maryland, the few coins that did circulate tended to come from ships paying customs duties and port fees, and from wheat sales in the north of the province to the merchants in Philadelphia who supplied Barbados and Jamaica, Britain's sugar islands. Read through the August 1764 issues of the *Maryland Gazette*—Jonas and Anne Catharine Green's newspaper—and you can see the old silver Spanish dollars everywhere.

The City of Philadelphia advertised a race to be held the next month—three-mile heats for four-year-old horses, for a purse of "ONE HUNDRED DOLLARS." Samuel Galloway advertised a "CARGO of healthy SLAVES," suitable for the ironworks in Baltimore Town. Dollars would be taken. Thomas Rutland asked for the return of a servant named John Ward, a round-shouldered, black-haired man with a great love of strong drink, and offered a reward of £3—payable in dollars. John Wilmot of South River asked for the return of a "country-born negro man" named Taney, who was about six feet tall and slow of speech and had a small scar on his forehead. Wilmot thought Taney might be waiting in Annapolis to get on a ship and offered a 4 dollar reward.

At the end of the eighteenth century, the flow of Spanish silver dollars continued to move along the same old paths, from Zacatecas east to Seville and Europe, and from Potosí west to Manila and the port cities of southern China. It was hard but not impossible for colonists to hold on to some of these dollars as they crossed the Atlantic. Merchants in port cities like Boston and Philadelphia shipped wheat, hogs, and lumber south to the sugar islands, and returned with rum, molasses, slaves, and silver dollars. There was some wheat in Maryland, which put Annapolis at the very southern edge of the North American colonies that could make this trade. In Maryland, dollars were big money for expensive things.

But the province had the same old problem as the silver miners in Joachimsthal. People held a few silver dollars and gold *pistoles*—a Spanish coin worth about 4 dollars. But there weren't enough of either, and there were almost no petty coins for small purchases. Colonists even used shears to clip the coins they had into smaller change, since a quarter of a piece of eight was worth just a little more than a shilling. The practice was particularly common in Maryland, enough so that the assembly tried to forbid it, then in 1729 finally gave up and accepted it. There's an old argument among economists and historians over whether colonists were just complaining about the lack of coins, as colonists do. But serious people in Maryland at the time certainly saw it as a problem.

In April 1761, Stephen West advertised in the *Gazette* that he was selling goods from Europe, as well as rum, sugar, molasses, and salt from the Caribbean. He would buy pork, wheat, corn, and wooden staves, but was so desperate for any kind of money to carry out the transactions that he offered in his ad to produce some himself. "As I daily suffer much inconvenience in my business for want of small change," he wrote, "which is indeed a universal complaint of almost every body in any sort of business, I intend, if not better method is proposed, to print, for the convenience of my neighbors and myself, a parcel of small notes"—paper money. He offered to publish the exact number of bills he'd issued, promised that the bills would be redeemable for "good Spanish dollars," and wrote that he hoped to talk it over with other prominent men. West was so desperate for small change he didn't seem to think he could run an import business unless he made his own.

In September 1763, the Greens had taken the unusual step of dedicating almost the entire front page of the *Maryland Gazette* to an anonymous letter on the nature of money. The lack of gold and silver, the letter reported, was "an Evil universally felt and complained of." Men normally willing to lend coins at interest couldn't meet demand; they literally couldn't supply the coins to lend. Even when there had been gold and silver in the province, the writer pointed out, the "Want of Small Money for Exchange" had been "attended by the Greatest Inconveniences to the People."

When Horatio Sharpe sent those two letters across the Atlantic to Lord Baltimore and his secretary, Parliament had just made the problem of small change worse. Since just before 1700, almost all the colonies had been slowly developing ways to print money and make it hold its value, but in 1764 Parliament had passed the Currency Act, essentially stopping this process cold. The act made it illegal for any of the colonies to issue paper money as legal tender. If something is legal tender, everyone has to accept it for everything—rent, debts, taxes. We don't think of paper money as a major political issue now, so it's hard to see what a shock the Currency Act was, but Benjamin Franklin would later tell the House of Commons that it was one of the colonists' main frustrations. Sharpe put his letters to Calvert and Lord Baltimore on a ship in August 1764 to thread a needle. He knew there wasn't enough small change in Maryland. He needed to produce some, while working within the letter of the Currency Act. Whatever he did, he couldn't print legal tender.

In the summer of 1764, Lord Baltimore had just returned from a tour to Constantinople, where he was underwhelmed by the Hagia Sophia and disappointed that the women of the city veiled their faces. In his letter that August, Sharpe released his standard volley of praise, welcomed his lordship home from his trip, and assured him that any trouble in the province was just the same few people, fond of their own popularity, "clamouring for Liberty." The letter to Cecilius Calvert didn't show quite the same deference.

With Calvert, Sharpe just listed what needed handling, in a voice of restrained frustration familiar to anyone today who works in an office. Lord Baltimore, for example, had asked whether he could build on any plots in Baltimore Town. It would not be possible, Sharpe wrote, since Lord Baltimore no longer owned any of the land. Sharpe also went on at length about Parliament's Currency Act. Parliament had made a mistake and trade would suffer, he wrote, "from the Want of paper Currency." To be sure, he added, Virginia and some other colonies didn't know what they were doing with their paper currencies. They had given Parliament too many reasons for a ban, and unless paper money could be "fixed at a certain & invariable Value" there wasn't much point to it.

Horatio Sharpe was a masterful bureaucrat. He was conceding the logic of Parliament's decision on paper money while also nudging Calvert toward a way to sneak around that decision. Maryland, like most of the rest of the colonies, had issued its own paper shillings. Those shillings stood out among the colonies even then as a successful experiment in paper money. But by sheer coincidence, they had been scheduled to be recalled in 1764, the year the Currency Act prevented any new legal-tender paper money. Horatio Sharpe knew that any new money in the province would have to both follow the letter of the act and work the same way the Maryland paper shillings had. If Sharpe wanted to print paper money, he would have to find a way to fix it to something of "certain & invariable Value."

That something would be the silver dollar. And to understand how Horatio Sharpe was so certain he could make a piece of paper worth the same amount as a big silver coin, we have to take a step back to see how money already worked in Maryland. At the time, merchants and philosophers on the far side of the ocean looked at colonial paper money as a questionable novelty, but all those paper shillings rested on English traditions the colonists had brought with them.

BILLS OF EXCHANGE AND PROMISSORY NOTES

The Calvert family founded Maryland in the 1630s as a tobacco plantation, modeled on the Virginia Company's practice of tending tobacco with a mix of indentured and enslaved labor. Until the early eighteenth century, Maryland had a simple economy: Tobacco was the only crop, and Maryland could ship its tobacco only on English ships, which meant that just a few agents in London were the only buyers. One product, one destination. Remember the distinction between the real money of coins in the hand and the imaginary money of agreements written down on ledgers. The money of the early tobacco economy in the Maryland tidewater was almost entirely imaginary, just bookkeeping on the water's edge. Trading ships from London arrived every fall, and planters rolled hogsheads of tobacco down to the river to meet them. A factor—a local agent for an overseas buyer—would note the value of the tobacco departing for London. These same trading ships carried tools and cloth for the province, and the factors would subtract the value of the goods that stayed on the shore from the tobacco that left with the ship.

If the planter shipped out more in tobacco than he bought in tools and cloth, the factor would write out a bill of exchange. This was a contract on a slip of paper, signed by the factor, promising that the tobacco buyer in London would pay out some kind of money to the planter's account when asked. Bills of exchange—a technology brought to England by Florentine bankers in the fourteenth century—remained remarkably consistent over several centuries: One person asks another person to pay a third person, all written out on a piece of paper roughly the dimensions of paper money today. Below is a bill of exchange from 1754, in which William Byrd in Virginia directed Robert Cary, a merchant in London, to pay £200 sterling to the account of David Mead, who could then spend that £200 on a luxury from Britain. Byrd's bill is almost identical to bills of exchange written in Florence or London in the time of the Medici.

Gent.

Virginia, Oct. 26th 1754 Exchange for £. s. d. 200 . 0 . 0

At Sixty Days Sight of this my First Bill of Exchange, my Second and Third (of the same Tenor and Date) not paid, pay to David Mead Esqr. or Order, the Sum of two hundred Pounds Sterling, (Value here received,) at Time make Payment, and place it to Account of Gentn.

To Robt. Cary Esqr. & Compa. Mercht. in London.

Your Most Hble. St.

W Byrd

A bill of exchange signed in Virginia in 1754. These bills guaranteed payment in London, but also passed hand to hand in the colonies. (Image from the New York Public Library.)

Bills of exchange served as big money in the colonies, reserved for wealthier planters who could run up surpluses on tobacco sales, get a bill of exchange from a factor, and then sign it over to another planter for land or a large debt. The bills would eventually travel back to London, where they could be redeemed for cash. When Horatio Sharpe sold land on behalf of Lord Baltimore, for example, he returned the profit to London in bills of exchange. The bills could pass hand to hand in Maryland, endorsed on the back, as we would with a paper check today. Maryland planters also sold some of their bills of exchange north to Philadelphia and New York, another source of the few coins in the province.

For smaller, local purchases, colonists relied on other habits they'd brought from England. Remember that merchants in provincial Annapolis kept book credits for their customers—records of money owed—neatly recorded in a bound ledger. Tavern keepers and tradespeople offered book credits on their own ledgers, leaving a record of debts that people in the community could trade with each other. Colonists also paid each other with promissory notes—a promise on a slip of paper to pay sometime in the future, something like an IOU. These, too, were not brand-new to colonial America. It's possible to find examples of promissory notes in Lombardy as far back as the eighth century; they showed up in England as early as 1300. Just like bills of exchange, the wording and layout of promissory notes are strikingly consistent over time. These were legal documents, and could be contested in court.

By the seventeenth century, it was common in continental Europe to endorse a promissory note—sign it on the back—and pass it to the next person. England and the colonies started doing this, too, at roughly the same time. A law in Maryland in 1642 laid out the rules for endorsing notes, suggesting it was common at the time. In 1647, a law in Massachusetts, copied by other colonies, declared all notes to be negotiable—they could pass hand to hand as money—so long as they'd been endorsed. Parliament followed the colonies, confirming in 1704 that any endorsed promissory note was negotiable in England, too. American colonists didn't have to retire their own note by handing over coins. They could do it with anything that held value—tobacco, for example. Below, in a form easily recognizable for several centuries, is a handwritten note from Edmond Brice of Annapolis in 1777 to buy an enslaved boy for £180. His wealthy brother James Brice signed the back as a guarantor, showing that he would pay the note if Edmond couldn't.

It was possible to manage most daily purchases with either book credits or promissory notes. But that constant desperation for small change in the colonial economy suggests that coins did play a role on the edges of how the colonists used credit to pay each other. Mutual credits never balance out perfectly, and sometimes colonists needed to just pay off a debt and walk away. After customers closed out book credit with some kind of payment, the merchant would record how—in labor or wheat, for example, or with a promissory note. Sometimes these records just read, maddeningly, "cash," leaving historians to argue about what cash even was.

In Maryland's early tobacco economy, there is some documentary evidence that colonists used beaver pelts as cash, or strings of roanoke—

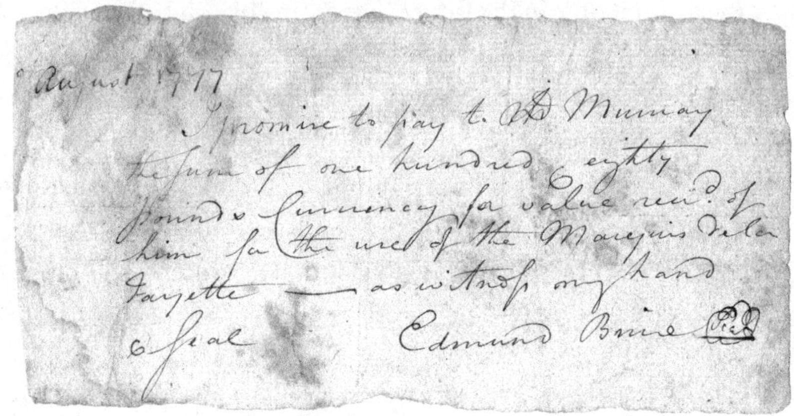

August 1777
I promise to pay t. [illegible] Murray
the sum of one hundred & eighty
pounds Currency for value rec^d of
him for the use of the Marquis de la
Fayette —— as witness my hand
& Seal Edmund Brice (Seal)

A promissory note, written in Annapolis in 1777. These notes were a common way of making an on-the-spot payment when no cash was available. (Image from the H. Furlong Baldwin Library, Maryland Center for History and Culture.)

beads made of whelk and clamshell that have since come to be known as wampum. One English traveler to the province recorded that a good porker—a pig—could also serve as money. But as early as 1637, the Maryland Provincial Court decided that it would pay, tax, and fine colonists in what everyone had sitting around, dried and packed in hogsheads: tobacco.

In September 1657, for example, the Provincial Court sentenced John Dandy to hang for murdering his servant, Henry Gouge, and dumping his body in a creek. Two surgeons had dissected Gouge's head to check for trauma; the court granted them an even split of one hogshead of tobacco. Major John Hallowes had detained Dandy after he fled across the river to Virginia; the court awarded Hallowes 498 pounds of tobacco from Dandy's estate. This doesn't mean the Provincial Court handed out actual tobacco. Major Hallowes didn't take 498 pounds of tobacco with him back to Virginia. A hogshead of tobacco was fragile and spoiled easily; planters would leave dried tobacco in their barns right until it was time to roll it down to the water's edge and put it on an English ship. Hallowes would have marked a hogshead with his own name, right there in dead John Dandy's barn, to collect later, after the tobacco sold. Planters eventually figured out how to write out tobacco notes that shifted ownership of a hogshead sitting in a barn somewhere from one person to another, and in 1747 the Maryland Assembly approved a more transparent, official system of printed tobacco notes, a kind of cash that proved ownership of a hogshead in a sealed provincial warehouse.

By the time Sharpe wrote his letters, Marylanders were paying all their provincial, county, and parish taxes in tobacco notes. They paid fees and clergy salaries the same way. Some merchants kept their books in units of tobacco. Money is a product, and the right to produce it comes with a lot of power. Tobacco notes worked as a currency, because two kinds of people had power in early Maryland: the London agents, who preferred to pay in bills of exchange, and the planters, who literally grew money every season. But it didn't work for everyone else in the province, who had to grow what was called trash tobacco to pay their taxes, no matter what their trade.

COLONIES FOUGHT EACH OTHER FOR DOLLARS

Maryland had what one historian called a direct economy: Tobacco grown by slaves left straight for London; then tools, cloth, and luxuries arrived on the return trip. Colonies to the north had an indirect economy: Wood, wheat, and hogs traveled to Barbados and Jamaica, and returning ships carried molasses and coins, which paid for manufactures from Britain. Planters in Maryland sold tobacco from their own docks and Annapolis was barely a town, but the Atlantic dockyards in Philadelphia, New York, and Boston had more specialized trades—wheelwrights and shipwrights, coopers and rope makers—which meant more tradesmen demanding cash for their work. The indirect economies surrounding the big Atlantic port cities had a better supply of dollars, but also a greater need for small change.

In 1691, Increase Mather and William Phips, who would become governor of the Massachusetts Bay Colony, begged the Council of Trade and Plantations in London to establish a local mint. Boston had briefly had a mint, the only one in the North American colonies, but the Royal Mint, guarding its own privileges, had advised the Crown to shut it down. Shopkeepers in the colony didn't have small change, and people were being cheated with counterfeits.

Mather and Phips also complained that there was "practically only Spanish money in New England." Estate settlements in Massachusetts, too, disclosed hoards of silver dollars, and letters mentioned both payments and savings in dollars. In 1699, Richard Coote, the Earl of Bellomont and governor of New York, made a payment of 500 Spanish dollars from what he modestly referred to as his "little stock." New York in particular had so many pieces of eight that in the 1690s merchants kept their accounts in dollars and pieces of eight. That is, for a time in early colonial Manhattan, dollars were both real and imaginary money.

A Dutch *leeuwendaalder*, known to colonists as a "dog dollar." Worth slightly less than Spanish dollars, these were more likely to stay in circulation in the American colonies. (Image from the American Numismatic Society.)

In 1701, Nathaniel Blakiston, the governor of Maryland, wrote to the Board of Trade and Plantations with his own complaint. There wasn't much money in the province, he explained, just a few pieces of eight and some underweight Dutch Republic dollars he called "dogg dollars"—the lion on the coin, rubbed with use, looked like a dog begging for scraps. Even worse, he wrote, the few dollars Maryland did have were being "carryed away by our neighbours." Blakiston was referring to Pennsylvania. He was flagging a practice that London had been aware of but had quietly tolerated. The dollar was so important to the colonies that they had been engaging in what we'd today call competitive devaluations—fighting with each other to pull dollars in.

London had set an official exchange rate of sterling to the dollar: Both Seville dollars from Spain and rix-dollars from Germany and the Baltic were worth 4 shillings, 6 pence. But to draw dollars in, different colonies began declaring that dollars were worth more than that, locally. To get dollars, merchants would simply record them at higher values in their books, offering more goods for payments in dollars. The colonies were competing to attract any Caribbean merchant or captain with pieces of eight. By 1700, a dollar was worth 6 shillings in New England. It was 6 shillings, 9 pence in New York. In New Jersey and Pennsylvania, it was 7 shillings, 8 pence. Each of these new dollar exchange rates created its own local currency, worth less than the sterling pounds, shillings, and pence of England. Merchants noted these distinctions in their ledgers, recording prices either in shillings sterling or in shillings current Pennsylvania money. Already in 1700, the colonies were no longer on England's monetary standard. They had what we would today call a managed exchange rate with the dollar.

You can see why Maryland's Blakiston was so frustrated. The Board of Trade and Plantations had allowed the northern colonies to nudge their exchange rates up, pulling in dollars. But a combination of the Crown and the board refused to allow Maryland and Virginia the same privilege. Merchants in London didn't want any confusion over the value in pounds and shillings in the debts they were owed by tobacco planters, and the board didn't want the tobacco colonies to have the more diverse, indirect economies that might encourage them to do anything other than grow tobacco. Maryland, with its simple, direct economy, had to value its dollars at 4 shillings, 6 pence, the same as in London. There was no reason for anyone to sail up the Chesapeake Bay to Annapolis or Baltimore Town with dollars that were almost twice as valuable in Philadelphia.

Blakiston's letter launched an inquiry. In 1704, a crown proclamation laid out exact exchange rates for every kind of silver that might wander into the colonies. Seville pieces of eight, Mexico pieces of eight, ecus from France, even "Old Rix Dollars of the Empire"—everything that passed in global markets for a dollar—had to sell for no more than 6 shillings. Northern colonists generally ignored the proclamation until it was followed by an act of Parliament in 1708. Even after the proclamation, local merchants continued to buy full-weight Spanish and rix-dollars at whatever price made sense. In Maryland, this was known as common money, where a silver dollar got you 7 shillings, 6 pence. The rate kept creeping up in Philadelphia, carrying dollars up to Pennsylvania. Merchants in Annapolis were always under pressure to match it, or else lose even more of their own dollars.

Parliament had exerted some sovereignty over money in the colonies, but it was the kind of sovereignty that mattered only to merchants in London, who didn't want to trade with a place where the value of a shilling could drop from one year to the next. The Crown and Parliament hadn't solved either of the colonists' two basic problems with money: They could never get enough silver dollars, and they barely had any small change to periodically clear all those small acts of credit. And as colonists in America began to trade more directly with each other, the big problem of the petty coins got worse.

"TRULY AND BONA FIDE SUNK"— PAPER BILLS OF CREDIT

In 1730, a man named Ebenezer Cooke published at his own expense in Maryland one of the strangest, most delightful documents I've ever read. *Sotweed Redivivus* is twenty-eight pages of often profane couplets in which a man gets on an old horse and rides to Annapolis so he can get sloppy on claret and talk about monetary policy. We don't know a lot about Cooke. He was likely educated in England, inherited a plantation at the mouth of the Choptank River, and held several local commissions in provincial Maryland. He is better known for another, longer work published in London in 1708, *The Sot-Weed Factor;* that epic, and the bare facts of Cooke's life, make up the source material of a novel John Barth published in 1960. In *Sotweed Redivivus,* Cooke's narrator arrives in Annapolis as the Maryland Assembly has taken up a bill to issue its first run of paper money. The bill was first submitted in 1727 and was argued every year until it finally passed in 1733. "The Case to me seems very plain," says Cooke's narrator, "And was for *Paper Currency:* / It's Money, be it what it will, / In Tan-Pit coin'd, or Paper-Mill, / That must the hungry Belly fill." It's a poem about paper money. And Cooke didn't have to explain what paper money was.

By the 1720s, it would have been familiar to anyone in Britain's North American colonies. In 1690, Massachusetts issued £7,000 in paper bills to pay for an expedition to Quebec that had failed to capture either Quebec or any silver. The bills were indented—marked with a design to prevent forgery. They carried the seal of the colony and a printed message that read a bit like a promissory note, in which the Treasury in Boston promised to receive the bills "in all Publick payments and for any Stock at any time." Massachusetts gave its indented bills to suppliers, soldiers, and widows. The colony essentially borrowed from its own colonists, handing over the bills as a contract, proof of the loan.

Just like the silver flowing to ports in southern China, though, paper bills needed a sink. Massachusetts couldn't just push its bills out into the world. Something had to be pulling them back in, giving them value. So the colony also prepared a tax, payable in the same paper shilling indented bills. Debt canceled debt. The colony borrowed from soldiers and widows while at the same time declaring that everyone together owed that same amount back to the colony. The bills were legal tender, so in the meantime everyone had to accept them as payment for any debt. In 1709, Connecticut, New Hampshire, New York, and New Jersey issued their own indented bills, which came to be known more generally as bills of credit. Rhode Island followed in 1710. To simplify dramatically, most of these bills were initially issued to pay for the costs of each colony's contribution to Queen Anne's War, fought on the New England frontier with the French.

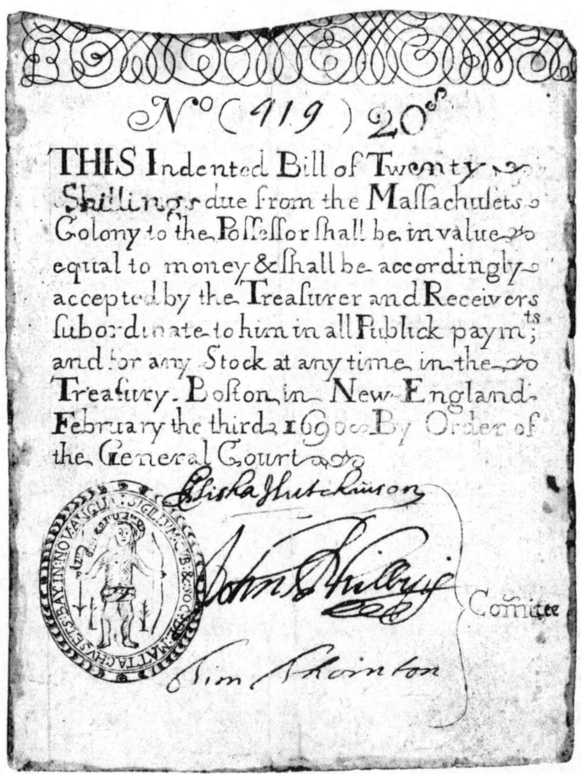

An indented bill issued by Massachusetts in 1690. These were copied and adapted widely across the colonies, and came to be known as bills of credit. (Image from the National Museum of American History.)

The bills of credit from the American colonies don't fit neatly into how we're usually taught about paper money. Somewhere in a textbook you probably learned that people dropped off gold coins for safekeeping and received, for that gold, slips of paper that could be traded back in for gold, on demand. Then the slips of paper themselves became a negotiable instrument: They could trade from person to person, as money. That explanation often comes with a history of how goldsmiths in seventeenth-century London took in gold for paper receipts. That did actually happen. Goldsmith bankers were real. A Maryland tobacco note handed out for tobacco was something like a receipt for gold, and gold and silver certificates circulated as late as the early twentieth century as proof of precious metals held by the U.S. Treasury.

That's one explanation. But it's selective and deeply misleading. To say that goldsmiths were the origin of paper money is to ignore centuries of other kinds of common promises on paper. What we think of now as a slip of paper money, printed by an American colony, came to be known at the time as a bill of credit for a reason. It bore the wording of a precise promise, just like the old promissory notes and bills of exchange. It relied on an understanding of how a promise on paper worked, both in custom and in law. By the end of the seventeenth century, for example, a "bill obligatory" was a more formalized promissory note, blessed with a seal by a notary. Those first indented bills, then, were a small step; instead of a person making a promise, it was the Massachusetts Bay Colony.

None of those slips of paper promised that there were coins or a commodity already tucked away somewhere. They were, instead, promises to pay something in the future. That story about the goldsmith bankers implies a progression: First there was metal; then it became paper, and then people made loans. But that progression isn't an actual history. In the markets we've talked about so far, coins and credit worked together. In early sixteenth-century Leipzig, the silver pouring in from Joachimsthal didn't replace credit on market days; it expanded it. At the Zocodover in late sixteenth-century Toledo, rural weavers came in to get supplies on credit, then delivered finished products to cancel out their debts.

When a tradesman in colonial America wrote out a note to a neighbor, or when a shopkeeper recorded a book credit in a ledger, they were *manufacturing money*. Instead of paying with a coin, they paid with a promise. That promise, explicitly worded on a piece of paper, became money as it passed from hand to hand. So when you try to understand why paper money might have value, you can't just think about a coin. You have to think about a promise—what was promised, who promised it, and whether the promise was credible.

Until the early twentieth century, historians and economists tended to dismiss colonial bills of credit as inherently untrustworthy and inflationary, because they couldn't be redeemed on demand for silver or gold. After the bank failures of the Great Depression, a few historians began to think about older forms of state currency. They took the colonial bills more seriously, looking at differences among the colonies. Some bills had credible promises and held their value. Some didn't. More recently, Farley Grubb at the University of Delaware has looked at the financial structures behind each colony's bills, examining them a bit like a credit analyst in a modern bond market. Christine Desan, a legal historian at Harvard Law, has encouraged historians to think about how law gave the bills value. Colonial assemblies put the bills into circulation as payments, then took them back out as taxes; it was laws that kept the bills moving, the same way the heart pumps blood through the body. Laws are important, but I am partial to thinking about bills of credit as part of a long tradition of financial contracts on slips of paper that passed from hand to hand as money; that's what the bills looked like, and they were printed with clear explanations of why they had value and how they could be redeemed.

Arguments about the substance of money, however, miss the importance of process and administration. Within New England, the paper shillings of Massachusetts, New Hampshire, Connecticut, and Rhode Island all circulated within a de facto common currency area. Each colony, however, only had control over its own paper money. Rhode Island began to embrace its bills of credit as a way to stimulate local trade and pay for ongoing expenses, the way a modern government might buy its way out of a recession. All this paper together, pushed out more quickly than it could be taken back in for taxes, began to erode the value of all of New England's money—not just the bills of credit, but all the local handwritten promissory notes and book credits as well. The value of New England's currency of local pounds, shillings, and pence dropped slowly at first, then rapidly in the 1740s, until Parliament passed its first Currency Act, in 1751. The act prevented the northern colonies from issuing any paper money as legal tender. It protected British merchants against what we now call inflation—from having to accept lower-value New England money as payment for old debts.

William Douglass, a physician in Boston who had become known through his arguments against large-scale smallpox inoculation, wrote excoriating essays about bills of credit in the 1730s and 1740s that were influential in Britain. Douglass saw any money issued by a popular assembly as inherently flawed, a "knavish device of fraudulent debtors of the loan money to pay off their loans at a very depreciated value." That is, people borrowed money in a currency controlled by a colony. Then the colony printed more bills in that currency, making existing debts worth less, and making it easier for borrowers to pay those debts off. This does not seem to have been the explicit intention behind the bills of credit in New England, though it is what ultimately happened.

As Douglass was writing, however, colonies outside New England had already begun to change how they administered their notes. New York issued its first bills of credit in 1709. Like Massachusetts, New York made its bills legal tender, and accepted them as payment for new taxes. Within a few years, however, New York's assembly had added what it called at the time a sinking fund. The fund was a way to buy back some of the bills of credit with silver on a regular schedule—to sink them. The colony passed an excise tax on anyone distilling strong liquors, payable in an eighth of an ounce of Spanish silver per gallon. So that the bills could be "truly and bona fide sunk," the silver from the excise tax on liquor would stay in an audited account, and twice a year the province would use that silver to buy bills of credit and burn them. Sinking the bills was both an administrative act and a public performance; burning the sunk bills supported the value of the bills still in circulation. In 1723, the New York Assembly added a new estate tax explicitly in silver dollars, which also went into the sinking fund. That is, dollars were so ubiquitous that New York sank some of its paper shilling bills of credit with silver dollar coins. The assembly kept its promise, sinking and burning the bills it issued with the silver it got from excise and estate taxes through the 1720s—usually well more than half of each run of new bills, and almost all of some runs.

In 1722, Pennsylvania issued bills of credit for another reason: what the historian Katie Moore has called an economic stimulus. Pennsylvania had been able to stay out of Queen Anne's War, and so didn't have to issue money to pay for troops. But by the early 1720s, global prices for flour—Pennsylvania's main export—had collapsed. And in London a stock bubble had burst limiting the credit that British merchants would extend to the colonies or anywhere else. Trying to increase the supply of shillings during this recession, Pennsylvania started handing out bills of credit in three different ways.

First, the assembly paid out bills of credit as loans from a public land bank; colonists could borrow bills against half the value of their land, handing them back over to a loan office as they paid down the principal. Crucially, though, borrowers paid the interest on these loans as "money"—silver dollars or gold pistoles. The loan office would advertise how much it had collected in coins as interest, and would use it to sink some of the bills. "The true and regular sinking of the said bills," the act read, "will very much conduce to the keeping up the value of the same"; sinking the bills was both administration and performance, just like in New York. More bills of credit went to public works; those would return right back to the Treasury as payment for new estate taxes. Even more would go to pay the colony's debts. Just as in New York, the Pennsylvania Assembly also promised to sink some of its bills through a dedicated sinking fund, topped up with excise taxes on wine and rum; import duties on wine, rum, brandy, molasses, cider, hops, and flax; and an import duty on slaves. These taxes would be paid only in "ready money"—silver dollars. The ships that brought in products—and humans—were more likely to carry silver and could be forced at the port to pay in silver. Supported by a land bank and a sinking fund, the Pennsylvania bills of credit held their value. They circulated into New Jersey, forcing that colony to issue its own land-bank currency.

Sinking funds and the loan office don't provide a complete explanation for how the bills retained their value. Both New York and Pennsylvania collected some of their bills of credit back as tax payments, just as colonies in New England had. But the thought that went into these arrangements shows that the bills weren't receipts for silver, nor were they just tickets paid into the economy and then taxed back out. Rather, they looked a lot like the promissory notes and bills of exchange that had already been in circulation. Some promises on paper passed hand to hand and never needed a coin. Some promises cleared with a coin. Coins and paper worked together, in a system built out of habits, confirmed by laws.

This is what was happening around Ebenezer Cooke in Maryland in 1730, when he sat down to write *Sotweed Redivivus.* From his perspective, Pennsylvania's paper money was working. At times, Cooke's narrator in Annapolis sounded a lot like Sancho de Moncada in Toledo a century before. Where Moncada thought that the silver industry was choking everything else off in Castile, Cooke blamed Maryland's dominant crop: tobacco. The province's old sotweed trade, with its simple yearly swap of tobacco for tools, had created a self-reinforcing problem. Without any other products, Maryland couldn't draw any kind of big-money coins up the Chesapeake Bay. But without little money—local, circulating cash—it was hard to create those products, since no one locally could buy or sell anything. "It's industry, and not a nauseous Weed," wrote Cooke, "Must cloath the Naked and the Hungry feed."

Cooke's narrator, after watching the assembly debate the paper money bill in Annapolis, meets an old friend, a planter. The two go to a bar to drink lemon punch, then end up at the planter's house, drinking claret until the planter falls asleep. The narrator, bored, jolts him awake and pours more claret. The planter, refreshed, spits out what economists now call an industrial policy—a plan for Maryland's economy. The province needs to plant wheat, hemp, flax, rice, and cotton, said the planter. It needs to fill its pastures with sheep and cattle. And the province needs its own ships, freeing itself from the British merchants who prefer the direct tobacco trade. Maryland will "never flourish," he says, "'till we learn to sound / Great-Britain's *Channel, and in Cash abound*." If Maryland could build ships and sail them, then it could sell all those other products and bring home actual money.

Ebenezer Cooke was not a great poet. But he was a reasonably capable development economist. Once there's cash in Maryland, he wrote, "*Mechanicks* then of ev'ry Sort, / And *Mariners* wou'd here resort, / When they hear *Money* circulates, / Within our Towns and City Gates." A supply of cash would help the province urbanize and industrialize, make even more products, and then sell those products abroad. "See how our *Staple* sells at Home," the old planter says, "*Barbadoes* and *Jamaica* drain; / Bring hither, from the Mines of *Spain, / Moidores, Pistoles,* and *Cobbs,* full Weight; / The very best of *Spanish Plate*." A cob was a crude dollar minted at either Mexico City or Potosí, and "Spanish plate" is a play on words—*plata* is Spanish for silver. Planters in Barbados and Jamaica grew almost only sugarcane, but if provincials from Maryland could sell them corn or pork or even tools, the planters could pay with the best kind of money: silver dollars.

Maryland was among the last of the colonies to consider bills of credit, because it was one of the last colonies left with a simple, single-crop economy. As Cooke's narrator was on his bender in Annapolis, though, that had already started to change. The population continued to grow—both free and enslaved—but tobacco production remained stable. And tobacco production had become more efficient, leaving more time for specialized work, like making cloth at home. This was particularly pronounced among the enslaved workers on the larger plantations. Free farmers started to plant more corn and wheat, particularly in the north of the state, where the soil didn't suit tobacco. The wheat sold to Europe, and the corn sold to the British West Indies. Both crops required plows, carts, and wagons, which also encouraged specialization.

Tools for crafts started to show up more frequently among plantation inventories in the decades after 1700. So did the kinds of basic imported household items that in the previous century would have been considered luxuries—silverware, Bibles, linens, even some spice boxes. Scottish tradesmen arrived on the Chesapeake, where they bought tobacco and sold tools all year, and not just when the tobacco ships arrived. There were more things to export from Maryland and more things to buy and sell at home. That meant a better supply of big-money dollars and pistoles from Barbados and Jamaica, but also a greater need for some kind of little money in the province.

Cooke's narrator and the old planter finish their drinks. Cooke hints that the planter has simply been talked into silence, a possibility I find easy to believe because I have read Cooke's entire poem. And in 1733, a printer in London began producing £90,000 of Maryland's first paper bills of credit. They were initially valued as "current Maryland money," using the same crown proclamation rate as the other colonies—6 shillings to the dollar. The new shillings were legal tender–ish. Provincials could use them to pay any contracts, so long as they were written in current money, not sterling. They could pay any taxes with them, except the ones due to Maryland's proprietors, the Lords Baltimore of the Calvert family. Parishes did not accept the new notes; in Maryland, you still had to pay God in tobacco.

The province did several things with its new paper cash. With £3,000 it started construction on a mansion for the governor, a white elephant that remained unfinished for decades. The mansion, now completed, sits at the center of St. John's College as McDowell Hall. Maryland also handed out almost £50,000 directly to provincials, something like what the economist Milton Friedman would later call "helicopter money."

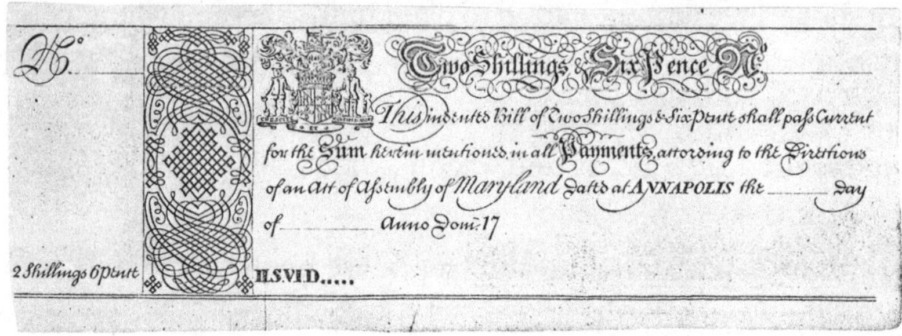

A Maryland bill of credit from 1733. Maryland was one of the last colonies to issue its own paper currency. (Image from the Newman Numismatic Portal at Washington University in St. Louis.)

Every head of household got paper shillings, in proportion to every "taxable"—every person, free or enslaved, living on his property. The rest of the new bills were reserved for future expenses and, just like in Pennsylvania and New Jersey, to lend to colonists who could offer land as a security. The province held the bills in an iron chest that could only open when three keys were turned at the same time. The keys were given to three commissioners, each appointed by the governor.

Maryland, too, created a sinking fund for its bills of credit. It had fewer imports than New York or Pennsylvania, though, and fewer opportunities to take in silver dollars. So at the same time the province started handing out its new shillings, it passed a tax on tobacco exports of 1 shilling, 3 pence on every hogshead of tobacco. The proceeds of that tax, taken in sterling bills of exchange, were shipped to London and used to buy stock in the Bank of England—a neutral, safe investment in Britain's most stable chartered company. The plan in 1733 was to let those taxes accumulate and grow in value as stock in the bank, then use them to buy back a third of the Maryland shilling bills of credit by 1749, then the other two-thirds by 1764—the year Horatio Sharpe would write those letters. The province wanted to sink its shilling bills of credit by carefully nurturing a dedicated investment fund.

Walk downhill from McDowell Hall today, along Prince George Street toward the Annapolis City Dock. Take a right at Maryland Avenue and at the end of the block you'll find yourself looking up at Maryland's statehouse. Right in front of you, on the lawn, sits a small brick building flanked by two short wings. I grew up in Annapolis, and my grandmother gave historic tours downtown. When I was a teenager, she taught me how to do it, too. I was wildly unqualified. It was just a simple performance of memorized facts. This, I would say, gesturing toward each wing of the little brick building, was the Treasury. It's the oldest public building in the city. It's where they kept the money.

I was right, but not in the way that I'd thought. The Treasury wasn't just for gold and silver. The province built it in 1735. It was designed expressly to manage the shilling bills of credit, a space to hold new bills in the locked chest, burn old bills as they came back in, and make notes in the accounts of the sinking fund. At the time it wasn't called the Treasury. It was called the Paper Currency Office, or just the Paper Office. It was there to guard the dollars, the pistoles, *and* the paper, and to guarantee that the whole process would work. After 1733, the province itself manufactured money. That money was all credit, all just a promise. The little brick office with the big lock was there for the practical purpose of security. But it was also a physical reminder, in the same way that commercial banks used to be columned and imposing. Maryland had made a promise with its paper money. Thirty years later, the strength of that promise was exactly what had begun to cause problems for Horatio Sharpe.

MARYLAND SANK ITS BILLS OF CREDIT ON SCHEDULE, CAUSING A DEFLATION

When the province first started handing out its bills of credit in 1734, they immediately dropped in value. By 1736, that exchange rate had fallen to 230 Maryland shillings to 100 shillings sterling. In April 1743, it briefly hit a low of 325 Maryland shillings. But then the exchange rate began to climb back up, particularly after the province sank half of its bills of credit, on schedule, in 1749. By September 1764, just as Horatio

Sharpe was writing to Cecilius Calvert about the money problem in the province, the rest of the Maryland shillings were right back at their original face value—133 of them would get you 100 shillings sterling.

The best explanation for why the value of the Maryland bills of credit dropped and then recovered is the simplest. The sinking fund was a novelty: a tax on tobacco in bills of exchange, invested in stock at the Bank of England. It built on the familiar experiences of other colonies, but was also a new structure for a sinking fund, in the care of a province that had never issued bills of credit before. At first, the proof was still thirty years in the future. People didn't believe that it would work. Then they did. Then they *really* did.

In March 1764, Cecilius Calvert wrote Horatio Sharpe a rambling letter on a list of subjects. Sharpe had asked for English hares, for his new private estate across the river from Annapolis; Calvert was happy to provide them. Calvert was exercised in particular about Edward Lloyd, a planter in Talbot County on Maryland's Eastern Shore. Lloyd, who owned forty-three thousand acres of land, was also one of Lord Baltimore's two rent-roll keepers, responsible for making sure that the Calverts got paid rent from their possessions in the province. His accounts had come in both late and confused; Calvert suspected Lloyd was unreliable because, like other men born in America, "in his Blood reigns a melancholy Damp."

Sharpe and Calvert had also been writing to each other about the sinking fund—the thirty years of tax revenue on tobacco that had all been invested in the stock of the Bank of England, waiting to buy back all the Maryland bills of credit. In 1733, this had just been a promise from the provincial legislature. In 1749, the province did in fact sink a third of its paper shillings on schedule. In 1754, the Paper Office distributed more paper shillings to pay the province's expenses in what would become the Seven Years' War. The commissioners then immediately began paying back into the sinking fund from new taxes—on tavern licenses and on the imports of carriages, wine, servants, and slaves. Over the next decade, twenty-two ships paid import duties into the sinking fund on roughly twenty-six hundred humans as cargo. The bills of credit had helped Maryland diversify its economy, but the fund to sink those bills was still inextricably bound to the province's old tobacco and slave system. By 1764 it seemed likely that the province would make good on its promise to buy back the rest of its shillings at face value. Calvert wrote that even though the value of the fund's stock in the Bank of England had dropped for a time, the slow accumulation of taxes and interest had ensured the fund would be enough to meet the original schedule from 1733.

In 1985, Bruce Smith, an economist, considered all the ways Maryland's provincials would have thought about their paper money in the eighteenth century. As the province spent and lent out its shilling bills of credit over three decades, the supply of those shillings continued to grow, even when taking population growth into consideration. According to the quantity theory of money, this should have caused inflation; it should have made the shillings less valuable. But that's not what happened. Smith argued that the *quality* of paper money was as important as its quantity. As it became clear that Maryland would manage the fund carefully, the fund provided backing for the bills of credit that was literally every bit as good as gold. The sinking fund was a real financial asset.

And by the middle of the eighteenth century, the province of Maryland had begun to fulfill Ebenezer Cooke's boozy prediction: It started making more things, expanding its economy beyond the simple exchange on a ship's deck of tobacco for goods. Marylanders continued to sell more wheat, pork, and wood through Philadelphia. More tools for making carts and cloth showed up in estate inventories. An ironworks opened in Baltimore Town. Even the tobacco planters, as they continued to purchase more slaves at the province's port towns of Annapolis and Patuxent, began to make more things on their own plantations.

But as people buy and sell more things in an economy, the supply of money has to expand, too. By the early 1760s, there were more transactions in the province, but the supply of those Maryland paper shillings had started to shrink, well before the planned date to buy them back. The problem, Calvert pointed out to Sharpe in his letter, was that "infamous Jobbers" had started pulling all the Maryland shillings out of the province's economy. "Jobber" was almost always an insult; it referred to someone who bought and sold stocks purely as speculation. Calvert was complaining that jobbers in Maryland, anticipating a full payout when the province sank its bills of credit, had begun buying up bills at a slight discount from people who needed to spend the money, and were then holding on to them, rather than using them to buy things. "Little currency has circulation," Calvert wrote, "the utility prevented, Lock'd up in the hands of merciless wretches that grind the very Poor." The Maryland shillings had become so valuable as an investment that people stopped using them as money.

Then, in early 1764, Parliament passed its Currency Act—the one that banned all legal-tender paper money in the colonies, period. Merchants in London and Glasgow had been complaining that they were getting paid in lower-value colonial paper currency, particularly in Virginia. But the Currency Act was also inspired by a theory about money. George Grenville, the prime minister, wanted the colonies to pay their taxes in silver. If they stopped using paper, Grenville believed, silver dollars would naturally flow in and could then happily be sent back on ships to London as taxes. He wanted to turn the colonies into a silver dollar farm. Grenville was following a line of reasoning that was widely shared in Britain: Coins were inherently the best kind of money, and they traveled naturally with trade to countries where they were needed most.

David Hume had articulated this idea in his *Political Discourses,* printed in 1752 and already wildly popular in Britain and on the Continent. If there is not enough gold or silver somewhere, then prices there will drop. As they drop, that place will be able to sell more products abroad, bringing coins back in. Hume described this cycle as a "happy concurrence of causes." Economists now refer to it as the Hume price-specie-flow mechanism, a neat proof that paper credit is unnatural, because it artificially creates new money, keeping prices high *and* interrupting the natural flow of specie—silver and gold.

In May 1764, England's Board of Trade in Whitehall demanded that Horatio Sharpe produce an account of every single Maryland paper shilling that had been issued. That meant Sharpe would have to take his private barge across the river to Annapolis and spend some time with the commissioners in the little brick Paper Office, going through account books. In July he reported back to London that of the £90,000 in Maryland shillings printed in 1733, there were £41,000 left outstanding, all scheduled to be sunk over the coming winter using bills of exchange, payable in London out of the sinking fund. The shilling bills of credit had functioned as money. They had worked. And as the jobbers bought them up, waiting to sell them back to the province, the bills were draining out of the economy.

By coincidence, credit was also tightening in London. Merchants were less willing to extend loans anywhere across the Atlantic, which meant that bills of exchange and Maryland's few silver dollars and gold pistoles flowed out of the province to pay down loans in England. Merchants in Maryland were so desperate for any kind of cash that between 1762 and 1764 they bought millions of copper farthings from Philadelphia and New York to use as small change. Henry Callister, a planter and slave trader on the province's Eastern Shore, wrote in 1764 that "there is no record, since the province was called Maryland, of such a scarcity of money, whether real or imaginary." There was no point in suing anyone for debts, he wrote; no one could pay.

If there are the same number of things to buy in an economy, but less money to buy them with, something has to give. Prices need to deflate—to drop. It's hard to come up with data on colonial prices; what little we have shows change on a year-by-year basis, which can make it hard to see the full problem. If prices change a little bit every year, then people should adjust a little bit every year. But the faster prices change, the harder it is to adjust. As things become less expensive, people should, in theory, just lower their prices and accept cuts in pay. But people don't like it when numbers go down, and sometimes they'll just refuse to adjust, which makes deflations a painful grind.

The historian Lois Green Carr is responsible for most of the numbers behind what we know about the Maryland economy in the eighteenth century. She died in 2015, but you can still see her papers at the archives in Annapolis. Reading through them, I found a short list of careful notes in pencil on a yellow legal pad, each taken from a probate record—what someone's estate owed and was owed after they died. Each line shows just a date, the name of someone who died, and an exchange rate of Maryland current money to British sterling.

When Nehemiah Birkhead died in January 1764, the assessors of his estate valued current Maryland money at 150 percent of sterling. But when Nathaniel Dare died in August of the same year, the exchange rate had already climbed to just over 133 percent. These notes never found their way into any of Carr's published work, but they show the beginning of an idea. Prices in Maryland weren't going through a gradual adjustment. They were deflating by the month.

We have been conditioned over the last hundred years to worry more about inflations than deflations. But historically, deflations were just as common and just as devastating. In theory, markets in a deflation should clear; eventually people agree on a lower price and start trading. In practice, people are obstinate. In a deflation, merchants will sometimes simply refuse to keep negotiating. If they're owed money, they'll just wait for the full amount. If they owe money, they'll watch helplessly as their own earnings drop, while their loan payments don't. If they have something to sell, they'll wait for prices to go back up. Or they'll just stop buying and selling, period.

SHARPE'S SOLUTION: THE SAME BILLS OF CREDIT, THIS TIME IN DOLLARS

This deflation was the source of Horatio Sharpe's undisguised annoyance in his letter about the Currency Act to Calvert in August 1764.

According to the prime minister's hopeful theory, borrowed from David Hume, without paper money prices would adjust down, and silver dollars would naturally flow into the province as needed—and from there to England. From what Sharpe could see from Annapolis, it wasn't working out that way.

A cameo of Sharpe from around the same time shows him solidly in middle age, with a full head of hair, a prominent nose, and a lower lip pouting over the beginnings of a double chin. The province had started building a governor's residence in 1764 but never finished, leaving Sharpe to work out of rented quarters in Annapolis. In the late summer of 1764, he had started building what he called a "small elegant lodge" at Whitehall, a hundred-acre tobacco plantation he had acquired through a land swap with a church parish.

Sharpe, the youngest of nine sons, was ambivalent about his work in Maryland, and in letters home was wistful about a return to the marines or a quiet, dependable income in England. He had become wealthy in America, though. Eight enslaved men rowed his private barge over the Severn River between Annapolis and Whitehall. He was fascinated with the possibility of developing more industries in the province and, like other planters, was making changes on his own property; he converted an old mill to a loom so the slaves at Whitehall could weave wool cloth from his flock of South Devon sheep.

Lady Matilda Ridout Edgar, Sharpe's biographer, suggests that he was building Whitehall and its gardens as a gift to Mary Ogle, daughter of a former governor. It's likely a cherry-tree story; it shows up in other Maryland histories, always sourced to Edgar. Mary Ogle did not choose Horatio Sharpe; she married John Ridout, Sharpe's thirty-two-year-old secretary. In the muggy Chesapeake summer of 1764, then, while Horatio Sharpe was trying to solve the problem of deflation in Maryland, he was possibly lovesick but definitely distracted with a construction project.

It's difficult to introduce something completely alien and have people accept it as money, so most new kinds of money come from something people already know. Horatio Sharpe had to find something that would work in the province as small money. But he had a precedent to work with: Maryland's shilling bills of credit. In 1733 they had been an innovation, backed by a promise of future taxes on tobacco paid as bills of exchange into a sinking fund invested in the stock of the Bank of England. Three decades later, provincials in Maryland understood how those bills of credit worked, and trusted them as money.

Sharpe had to step delicately around Parliament, though, which had made clear there was to be no more legal-tender paper money in America. This left him a slim path. The province could print bills, but it couldn't order people to accept them. The Currency Act had also made the ancient Carolingian currencies of pounds, shillings, and pence problematic. In Annapolis, shopkeepers understood the difference between Maryland currency, common currency, and sterling. But that nuance got lost in London, particularly for the merchants who were adamant that they would not be forced to accept lower-value provincial goods and bills for higher-value debts in sterling.

There was another currency available, however. There's a clear picture of money in Maryland's economy in the back pages of the *Gazette* that summer. On August 1, a subscriber offered a 20 dollar reward for three servants who had run off, possibly posing as sailors. Hugh Maguire was offering singing lessons at St. Anne's church for 15 shillings a quarter, with a dollar up front. A gray mare a little over thirteen hands had strayed from a subscriber in St. Mary's County, who offered a 7 dollar reward. Dollars were not the only currency offered; some subscribers offered rewards in English shillings or gold Spanish pistoles. But the silver dollar was everywhere. There was both a precedent for bills of credit in Maryland and a commonly accepted denomination other than the old shillings and pence—the dollar. But a solution that would create a new supply of money wouldn't just have to adhere to the letter of Parliament's Currency Act. It would have to be snuck past Lord Baltimore. As the proprietor of the Province of Maryland, Baltimore retained some of the rights of a feudal lord, and could reject legislation from the Maryland Assembly, if he cared to.

Getting Lord Baltimore to care about anything was a challenge. He left behind a record of encounters with people who loathed him, universally describing him as charmless and grossly indecent. He was suspected of killing his ex-wife by pushing her out of a carriage in 1758 to settle a dispute over money. He let his rambling and disorganized uncle Cecil do all the boring stuff for Maryland; Baltimore had never visited the province and never would. He got an annual income from taxes on tobacco exports from Maryland, as well as the lands managed by his rent-roll keepers, which paid him in tobacco sales. His fundamental problem in life was that he had inherited a slave plantation that paid him so much every year he was bored. And by the end of his trip to Constantinople, he had decided he was done with Maryland altogether.

In January 1765, Baltimore wrote to Sharpe to complain that the surveys of his lands in the province weren't flattering enough. He was cashing out of Maryland, and his only concern was how much money he could come up with, as quickly as possible. By the summer, Baltimore began complaining that his rent collectors in Maryland were skimming off his account by accepting rents in pistoles or dollars, rather than sterling bills of exchange. Sharpe explained patiently that this had become common practice in the province and blamed the disarray in Baltimore's rent-rolls on a familiar scapegoat—Edward Lloyd, one of Baltimore's two keepers of the rent-roll.

Any new run of bills of credit would have to wait. As governor, Sharpe had prorogued the Maryland Assembly—delayed calling it together. He gave as his reason an outbreak of smallpox in Annapolis, but his letters show him much more worried how the provincials in Maryland were responding to the Stamp Act, which forced colonists to pay for a stamp on any official or legal papers. In September 1765, the province's stamp distributor was hanged in effigy in Annapolis, and a mob burned down a house he'd rented. In October, Sharpe finally wrote to Lord Baltimore to explain that he had no choice but to finally call the assembly, because he was worried they might meet without him—better to have a public fight over the Stamp Act than to let the assembly make a private move.

There was also some urgency over the province's debts. Maryland had not yet paid the officers in the west of the province who had raised troops to fight in the Seven Years' War, or the provincials who had quartered and fed those troops. Sharpe informed the assembly in December, in his understated way, that several hundred men were on their way from western Maryland, armed with guns and tomahawks, to settle up in some kind of money. "I recommend it to you to consider seriously the Consequences," he wrote, "of large Bodies of People being prompted to come hither."

The assembly also had to close out the books on the old bills of credit. A committee unlocked the chest in the Paper Currency Office to update their last report, from 1763. The province had redeemed £56,000 in paper shillings and burned them, with only £4,800 left outstanding. Some of the accounting is grim; Maryland had paid out £200 in bounties on four Native American scalps collected in the west of the province and burned another £1,920 that had been appropriated for more scalps, but never paid out. The province had also continued to take in revenue, including £930 of "Duties on Servts & Negroes"—the tax that had been imposed to make sure the province could continue to top up the sinking fund invested in Bank of England stock.

It was hard to get precise numbers on the value of that fund, since it depended on the value of the stock of the Bank of England. It was a crucial bit of financial data for the province; the *Gazette* would sometimes report the price of a share in the Bank of England when a ship arrived from London. But the committee estimated that even after all those paper Maryland shillings had been redeemed and burned, there was £20,000 left in the sinking fund in London; the province had actually made a net profit on the fund. The iron chest in the Paper Currency

Office also contained £142 in sterling bills of exchange, £10,108 in gold, and £1,464 in silver—the latter two probably in the form of pistoles and dollar coins. With some assumptions about what the province's treasurer might have, the committee got to a total balance of £36,000 on hand.

They didn't recommend the province spend this cash, however. On November 28, they proposed that the province turn its portfolio of gold, silver, stocks, and bills of credit *into dollars*. They wanted to do the exact same thing the province had done in 1733, with its paper shillings. Maryland would print 135,000 dollars of bills of credit, "to support the Trade and Commerce of this Province at this Time when Specie is so scarce among us." At the same time, the province would invest all £36,000 in another sinking fund, again wholly allocated to stock in the Bank of England, which would grow over ten years, then buy back the entire issue of dollar bills of credit. The province could have bought anything. What it proposed instead was to manufacture what it needed most: small change, this time in dollars instead of shillings.

There doesn't seem to have been any debate in either house over the proposal to issue the bills in dollars. Sharpe explained in a letter to Calvert in late December that the bill was unproblematic and would have passed were it not for an unrelated fight about who should pay the Maryland officers—the assembly or the lord proprietor. Spanish silver dollars were so familiar in Maryland that it's how the province calculated its own debts; public debt was 135,000 silver Spanish dollars, Sharpe wrote, exactly the same sum of dollars the proposal would produce. He didn't seem to feel any need to explain or justify the use of dollars as a unit of account, which suggests that it would have been unsurprising in London as well. The bills wouldn't be legal tender, he explained, and would have the same "bottom" as the sterling bills produced at the Bank of England.

By "bottom," Sharpe meant what we might think of today as "backing." The Maryland dollars would be backed by a commitment to buy them back with shares in the Bank of England. The new Maryland dollars, Sharpe wrote, could stay comfortably within the letter of Parliament's law banning paper legal tender in the colonies, because Maryland wouldn't need to make them legal tender—payable for all debts. The law would not force any provincials to accept the new dollar bills of credit, but the bills would pass as money anyway, because the province had made a credible promise to buy them back in a decade, just as it had with its shilling bills of credit in 1733.

Sharpe also found a way to sweep away the one other argument against paper money, the one preferred by the prime minister: that it would drive all the silver out of the province. Whether or not there's silver or gold in the province, he explained carefully, depends on whether Maryland makes any products it can sell abroad for silver coins. It's the exact same argument that Sancho de Moncada tried to make to Philip III: If you want to hold on to your hard currency, industry and exports are all that matter. But for good measure, Sharpe carefully discharged a rhetorical weapon he'd been holding, cocked, for more than a year. "For my own part I see no Objection to the Scheme," he wrote, *but* "I have heard it said that Col. Lloyd seem'd apprehensive that the Emission of Paper Money might be a means of the little Specie now in Circulation here being carried out of the Country."

Horatio Sharpe, a frustrated middle-aged administrator, possibly unlucky in love, who wanted more than anything to return home to a modest income in England, was so skilled as an infighter that he took the strongest objection to the new paper dollar plan and put it in the mouth of the one person in the entire province Lord Baltimore hated the most: Edward Lloyd, who was at that very moment thwarting Lord Baltimore's plan to squeeze the province for cash.

THE MARYLAND DOLLAR PASSES

Mollie Ridout, one of John and Mary's many descendants, doesn't think the story about how Horatio Sharpe built Whitehall for Mary Ogle is true. Sharpe stayed with John and Mary when he was in town in Annapolis; after the American Revolution, he sold Whitehall to them. Mollie finds it hard to believe that Sharpe would remain so close if Mary had actually spurned him. It's far more likely that Matilda Ridout Edgar, writing Sharpe's biography in 1912, was troubled by his lack of a wife, and preferred to think of him as unrequited, rather than as a bachelor.

I asked Mollie about Sharpe and the Ridouts as we sat on the porch at Whitehall, looking down a stretch of lawn that reaches to the Chesapeake Bay, a quarter mile away. Ridouts still have the family cemetery at Whitehall, and they own and farm bits of property on the surrounding peninsula. When we spoke in 2021, Mollie was done with farming and had begun work on a history of the family. She had been digging through her own father's papers, finding grocery receipts from 1970 mixed with letters between Horatio Sharpe and his secretary.

Annapolis is still a small town, and Ridouts are everywhere—a Ridout was my junior high band teacher. Mollie knows my family, and had agreed to take me around Sharpe's old property. The house itself is now just an event space, hosting about a dozen weddings a year. We couldn't get in, and so we just peeked in the windows. It was small, open, and empty; even when it was built in 1764, Mollie said, it was never supposed to be much more than just a place to hold parties in the summer.

The last son of a large family, Horatio Sharpe was born into status but not great wealth; he owed his position in Maryland to the influence of his brothers in London. In the late 1760s, Sharpe continued to build out at Whitehall, running arcades out from the main house, east to kitchens and a council chamber that was never finished, and west to the bedrooms, finished in marble and Delft tile. These were the kinds of details that had to be imported from abroad, payable only in the bills of exchange that, for Sharpe, came from tobacco sales; he owned hundreds of acres of tobacco land around Annapolis and Baltimore Town, and in the west of the province.

For several years, as Sharpe worked on Whitehall and took his barge back and forth to Annapolis to deal with the assembly, Lord Baltimore never seemed to care about the province's plan to print dollar bills of credit, at least not enough to ever address them directly. The bill to print them did not pass in 1765, since Maryland's upper and lower houses still couldn't come to an agreement on who was supposed to pay the officers of the province. But the mood between the royalists of the upper house and the provincials of the lower house improved when Parliament repealed the Stamp Act in March 1766.

By this time, Cecilius Calvert, Lord Baltimore's rambling uncle and secretary, had died in London. His replacement, Hugh Hamersley, began communicating with Sharpe in the clear, efficient sentences of an actual secretary. Just after the repeal of the Stamp Act, Hamersley wrote to Sharpe that he had discussed the dollar bills of credit with his lordship, who was inclined to agree with it. Hamersley himself couldn't find reason why the bills wouldn't work, and this is as close as we get to an approval from Lord Baltimore. He never put his consent to the bill in writing. Either he didn't want to get in trouble with Parliament, or he didn't care enough about Maryland to bother with its problems.

Mollie Ridout and I stepped off the porch at Whitehall to walk down to the water, looking almost straight south down the Chesapeake Bay. Across the river in Annapolis it was ninety degrees, but with the breeze from the bay coming up the lawn, it felt at least ten degrees cooler at Whitehall. It's clear why Horatio Sharpe swapped holdings with St. Margaret's Church, still today located one peninsula to the west, to put a summerhouse on this particular spot of land. Like much of the Maryland Assembly, he was enthusiastic about transforming Maryland into a more diverse economy, with domestic industry selling to the whole world. But his own wealth came from tobacco, planted and tended by enslaved men and women whose own descendants still live on the peninsula around Whitehall. Maryland's paper currency took its value from taxes on slave-grown tobacco. The bills of credit weren't a clear, immediate step away from a slave economy. They were a complement to it.

By 1766, pressure had increased for the assembly to come to an agreement over whose job it was to pay the province's official salaries and pass the act to print the dollar bills of credit. European markets had recovered after the global disruptions of the Seven Years' War, which had ended in 1763. Maryland exports of grain, staves, and shingles had shot up in 1764 and remained high, making the demand for some kind of local currency even higher. As exports went out from the colonies, merchants in England paid for them by sending back the bills of exchange that were ultimately good for buying things in London. Provincials could pay for land in Maryland with bills of exchange, but any other local purchases took coins or credit; with all the old shilling bills of credit sunk and burned, there just wasn't enough money to do all the buying. Pennsylvania and New York had the same problem and were themselves fighting for a share of the colonies' dwindling stock of coins, making it even more expensive to borrow any kind of cash in Maryland.

In mid-November 1766, Horatio Sharpe informed the lower house that he would need to wrap up the session soon, since he had to travel across the Chesapeake Bay to help Lord Baltimore liquidate more of his family's hereditary estates on the Eastern Shore. That month the lower house had also updated the accounts of the Paper Currency Office. As of May of that year—remember, financial data traveled by sail—the province had invested £28,600 of capital in the stock of the Bank of England, which had grown to the fantastic market value of £33,357. The Paper Currency Office also recorded three and a half reams of writing paper, fourteen bundles of quills, seven dozen bottles of ink powder, a pair of fire tongs, several writing tables, an oval meeting table, and nine leather-bottomed chairs. Like the mine faces of Joachimsthal or Potosí, the office was a money factory. The quills, the chairs, the tongs for the fire that had burned the sunk paper shillings—these were tools for the production of money.

In December 1766, both houses finally passed "An Act for the Payment of the Publick Claims for Emitting Bills of Credit and for Other

Purposes Therein Mentioned," which approved the dollar bills of credit. Horatio Sharpe took a risk and signed on behalf of the proprietor, Lord Baltimore, who hadn't yet granted explicit permission. It's clear from the arguments that led to the act and in the text itself that the assembly didn't believe they were printing new dollars just to pay Maryland's debts. As Sharpe pointed out in letters to London, the province had debts with many members of both houses, including Sharpe himself. They could have decided to pay themselves from the province's stock of silver dollars and gold pistoles or in bills of exchange that would pay out in London. Instead, the act called for specific denominations of printed dollars, with larger runs of smaller units, all the way down to twelve thousand bills of one-ninth of a dollar each; the odd fraction made those bills worth about half a penny in sterling. To the assembly, this act solved the problem of small change. It would make it possible for provincials to pay for small items and clear small debts.

Each dollar would be worth 4 shillings and 6 pence, the official conversion rate for sterling. And in 1777, just as with the old shilling bills of credit, a commissioner would be on hand at the Paper Currency Office to sink the dollars by buying them back, again with bills of exchange, denominated in sterling and paid out of the sinking fund held in the stock of the Bank of England. The Maryland Assembly understood, building on long experience in the colonies, that paper money needed a sink. They couldn't just print it out and declare that it had value.

The act also shows what the province had learned about the production of money. For paper money to have value, all the processes that print and sink it have to be transparent and almost performative. A bill of credit was ultimately an act of trust, and that trust had to be earned and re-earned, in a way that would be clear to any provincial who might spend a paper dollar. There were instructions on how and when to open the iron chests in the Paper Currency Office, and office hours for the commissioners to pay out the province's debts in the new bills. There were salaries for the commissioners who would carry out the work, a clerk to help, even an allowance for pens and paper. Just as the Federal

Reserve today takes torn and defaced bills out of circulation, there's a provision in the act to trade in and burn torn Maryland dollars.

All the histories of this act that I've been able to find conclude that Lord Baltimore approved it. This doesn't seem to be true. I can't find a single instance, in any of Sharpe's letters, where the lord proprietor explicitly grants his permission to print dollars. What we read instead in those letters is an increasingly frantic Sharpe, reminding both Hugh Hamersley and Lord Baltimore of all the times they'd sent encouraging letters about the act in the past. Sharpe seems to have been worried that he was all on his own on the far side of the Atlantic with a run of brand-new, potentially illegal bills of credit—with his signature on the act that had created them. Hamersley's responses were noncommittal. Baltimore seemed concerned mostly about selling his land, in one case even offering to co-sign on a loan for a potential buyer. He was also annoyed that he had to take care of his uncle's estate.

Sharpe's letters begging for approval of the bills of credit stretched well into 1767; in August, Hamersley offered only that it was difficult to say whether Parliament would ultimately take exception to the act. But already on January 1 of that year, there's a brief item at the end of the news section of the *Gazette,* informing readers that the first new dollar bills had been deposited in the iron chests at the Paper Currency Office. The *Gazette* knew, of course, because the printers who ran the paper, Jonas and Anne Catharine Green, had also printed the new dollars. No one in London gave permission for the first paper dollars. The Greens began printing because no one said no.

The Greens printed up their dollar bills of credit with an explicit nod to the silver Spanish dollar, re-creating the coin on the bills themselves. This was not an old name for a new denomination; it was a financial instrument bound tightly to a physical object that was already both universal and familiar, a silver coin from another empire that both Parliament and the Maryland Assembly had found difficult to control. Those bills the Greens printed don't mark the moment America created its dollar. They just mark one more moment when the dollar won.

A dollar bill of credit, printed by the Province of Maryland in 1767. It is the first printed American dollar. (Image from the Newman Numismatic Portal at Washington University in St. Louis.)

HORATIO SHARPE RETURNED TO LONDON, AND LORD BALTIMORE LEFT LONDON ON THE RUN

Horatio Sharpe did not remain governor for long. In July 1768, Hamersley informed Sharpe that he had been replaced by Robert Eden, the younger brother of one of Lord Baltimore's brothers-in-law. It's not clear why. Two of Sharpe's older brothers, who had protected him in England, had died. It's also possible that Lord Baltimore was frustrated by the pace of revenues from Maryland and thought he might do better.

Lord Baltimore was also on the run. In March 1768, he was brought to trial in Surrey for the rape of Sarah Woodcock, an unmarried milliner. He was acquitted; the jury found that she had consented, since she had waited a week to report the assault. But with his title the trial became a spectacle. Court transcripts were printed and sold as illustrated pamphlets. That year, a woman claiming to have lived with him published *Memoirs of the Seraglio of the Bashaw of Merryland, by a Discarded Sultana,* a barely veiled account alleging that Lord Baltimore, an "impotent lecher," had taken careful notes on the harems he had seen in Constantinople and modeled his own household on them. There was a list of rules for the sultanas: There was to be no reading in bed, no fewer than three baths a week, mandatory inoculations for smallpox, and no more than four glasses of wine at dinner. Lord Baltimore left England after the trial, and accounts of ambassadors he met in Europe suggest similar arrangements while he was traveling.

Horatio Sharpe, waiting for the new governor to arrive, continued to sell Baltimore's land and send bills of exchange back to London. He asked, as a favor, to buy some of the proprietor's land near Whitehall. Letters from Hamersley show Baltimore in the Netherlands, then St. Petersburg, then Dresden in Saxony, then on Lake Constance, where according to Hamersley his lordship "Contradicts all the Reports Spread of him from Florence Vienna &c of Duels, Murthers and hairsbreadth Escapes." His last letter to Horatio Sharpe, from Nuremberg in 1770, offered only some ambiguous lines about the land Sharpe wanted to buy. Baltimore apologized that he would have written earlier, but he had nothing to say. Frederick Calvert, the sixth and last Lord Baltimore, died in Naples in 1771.

At Whitehall, Mollie Ridout walked me back from the gardens to the road, past the parapets and defensive ditch Horatio Sharpe had designed himself in case the American Indians he had encountered in the Appalachian Mountains during the Seven Years' War ever made it east to Annapolis. The road itself is a straight shot out the front door of Whitehall to Route 50, a mile and a quarter away—Sharpe laid it out that way, to race his horses. That's still how it's used today. Young men know what a straight road is for, said Mollie. They come out to Whitehall on weekend nights to drag race.

Horatio Sharpe stayed in Maryland until 1773. He wrote to one of his brothers that his gardens at Whitehall had become his principal amusement. He bred and raced horses out of an octagonal barn on the property. He visited the Ridouts in Annapolis, and held parties at Whitehall. In 1773, he sailed to England on family business and moved in with his mother on Savile Row; his health and the war kept him from ever returning to the colonies. In 1782, he finally gave up Whitehall, selling his entire estate—thirty-one enslaved men and women, the land, his silver, a cabinet of liquor, his furniture, and eighteen horses—to the Ridouts for £7,000. Horatio Sharpe died in 1790 in Hampstead, England. The Ridout family tried to make the transition to wheat farming at the end of the eighteenth century, but could never make a profit the way they had with tobacco.

There are a lot of Maryland dollars left today. They never got sunk, and so you can still find stacks of them in museums and collections. Like Confederate dollars, they're easy to get ahold of because ultimately their value dropped to nothing during the Revolutionary War. The province and its commissioners in the Paper Currency Office faithfully administered the dollars; the dollar bills of credit worked so well the assembly even issued more of them in the early 1770s to lend out against land. There's an argument among academics now over how the dollars held their value as long as they did. Farley Grubb has argued that before the war provincials saw the dollars as a kind of bond, redeemable in a decade, that held what we'd now call a "liquidity premium": The province had printed enough of them that they traded easily. Ronald Michener at the University of Virginia makes a simpler argument. Looking at contemporary account books and letters, he concludes that provincials simply traded paper dollars as if they were silver dollars. The sinking fund had made the dollars so trustworthy that to the provincials they weren't bonds. They were money.

The Maryland dollars lost their value when the war severed their connection to the sinking fund, invested in the stock of the Bank of England. The commissioners could not, as scheduled, open the office in March 1777 and begin redemptions on time, because they no longer had access to the province's accounts in London. There was nothing an independent province could do to fix this. Governments have some control over what money is and how it works, but that control is not infinite. There are limits to monetary sovereignty. For Maryland's dollar bills of credit, the backing—the bottom, as Sharpe called it—was definitional. Without it, the whole system of trust that underpinned the bills of credit collapsed.

We are used to thinking about dollars as a unit of measurement, like a foot or a gallon. I have found that unhelpful when trying to understand Maryland's dollar bills of credit, the first American dollars. The dollar wasn't an abstract idea to Horatio Sharpe or any of the people advertising in the back of the *Maryland Gazette*. It was still an actual, physical coin, a piece of metal that clanked on a desk. Maryland didn't just print something up and declare it a dollar. The assembly had to design a tight, transparent set of controls to get slips of paper to work the same way that coin did.

In the second half of this book we'll see how that changed slowly over the nineteenth century, and how Americans and ultimately the world started to think of the dollar not as a silver Spanish coin but as a printed note or a deposit produced by an American bank. In this colonial moment, however, when the Maryland Assembly and its distracted governor began printing dollars, it didn't take over the idea of a dollar from the Spanish crown. The Maryland Assembly did not suddenly own what a dollar was, not even in its own province. It took the dollar as it found it—a big silver coin, still mined at Zacatecas and Potosí, minted in Spain's empire, and shipped all over the world—and adapted to it as best it could.

Part II

The Bank Dollar

Introduction

THE JACKSON HOLE SYSTEM

On the last weekend of every August central bankers, economists, and a few journalists fly to Jackson Hole, Wyoming, pile into vans, and drive into Grand Teton National Park for three nights at the Jackson Lake Lodge. The bankers and economists give presentations to each other. They hike together. They ride horses together. The Federal Reserve Bank of Kansas City runs the conference, and makes sure every year that it's a safe space for central bankers. What is said on the dais can be shared. What is said over cocktails or breakfast—that stays at the lodge.

Financiers know the event simply as Jackson Hole. It's an academic conference, but it's also a social ritual and a public performance. Every year, the chair of the Federal Reserve takes a scheduled walk on a patio with a view of Mount Moran. Every year the chair is joined by the most important central bankers at the lodge—the head of the European Central Bank, the head of the Bank of Japan, whoever happens to be there. They stand together for a second, just a couple of friends, chatting. Press photographers know this is coming, and catch them there: together, powerful, stable, calm.

When things start to collapse in global finance, these are the people who will ultimately be asked to hold it all together. They know each other, and often trained as economists under the same advisers at just a few prestigious universities. Central banking is one of the few areas of national politics where it's perfectly normal to hold citizenship in one country and serve as a policymaker in another. The hikes at Jackson Hole, the breakfasts, even a yearly party in cowboy boots—these are all ways to reinforce social ties that will eventually have financial significance. The walk on the patio together is a public performance of private relationships. There's a reason this summer retreat for the world's central bankers is in the Tetons and not in the Alps. The yearly ritual of Jackson Hole comforts all who come with the reassurance that in an emergency they will be blessed with American bank dollars.

DOLLARS COME FROM BANKS

In the first half of this book it was easy to be precise about what a dollar was. In northern Europe in the sixteenth century, the seventeenth-century Iberian Peninsula, and Britain's Atlantic colonies in the eighteenth century, a dollar was any one of those copies of those original silver joachimsthaler coins. In some of these places, merchants began to keep their accounts in dollars as well, but that shift took decades and in some cases centuries. Silver joachimsthaler began moving through the Leipzig market in 1520, but the city itself didn't begin keeping its accounts in taler until 1722. In Potosí, the mint didn't start keeping records in reales de a ocho until the 1580s, well after the coins themselves had started streaming west from Acapulco and east from Veracruz. In provincial Maryland, even as merchants calculated exchange rates in dollars, they kept their own books in shillings. The dollar was copied as real money first—a big silver coin—and then only over time became an imaginary money, written down on ledgers and scraps of paper that passed from hand to hand.

By the middle of the nineteenth century, however, Americans had started to think differently about what a dollar *was.* They stopped thinking of a silver coin that came from abroad and started thinking of the dollar as paper notes and deposits on the ledgers of commercial banks. It wasn't the existence of the United States that drove this change, or even necessarily the massive, bloody disruptions of the American Civil War. Again, the biography of the dollar is not the biography of America, and as we saw in provincial Maryland, silver dollars were already embedded in the American economy well before the Revolutionary War. Far more consequential was a decision written into the Constitution that took the production of money away from the states. Over the next half century, the states snuck around this ban by chartering their own banks to manufacture dollars instead.

This is still the system we have today. You might have read in a textbook that the Federal Reserve makes our dollars, or you may believe that the Federal Reserve is just an accounting fiction and the Department of the Treasury makes our dollars. If I achieve anything with this book at all, it will be to explain, in plain English, one uncomfortable thing I know to be true: Commercial banks make our dollars.

This system leaves many people in America and abroad poorly served. Many Americans don't have access to banks, for loans or even just for deposits and transfers. Bank regulations are inadequate. The bank lobby in Washington is so entwined with its own regulatory agencies that journalists call all of it together the Blob. I'm not saying it's a good system. I'm saying it's the one we have. And so in the second half of this book we will take some time first in antebellum New Orleans and then in Depression-era Iowa to understand how people stopped thinking of a dollar as a big silver coin and started thinking of it as either a piece of paper produced by a bank, or a deposit marked down in a bank ledger.

The economists' story of money isn't very precise about what banks do. It teaches that silver and gold coins simply became less important over time. As they did, the dollar became something we now call fiat. This is a legal term, from the Latin for "let it be done." Under a fiat system, the United States now declares that there shall be dollars, and then there are. The Department of the Treasury demands taxes in dollars, and so that's how we pay them. In this story, the value of a dollar rests on command and belief. People were told to believe they didn't need coins, and so they came to believe they didn't. The fiat story dissolves the distinctions among kinds of dollars, and it ignores the financial agreements that make dollars possible. It leaves only one government dollar, which can be whatever America wants it to be.

In the fiat story, the Federal Reserve is the ultimate origin of dollars. It creates a special kind of dollar called M0, or base money or high-powered money, out of nothing. Then commercial banks use those high-powered Fed dollars through a process called the money multiplier to make loans. In the economists' fiat story, it doesn't really matter how the Fed creates dollars. It just does. I can squint my eyes and make this story kind of true. The banks of the Federal Reserve System do manufacture what we call reserves, an incredibly valuable form of dollars. But it's important to remember that the banks of the Federal Reserve System are still just very special banks. When the Fed produces new dollars, it does it exactly the same way commercial banks do. When we think of the Fed as a magical fiat money printing machine, we lose our ability to understand how it works, and why it has so often failed to do what it was supposed to. And to do that, we have to understand how commercial banks work.

In 2011 researchers at the Bank of England published a paper that journalists and academics still pass around like samizdat. The paper argued that the old story about the base money and the money multiplier had gotten it exactly backward. Commercial banks manufacture money, on their own—almost all of the money we actually use. A license to print money exists. It's a bank charter. Bankers understand this, though as practitioners they don't often talk about their work as a theory of money. To see how a loan produces new money, though, it helps to think like a banker, using a diagram we call a T chart.

Bankers see the world as matched sets: assets on the left, liabilities on the right. To a banker, a loan to you is an asset; it's a contract, binding you to pay the bank back with interest. The bank can wait for you to pay, or it can sell the loan. On the other side of the chart, the banker sees

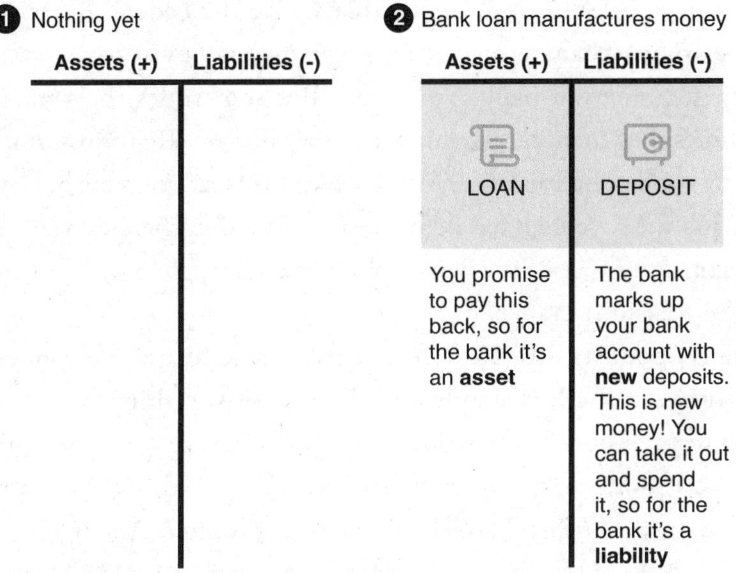

Illustration by Evan Applegate.

your deposits as a liability; you can withdraw them whenever you want, or transfer them to someone else in another bank.

If you've ever seen a T chart before, please clear your mind. There are no reserves or investors in this chart; we are simply trying to establish how a bank manufactures money. In step 1 above, we have done exactly that. There is nothing going on, no deposits, no loans, nothing, just a bank with the intention to produce money. In step 2, the bank makes you a loan. It's a trade, dollar for dollar. You give the bank a contract promising to pay the bank back, and the bank marks up your account with brand-new deposit dollars. It did not take them from anywhere. It did not transfer them from another bank or borrow them from the Federal Reserve. Those are brand-new deposits. They are brand-new manufactured dollars. It can get more complex, but it will never be fundamentally different. That's it. That's how dollars are made now. We could perhaps imagine a simpler system, or a better system, but again this is the one we have.

Banks began producing money—and dollars—well before anything like a central bank existed. Central banks like the Federal Reserve are not the origin of bank money. They are an imperfect way to *control* that money. Commercial banks are useful. But sometimes they fail, and sometimes they manufacture too many new dollars. There's nothing inherently good or bad about a central bank; it's just a tool, a big bank that does a job the sovereign has defined for it. That job changes over time; the original purpose of the Bank of England was to help with "carrying on the war against France."

The economists' story, where a central bank creates fiat money, is powerful because it's so simple. But there's an astonishing lack of curiosity and precision in the word "fiat." When we say that the United States now produces dollars by fiat, we don't have to think about any of the mechanics of *how* it happens, or who's responsible. And it allows us to say that the dollar is powerful because America is. The story lets otherwise thoughtful people say vague things like "The dollar is the world's currency because America has aircraft carriers," and then let their argument rest. But there is no such thing as a fiat dollar. There are all kinds of financial assets denominated in dollars, and there are deposit dollars. Commercial banks hold most of the deposit dollars, but the Fed holds some, too. These bank dollars have value because regulations, developed over time and usually after painful financial collapses, make sure bank deposits have value. And so the story of the dollar doesn't start with a coin and then end in a country. It starts with a coin *and then ends in a bank.*

THE PRODUCTION OF MONEY IS ALWAYS POLITICAL

I went to Jackson Hole in 2019 as a correspondent for the *Financial Times*. There were only two central bankers who took the public walk together that year: Mark Carney, governor of the Bank of England, and Jay Powell, chairman of the Federal Reserve. They both wore suits. Carney wore tennis shoes. They pointed at Mount Moran. They did not appear to be panicked. And in what's become a standard part of the pageant, on Friday morning Powell gave a policy speech in the Explorers Room.

Central bankers place great value on communication. Their speeches are hard to parse, ambiguous even if you know what to look for. But each one is a ritual, staged well in advance. When policymakers at major central banks speak, their staff release a copy an hour ahead of time under heavy embargo to a few journalists at major papers, who frantically write a story that will publish at the exact same time as the speech begins.

I got my early copy and picked over it with my editors for news. There was little. For almost a year, businesses had been holding off on making big decisions as they waited for the United States to reach a trade agreement with China. But trade policy, Powell said in his speech, "was the business of Congress and the administration, not that of the Fed." He didn't indicate that the Fed had planned any changes in monetary policy that might encourage or discourage American banks from making loans. I finished my news story, my editors published, and Jay Powell began to read his speech to the lodge. The rest of us waited for what we knew was coming.

"As usual, the Fed did NOTHING!" This just under an hour later on Twitter, from the president of the United States. "It is incredible that they can 'speak' without knowing or asking what I am doing, which will be announced shortly. We have a very strong dollar and a very weak Fed. I will work 'brilliantly' with both, and the U.S. will do great."

"My only question is," he followed, "who is our bigger enemy, Jay Powell or Chairman Xi?"

Donald Trump spent a fair amount of time in his first term as president yelling about the Fed in general and often Powell in particular. He has sharpened those attacks in his second term, claiming in August 2025 to have fired the economist Lisa Cook from the Fed's Board of Governors to free up a seat for his own pick. It is an accepted norm in

Washington that the Federal Reserve is both independent and apolitical. It's not supposed to answer to any political party, or help anyone in particular. Trump continues to violate that norm, but it's just one in a long list of violations.

I was struck, covering the Fed during some of the Trump years, at how much he knew about banks, lending, and the Fed. He had to. He had been borrowing huge amounts of money his entire life. He knew that the Fed had some ability to encourage banks to lend, and as president he wanted more lending; more lending can help more businesses expand, which can create more jobs. But you don't have to agree with Donald Trump to see that money is inherently political.

We still live in Carlo Cipolla's world of big money and little money, where different kinds of new bank loans move dollars to different kinds of people. Just as it was a bad business for medieval mints to make petty coins, it's bad business for banks now to make small-dollar loans. Banks, like mints, tend to favor big money, and for the same reasons. And every time the Fed acts to encourage or discourage lending, its tools help some banks more than others, some loans more than others, some people more than others. Central bankers tend to look down on politicians of all parties as irresponsible spendthrifts, itching for more lending and willing to risk inflation. Trump, in his abusive way, was calling the Fed's bluff. He knew that central bankers themselves are in the trade of highly political decisions.

After lunch at the lodge in the Grizzly Room it was Mark Carney's turn to talk. He was leaving his job as governor of the Bank of England, and he said the kinds of things you can only say when you're on your way out. The problem, he said, was the dollar. It was too strong, too ubiquitous, and too many people in too many countries relied on it. Old theories die slowly. Everyone in the room was familiar with the academic literature on how powerful the dollar had become. Several people sitting there drinking coffee had their names on that literature. But it was time, Carney said, to move on from a couple of old assumptions: that countries control their own money; that everyone makes adjustments on their own; that everything kind of works out over time. It was not working out.

Currency theory in the late twentieth century assumed a basic structure. To buy something in another country, you had to buy some of that country's currency first. If the dollar became more important globally, it was because a lot of people wanted to buy from Americans or in America. This seems straightforward, and it makes sense. If you fly from Washington to Frankfurt, you hand over your dollar cash at the airport for cash euros. Or if more people want to buy things in or from Germany, more people want bank deposits in euros, and the euro becomes more valuable. But that's not what really happens.

When a company in Brazil imports something from anywhere else in the world, there's close to a 90 percent probability that it will write out the purchase order not in Brazilian reals but in dollars. Most invoices in global trade are written in just a few vehicle currencies that carry value from one country to another—yen, yuan, euro, pound. But the only vehicle currency that matters is the dollar. The old theories assumed that companies simply wrote out invoices in their own domestic currencies. But work by a few economists who were right there in the Grizzly Room at Jackson Hole shows that companies make clear, rational decisions about how to invoice. Importers and exporters want stable, predictable prices. When they all invoice in dollars, prices are sticky; they don't change.

In the old currency theories, global use of a country's currency was proportional to the size of its international trade. Big exporters had big global currencies. But companies actually invoice in dollars wildly out of proportion with the size of America's trade. As Carney pointed out, even as America's role in global trade had dropped, the dollar's importance had risen. This is also true for central bankers. Foreign central banks hold far higher proportions of dollars as reserves than their trade with America would predict. And it's true in finance as well. When non-American companies and countries borrow abroad, it doesn't matter where they are, or whom they're borrowing from; they almost always borrow in dollars. Economists now refer to the disproportionate use of dollars as the dominant currency paradigm. Note that the country isn't dominant. The currency is.

I have found it helpful to think of America not as a country that happens to use dollars. Rather, it's a country where commercial banks and the federal government have together become really good at manufacturing a lot of different kinds of dollars. When the United States borrows bank dollars from investors, it sells a bond we call a Treasury. The sheer volume of Treasurys alone sold at auction every week beggars comparison with any other financial asset, anywhere in the world. Politicians and voters think of Treasurys as debt, but traders and advisers in financial markets think of Treasurys as a kind of dollar. When someone on a trading floor says "go to cash," no one's buying briefcases of dollar bills. They're buying Treasurys.

In addition to Treasurys, financiers describe America's markets as deep and liquid, which means that there are a lot of private assets in America—houses, stocks, bonds—all with clear dollar prices and lots of buyers and sellers, all using deposit dollars in American banks to pay each other. Like the borderland mines of St. Joachimsthal and the mita mines of Potosí, the federal government in Washington and the country's banks and financiers together manufacture a flood of big dollars—not always useful for domestic payments, but invaluable for investors, traders, and financiers all over the world.

Just as with the old silver dollars, this volume and predictability has inspired what Cipolla called faithful copies. Foreign commercial banks make their own dollars, on their own balance sheets, outside the United States, without any meaningful American control or regulation. They do it the same way American banks do: They just do it. The United States is not sovereign over these dollars. The Federal Reserve did not create them. There is no room in the fiat story for these dollars. But they exist, so many of them that, perversely, sometimes in a crisis the Federal Reserve is called on to rescue them. The United States protects dollars made abroad, for foreigners. This is hard to grasp, and we'll spend a chapter walking through how these dollars work, what they do, and how the Fed bails them out with emergency loans.

I have come to believe these periodic emergency dollar loans are the main reason foreign central bankers come to Jackson Hole. They want to be trusted and familiar to the Fed, from hikes and horseback rides, when it comes time to ask for help with their own dollars. When the Fed protects those foreign dollars in a crisis, it's being pulled, by necessity, to act as what economists often call the central banker to the world. The way the dollar works now, it isn't necessarily America's money. It's a single currency that serves a lot of different people, including foreigners who hold offshore dollars in foreign banks.

For Mark Carney, the problem with the dominant currency paradigm was that even if America wasn't completely sovereign over the dollar, other countries weren't sovereign at all. A country could attempt to devalue its currency, making its exports cheaper and encouraging buyers at home to avoid expensive imports. But if that same country has borrowed in dollars, its debts suddenly become more expensive, and so it's trapped by the dollar. In 1971, John Connally, the secretary of the Treasury under Richard Nixon, told a group of finance ministers in Rome that the dollar was "our currency, but your problem." Speaking at Jackson Hole almost fifty years later, Carney rewrote the quotation for an audience he knew would get the reference. "Our dollar, your problem," he said, "is becoming any of our problems are your problems."

Short term, said Carney, countries might have to learn how to coordinate better in a system where they're all already on the same currency anyway. Long term, the global economy might need a new system—a replacement for the dollar, what he called a "synthetic hegemonic currency." Carney nodded in the room at Barry Eichengreen, an economic historian who researches global transitions from one dominant currency to another. Transitions "don't always go smoothly," he said. "But what I'm trying to argue is that blithe acceptance of the status quo is misguided."

The first response to Carney came from Stanley Fischer, senior to everyone else in almost any way imaginable. Fischer had been both the governor of the Bank of Israel and the vice-chair at the Fed's Board of Governors. Just as important, as a professor at MIT for two decades, he had served as either dissertation adviser or teacher to many of the people in the room. "The trouble one has," he said, "is the problem is not with the IMFS"—the international monetary financial system—"it's in the president of the United States." The room murmured in discomfort. Fischer, who had ended his term at the Fed early after Trump became president, had the authority to make everyone squirm. But he had also articulated an important idea.

For Carney, the dollar system itself had structural flaws. It was inherently unsustainable. For Fischer, there was no reason to move on from a system that had been working when the problem was not structural but political. The United States can only be a dollar-manufacturing machine if it's stable and predictable. The system could work so long as America passes budgets, continues on a path of free trade and economic growth, pays interest on its Treasurys, and keeps its banks safe. For Carney, the dollar system must necessarily pass. For Fischer, it can only collapse if America is foolish enough to let it. Every disagreement about the future of the dollar comes down to one of those two arguments. Carney finally released the tension with a joke, asking whether there were any more questions.

Within months, financial markets would begin to panic as a pandemic, a kind of instability unanticipated in any economic model, kept workers and customers home, stopping payments in every imaginable kind of transaction. As they had during the global financial crisis, foreign central bankers again asked the Federal Reserve for emergency dollar loans to help with their own commercial banks, and again the Fed obliged. It is hard to imagine that the global dollar will continuc forever. It is equally hard to imagine any other central bank providing that kind of global service. But the pandemic also showed what the Federal Reserve and the federal government hadn't paid attention to and couldn't do. The Jackson Hole system worked, moving dollars around the world cleanly when needed. But the Federal Reserve and the federal government didn't have any way to get dollars to Americans in America. The systems weren't in place to hand out dollars to people, either directly or through forgivable bank loans.

The dollar is not America's currency. It works for the world—for now. But it doesn't always work for America. In the second half of this book, we're going to look at how Americans produced dollars, and how consistent choices over two centuries made sure that dollars worked as a global financial instrument first and a domestic currency second, if at all. The dollar is no longer a big silver coin. It is now the U.S. bank dollar. But America is still not in charge.

4

Silver Dollars Become Bank Dollars

New Orleans, 1842

"À BAS LES COURTIERS!"

On the morning of May 20, 1842, several thousand people gathered at the Place d'Armes, a weedy parade ground marked with dirt footpaths in front of the St. Louis Cathedral in New Orleans. They were small merchants from the grocery stalls and coffee tables of the covered markets along the waterfront; *The Daily Picayune,* an English-language newspaper for the Americans in the city, described them as "Frenchmen, Spaniards, Italians," but there were likely also some Greek merchants and even Choctaw, who sold plantain-leaf baskets and sassafras root at the market. A Frenchman, in the language of the *Picayune,* was one of the city's Creole population—maybe Latin, probably Catholic, but definitely not American. Some of the merchants gave speeches, and then they all walked through the trees at the edge of the parade ground to the office of the mayor, where they started to get loud and threatened to do more than just talk.

The Frenchmen were worried about their money. It had dropped in value, almost overnight. Small trade along the waterfront in the late 1830s and early 1840s relied on municipal notes—paper dollars printed by each of the city's three municipalities. The notes functioned a lot like the colonial bills of credit, but they were only one of many kinds of dollars on paper circulating in the city. To handle the trade in paper dollars, bill brokers along Camp Street took different kinds of paper in at different rates for silver dollars—by then mined and minted in an independent Mexico. A week before the merchants had gathered on the Place d'Armes, the bill brokers would still take a dollar of municipal notes at only about a 1 percent discount below a silver Mexican dollar. By Thursday, May 19, that discount had dropped to as much as 10 percent. By Friday it was as low as 40 percent. The Frenchmen had seen the value of their dollars cut almost in half in two days, which is why on Saturday they arrived, angry, at the mayor's door.

Denis Prieur, a Jacksonian Democrat in his second stretch as mayor, stepped out to meet the crowd. A refugee from the Haitian Revolution, Prieur was comfortable among the small merchants and likely spoke to them in French. He assured them there was a plan for every municipality in the city to buy back its notes at par—at 100 percent of their value. When the crowd didn't believe him, he invited a few of them up to his office for a meeting. It wasn't enough. Someone yelled "À bas les courtiers!" and the rest of the merchants began to repeat it, running down Chartres Street, headed for Camp. *À bas les courtiers* means "down with the brokers." If the merchants couldn't get silver at par on Camp Street on Friday, on Saturday they were just going to take it.

To get there, they had to cross Canal Street. Running north from the river, Canal marked the border between two of the city's municipalities, and two often hostile cultures. To the east was the First Municipality, which held a century and a half of the city's history—cultural layers of Creole French, imperial *criollo* Spanish, and white and free colored refugees from Haiti. To the west was the Second Municipality, swelling with merchants and chancers newly arrived from Maryland, Virginia, Kentucky, Tennessee: the Americans. The land in the middle of Canal Street was called the neutral ground, a political joke at the time and still today what the people of New Orleans call the grass in the middle of a road. The street was a real, physical barrier; in the 1840s vendors had to clear brush from the middle of Canal to sell bananas and coffee, and children caught crawfish in ditches on Canal just north of Claiborne Avenue.

Canal Street also marked a porous border between two different kinds of finance. The Americans had arrived in New Orleans as part of a boom in long-distance trade, moving American cotton from the mouth of the Mississippi to Britain and Europe; wood, lard, and flour to Cuba and Haiti; sugar to the U.S. East Coast; and taking in coffee and more sugar from Cuba. Moving things across oceans required big finance and big money, and the cotton trade in particular made New Orleans a center for bills of exchange that paid out in London or Paris.

The early decades of the nineteenth century also marked a dramatic expansion of banking in America. In 1789 there were 2 banks in the United States. By 1837 there were 729. With new banks came new bank notes—paper dollars, guaranteed by a commercial bank. One line in the U.S. Constitution had forbidden the states from issuing bills of credit, and so instead the states chartered banks to do it for them. The chartered banks in Louisiana—16 of them by 1837—issued their own notes, each with its own unique design. Within the city, the bank notes traded equally for each other, at par. Banks tended to print their notes at much higher face values—some $1 or $5 notes, but a lot of notes for $10 and even $100. It's not an absolute distinction, but bank notes worked better as big money for wholesalers or merchants moving cotton and coffee and sugar up and down the river.

The covered markets on the French side of Canal relied on small money. Cut slivers of Mexican dollars passed hand to hand with municipal notes, alongside an older French tradition of promissory notes, called *bons* or *doits.* In the blocks around the parade ground, what we now know as the French Quarter, dry goods merchants and even tailors offered short-term loans in silver or bank notes, guaranteed by bons, a private system of social finance that was both distinct from and complementary to the wholesale commercial loans coming from American banks on the other side of the neutral ground. These two systems moved back and forth across Canal; Americans would write out bons to Creole merchants, and Creole sugar factors would sell bills of exchange to American banks and the bill brokers on Camp Street. The French habits were older, designed for an outpost on the edge of an empire. The bank dollars were a novelty, an innovation that fueled what historians call America's market revolution.

Bank dollars were fragile. Their value became uncertain when banks began to wobble, and during an 1837 panic over cotton prices banks had wobbled all over America. The municipal notes in New Orleans were a response to that panic. The city's banks stopped issuing new notes; their old notes dropped in value, in a few cases by more than half. Something had to work as money. The Constitution had forbidden the state from printing bills of credit, and so the city did instead, grasping at an old technology out of necessity.

By 1842 the city's municipal dollar notes had become reliable and useful; they were good for the kinds of small purchases of coffee or pork someone might make in the markets on the French side of the neutral ground. That meant a lot of people in the French municipality held the city's notes. The American bankers and cotton factors on the other side of Canal didn't have to rely on the municipal notes, and saw them as either inconvenient or irrelevant. The *True American,* a newspaper that catered to the same audience as *The Daily Picayune,* referred to the municipal notes as "dirty fractional parts of bons," an efficient way to make clear that the notes were small, untouchable, worthless, and French.

The municipal notes lost almost half their value in two days because Louisiana had passed a law guaranteeing that every bank could redeem its own bank notes for silver or gold. Well into the twentieth century that law served for financial historians as a model for bank regulation, an achievement in what we now call sound money—money that never, ever drops in value. Perfectly sound money seems ideal and even natural, but it comes at a price. Laws that make paper *always* redeemable for a coin make other, more flexible arrangements impossible. The municipal notes worked at the covered markets, but the city wouldn't take them for silver on demand, and so the law that made the bank notes finally sound for the Americans made the municipal notes suddenly questionable for the French, Spanish, Italian, Greek, and Choctaw merchants by the river. And the people who had questioned the municipal notes worked the counters at the bill brokers on Camp Street.

After they crossed Canal, the crowd pushed into four brokers' offices and sacked them. Some ran away with gold and silver coins, between $5,000 and $10,000 worth. Some ripped up the exchange counters, smashed windows, and scattered piles of silver dollars. By the end of the day twelve men with French or Spanish names were in jail in the American municipality, private militias had been called up, federal troops had occupied the Place d'Armes, and the French municipality had announced a hasty plan to redeem its notes for silver dollars, at par. It was a riot for silver dollars, but it was also a riot *about* dollars, an undamming of anger over how dollars worked and whom they worked for.

Between the founding of the republic and the Civil War, a solid, 250-year-old definition of a dollar began to loosen in America. Commercial banks got the power to issue their own dollars, and Americans began to think of dollars as things that came from banks in their own cities, not mines far away. That is still the system we have today: Commercial banks make American dollars, almost all of them. But we never completely fixed the problems that pushed that crowd across Canal Street in May 1842.

Banks are unreliable. They fail all the time, and when they don't fail, it's because of the rigorous application of the regulations that Americans have developed, imperfectly, over two centuries of watching them fail. Banks never stopped favoring big accounts and big borrowers, which has meant that small merchants still had to build their own kinds of dollars to get by; these dollars then became particularly important when a lot of banks failed together, as they periodically did. All these challenges were etched into the dollar by the U.S. Constitution. There is no perfect system of money. But Americans made a choice at the very beginning of the republic: They took the dollar away from the states and gave it to the banks.

THE CONSTITUTION COMMITTED AMERICA TO BANK NOTES

Article I of the Constitution presents a list of things that states *can't* do; it includes clear instructions on money. States may not mint coins. They may not issue bills of credit—no state paper money. And states can't force anyone to accept anything other than gold or silver as a payment. Economic historians often present the Constitution and the financial legislation of the early 1790s as a kind of housecleaning, sweeping up unreliable, inefficient forms of money and replacing them with a clear, unified bank dollar system, an architecture for investment and growth. But that story rests on the assumption that the old colonial system of bills of credit had to be stopped. It's not clear that it did.

The Continental Congress began issuing paper dollars in 1777. These were bills of credit, just like the ones the colonies had issued, printed with a promise to redeem them for silver Spanish dollars in the future. Bills of credit had held their value before the war because the colonies could collect taxes, both in the bills themselves and in some kinds of coins that would sink the bills. This was difficult for the states to maintain during the war. It was impossible for the Continental Congress, which could only beg the states to contribute to what was essentially a sinking fund. Even so, the continental bills of credit held their value fairly well until the middle of 1778.

By January 1779, though, Congress had stopped even giving a definite date when it would redeem its dollars with silver, and they were trading at more than 7 continentals to 1 silver dollar. A year later, they were trading at 30 to 1, the last quote before they became essentially worthless. State currencies printed during the American Revolution didn't do much better. By the last summer of the war in 1781, New England bills were trading at 90 to 1, Pennsylvania bills at 225 to 1, and Maryland bills at 280 to 1. During the war, George Washington kept his own account books in Pennsylvania shillings, then New York shillings, then continental dollars. By the end of the war, Washington's currency on hand was depreciating as he held it.

That wartime inflation wasn't the end of the story. The new American states didn't descend into chaos under the Articles of Confederation. Neither did their money. After the Revolution, the new states returned to their old practice of issuing bills of credit. And every state—except again Rhode Island—was able to buy back its paper at full value, on schedule. By the mid-1780s the state exchange rates for current money to Spanish milled dollars were back where they had been before the war. The conflict that led to the ban on state bills of credit in the Constitution wasn't between chaos and order. It was between the Americans who wanted their states to keep printing money and the Americans who wanted to have banks do it instead.

America's first chartered bank was almost single-handedly the work of Robert Morris, a Philadelphia merchant appointed to the office of superintendent of finance in May 1781. Within a month Congress had approved his plan for a single bank, with a monopoly on bank notes. Morris modeled his Bank of North America on the Bank of England—a private corporation, run by merchants, that got privileges *from* the sovereign in return for loans *to* the sovereign. Like the Bank of England in Britain, the Bank of North America was simply referred to in America as the Bank. For several years it was the only one.

Banks aren't complicated—really! The way Morris set up the Bank of North America was ultimately a model for banks all over America in the early republic. Much of it would still be recognizable to any commercial banker today. Morris started by putting out a call for subscribers, what we'd think of today as investors. There were one thousand shares in the Bank, each initially worth 400 Spanish milled dollars. Subscribers paid for each share in gold or silver coins, half up front, half within three months. It's crucial to understand here that the subscription wasn't a deposit. The classic, simplified, textbook model of a bank starts with customer deposits, which the bank lends out at interest. This is not at all how banks start, then or now. A bank starts when people agree to risk their own wealth in a business venture. The coins from subscribers became the bank's capital, and in return they got what we'd today call equity—a share in the bank's profits.

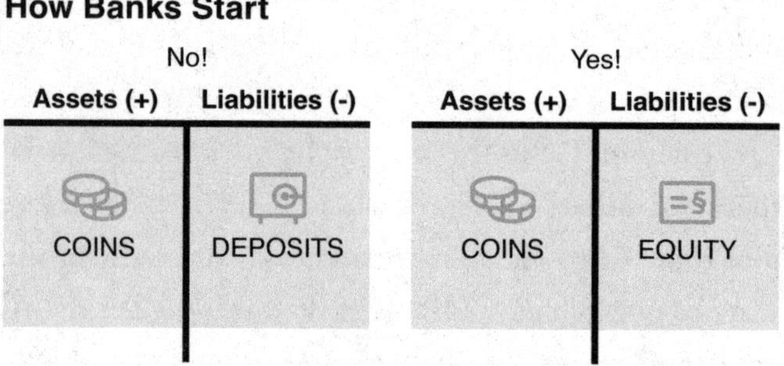

Illustration by Evan Applegate.

Subscriptions for the Bank of North America came in slowly at first, most of them from other Philadelphia merchants. Just before the Battle of Yorktown in the fall of 1781, a loan to the Continental Congress of 470,000 silver dollars arrived in Boston from France. Morris had 254,000 of these dollars carried in a convoy of sixteen oxcarts down to Philadelphia and handed over to the Bank's treasurer. By the time the convoy arrived, Yorktown had been decided. The Bank didn't have enough capital to open until the war was already effectively over.

The Bank of North America made most of its profit through a specific kind of commercial loan—the discount. As we saw in the last chapter, Americans were already familiar with handwritten promissory notes. But those notes weren't always perfectly negotiable. They were often made out in odd amounts, and their value relied on the personal reputation of whoever had signed or countersigned them. A merchant could get cash for a promissory note, however, by leaving it with the Bank in return for a short-term loan, sixty days or less. The Bank would hand over slightly less cash than the promissory note's face value and would eventually receive the full value as it closed out the loan. The difference—the discount—was the Bank's profit. In addition to promissory notes, merchant banks like the Bank of North America discounted commercial paper, promissory notes guaranteed by actual physical goods. A merchant could discount commercial paper against wheat shipped but not yet paid for, for example, or molasses arrived from the Caribbean but not yet sold.

I have been vague so far about the word "cash," because the *way* the Bank handed out cash is crucial to understanding how banks worked. When the Bank of North America discounted a promissory note, it did not lend out any of its Spanish milled dollars. Instead, the Bank handed out its own bank notes—something like a printed bill of credit issued by a bank, instead of a colony. A merchant asking for a discount at the Bank was just swapping notes, handing in a promissory note of an odd amount, guaranteed by a person, in return for bank notes, made out in regular amounts and guaranteed by the Bank. The bank notes were convertible—they could be redeemed on demand at the Bank for silver dollars—but people didn't always immediately run with their notes back to the Bank for coins. Just as had already been true for the Bank of England for more than a century, notes from the Bank of North America circulated as cash. Think of "cash" as real money: anything accepted as payment, from a stranger, without question.

Bank notes from the Bank of North America were from the very beginning designed as big money. Issued at face values of $10, $25, $30, $40, and $50, they were useful as big-money cash for the merchants who discounted promissory notes. We now use the word "backed" as a catchall for why money has value. But we have to think of the Bank of North America's bank notes as both backed *and* convertible. They were backed by the Bank's most important asset: not its silver, but the quality of the promissory notes the Bank had discounted. Better loans from reputable merchants were more likely to be repaid. But the bank notes were also convertible, since merchants could trade them in for coins on demand.

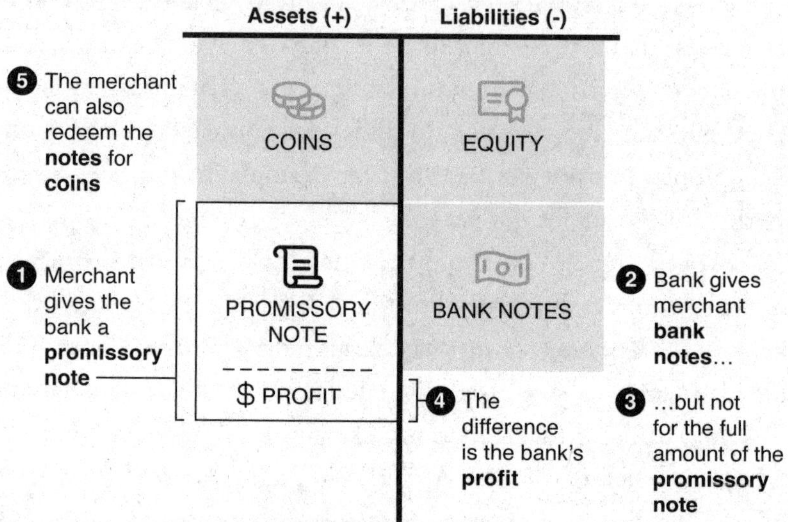

Illustration by Evan Applegate.

Even as the Bank of North America began handing out its dollar notes for discounts in the 1780s, new American states continued to print their own money. In 1785, still under the Articles of Confederation, Pennsylvania printed a new run of bills of credit. They were denominated in the old money of account, Pennsylvania shillings and pence, for much smaller amounts—3 pence, 9 pence, and 1, 2, 5, 10, 15, and 20 shillings. The Bank didn't have a commercial interest in producing small money in Pennsylvania shillings, but the assembly agreed that the commonwealth was "suffering much inconvenience for want of a sufficient circulating medium." The bills of credit went to farmers, who could borrow them through a land bank, and to interest payments on Pennsylvania's share of Congress's debt from the war. The bills were also backed by a sinking fund: taxes on imports into Philadelphia, payable in coin, dedicated to buying the bills back, starting in 1787. The commonwealth's bills were convertible on a schedule, unlike the Bank's notes, which were convertible on demand. The assembly accepted its bills of credit for tax payments, but did not make them legal tender. No one had to accept them as a private debt.

We have been conditioned to think of different kinds of money on a scale from good to bad. But Pennsylvania's bills of credit and the notes of the Bank of North America were both useful—in different ways, to different people. The Pennsylvania shilling bills of credit complemented the book credits in local shillings that shopkeepers still kept with their customers. The bills traded below par, at between 10 and 20 percent off their face value. The dollar notes of the Bank of North America traded at par, at one to one with the Spanish milled dollars. The bank notes, just like the silver dollars, were never designed to work for the economy of the entire commonwealth. They served a purpose for merchants, who needed money firmly anchored to the value of the one coin that was ubiquitous in Atlantic trade.

Farmers in Pennsylvania argued that the Bank was too focused on short-term discounts and wouldn't lend on the longer, seasonal terms needed for agriculture. Both farmers and the trades believed that the state's limited stock of silver dollars and gold pistoles was locked up in the Bank's capital, driving up interest rates on smaller loans. They were also concerned that the Bank's notes, which were convertible on demand, would drive down the value of the commonwealth's bills of credit, which could only be converted to coins over a schedule of several years. And the Bank was profitable only to the small group of people who had invested in it. As a delegate to the Pennsylvania Assembly pointed out, both Pennsylvania and the Bank of North America printed paper money; the question was only which institution got 6 percent for lending it out.

This argument between bank notes and state bills of credit was still current when delegates began to gather in Philadelphia in the summer of 1787 for a constitutional convention. Robert Morris was openly hostile to Pennsylvania's bills of credit, but he wasn't alone. Correspondence among the framers of the Constitution reveals a skepticism of the kinds of unrestrained democracies that had flourished in the new states, and of the one thing in particular that all unrestrained democracies seemed to produce: state bills of credit. If the value of those bills fell against the silver dollar, even a little, anyone who had lent money in state shillings saw the value of that loan drop, too. As James Madison wrote to Thomas Jefferson just before the convention, state bills of credit were an "indulgence to debtors."

Over the course of the convention, initial objections to making state bills of credit legal tender quietly became a ban on state bills of credit altogether. The Constitution stripped the states of their power to produce money; even though the word "bank" doesn't appear in the Constitution, that's where the power went. Economic historians have described the turn toward banks as a victory for economic growth in the early American republic: Banks and bank notes made early industrial investment possible, and made transactions clean, liquid, and consistent. This is a plausible argument, but it's also selective. After the Revolution, bank notes were still just as experimental as state bills of credit. Banks would periodically fail in a financial panic, or sometimes just because they were poorly managed. When a bank failed, its circulating bank notes failed, too. The Constitution didn't end chaos and replace it with the dollar. It just guaranteed a different kind of chaos.

BANK NOTES IN NEW ORLEANS

Randy Haynie started collecting coins for a Cub Scout badge in the 1960s. Once a week, he would ride his bike through the drive-through of a bank in Houma, Louisiana. The tellers had promised to look for rarities; when they found something, they'd wave him into the branch, where he'd get in line and buy whatever they'd found at face value. One week the bank's president pulled Randy into his office, opened a drawer, and handed over a red seal $2 bill from 1928. The seal, a red watermark, meant that the bills had been issued directly as notes by the U.S. Treasury. Red seals passed as dollars, but functioned like a loan to the federal government. In good condition today, a 1928 red seal $2 bill will sell at auction for $7,000.

Not many people collected paper money in the 1960s. At the time, there were still personal memories of a gold standard, and Randy suspects that other collectors were nostalgic for hard coins. But old paper was relatively cheap, and so he started buying it. Randy has now collected more than five thousand notes and bills, which he keeps in albums locked in safes in Lafayette, where he lives. He only buys paper dollars from Louisiana, and has managed to build the largest collection of southern American paper currency in the world.

Randy commutes to Baton Rouge to work as a lobbyist at the state legislature. His office in the capital is the former home of Earl Long, governor of Louisiana for two terms in the 1940s and 1950s. Randy has decorated the house with framed currency; when I arrived to talk about his collection, he spread several of his albums across a table in what used to be Earl Long's dining room. I have found, trying to understand the dollar, that collectors like Randy and the numismatists who study coins are just as helpful as economists and historians. Most academics working on money and finance start with documents like old letters, or with reconstructed data sets. But collectors and academic numismatists start with actual physical money. The properties of money—the way it was stamped or printed, or what was written on it—can tell us a lot about how things functioned as money and why they had value.

Randy is a completist, and his collection starts in 1803, the year Louisiana became an American territory. His promissory notes in French from the territory—bons—were often denominated in *piastres,* which in French at the time meant the same silver Spanish dollars that were current on the East Coast. French and Spanish settlers in the Louisiana Territory did not start counting in dollars because they became American. They already lived on the edge of the same global flow of silver, and had already counted in dollars before the Americans arrived. It's likely the dollar sign, $, entered English from the South, as American merchants on the lower Mississippi in the late eighteenth century adopted a stylized *P* and *S* as an abbreviation of *pesos,* another Spanish word for dollar.

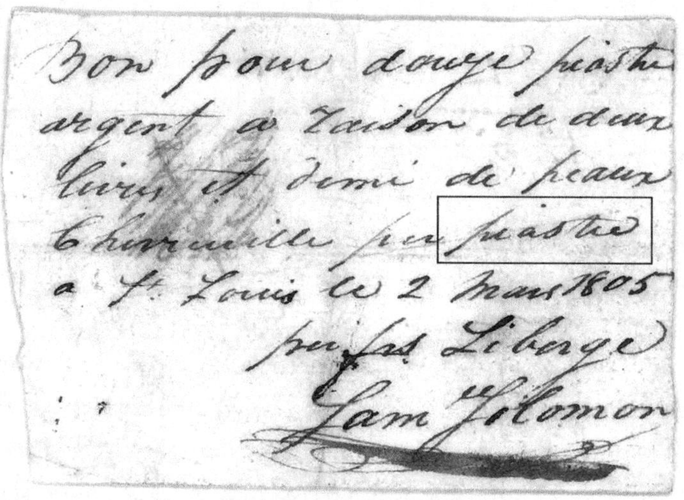
Bon pour douze piastre
argent a raison de deux
livres et demi de peaux
Chevreuille par piastre
a St Louis le 2 Mars 1805
pour Jas Liberge
Sam Solomon

An 1804 promissory note written in *piastre,* a French word for silver dollars. (Image courtesy of Randy Haynie.)

Until the arrival of regular steamboat traffic in the 1820s, trade flowed downriver on the Mississippi. Flatboats full of whiskey and corn, salted hams and live cattle floated down from western rivers and the Ohio valley. On arrival in New Orleans, boatmen known locally as Kaintocks—from Kentucky—haggled along the levee in front of the covered markets, sold their flatboats as lumber, stayed awhile to drink, and then either walked home or sailed around the coast, silver strapped around their waists. In the 1820s steamboats became reliable enough for regular traffic up and down the river, turning a colonial outpost into an American port.

New Orleans finance in the first decade of steam travel was relatively simple. Cotton left New Orleans the same way tobacco had left Maryland a century before. Local factors working for foreign buyers would pay for cotton with bills of exchange on London, useful for buying things made in Britain. At first, banks in New Orleans were just for merchants; bankers bought and sold bills of exchange, and offered short-term discounts on promissory notes and commercial paper backed by goods on the levee. By 1830, banks in Louisiana had circulated just over half a million dollars in bank notes, still well under the $8 million from Pennsylvania banks and $6.5 million from banks in New York. By the middle of the 1830s, however, there were thirteen new banks in Louisiana and almost $8 million in bank notes. This was still fewer than in New York or Pennsylvania, but on a crude measure of bank notes to population Louisiana was far better supplied than any other state. Banks had taken on two new jobs in New Orleans: financing the physical growth of the city itself, and financing sugar plantations up the river.

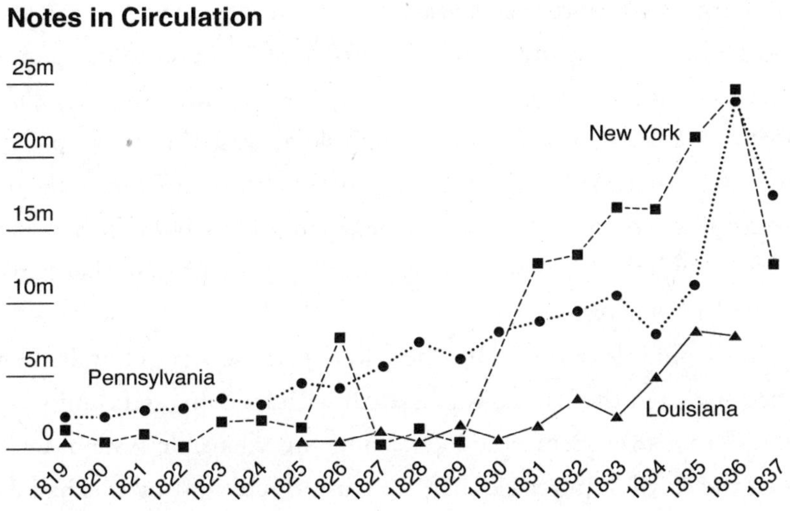

Notes in Circulation

25m
20m
15m
10m
5m
0
New York
Pennsylvania
Louisiana
1819 1820 1821 1822 1823 1824 1825 1826 1827 1828 1829 1830 1831 1832 1833 1834 1835 1836 1837

Graph by Evan Applegate. (Data from J. Van Fenstermaker, *The Development of American Commercial Banking, 1782–1837.*)

Anyone could operate a private bank, but a state charter—a specific grant of incorporation to a single bank—gave a bank a few important privileges. A charter from a state limited the liability of a bank's officers and investors if the bank failed. A charter also granted a bank the power to issue bank notes; it was literally a license to print money. In return, the state demanded certain protections. The bank would need a certain sum of capital to get started, for example, or have to hold a minimum amount of silver against its loans. Investors also often had to promise to provide loans that would be useful to some powerful group in the state legislature.

In the early 1830s, Louisiana chartered five improvement banks, something like what we would call an infrastructure bank today—a way to build something the state wants. We think of commercial banks now as agnostic, out to make money however they can. But in nineteenth-century Louisiana, each improvement bank had a job to do. In 1829, the New Orleans Gas Light and Banking Company got a charter in return for a promise to install gas lamps on streets all the way out to the city's growing suburbs. Two years later, Louisiana chartered the Canal and Banking Company, which used some of its notes to pay gangs of Irish immigrants to dig the New Basin Canal with shovels, six miles north to Lake Pontchartrain through what was still a swamp. Those notes were, in turn, backed by the promise of future revenue to the bank from flatboat tows up the canal. The Exchange Bank built the St. Charles Hotel, a hub for the new American business district. Another bank financed a water system.

In the middle of the 1830s there were just over seven hundred chartered banks in the United States, each with its own assets and its own notes. That may seem now like an incomprehensible system, making even the smallest purchases hard to trust. But almost no one had to be familiar with the balance sheets of seven hundred different banks. The United States in the early nineteenth century was not what we'd today call a currency union. Brokers in New Orleans published in the *Picayune* a single list of rates for bills of exchange payable in London, Paris, Boston, New York, Philadelphia, and Baltimore; to transfer money, Baltimore was as foreign as Paris.

This was true for bank notes, too. They normally circulated within an American city, or among farming communities around that city. In

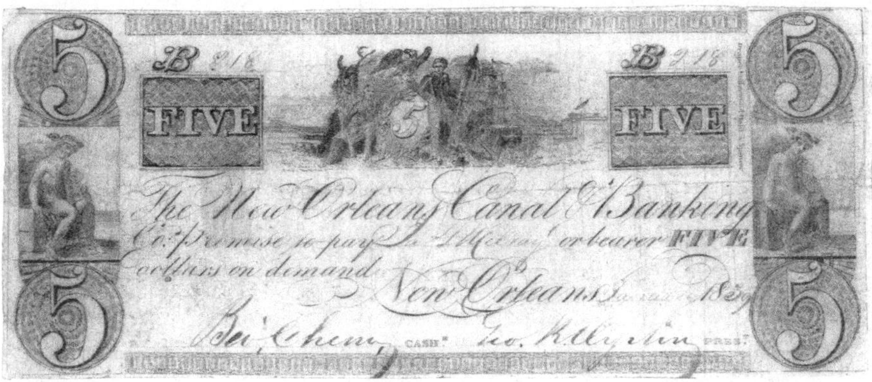

An 1839 bank note from the New Orleans Canal & Banking Co., which agreed to finance a canal through New Orleans in return for a banking charter. Like a promissory note, the note is dated by hand and made out to a customer by name, and the bank's cashier and president have both signed it. (Image courtesy of Randy Haynie.)

New Orleans, brokers took local bank notes at the same price, as "bank notes of this city." In northern merchant cities like New York, bill brokers published bank note reporters—lists of bank notes from different states, with their prices—but took all notes from New Orleans at the same slight discount. Traveling paper money men did move notes from city to city to redeem them, and banks found ways to use those same paper money men to circulate their own notes far from home to prevent redemption. But for most people, and particularly the Creoles and Americans in New Orleans, each city had its own banks and its own bank notes—its own dollars.

The new bank notes didn't crowd out the old habits of money in New Orleans. Randy's collection includes several bills of exchange from the same period, signed in New York, payable in New Orleans, and countersigned several times on the back to pass from hand to hand, just as bills of exchange had passed as cash in seventeenth-century Maryland. Promissory notes still paid for larger purchases, too. In Randy Haynie's collection are two notes from the 1830s in French from a Mr. DeBlanc: one for 1,500 piastres due in a year, and another for the same amount, due in two years. Both cleared.

Cecee Macarty, a free Black woman in New Orleans who built an importing house worth $155,000 by the time she died in the 1840s, used the flow of cash from her business to discount promissory notes on the side. François Lacroix, a free Black man, was a partner in a tailor shop on Chartres, a short walk across Canal from the brokers' windows on Camp Street. He discounted notes for his customers, and occasionally sued when they couldn't eventually clear their accounts with some kind of cash. This kind of private banking was common in other states as well, where free Black merchants couldn't get a bank charter. Bank notes, says Randy, were just refined promissory notes, and the millions of new bank notes in New Orleans were a complement to the old system, not a replacement. And they hadn't dislodged the silver dollars from Zacatecas and Potosí, still the most important kind of money in America.

THE SILVER PICAYUNE ECONOMY

The Daily Picayune was named for its price: 1 picayune. The word "picayune" has come to mean a small thing of no significance, but in New Orleans in the early nineteenth century a picayune was the same thing other Americans knew as a bit—one-eighth of a silver dollar, clipped with shears to a tiny pie slice, sometimes punched with a hole so it could hang on a string. It came through French from *piquar,* which in an archaic Romance language from southern France meant to ring, like a bell. A picayune was a little coin from somewhere else that rang in your pocket. In New Orleans and all over America as late as the 1840s, little pieces of foreign silver still mattered as small change. Picayunes rang in the offering box at the cathedral. The rioters in 1842 would have run by a shop on the corner of Chartres and Canal that sold soda for a picayune. A cup of coffee at the covered markets went for a picayune; a soup bone went for two. Street vendors offered flowers in picayune bouquets, herbs in picayune bundles, and sugared popcorn in picayune piles, all sized to sell for exactly one-eighth of a silver dollar. The history of all this silver was clear in New Orleans at the time; in its inaugural issue in 1837, the *Picayune* promised that "when we exchange *our* picayune for *your* picayune, and when we *derive a profit,* it will be time enough to *touch the Spanish.*"

Silver dollar coins from Mexico hadn't become any less important in the United States, even decades after the Constitution. America's new Congress had established a mint in 1792, laying out the weight and fineness of new American coins. The U.S. dollar, a coin in silver, would be "of the value of the Spanish milled dollar as the same is now current." There would also be gold eagles, worth 10 silver dollars. Economic historians usually refer to this as a bimetallic standard, one that defined the dollar through fixed weights of both gold and silver. This was true in law, but in practice very few gold eagle coins ever circulated before the 1850s. The Spanish milled dollar was still the accepted standard for Atlantic trade, a coin Americans knew well from handling it themselves. Congress did not create an American dollar in 1792. It simply consented to the silver dollar standard that had already been in place well before the American Revolution.

The way money worked in the early American republic wasn't completely different from the way it had worked under British rule. It is difficult to pass a law to change the way people count, and so shopkeepers and small merchants kept their accounts in shillings and pence into the first decade of the nineteenth century. The new mint in Philadelphia did produce coins, but nowhere near enough of them, or the right mix. And so Congress kept allowing foreign coins to pass as legal tender for a time, then kept pushing the deadline back by two or three or ten years, all the way to 1857. For the first half of the nineteenth century, there was no U.S. dollar. There was still the old silver dollar that continued to arrive on ships, and a variety of American attempts to recreate it.

Actual silver Spanish milled dollars continued to be hard to find in America. Still the best thing to do with a real silver dollar was to ship it in the direction of Europe or China, to pay for high-quality manufactured goods. In the first few decades of the nineteenth century, American merchants almost completely replaced European silver shipments into China, and New Orleans sat at the center of the American dollar trade. Traders along the levee moved American wheat and pork to the Caribbean, taking Spanish and then Mexican dollars as payment. Or they bought silver dollars outright, swapping them with bills of exchange that paid out in London; merchants in Mexico or Cuba could use the bills to pay for British imports. Those silver dollars sailed on small packet ships from New Orleans to merchants in the Northeast, then on fast clippers to Canton, to buy the same silks and porcelains that Cantonese merchants had always sold for silver. Politicians in the early American republic fought over the silk trade for the same reason Sancho de Moncada had complained to the king in Madrid two centuries earlier: All the dollars were going to China.

The coins that did pass in the early republic tended to be either foreign gold or smaller and cut pieces of foreign silver. Americans took gold guineas, crowns, and pistoles from abroad, and American textbooks taught arithmetic rules to convert gold on a ledger into silver dollars. In silver, smaller Spanish 4- and 1-real pieces were more likely to stay in circulation in America, as were the bits and picayunes, cut with shears and worn smooth. As late as the 1850s, people still quoted prices for smaller purchases in shillings, or levys, both names for a Spanish 1-real piece. A half-real piece was known as a fip. In New Orleans in the 1840s, the municipalities printed their notes and assessed fees in multiples of 12½ cents—a picayune. The early American republic remained a picayune economy, still ringing with foreign coins and inherited English ideas about money.

Between 1806 and 1835 the United States even stopped minting silver dollars altogether. Economic historians blame the official U.S. silver-to-gold ratio, which undervalued silver coins, encouraging Americans to buy cheap silver at home and ship it abroad for a profit. But the records for the U.S. Mint tell a different story. That whole time the mint had continued to stamp increasing numbers of silver half-dollars, along with periodic runs of quarters and dimes. These were all the same fineness as the dollars, just a smaller size. In his annual report to the White House for 1806, the director of the mint gave two reasons for its decision to avoid producing silver dollars. First, the mint's customers preferred small change for daily purchases. There might have been some truth to this, although mint customers consistently complained that they wanted even smaller coins, but had to settle for the half-dollars, which were cheaper for the mint to produce but tended to end up in banks.

Second, the director of the mint wrote that smaller coins were more likely to stay in the country. Anything that functioned as a silver dollar was too useful in global markets to remain at home. The mint's officers repeated this argument for the next several decades. It was clear to them that not all silver was the same; the mint made the half-dollars to get them to stay in America. The few silver dollars minted in America were slightly smaller than Spanish milled dollars, likely as an attempt to keep them from leaving the country, but even these tended to pool in the Caribbean, where they passed as full dollars. It wasn't silver that was in high demand for export to Europe and China. It was silver dollars, still moving around the world.

LOUISIANA'S TOP-HEAVY PROPERTY BANKS

As Louisiana's legislature was chartering improvement banks to build out the city of New Orleans in the early 1830s, it also began approving property banks, developed as tools for wealthy landowners in the American South. Property banks in Louisiana took land and humans and turned them into dollars and sugar. These banks also introduced a new scale to banking; at its founding, the Citizens' Bank, the last and largest of these banks, was by assets the second-biggest bank in America.

The sugarcane fields that ran along the river upstream from New Orleans to Baton Rouge demanded a much bigger up-front investment than the large-scale cotton plantations in Alabama and Mississippi. Cane had to be crushed in a mill immediately as it came off the field, then boiled down several times in a series of pans elevated in a brick structure over a massive fire. During the harvest season, planters had slaves run the mill around the clock in shifts; the work required training, judgment, and technical knowledge. Sugar was an industrial product, and the Portuguese planters who developed the model of slave sugar called a plantation an *engenho:* a machine. The sugar machine was expensive, and it became even more expensive after planters began to convert their mills to steam power. In 1827 there were twenty-one thousand slaves working cane fields in Louisiana, and 82 steam engines. By 1841 there were fifty-one thousand slaves and 408 engines.

Sugar planters needed longer loan terms than they could get discounting promissory notes at merchant banks. And if they were going to pool capital to start their own bank, they couldn't do it with the silver that merchants were far more likely to have. What the Louisiana sugar planters did have, however, was what to a bookkeeper looked like assets: land and enslaved men, women, and children. America and Louisiana were approaching what turned out to be the absolute top of a banking boom, convinced that the value of land and humans could never go down.

In 1827 the state chartered the Consolidated Association of Planters of Louisiana, which became a model for other property banks. Planters took out a mortgage with the bank, against their land and human property. The mortgage gave the planter shares in the bank, and the bank sold bonds in Europe, using the mortgaged land and slaves as collateral. These bond sales brought in bills of exchange, payable in London, which returned to New Orleans to serve as the bank's capital; the bank could sell them to bring in silver dollars as needed. Finally, the bank made loans to its shareholders of up to half the value of their property, paying them out as bank notes.

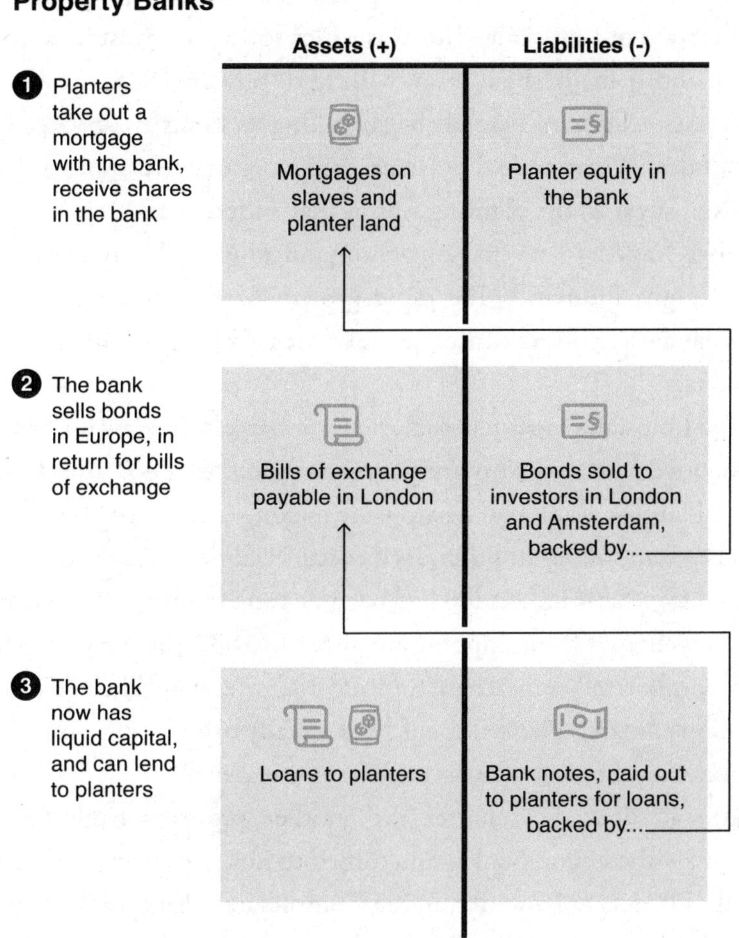

Illustration by Evan Applegate.

At first, agents for the Consolidated Association of Planters had trouble selling the bank's bonds, even in the United States. Bonds on new railroads or canals were popular at the time, but those rested on clear plans for future revenue. A bond on a collection of planters' mortgages, however, looked slippery; it wasn't clear what the returns were, who guaranteed them, or how it was possible to even pursue that person in another state if the bank failed. And so the state assembly amended the bank's charter and agreed to issue the bonds in the name of the State of Louisiana. This was easier for bond investors abroad to grasp, and it made them more willing to buy. In 1828, the Consolidated Association of Planters began selling its Louisiana-backed bonds in London. Planters in Louisiana shipped forty-five thousand hogsheads of sugar in the planting season that ended in 1829. In 1830, that number leaped to seventy-one thousand hogsheads; in 1831, it was eighty-eight thousand. The rapid growth of new sugar machines in Louisiana was a direct consequence of the new property bank for sugar planters.

The Louisiana sugar planters and their bankers in New Orleans were productive but also constantly overextended. In 1831, the Consolidated Planters' Bank had a hard time making interest payments on the bonds it had sold in London. Its directors claimed, weakly, that bills of exchange payable in London had become too expensive and that storms had prevented it from shipping any silver. In 1832, the sugar crop failed. Edmond Forstall, a merchant and sugar planter who'd helped establish the Consolidated Planters' Bank, had already begun work on a solution for indebted Louisiana sugar planters: more debt.

Forstall drafted a charter for another property bank for sugar planters—the Union Bank—and turned to London again to sell the new bonds. Planters borrowed from the Consolidated Planters' Bank, bought land and slaves, couldn't make their payments, then fixed the problem by borrowing from the Union Bank. The new bank, Forstall later explained, had "been the means of saving many and many of our planters from expropriation." He saved Louisiana's sugar planters *again* in 1835 with a third property bank, the Citizens' Bank of Louisiana. Had it not been for the third bank, he said, "a sweeping mutation would have taken place in the ownership of the sugar estates"—a wave of bankruptcies. Sugar planters were a bad risk, and the Louisiana property banks weren't reliably profitable. But powerful people got the bank charters they wanted, and each new property bank kept the sugar machine running.

Notes for $10 and $100 from the Citizens' Bank of Louisiana. Printed in English and French, both notes circulated, were redeemed at the bank for silver, and were then canceled with slashing pen marks. (Image courtesy of Randy Haynie.)

In a letter to a bank in London, Forstall praised the new bonds of the Citizens' Bank as "equal to any ever tendered to the Capitalists of Europe. It is bound upon the best property of the Country. It must ultimately succeed." Sharon Murphy, a historian who has written about the Louisiana property banks, has argued that finance erases human stories. You can still read an almost-complete record of mortgages, ledgers, and minutes of the Citizens' Bank at the Tulane University Archives in New Orleans. This archive is numbing, as long lists of the names of slaves on the mortgages become numbers in the clean, amoral lines of double-entry bookkeeping. Every bank note in America was backed by some kind of asset. To understand how Louisiana was able to print so many bank notes, we have to take a hard look at the word "asset," and what Edmond Forstall actually meant by "the best property of the Country."

David Morgan fought in the Battle of New Orleans in 1815, and in 1824 acquired twelve hundred acres in St. Tammany Parish, "by donation from the government of the United States as an actual settler." In 1826, Morgan purchased six enslaved men and women from Abner Robinson of Richmond, Virginia, for $3,484, signing a mortgage on his land to Robinson that guaranteed four promissory notes. Six people, "all slaves for life," are named in the sale with their ages, including Yorrick, twelve, and Delphia, fifteen.

Legal documents at the time were folded in tight packages; on the front, a notary would record a date and the parties to the contract, and a summary of the collateral. For the mortgage with Robinson, the notary wrote "4," for the four adults in the sale, and then added "Yorrick," then "Delphia," and then "2 children"—meaning Yorrick and Delphia. In 1826 children were treated as collateral for a slave mortgage, but they were also distinct from the adults.

In 1832, Morgan and his wife, Mary Baham, mortgaged their land and the people they had bought for stock in the Union Bank. By then, there were twelve enslaved people listed with the property. Only Yorrick and Delphia were left from the original six. Delphia had by then had two children—Tom, three, and Nelson, one. The penciled summary on the loan just reads "12 Slaves—." In a time of easy credit for sugar planters, Tom and Nelson counted as full collateral. By adding two toddlers to their list, Morgan and Baham could borrow more dollars. Three years later, they signed a promissory note to the Union Bank for a $5,000 loan.

In January 1838, Edmond Forstall, in his capacity as the president of the brand-new Citizens' Bank, appeared at a notary's office to confirm receipt of the mortgage of David Bannister Morgan and his wife, Mary

Constance Baham, in return for two hundred shares of stock in the bank, worth $20,000. This time Morgan and Baham counted twenty-one slaves on the land in Tammany Parish. The new arrivals on the plantation were mostly men in their twenties, likely there to work the field and the mill. Delphia remained, by then with another infant: James. There are six other children named in the mortgage, but again the summary of collateral reads only "General Morgan Plantation x 21. *Slaves.*" The document also carefully confirmed that Morgan and Baham had already mortgaged the same property to another bank. The 1838 mortgage for shares in the Citizens' Bank was conditional; it had to be used to pay off the $5,000 1835 note with the Union Bank.

And 2° Twenty one Slaves, described on the back
of the Commissioners certificate of appraisement as
follows viz Frederick, aged twenty five years, Yorrick aged
18 years. Henry aged 18 years, Sally, aged 22 years. Agnes
aged 7 years, Jourdan, aged 5 years, Eliza Jane aged
3 years. Richard aged 1 year Maria aged 22 years.
Robert aged six years. Jefferson aged 4 years. Edmund aged
1½ years. Delphia aged 25 years. Tom aged 7 years.
Nelson aged 5 years. James aged one year, Tom aged
15 years. Nancy aged 13 years. Grace aged 14 years.
Louisa aged 11 years and Jim aged 12 years.

David Morgan and Mary Baham's mortgage with the Citizens' Bank of Louisiana. (Image courtesy of the author.)

Over a decade, David Morgan and Mary Baham strung a land grant from the federal government into a series of promissory notes to a slave trader, then stock in a property bank, and then a loan to build out a sugar plantation. Then they turned the same sugar plantation into stock in *another* property bank in return for the right to take out an even larger loan. These transactions show up in historical data as a rapid expansion in the production of bank note dollars in Louisiana. Obscured behind that data is Delphia, born enslaved in Richmond. She sailed to New Orleans at fifteen, and was tallied as a child on the mortgage for her own purchase. Then she became an asset on the balance sheet of two banks as an adult, then bore three children, all named as capital, who joined her on the ledgers. Then and now, bank dollars don't just happen. They have always been produced for specific people, for specific reasons, against specific assets.

In New Orleans, bank notes were an expression of power, a kind of monetary sovereignty for the planters and merchants. The supply of bank capital and the value of bank notes rested on confidence, and Edmond Forstall liked to assure his correspondents in London that Louisiana and its sugar machine would always generate wealth. That confidence collapsed during the panic of 1837, and the bewildered reckoning that followed changed the way we think about bank dollars still today.

"NEVER WAS THERE SO MUCH LIQUOR DRANK IN NEW ORLEANS IN ONE DAY"

In 1835, Andrew Crane left New Jersey for Louisiana, where he began shipping down carriages built in Newark and selling them on commission to some of the wealthiest families in New Orleans. Crane was a careful bookkeeper; his papers ended up in the archives at Louisiana State University in Baton Rouge, and they give us a picture of how dollars moved in and out of banks in Louisiana. On arrival, Crane bought a workshop from Mark Walton with four twelve-month promissory notes, at least one of which Walton promptly discounted for bank notes at the Union Bank of Louisiana—the same property bank where David Morgan had gotten one of his sugar loans.

Crane occasionally took in cash for repair work, but his customers usually paid for their carriages with promissory notes, on terms of six months. The only record we have of these notes is Crane's journal, a running record of each day's accounts. The notes themselves he would hand back to be destroyed after his customers had paid them down. In the late 1830s, however, we can see a change. Crane began holding on to his customers' promissory notes; the only reason to keep a note was to show it to a court, when something had gone wrong. In 1838, for example, George Bostwick wrote a promissory note for $425 that two more people endorsed and passed on, before someone handed it to Andrew Crane. Bostwick rented horses and carriages out of a stable on Girod Street, but business must have been bad, because he failed to pay down the note. Crane had a notary chase Bostwick down at his home, where his wife said he wasn't there and couldn't pay. Then the notary went to the stable on Girod Street, where Bostwick had started sleeping, only to learn that Bostwick had left town altogether.

In his own collection, Randy Haynie has noticed the same shift that's in Andrew Crane's papers: In the late 1830s and early 1840s, there are fewer bank notes, and more handwritten promissory notes. The handwritten notes had become either more common or more likely to fail and stay in the record—or both. This is what we would expect to find during a banking contraction, and that's certainly what was happening at the end of the 1830s. In New Orleans, the city's bank notes were worth less than they should have been or nothing at all, and even the old system of promissory notes had started to unravel. In 1837, Americans went through something that was still novel and bewildering: a financial panic.

Both banks and bank notes had grown dramatically. In 1830 there were 330 banks in America with $61 million in circulating bank notes. By 1837 there were 634 banks, and $149 million in bank notes. This growth was even more pronounced in Louisiana, as the state added improvement banks to build out New Orleans and property banks for the sugar planters along the Mississippi. Americans were in what we now call a bubble, like Edmond Forstall's optimism about an ever-increasing flow of profits from agriculture.

One explanation for the panic of 1837 comes out of what historians call the Bank War, a political fight between Andrew Jackson and the Second Bank of the United States. The Second Bank was the only bank in America with a national charter and branches in multiple states; Congress

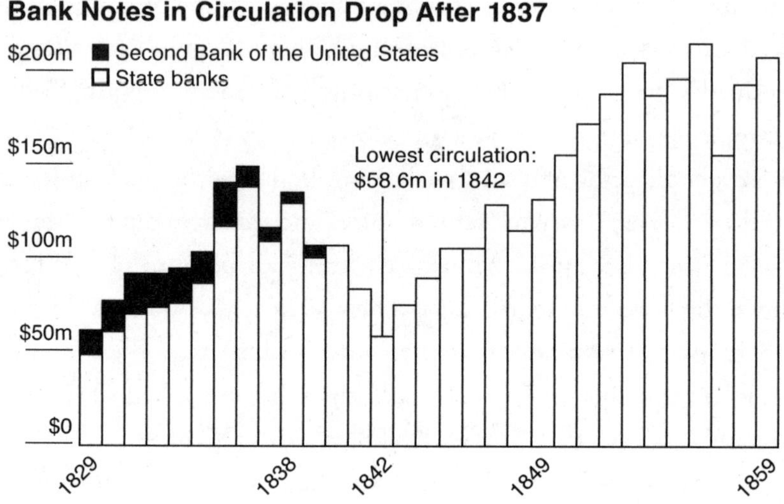

Graph by Evan Applegate. (Data from U.S. House of Representatives, *Condition of State Banks,* 1841.)

had created it to handle payments for the federal government. The bank took in dollar bank notes and certificates of bank deposits as payment for federal land, and silver dollars for tariffs paid at the ports. It also held bills of exchange to make payments on federal loans held abroad. But the Second Bank was also a merchant's bank, with private investors. It took in commercial paper on discount, and used its network of branches to sell bills of exchange that moved dollars among American cities.

Money and banking didn't map neatly onto political parties in the 1830s, but Andrew Jackson's Democrats resented banks in general and the Second Bank in particular. Rural Democrats and city labor movements allied with the party were frustrated that state-chartered banks, cozy with state legislators, failed to make sure bank notes and loans worked for everyone. Some wealthy Democrats, mostly in the South and West, were happy to have mortgages and discounts from their own locally chartered state banks, but disliked the way the Second Bank restrained those banks by pulling in their notes from around the country and redeeming them for silver.

Under Jackson, the Treasury began diverting its business to a small group of state-chartered banks instead, which encouraged the state banks to make more loans. Silver in the till didn't *cause* loans to happen, but it did make banks feel more confident, and perhaps incautious. Then, in 1836, Jackson's administration issued its specie circular, discouraging land speculation by demanding that people buying public land in the western states pay not with any kind of bank paper but with specie—with coins. One story of the panic of 1837 blames Jackson; he inflated a bubble, then popped it.

New Orleans also sat at the end of a chain of loans that stretched all the way across the Atlantic to the Bank of England. The financial relationships that bound merchants and banks over long distances were complex. They rested on confidence that assets in the present would continue to have value in the future. If any asset in the chain lost value, it put stress on every link, as news traveled by sail and each person along the way had to guess—or panic.

In 1837, cotton sold in New Orleans for 13 cents a pound. By the next season, it had dropped to 9 cents a pound. When prices in any commodity are uncertain, sometimes there are no sales at all. In April 1837, the *New-Orleans Price-Current* reported that the city's cotton market "is in a most strange situation; indeed, it might with propriety be said that we have none, as transactions are so nearly suspended." The paper couldn't quote a cotton price for shipment to Liverpool; sales were so sporadic, at so many different prices, that the paper didn't feel that quotes had any real meaning.

When the price of a commodity like cotton drops, anyone holding it has to adjust, selling more than planned for less than hoped. But when there's no price at all—that's when things break. As cotton factors in New Orleans realized they couldn't sell any of their stock to raise money, lenders all along the chains connecting them to New York, Liverpool, and London realized they were in trouble, too. To the banks, loans were assets. When someone couldn't make a payment, the asset stopped performing; it could no longer bring silver or the bank's own notes back on schedule. When this happened to enough loans, a bank could decide to suspend redemption; it would stop paying out silver dollars for bank notes. Bad bank loans meant bad bank notes. In 1837, banks holding suddenly questionable loans didn't fail, necessarily, but they did suspend. They stopped handing out silver for their bank notes.

Each city in the United States had its own banking system, and suspensions tended to roll across an entire city at the same time. Andrew Crane's journal for Thursday, May 11, 1837, records that he was able to discount three promissory notes for bank notes from the Merchants Bank and the Bank of Louisiana for just over $4,500. That was a lot of credit in a single day, and he was likely borrowing as much as he could, while he still could. The following day, several New Orleans bank presidents agreed to stop paying out silver dollar coins for dollar bank notes, and on Saturday morning people began literally running to the rest of the city's banks to redeem notes for handfuls of silver—a bank run.

Some banks continued to redeem notes smaller than $10. Some redeemed none at all. People turned away at the banks tried to discount their notes at bars; barkeepers refused to pay silver, but still took some notes for juleps and gin slings. "Never," according to the *Picayune,* "was there so much liquor drank in New Orleans in one day." On Sunday, Edward Plant, who ran a dry goods store on Chartres Street, advertised that he would continue to take bank notes "AT PAR!!" for the next ten days only. Suspension didn't make bank notes immediately worthless. It just turned every transaction into a fraught negotiation.

A week later, seven of the city's sixteen banks had stopped handing over coins. Five more redeemed only $5 and $10 bank notes. The normally dry remarks on the city's markets from the *Price-Current* grew philosophical. "We know not which way to turn," the paper admitted, "and the troubles of to-day go for nothing, when compared with the anticipations of tomorrow." By the end of the month, the paper had arrived at despair. Bills of exchange with the Northeast were no longer available. No one parted with silver except to settle old accounts or ship it abroad; with the value of bank notes uncertain, silver dollars were the only real money left. In the city, anyone with coins could buy hard merchandise at a discount. And, already in 1837, the *Price-Current* reported that people in New Orleans were beginning to write their own promissory notes for smaller purchases. "The whole machinery of our commerce," the paper wrote, "is deranged."

Since the Constitution, American states had been running an experiment: to let commercial banks issue paper notes that functioned as dollars. That experiment came with a risk, one we still live with today: When the banks fail, the dollars fail. After the panic, dollar bank notes didn't just drop in value. There were fewer of them. By 1838 the number of bank notes in circulation—dollars—had shrunk from $149 million to $116 million. Some banks had failed, and the rest had become chastened. They made fewer loans, and since loans create bank notes, there were fewer bank note dollars.

In January 1837, just before the panic, there were $7.7 million in notes outstanding from Louisiana's banks. We don't have good monthly data, but by March 1838 that had collapsed to $4.7 million. This begins to explain what Randy Haynie sees in his collection. In the late 1830s and early 1840s, people in Louisiana returned to the older habits of handwritten notes guaranteed by a person, not a bank. In theory, when the amount of money in an economy drops, prices should drop, too. In practice, prices drop slowly and painfully, and people come up with their own ways of replacing the money that's disappeared.

NEW ORLEANS REPLACED ITS MISSING BANK DOLLAR NOTES WITH MUNICIPAL DOLLAR NOTES

Already by May 20, 1837, a week after the city's banks stopped offering silver for bank notes, the American municipality in New Orleans had begun printing its own notes in denominations as small as 12½ cents—one picayune, or an eighth of a silver dollar. Randy has several notes from that first summer after the panic. They were guaranteed by future income from wharf taxes and drayage fees to move goods around the levee, which local merchants like Andrew Crane would have paid in silver. The municipal notes were just bills of credit, good for some city fees and guaranteed by a sinking fund. It was the old state money from before the Constitution, reimagined as city money. The notes were printed locally, with crude block images of whatever the printer had on hand—wreaths, trains, soldiers with shouldered arms. The paper was cheap and fell apart in pockets. But you can read through the lines of the complaints in the *Picayune* and see that the municipal notes passed as useful dollars.

A merchant in the city reported that he had paid off a $4,000 loan to a bank and received as small change a $2 note from the American municipality and an offer to start a deposit account for 50 cents. By August, a German man named Hartman had killed himself in a city jail, under suspicion of printing his own American municipality notes; there's not much point in counterfeiting something if it's worthless. Even the staff of the *Picayune* came around. An editor dismissed the notes as "sickening," but when a frock coat was stolen out of the paper's offices in 1838, in its pockets were $15 in municipal notes. Someone else at the *Picayune* was attacked by a man with a long black beard, got away, and remarked with irony that he had held on to all the small change in his pocket: "a 12½ cent note on the Second Municipality, a check 'good for one bit' on the City Hotel, and a 6¼ cent on the Post Office." The article referred to both the municipal note and the hotel check as "shinplasters," an older term used for the slips businesses handed out as small change. Both circulated as cash, in place of the clipped picayunes of silver that had suddenly become too important for small payments.

At first, the municipal notes were only ambiguously legal. When the city passed a law in 1822 allowing itself to issue what we would today call bonds, it made it explicitly clear that the city could not act as a bank, nor "issue notes payable to bearer." That prohibition had been handed

Notes from the First Municipality, in the older, French part of New Orleans, and the Second Municipality, where the Americans lived. The note from the Second Municipality was printed crudely in 1837, right after the panic. It's worth 12½ cents, or one picayune—an eighth of a dollar. The First Municipality's note was printed at much higher quality two years later for a full dollar, or in French, *une piastre.* (Image courtesy of Randy Haynie.)

down to the municipalities when they were created in 1836. The notes passed because the city needed them, and no one objected strenuously enough. Businesses and cities all over the country, including Baltimore and Philadelphia, were producing what came to be known as hard-times money—notes and copper tokens, often struck or printed with satirical, political themes. By the end of the year, all three municipalities in New Orleans had begun to issue their own notes, backed in similar ways. Smaller towns in Louisiana adopted the same solution. Randy has hard-times notes in his collection from storekeepers in Clinton and St. Francisville, and from the police jury—something like a city council—in Opelousas.

These notes show the beginning of a slow shift in the understanding of what a dollar was. Before the panic, Americans had come to accept bank notes as proxies for the old silver dollars. But the hard-times notes, in New Orleans and elsewhere, were issued as proxies for bank notes. "A dollar" had been for three centuries a big silver coin; it was becoming a piece of paper from a bank. Even after the panic, there was some faith left that the bank notes still had value, that the crisis would pass, and that bank cashiers would hand out silver again. The municipalities in New Orleans offered to redeem their own notes "in bank notes of this city," meaning that whatever value the bank dollars still had, that was the value of the municipal dollars, too. You can read similar wording on hard-times notes from other American cities. The Deer Creek Iron Works in Harford County, Maryland, issued what it called a "bill," redeemable at its offices in store goods, iron, flour, or current bank notes of the City of Baltimore. The hard-times notes weren't pegged to a Spanish silver coin. They were pegged to what a dollar was becoming: paper bank notes from America.

In December 1839, the American municipality passed a new law explicitly authorizing it to issue notes. Even though the banks had failed and left the city scrambling for useful dollars, the mayor of New Orleans objected to the law, arguing that issuing notes was still properly a privilege for banks only. He had heard that the state legislature would soon force the banks to start handing out silver coins for paper dollars again, and insisted that it would be better to wait than to "encumber this community with a new circulating medium incomplete and inefficient." The council voted unanimously to pass the law anyway. The next day the American municipality ordered $150,500 in mostly small notes from Draper, Toppan & Co. in Philadelphia, one of the most prominent bank note engravers in America, signaling a commitment to better print quality. In 1840, the council agreed to pay its treasurer $3 per thousand for the overwhelming task of signing the notes as needed. What had been a quick solution in a crisis was now policy.

BUDDHA HEADS AND BAT WINGS: THE BEGINNING OF THE END OF THE CHINA SINK

The panic of 1837 wasn't just about Andrew Jackson or the price of cotton; it also followed a disruption in the old patterns of how silver dollars moved around the world. By the middle of the 1830s, the market for silver coins in China had begun to change in ways that were felt in America but were completely beyond the control of the White House, the cotton financiers in Liverpool, and the bankers in the City of London. New silver dollars were arriving in Guangzhou, but they were not as welcome as the old ones.

After reforms in the middle of the eighteenth century, the mints in Mexico City and Potosí had started producing more uniform coins with milled edging, already familiar in Europe from mints on the Iberian peninsula; these were the coins recognized in the American colonies as Spanish milled dollars. This meant that the reales de a ocho that shipped through Manila to China began to arrive not as hacked-off, stamped bits of silver but as consistent, high-quality coins. By the end of the eighteenth century, coined silver dollars from abroad were in common use as far north as Beijing and deep into China's domestic trade routes. Just as it had in Britain's Atlantic-coast colonies, the silver Spanish dollar became a standard for imaginary money in China, a unit of account for contracts and trade ledgers.

Traders in China developed a language to distinguish among the different kinds of foreign silver coins. The Dutch dog dollar became the "horse sword coin," for example, named for the image on the other side. After 1772, the reales de a ocho from the Americas began to feature the serene, jowly busts of Charles III and IV, the Bourbon kings of Spain;

these traded in China as "Buddha head coins." Already by 1800, almost half of the transactions in the southeastern port city of Quanzhou were denominated in Buddha heads, and local factors for the East India Company noticed that those coins in particular traded at a premium over other kinds of silver. The Buddha heads were counted, not weighed; in China, just as in the Baltic in the sixteenth century, the dollar had become something more than just silver.

Then, for the first time in arguably five hundred years, the global flow of silver began to shift direction. European traders, in particular the East India Company, had figured out a way to supply opium to China, selling it there for silver. In the second half of the 1820s, the net flow of silver swung sharply negative, away from China. Traditionally, economists explained this shift in terms of the balance of trade: Merchants in southern China started importing opium and stopped importing silver. More recently, however, Alejandra Irigoin of the London School of Economics has pointed out that the demand for silver imports in the port city of Quanzhou collapsed in the early 1820s, as growth in opium imports was only just beginning to take off. It wasn't just any kind of silver that paid for opium. Irigoin makes a crucial distinction among *types* of silver.

When the trade began, merchants in southern China paid for opium with tael, the lumps of silver that traded by weight. But they didn't buy opium with the dollar coins. China did not have its own silver mints. The high-quality, reliable silver dollars with the milled edges and the Buddha heads had become too valuable within China to leave. In the 1810s and early 1820s, however, as Spain's empire in Latin America collapsed, newly independent countries allowed private mints to open and began exporting new dollar coins of the exact same weight and purity, but with new designs. In 1823, for example, the mint at Mexico City started stamping dollars with the Aztec eagle and snake; these arrived in China as the "bat coins." The consistent quality of the Buddha heads had been part of what made the real de a ocho a unit of account in China. But now that the Bourbon kings were no longer in charge in

Mexico, their Buddha heads were no longer on the money. Nothing had changed about the quality or size of the silver dollars minted in Mexico City. New rulers meant, simply, a new design on the face of the coin.

Merchants in China didn't want to trade with the new bat coins. They trusted the old Buddha heads, and that's what they demanded as payment for tea. Even in 1831, the Court of Directors of the East India Company grumbled that they were having trouble finding silver to send to China, "the Chinese having hitherto obstinately refused to receive any Dollars excepting those of the old Spanish Coinage which since the Independence of the Colonies, having been yearly decreasing in Quantity." The collapse in Chinese demand for silver imports in the 1820s wasn't about silver. It was about the new Mexican dollars. Chinese merchants wanted the old silver dollars with the Spanish kings on them, but Spain wasn't making any more of those, because its empire had collapsed.

Around the same time, we can see a mirror image of China in the United States. Imports of silver dollar coins into the United States didn't change that much in the 1820s. The Spanish Empire had been built as a machine to supply dollar coins to the world, and independence didn't make the machine stop. Exports of silver dollar coins *out* of the United States, however, dropped sharply, from almost $10.5 million in 1821 to a brief low of $731,000 in 1830. Then, during the boom years of the 1830s, imports spiked briefly to $13 million, while exports stayed between $1 million and $5 million. There is a ton of noise in this data from year to year. Broadly, though, dollar coins continued to arrive in America and then, for the first time, stayed there. The new silver dollars from an independent Mexico—the bat coins—were unwanted in China. They got stranded in the United States, then encouraged bankers to make more loans.

Those silver dollar coins pooling in banks in the United States formed what we now call a reserve—a stock of reliable and universally accepted money. Bankers knew they had to hold a reserve out of basic prudence, to redeem their bank notes on demand. But they wanted to keep that reserve as small as possible. Silver was expensive to acquire and didn't earn a return, sitting there in the vault. State charters demanded that banks hold a reserve, but the exact requirements differed from state to state, and even charter to charter.

The basic monetary theory you can read in any introductory college textbook says that when the government either lowers the cost of reserves or lowers the requirement to hold reserves, banks will make more loans. This process is called the money multiplier. It assumes a constant relationship: more reserves, more loans, more money. The problem with this model of banking is that it assumes that governments have way more power than they actually do. As we relearn every recession, bankers make loans when they feel like it. When they don't, they don't. "When they feel like it" doesn't seem very technical or precise, but the money multiplier isn't that technical or precise, either.

Before the boom of the 1830s, bank lending in America had been restrained by both silver reserves *and* banker confidence. To make loans, bank officers had to believe both that there were good loans to be made and that there would be foreign silver dollars or gold coins around when needed. Banks expanded across the South and West of America as bankers saw opportunities to lend—as the Jackson administration forced Native nations west, as cotton plantations found markets in London and sugar plantations found markets in Philadelphia and New York, as farmers in the Midwest floated hogs and whiskey to New Orleans on flatboats.

Starting in the mid-1830s, banks also began to hold more coins, both in absolute numbers and as a proportion of their loans; their reserves went up. Chinese merchants had rejected the new Mexican dollars, which began to move into America. Again, the new silver didn't *cause* new loans. But Americans did have a lot of loans to make, and the new Mexican silver dollars that remained in the United States made banks feel confident that silver would be available when needed. The banking bubble in America inflated in part because the old path of the silver dollar, from Latin America to China, started to break down with the end of the Spanish Empire.

SOUND BANK DOLLARS IN LOUISIANA

In most years of the 1820s and 1830s, close to half of the total American imports of precious metals—silver, gold, bars, coins, everything—came from Mexico. New Orleans sat on the old silver routes that left Veracruz and passed through Havana, and imported more silver than any other American city. It took trust to move bills of exchange and silver around an ocean; in Louisiana, the most reliable way to get silver dollars from Mexico was to use the Lizardis, a family of merchants who left Mexico after independence, taking their wealth and their connections with them to Paris, London, and New Orleans. Some of the Lizardis likely settled in New Orleans because that's where the silver was coming ashore in America; they simply put themselves at the other end of the same trade. In 1833, Manuel Julián de Lizardi became an American citizen, vouched for by Edmond Forstall, the man who would become the president of the Citizens' Bank of Louisiana.

Forstall shows up now in histories as one of the architects of the property banks that borrowed in Europe against the value of slaves and land in Louisiana. But there's another tradition that sees him as a hero of sound money—where pieces of paper are always worth the same predictable amount of silver or gold. Forstall had his hands on the flow of silver coming into New Orleans, and as president of the Citizens' Bank and then later as a state legislator he consistently argued that banks should have to hold enough silver and gold to survive a run and always redeem their notes at par—at exactly their face value.

Just before the panic of 1837, several members of the city's Association of Bank Presidents considered offering a premium on Mexican silver dollars, paying more than a bank dollar to buy them. Forstall, as president of the Citizens' Bank, was worried that this would mean that New Orleans bank dollars would be worth less than silver dollars, and so he persuaded the association instead to use his own bank's bills of exchange payable in London to import silver from Cuba and Mexico, through the Lizardis. The silver dollars started arriving in 1836, but by the summer of 1837, several months into the panic, the banks started turning down the extra dollars. They didn't need to buy silver if they weren't going to hand it over for their own bank notes. People in New Orleans had run to banks and then bars demanding silver in the spring of 1837; there was no reason to encourage them to keep asking for silver in the summer.

The banks didn't all collapse when they stopped handing over silver, and neither did their bank notes. In New Orleans, most banks didn't suspend because they *couldn't* pay out silver; silver in the city's bank vaults remained roughly steady over the same period. They suspended because they *didn't want to* pay out silver. They stopped the run by holding on to the silver they had left. That was just something a bank could decide to do, and there wasn't much recourse. Every bank charter had been granted to serve a specific purpose, for a specific group of people. Sometimes that purpose and those people were important enough that the state looked the other way while the bank looked out for its best interests. This left the value of bank notes uncertain. For someone holding a bank note in New Orleans, there weren't any silver dollars after the panic. But there might be some, sometime.

The bank presidents of New Orleans spent the summer of 1838 negotiating when they would start redeeming their notes for silver again. It was a decision they had to take together. The banks were all holding each other's notes, both as a favor to each other and as a threat: Any bank that paid first and alone would immediately run out of silver. Forstall continued as the strongest voice among the presidents to start redeeming immediately, without conditions. By September of that year, however, he had resigned as president of the Citizens' Bank, after losing a vote among the stockholders. The bank claimed that Forstall had been too close to lenders in London, but it is also likely that the stockholders—the only people who could get loans from the bank—wanted looser terms than Forstall would offer.

After the panic, Americans realized they didn't have enough control over their banks under the charter system. The public mood in Louisiana had swung hard against banks, and property banks in particular. Already in May 1837, on the day after the run on banks and bars for silver in New Orleans, the *Picayune* consoled itself by saying that "things *cannot become worse*"—its italics, not mine. There would be no choice but to open up the ledgers and clean up the banks, making them both simple and stable. "Banks are necessary," the paper concluded, "but then Banks must be under wholesome restrictions and salutary influence." America had given its banks the exclusive right to print dollars. In return they had been irresponsible and made too many dodgy loans. The old bank charter system wasn't working anymore. In Louisiana, a few well-connected merchants and planters had gotten exactly the banks and loans they wanted during the good times, and now everyone else was getting by in the hard times with a hastily assembled system of handwritten promissory notes and municipal paper dollars.

This frustration was shared all over the country. More than half of the states watered down the privileges of the charter system by passing a free banking law before the Civil War. Under the new laws, bankers no longer needed pull with the legislature to get a charter with other shareholders as a limited liability corporation; they just got together and opened a bank. This wasn't deregulation. Rather, it was a new, consistent set of regulations, available to anyone.

New York's free banking law in 1838—the most influential, and one of the first—made a profound change to the way its banks issued their notes. Under the charter system, bank notes had been backed by whatever assets the bank happened to specialize in—short-term commercial discounts, for example, or longer-term agricultural mortgages. Under New York's free banking law, to issue a note, a bank had to buy exactly one kind of asset: public debt. A bank could buy bonds from the federal government, from New York State, or if approved even the debt of other states. The New York law was supposed to make bank notes more reliable, and there's some evidence that it did. But it also did the state a favor, by creating a market for New York State bonds. This is essentially the same arrangement we have today. The Federal

Reserve notes you hold in your wallet are backed, one to one, by federal debt.

Chartered bankers in Louisiana proved more resistant. In 1839, Henry Dawson in Natchez, Mississippi, sued the Atchafalaya Railroad & Banking Company in Louisiana, arguing that since the bank no longer paid out silver for its notes, it had violated the terms of its charter, was therefore no longer a corporation, and could no longer collect on his note. The district court in New Orleans dismissed the suit, pointing out that the state had an "immense pecuniary interest in maintaining the credit of its banks, which in point of fact furnish the currency of the country"—dollar bank notes. Banks were so important that even when they had clearly violated their charters, the state could still decide to keep them going. To make this clear, the legislature then passed a law confirming that banks could stay open even if they weren't redeeming silver for notes.

Anyone who's worked as a banking reporter will tell you that a bank in trouble *always* says it's not insolvent, just illiquid—it needs some time to get cash. It's not a bad tactic. The bank might get some help from the state, or it might get lucky with a private loan. For a bank to fail, the state has to actually step in and say the bank is insolvent, that help and luck are never coming. In Louisiana, the state's sixteen chartered banks just stumbled along with a smaller stock of notes, most of which were worth less than they had been before the panic. After 1839, though, the problem became harder to ignore. Prices for cotton and sugar fell again, and prices for everything began falling precipitously; this is true whether you look at national prices for consumer goods or prices on the levee for flatboat products like pork and whiskey. The country was going through a deflation, one that New Orleans couldn't avoid by keeping its banks alive.

Just letting prices drop again after an inflationary boom is a simple solution, yet historically people caught in deflations seem to have consistently hated it. Sellers don't like to negotiate prices down. Deflation is a painful, slow process. Hard-times dollars like the municipal notes in

New Orleans were a way for cities to stall deflation, issuing dollars into an economy as the banks pulled them out. But they were not enough to resist the drag of collapsing cotton and sugar prices, commodities beyond the control of any city. Old loans made at the top of an inflation became harder to pay off after prices dropped again, which made the assets on bank balance sheets even more likely to fail. By 1842, as Forstall later wrote, "the Banks were prostrated, public and private credit were ruined," and Louisianans were more openly considering repudiating the debt the state legislature had taken on to support the property banks. As the property banks failed to make payments on their bonds to foreign investors, Louisiana's potential debt for its banks was vastly higher than that of any other state. Other states had borrowed money for canals; Louisiana was on the hook for almost $23 million, almost entirely for its property banks.

"WE HAVE FALLEN ON EVIL TIMES"

There was enough frustration with banks that in 1842, Louisiana finally passed a bill Forstall had written and championed: All banks in New Orleans would have to hold a painfully conservative reserve of silver or gold against notes and deposits. Bank charters had always instructed banks to hold some silver dollars out of prudence, to ensure that the banks could redeem their notes. Now the banks would be forced to hold a lot more silver. Virginia had already passed a bill in 1837 requiring a silver or gold reserve of at least a fifth of bank notes. Georgia in 1838 demanded a quarter. Ohio in 1839 got to a third. Louisiana's bank bill added two more restrictions. Banks would have to carry a one-third silver or gold reserve against both notes *and deposits:* If it was a liability and someone could demand a silver dollar for it, the banks had to hold a reserve against it. The other two-thirds of the assets held against bank notes and deposits would have to be commercial paper—again, short-term discounts against promissory notes from merchants, secured by the actual, physical inventory of the city's cotton and sugar factors.

Praise for Forstall's bill can get flowery. *The Banker's Magazine,* looking back in 1877, described it as "among the most enlightened pieces of banking legislation to be found on the statute books of any country." A banking historian writing in 1951 described it as "progress over everything that had as yet been achieved in America." Bray Hammond, who in 1957 published what's still the standard account of nineteenth-century American banking, concluded that the law "seems to me in substance the wisest adaptation of practice to environment in any banking law I know." Before that law, Hammond argued, a bank note was just a promissory note. With the law, it became far easier to believe that a bank note wouldn't just be ideally worth a silver Mexican dollar sometime in the future, but that it would always and reliably be worth nothing less. Forstall had laid out one side of an argument we still recognize: Should a dollar always be worth the same thing? If so, what are we willing to give up to keep it? For Forstall, sound money was worth closing the city's weak banks and radically shrinking the number of dollars in circulation, regardless of how it might halt lending or accelerate an already painful deflation.

For most of the city, the new banking law was a disaster. "We have fallen on evil times," one bank cashier wrote after the bill passed, "and our Legislature are doing every thing in their power to hasten the ruin of our state." To buy enough silver to meet the reserve requirement, banks had to sell some of their loans and hold off on making new ones. It became even harder to get a loan. In July 1841, banks in New Orleans held $46 million in loans. By January 1843, that had dropped to $20 million. Over the same period, Louisiana bank notes in circulation dropped from almost $7 million to just over $1 million.

Part of the city's problem was the disappearance of banks themselves. Over the same eighteen months, the total number of banks in the city dropped from sixteen to six. For a few of the stronger New Orleans banks, where notes were discounted at only 2.5 percent, the law had worked. Notes from the Citizens' Bank, though, were discounted at 50 percent, and notes from the Atchafalaya Railroad & Banking Com-

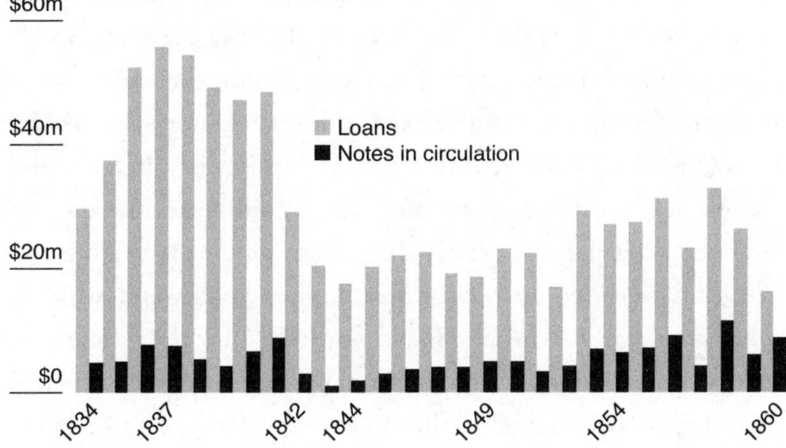

Illustration by Evan Applegate. (Data from Stephen Caldwell, *A Banking History of Louisiana.*)

pany were worth nothing. After the panic of 1837, the banks of New Orleans had remained in suspended animation, waiting for someone to declare them dead. It was Edmond Forstall's banking law that did it.

Before Forstall's bill, all the bank notes and municipal notes in the city traded at roughly equal discounts. After the law passed, the difference between bank notes and municipal notes became clear. Good bank notes could be sunk at the bank and converted to silver at any time, under a rigorous law that forced the banks to make it possible. Municipal notes could sink as payment for city fees, or for bank notes, only sometime in the future. Forstall's bill destroyed the value of the municipal notes.

On Monday, May 16, 1842, seven of the city's banks started handing out silver again. There was a run on those banks, for a day; they put all their clerks to the task of handing out silver, and they survived. On Thursday the value of the municipal notes began to drop, and on Saturday the Creole merchants from the covered markets marched over the neutral ground and sacked the bill brokers on Camp Street. Sound money was good for confidence in the American bankers who kept their doors open, but it shattered the value of the dollars in the pockets of grocers and butchers, the same dollars that had been issued to make up for the hole the banks had left after the panic of 1837.

The day before the currency riot, Denis Prieur, the mayor, was already alarmed by the drop in value of the municipal notes; he asked the councils of all three municipalities to meet within a day. In front of the crowd the next morning, he promised he would make sure the notes were redeemed at par—at exactly their face value. That evening, however, he sat with the council of the French municipality and made clear what he actually had in mind. He did not intend for the notes to keep circulating at par. He wanted them out of the city's economy at par. The municipal notes had offered a solution after the panic of 1837. In parts of New Orleans, they had been the only money available. But with the panic over, the power to manufacture dollars went back to the banks.

That night the French municipality approved a loan from the city's banks of $200,000 to buy back its notes. Meeting at the same time on the other side of the neutral ground, the finance committee of the American municipality presented a report with a plan to buy back the municipal notes by issuing treasury certificates that would bear interest, at face values between $20 and $500—swapping out small money for big money. The measure passed that night, and Prieur signed it the next day.

The councils continued to offer discounts on taxes paid in municipal notes. The discounts indicate that the notes were still trading under par; a New York bank reporter the next year listed the notes at a discount of 50 percent. The finance committee of the American municipality, meeting as a group to prevent fraud, began keeping records of the notes that returned, and regularly burned stacks of them to keep notes from slipping back out into the city. In December the council destroyed the plates used to print the notes shipped down from Draper, Toppan & Co. in Philadelphia. Just as had been true in Maryland before the Revolution, the city's notes didn't have value just because they had been issued. Sinking them—pulling them back in while maintaining at least some value—took a careful performance of both finance and public rituals. There had been $345,000 of the Second Municipality's notes in circulation in May 1842. By June 1845, that had dropped to just under $23,000.

There has always been tension between the goals of sound money and those of functional money. As we'll see in the next chapter, sound money is inflexible; in a panic, it can leave some people without any money at all, forcing a painful deflation on everyone. A reserve of silver Mexican dollars offers what seems like a simple mechanism. If you can make only three times the loans as the coins and bars that you hold, then you can't get into trouble. But people are creative. They will find ways of getting into trouble. The advent of sound money in America did not end financial panics, and it did not ensure that dollars work equally well for everyone who uses them.

NEW GOLD FROM CALIFORNIA AND THE END OF THE SILVER DOLLAR IN AMERICA

Andrew Crane, the carriage dealer who had moved to New Orleans in 1835, continued his trade through the 1840s, moving in 1845 to a warehouse with a private entrance to the St. Charles, the city's first luxury hotel. Crane had been a stockholder in the bank that had built the hotel; the bank closed with the sound banking law in 1842, but the hotel remained, built to the neoclassical look and scale of the U.S. Capitol. The St. Charles also held regular slave auctions in a seventy-foot-wide octagonal bar with a dome at its center, surrounded by a gallery and supported by columns. Crane's move had put him at the center of the city's slave trade, and in 1850 there's an abrupt shift in Crane's accounting, new records of a completely different trade: He had decided to become a sugar planter.

Crane auctioned off the entire contents of his warehouse: buggies and phaetons, his last yards of lace and fringe. He netted about $8,000. It must have been handed to him in bank notes, because he began buying with cash at the slave auctions, probably in the octagonal bar of the St. Charles Hotel. On January 11, he paid for Henry, about twenty-seven years old, $774 in cash, "the Vendor here by acknowledging the Receipt of the same." On the same day he paid for Mariah, about eighteen years old, $575 in cash. On March 15, for $3,325 in ready money—cash, handed over that day—he bought Noel Archer, about twenty-five; Andrew Brown, about twenty-five; Sam Royal, about twenty-three; and Primus Brunton, about twenty-five.

In February, Crane opened an account with the plantation supply merchants Druilhet & Laboval and began buying salt, flour, clothing for slaves, things he'd need to live upriver. He began shipping it on the *Gypsy,* a steamer that stopped at a landing near the convent in St. James Parish, and contracted with Irish ditchers to begin digging. In April he bought land, a strip running straight back from the east bank of the river, just above the convent. Crane handed over $900 in cash to Adolphe Malarcher, the heir to a sugar planter who had fled Haiti during the revolution; then Crane began to run out of the cash from his warehouse auction. He signed a stack of $500 promissory notes to Malarcher, written in French in units of piastre—still the French word for a silver dollar coin. Malarcher held the notes without bothering to discount them, handing them back over the next five years as Crane paid them off, and then canceled them with his characteristic slashing ink blots.

Andrew Crane made his move upriver on cash and credit at the beginning of another period of confidence among American bankers. This came in part from the long nineteenth-century story of expansion in America's industries and its exports—wheat and hogs, cotton and sugar. But in the 1850s, American bankers also had a brand-new source of reserves. John Sutter, a serial debtor from Switzerland who had lost his dry goods business in Missouri in the panic of 1837, had found gold in the chutes of his sawmill in California in 1848. That year the territory of California produced $10 million in gold. The next year it produced $40 million. By 1850, the year the territory became a state, production had grown to $50 million. It stayed at or above that level for the next decade.

The United States had already been through a gold rush in the late 1820s, after the discovery of gold placers in North Carolina and parts of the Cherokee Nation that would later become Georgia. That new gold from the South, and the Mexican silver that stayed in America instead of going to China, had begun to change the politics of minting in the 1830s. Congress recognized that the U.S. Mint had an obligation to provide small change, and made it cheaper and quicker for customers at the mint to arrive with silver and leave with exactly the coins they wanted, including dimes and half dimes for small purchases. This steady increase in small change made it more tolerable for cities all over America to start to wind down their municipal note issues, just as New Orleans did in 1842. For the first time in the United States, small silver coins had started to work for everyone.

California was wildly out of scale with everything that had come before. In that first decade of panning and mining, most of the California gold stayed in the United States, absorbed into American purses and American banks. Before the find at Sutter's Mill, the New Orleans branch of the U.S. Mint had never received more than $25,000 a year in gold, all of it foreign pieces for recoining. New Orleans was one of the first ports for the newly wealthy who returned from California, and in 1849 it took in $678,000 in gold, all of it from the Sierra Nevada. By 1850, the *Picayune* reported that the New Orleans Mint, like the one in Philadelphia, would get its own fund to stock gold bullion so that it could hand out coins on demand for the dust coming in on ships from California. Gold coins were suddenly so culturally important in New Orleans that in April 1850, the same month Andrew Crane bought his sugar plantation, a brand-new gold double eagle was placed in the cornerstone of a new building on Lafayette Square.

In 1851, the director of the U.S. Mint reported to Congress that operations in the past year had been "unprecedented in our history." The value of the coins coming out of Philadelphia, he explained, was twice what it had been in 1847, and four times what it had been in 1843. The mint had never made $20 gold double eagles before 1850. That year, the mint at Philadelphia made 1.2 million of them. The branch mint in New Orleans made 141,000. The amount of gold and silver in American banks and pockets more than doubled in a decade, from $120 million in 1847 to $260 million in 1857. Bank notes in circulation made the same climb, from $105 million to $214 million.

By 1857, Congress was finally ready to decide that the United States could get along without letting foreign coins circulate as legal tender—including the silver dollars from Mexico. After Sutter's Mill, Americans had their own source of precious metal. They took the system of bank notes, bills of exchange, and promissory notes they had built atop the silver dollar, and simply swapped in gold as a new reserve. In the United States, the silver dollar, a standard essentially unbroken since the first joachimsthaler of the 1520s, had become the American dollar.

Andrew Crane wouldn't have experienced the gold from California as a revolution in money. For him it was just a year of easier credit, a good time to become a sugar planter. At his plantation upriver, he didn't need the cash economy of bank notes anymore, and he likely never touched a gold eagle coin. In St. James Parish, Crane returned to an older kind of trade in paper, one that would have been familiar to a tobacco planter in Maryland or Virginia 150 years earlier. He opened an account with a sugar factor in New Orleans, Richard Nugent & Co., which credited Crane's account with sales to sugar buyers on the East Coast, then paid off accounts Crane kept with other merchants in New Orleans: D. W. & F. Belden, which sold fur, silk, and wool hats; I. Hobbs & Co., a bootmaker; Richards, Slocomb & Co., which provided tools, nails, and lumber. Crane also purchased more enslaved men for promissory notes. The notes passed hand to hand as cash before they returned to Crane, each time duly signed on the back.

In 1853, as credit continued to ease, the Louisiana legislature let the Citizens' Bank lend to sugar planters again. Crane negotiated a mortgage for stock in the bank, which he renewed later that decade. Then he borrowed by writing out four promissory notes, good for payment over time at his factor's office, for $3,000 each. The Citizens' Bank did not pay out any kind of cash, but opened a deposit account for Crane, who sent checks to New Orleans, payable at the bank. Crane hired enslaved workers from his neighbor, Euphiman Hebert, who wrote that "the girl Emma" had complained about conditions at Crane's house. A year later Crane gave Hebert a promissory note for $80, payable at his sugar factor's office in New Orleans, for "services of a girl Emma." Crane instructed the factor to charge the note to his account.

Most of us learned a story of money where silver or gold became paper. First, people handed coins to each other. Then the paper represented the coin; then the paper ascended to something else. I hope if you're still attached to that history, you can start to let it go. Since the beginning of this story, paper promises and silver coins have moved together in the same markets, providing different kinds of dollars to different people for different uses. Crane hadn't ascended past the physical dollar. Rather, he had reverted to an older kind of exchange, where promissory notes and ledgers moved nails and hats and whiskey upriver, sugar back downriver, and enslaved men and women around St. James Parish. The story of money—and the story of the dollar—don't pass cleanly, medium to medium, metal to paper. We never got rid of the dollars that sit on ledgers. As we'll see in the next chapter, that's still how we manufacture almost all our dollars today.

5

Bank Notes Become Bank Deposits

Hawarden, 1932

IRVING FISHER'S BIG IDEA

In October 1932, Irving Fisher spent two days at Iowa State University. Fisher liked to talk. He met with students, gave a speech about the economics of Prohibition, then gave another speech about the Depression, this one broadcast to most of central Iowa on the university's AM radio station. That year bank failures had again drained dollars out of the economy. Prices and wages had begun to drop, which meant that people were earning less money while their debts remained the same. This was particularly a problem in Iowa, a state of indebted farmers whose banks had been hit hard.

Herbert Hoover, the president of the United States, was frantically trying to keep banks open and dollars stable, but the problem was so broad that solutions became a parlor game in America. Everyone either had an idea or was ready to listen to one. After Fisher's broadcast in Iowa, the professor in charge of the station sent Fisher a letter, forwarding cards from all over the state, asking for more details—from a farmer, from two hardware store owners, from an assistant cashier at a bank who was grateful the station didn't play any jazz. They had all asked about one of Fisher's solutions for the bank problem: scrip dollars.

"Scrip" is a broad term, but it usually refers to locally produced money, used when nothing else is available—like the colonial bills of credit, or the municipal notes in New Orleans. In his broadcast, Fisher had mentioned Hawarden, Iowa, a small city on the Big Sioux River on the border with South Dakota. Charles Zylstra, a Dutch immigrant with some experience in community banking, had talked the town into an experiment: Storekeepers in Hawarden were already accepting scrip dollars, guaranteed by the city itself. Once again, bank dollars had failed so spectacularly in 1932 that there was panicked interest all over Iowa and all over the country about ways to replace the dollars that were locked behind bank doors. As late as the 1930s, Americans were still relying on a colonial idea to save their local dollars.

It wasn't paper bank notes that had failed that year, though. It was bank deposits. Since the panic of 1837, the United States had steadily found ways to make paper dollar notes more secure, ultimately taking the privilege of note printing away from commercial banks and handing it to twelve new regional public banks—the Federal Reserve. But bankers are creative. By the end of the nineteenth century, they had again changed how dollars worked in America, a change so thorough it's easy now to take it for granted. Banks in America stopped producing new dollars as printed notes, and started producing them as deposits, written down on a ledger. Dollar notes became dollar deposits.

The bank deposits were just as fragile as the bank notes had been. At the start of the Great Depression in 1932 and 1933, Americans ran scared to their banks, ready to swap deposits on a bank ledger for the secure, physical certainty of paper notes from the Federal Reserve banks. But a lot of Americans found their bank doors closed, their deposits frozen. The decisions that led to all those closed doors rested in part on a new set of ideas about money, tested in Britain and adopted in America: the gold standard. Over the nineteenth century, banks in America had started holding more gold than silver as a reserve, as new gold from California flooded into the rest of the country. The U.S. Department of the Treasury turned every remaining bank note dollar into sound money, building an intricate system that would swap any paper dollar for a fixed amount of gold. As we saw in the last chapter, sound money is a good idea in theory, and it works well for some people. But perfectly sound money forced a long deflation in America at the end of the nineteenth century, and during frequent panics it forced bankers to liquidate everything they could, then close their doors, leaving the fate of their remaining deposits uncertain. That is what had happened, again, in the fall of 1932.

The city of Hawarden became famous for its scrip dollars. Charles Zylstra had not invented the idea. But in Hawarden, for the first time that Irving Fisher knew of, actual merchants were accepting real paper scrip. After his speech at Iowa State that October, Fisher took the train west to Hawarden to see for himself. He stayed only a couple of hours. Zylstra was out of town, but the president of the city's Chamber of Commerce arranged some conversations at city hall. Then Fisher did what he always did: He made sure there was a quote for the paper.

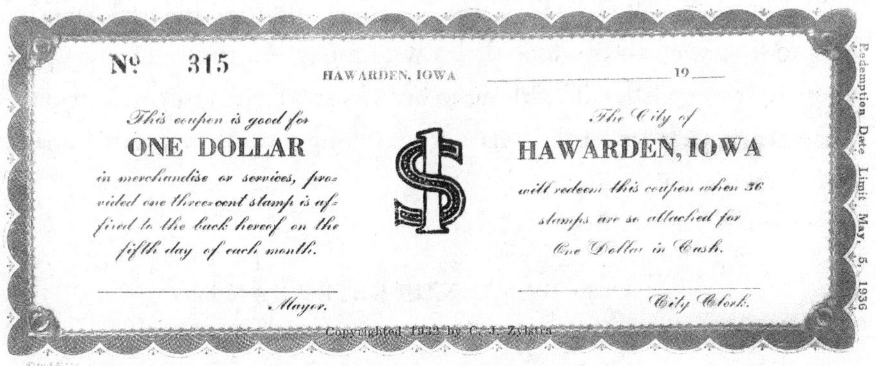

Nº 315

HAWARDEN, IOWA ______________ 19___

This coupon is good for
ONE DOLLAR
in merchandise or services, provided one three-cent stamp is affixed to the back hereof on the fifth day of each month.

____
Mayor.

The City of
HAWARDEN, IOWA
will redeem this coupon when 36 stamps are so attached for One Dollar in Cash.

____
City Clerk.

Copyrighted 1932 by C. J. Zylstra

Redemption Date Limit May, 5, 1936

A scrip dollar printed and used in Hawarden, Iowa, during the Great Depression. The Hawarden scrip was copied all over the country. (Image courtesy of Sean Trask.)

"The stamped money or scrip used by the city of Hawarden, Iowa is the most interesting experiment I know for combatting the depression," Fisher told the *Hawarden Independent.* A correspondent for the Associated Press picked up the remarks and filed them for national distribution; anything Dr. Irving Fisher of Yale said was news. On November 28, Fisher's column for papers all over the country declared

Hawarden's experiment a success. Reporters, politicians, and the curious all over America began to think of Fisher, Hawarden, and scrip dollars as inextricable parts of the same idea. Delegations from cities all over the Midwest arrived to see how the scrip worked. By December, Hawarden could watch itself on a Pathé newsreel about scrip at the Tivoli Theatre on Central Avenue. Irving Fisher had put a railroad town in northwestern Iowa at the center of the last widespread experiment in making dollars outside America's banks, an experiment still less than a hundred years old today.

It's easy to forget about what dollars are when they work, but in 1932 dollars held as bank deposits weren't working. One outcome of the New Deal in the early 1930s was to finally force banks to start paying to insure their deposits. The insurance made bank dollars more reliable, and over the rest of the twentieth century dollar deposits in an American bank became the most prized money anyone in the world could hold. But in the fall of 1932, it was once again up to individual Americans to find ways to produce their own money. All those Iowans who wrote to Irving Fisher after his radio broadcast weren't just reaching out to a celebrity. Their bank dollars were failing, and they needed a replacement.

STATE BANK NOTES BECAME STATE BANK DEPOSITS

The shift from bank notes to bank deposits started during the Civil War. In a war, a lot of things need to be paid for very quickly, and governments get creative about money. In the 1830s Andrew Jackson had vetoed the national charter of the Second Bank of the United States, ending its special status with the federal government and turning it into just a big bank in Pennsylvania. Abraham Lincoln had always been critical of that decision. To pay for the war, he yanked control of Union dollars back from the states.

In 1862, the Union Treasury issued its own U.S. notes—what came to be known as greenbacks, named for the color of their ink. We now colloquially call any U.S. dollars greenbacks, but functionally those original U.S. notes don't bear much resemblance to the way dollars work now. Greenbacks were structured like the colonial bills of credit, and were explicitly modeled on bills of credit Britain had used to pay for the Napoleonic Wars. The federal government could use its notes to pay for anything except interest on its debt, which it still had to pay out in coin. The new notes were legal tender, and Americans could hand them back to the Treasury for any taxes except tariffs on imports, which also had to be paid in coin.

Just as with the colonial bills of credit, the Union created a sinking fund for its greenbacks. Some of the coins paid in as tariffs went into the fund, which the secretary of the Treasury could "from time to time" use to redeem the greenbacks—to buy them back with silver or gold coins. It was a weak promise, but the fund held some financial meaning as backing for the notes. During the war, the private markets in New York that swapped greenbacks for gold swung frantically back and forth with the outcome of each battle. Union victories raised the likelihood of an eventual redemption and therefore the value of the greenback.

The Union government also created a brand-new national bank charter. Remember that before the war almost every bank answered to a state, with a state charter to offer local loans and local bank notes. The new federal charter created national banks—commercial banks that answered to the federal government instead of a single state. If your town has a First National Bank of Your Town, it was chartered under this law. National banks issued their own dollar notes, known as blackbacks—again, for the color of their ink. Just like the old printed notes that state-chartered merchant banks in New Orleans handed out for discounts, the blackbacks sat on a national bank's balance sheet, paired to an asset—a loan—that would provide a return over time. What had changed was the asset. To print blackbacks, a national bank had to buy bonds from the U.S. Treasury. National banks, whether they specialized in loans to merchants or farmers, always lent to Washington.

The new national bank charters also guaranteed that blackbacks would be sound money—always redeemable for gold. If a national bank failed to redeem its own notes at its own counters, a brand-new federal bank examiner, the Office of the Comptroller of the Currency, would take over the bank and all its federal debts, and any remaining notes from the failed bank could be redeemed directly at the Department of the Treasury. The Union government also taxed state bank notes at a punishing 10 percent. Salmon Chase, wartime secretary of the Treasury, wanted to get the state banks out of the precarious business of printing dollars, and he did. State-chartered banks stopped issuing their own bank notes.

Before the war, when state banks had to settle accounts with each other over long distances, they used the old silver dollars or, far more often, wrote each other drafts, a kind of check for bankers. Just like the dollar bills printed by state banks, the drafts were accepted at a discount—the farther they traveled and the worse the reputation of the issuing bank, the steeper the discount. But during the war, banks began to buy Treasury bonds and ship them to each other, to avoid having to pay the discount; a bond from the federal government functioned as big money, for one bank to pay another. The new blackback notes from the national banks moved around the country at a lower discount as well. Bank note dollars were no longer defined by a state or a city or an individual bank. Under the dramatic consolidation of power during the Civil War, bank note dollars in the Union began to resemble what we would think of now as a single national currency.

Monetary sovereignty is imperfect, though, and people are clever. Both national banks and state banks began to get around the restrictions on bank notes by producing more of a different kind of dollar: deposits. This is the same kind of dollar you have right now in your bank account. Deposits appear to be an operation that starts with you: You hand your dollar bills over to a bank teller, and those dollars show up in your account as a deposit. From your perspective, it looks as if the bank is keeping your dollars safe. From the bank's perspective, it looks as if the bank has borrowed your dollars. That much is all true, but it's not the full story. Deposits can also start with the bank: When the bank gives you a brand-new loan, it's also producing brand-new deposit dollars from scratch.

How Deposits Happen

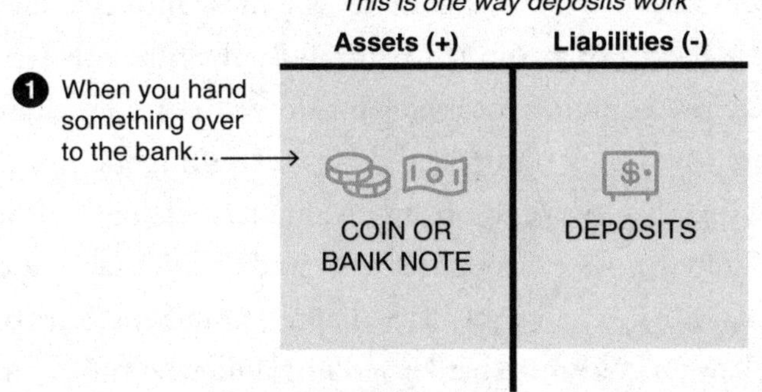

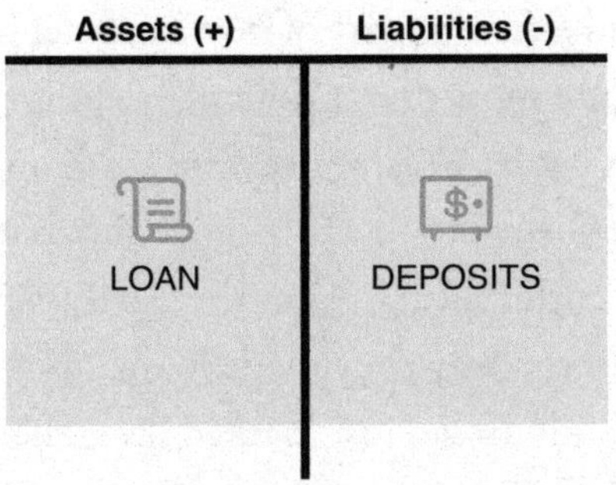

Illustration by Evan Applegate.

Think back to how banks in the early nineteenth century discounted promissory notes by handing out bank notes. The bank made a loan, and the bank notes it handed out were brand-new dollars. Banks did the same thing with deposits. Just as they had printed brand-new bank notes, commercial banks would credit a borrower's account with a record on a ledger of brand-new deposit dollars. This is still what happens when you take out a bank loan: The bank simply credits you with new deposits. You can then transfer these to someone else's account at another bank, to pay a bill from a contractor or the electric company. The bank sees your loan as an asset, paired with the liability of the brand-new deposits, which you can withdraw or transfer whenever you like.

Deposits are an old idea. Money changers in twelfth-century Venice kept an oral record of what they held on deposit, calling out transfers among different depositors. This matches the most intuitive idea about deposits, as a record of a coin left behind. By the fifteenth century, though, it was also common for merchants in Venice to overdraw their own accounts when they transferred deposits to someone else—essentially borrowing that overdraft from the money changer. This Italian system migrated north through Bruges and Amsterdam, and eventually to England. As we saw in the last chapter, simple histories of banking tend to focus on goldsmith bankers in England, who took gold on deposit. But again, that kind of deposit is only part of the story. The older Italian tradition, where the banker notes a loan as a brand-new deposit—that's still a crucial part of how banking works today. It's how we now manufacture most of our dollars.

Dollars did not evolve in America *from* bank notes *to* bank deposits. Both notes and deposits sat on the balance sheets of commercial banks in the early nineteenth century. After the Civil War, the state-chartered banks just changed the way they made loans; they avoided the heavily taxed bank notes and instead just marked down new loans on their balance sheets as new dollar deposits. Just after the Civil War, Americans held $590 million in cash—coins and printed dollar notes—and $1 billion in deposits. By 1900, cash in hand had grown to $1.2 billion, but deposits had grown out of proportion with cash, to $7.3 billion. By 1930, Americans held $3.8 billion in cash, and almost $51 billion in deposits.

This is the system that began to unravel in the early 1930s. There are a lot of things that caused the Great Depression. But one way to think

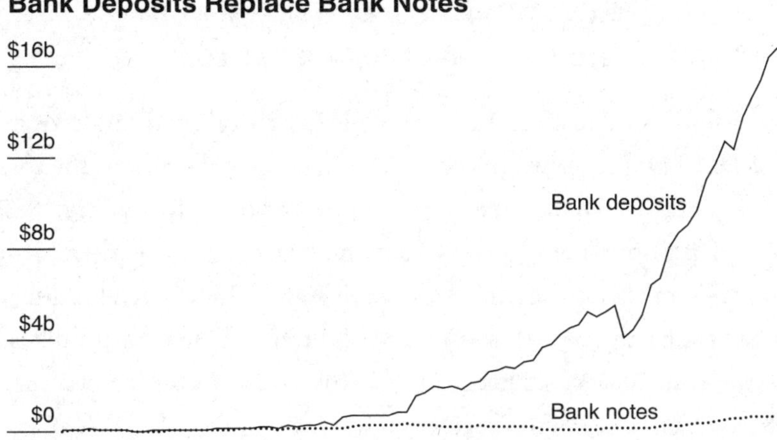

Illustration by Evan Applegate. (Data from Milton Friedman and Anna Schwartz, *A Monetary History of the United States, 1857–1960.*)

about how it accelerated around America is that as mortgages and business loans began to fail, the deposits at the banks that held those loans looked uncertain. People withdrew what they could, forcing banks to either convert deposits to cash or suspend—prevent withdrawals altogether, leaving the value of any remaining deposits uncertain.

There were about five hundred bank suspensions in 1928. In 1932, there were about fifteen hundred. In 1933, there were just over twenty-seven hundred. In October 1932, when Hawarden introduced its first scrip dollars, Americans held $4.9 billion in cash, but deposits had dropped to just under $40 billion; they had collapsed by a fifth in just two years. Even these numbers are somewhat optimistic. A lot of banks stayed open in the early years of the Depression, but came to quiet agreements with their customers to leave deposits untouched. The panic of 1837 started a decades-long process of regulation to make bank notes both safer for Americans and more useful to the federal government. At the beginning of the Great Depression, it was the bank deposits that failed.

BANKS WERE FRAGILE WELL BEFORE THE DEPRESSION

Hawarden, founded almost a century and a half ago, still thinks of itself as a relaxed English town in a prim Dutch county. Ask about the town's origins, and you will inevitably hear about the theft. In January 1872, a party of fifty-five men in horse-drawn sleighs, many of them armed Union veterans of the Civil War, stole the safe in Hawarden holding the county property records, took it to a Dutch settlement, and declared that the county seat had been moved. The safe was eventually returned to Hawarden. The county seat was not.

"It was a bunch of drunken Hollanders," said Mary Johnson. "It was a happy bunch of guys." Mary volunteers as Hawarden's city historian; her own grandmother told her stories about homesteading. Mary laughed as she told her version of the theft of the county seat, where the man in Hawarden in charge of the property records escaped out the back disguised in his wife's dress, afraid for his life. Julie Hummel, sitting beside her, started to laugh as well; she hadn't heard the part about the dress.

Mary and Julie met me in the summer of 2021 at the offices of the Hawarden Chamber of Commerce, tucked on the second floor of a 1935 brick building on Central that used to be the high school. They were wistful about the 1950s and 1960s in Hawarden, when Central was packed on Saturday nights and the merchants once flew Santa Claus in on a helicopter. Julie pointed out that farms had gotten bigger and more automated; it just didn't take as many families anymore to do the same job. Hawarden was founded as a railroad town, and when the trains stopped moving through, the town withered. The old story about the heist is a way to talk about culture: All around us the Dutch have prospered, keeping their children in town. We, the English, have struggled.

I had traveled to Hawarden to talk to Mary and Julie about any family memories of the Depression, but Mary remembered only that her family had to work long hours to keep their drugstore open. She said her family talked more about the Flood of 1926, and that her mother had money in the Hawarden State Bank when it failed the next year. Like any two people who have spent a lifetime in the same place, Mary and Julie can navigate Hawarden through landmarks that have disappeared, and together they figured out where the Hawarden State Bank had been by working their way through all the stores that had replaced it. They agreed that the old bank building still sits on the corner of Central and Ninth, a stylized granite castle with a front door set a couple of steps above the street.

The State Bank of Hawarden closed its doors well before what we think of as the Great Depression. It wasn't a dramatic global collapse in trade and lending that kept Mary's mother from her deposits. It was two years of bad harvests and low global prices for corn and hogs, and then a fifty-year flood, which stressed the community and then stressed its bank. Well before what we think of as the Depression, America's banks were already fragile, particularly in the Midwest, a problem the federal government had never fixed. It wasn't an accident that Hawarden, a small town in northwestern Iowa, became a model for scrip dollars during the Depression. Places like Hawarden already knew what happened when a small bank failed and drained a town of its dollars.

What would become the Hawarden State Bank opened in 1889 as the Sioux County Bank in a single room on Central Avenue next to a hardware store. Founded with a state charter, it reorganized two years later as a private bank, making its owners fully personally liable for the bank's debts. This was a common step in smaller communities in Iowa, where it was difficult to assemble the capital to meet the requirements of a state charter. The bank reorganized in 1904, with new investors. This could have meant that the town was growing, but it likely meant that the bank was in trouble and needed more cash to keep it stable. With the reorganization, the bank also took on a state charter and became the Hawarden State Bank.

That word again: "cash." In every age, it's obvious what counts as cash to the people using it. But the actual substance of cash changes slowly over time. By the time of the bank's reorganization, investors could have handed over several different things, each one of them an artifact from a long fight after the Civil War over what cash would be—greenbacks, blackbacks, silver, or gold. In 1873, Congress passed a law quietly dropping the legal definition of a dollar as a fixed weight of silver, defining the dollar as only a fixed weight of gold—severing the last remaining legal link to the joachimsthaler. Then, in 1875, the federal government decided that it would make good on its wartime promise: It would sink its greenbacks with gold. The Department of the Treasury sold bonds to raise $50 million in gold coins, and after January 1, 1879, anyone with more than $50 in greenbacks could hand them in at the office of the assistant treasurer in New York. This is the day the United States became what we think of now as a gold standard country. By law, the U.S. Treasury was ultimately responsible for making sure both blackbacks *and* greenbacks could be redeemed, on demand, for gold and gold only.

By the end of the nineteenth century in America, there was a long list of things that people thought of as cash dollars. There were gold coins. Even though the federal government had stopped defining dollars in terms of silver, the old silver coins still circulated, too. Anyone with gold or silver could also hand it in to a branch of the U.S. Mint for a gold or silver certificate, a note that represented metal held by the Treasury. National bank notes circulated, redeemable for gold at banks; greenbacks circulated, redeemable for gold at the Treasury. All of these were restrained by the gold standard, an elaborate mechanism that tied the total supply of American dollars to the total supply of gold in America.

Fights over money in the nineteenth century were intense, technical, and partisan, but we can sort Americans into two broad categories. Financiers in banking centers on the East Coast tended to favor the gold standard and the restrictions of the national bank charter. Gold convertibility offered them two advantages. First, it guarded against the danger of inflation; as prices rise, loan contracts signed at the old low price become less valuable. Second, a long-term commitment to a gold standard made it cheaper for Americans to borrow from financiers in Britain, who didn't want to see their loans inflated away, either.

Farmers and wage earners in the South and West worried most about deflation; as prices drop, loans and leases made at the old high price become harder to pay off. The Greenback Party wanted the federal government to keep printing greenbacks, without guaranteeing convertibility. There had also been new silver strikes in Nevada in the 1860s—finally, an American source of silver—and the Free Silver Movement argued to bring back a silver standard, to mint new silver dollar coins or let the supply of national bank notes expand with a silver reserve.

The new silver offered another front in the same old war. Financiers wanted to stick to the more restrictive, deflationary gold standard. The financiers got what they wanted, and America stayed on a gold standard. The global supply of gold continued to grow, with new finds in Australia and South Africa. But the American economy grew more quickly. The supply of what Americans thought of as dollar cash and reserves couldn't grow as fast as American farming and industry, and so prices dropped through the end of the century. The United States suffered a long, slow deflation.

THE PANIC OF 1907 AND THE CREATION OF THE FEDERAL RESERVE BANKS

In July 1908, the Hawarden State Bank reorganized *again* and once more had to add more capital. The timing could be a coincidence, but it's likely that the bank got caught up in a financial panic that had begun in the fall of 1907. Banks had not been stable in America during the national bank era, even under a gold standard; there had been waves of failures about once a decade. The sound money of the gold standard had guaranteed the reliability of dollars held as cash. But it didn't make banks more stable; it simply pushed the inherent fragility of banking away from notes and toward deposits.

When people get scared, they often go through a flight to safety;

they trade one questionable kind of money for another that feels more secure. In any kind of banking panic, what matters in your flight to safety is whether your bank has access to a reserve of cash. After the Civil War, people tended to hold their dollars as deposits at banks. When they got scared, they wanted what they had come to understand as reliable cash: blackbacks, greenbacks, gold certificates, or silver certificates. And whether a bank had cash depended on a daisy chain of reserve relationships *between* banks that looped all the way to New York.

Country banks—small, rural, state-chartered banks—kept their own deposits, called bankers' balances, with bigger correspondent banks with national charters in regional cities and financial centers like Chicago and St. Louis. These big regional correspondent banks, in turn, kept bankers' balances in even bigger banks in New York City. Banks in New York competed to draw in bankers' balances, offering attractive interest rates and advertising directly to correspondent banks in regional bankers' magazines. The New York banks often also balanced the liability of all these deposits from other banks with a risky asset: loans to speculators on Wall Street who wanted to buy stocks.

Financial panics in America tended to happen in the spring and fall; the banking system at both the state and the national levels tied private finance in the entire country to the agricultural rhythms of the country banks. Farmers borrowed heavily to plant in the spring, and then again to harvest in the fall. These were also the times when farmers were paying suppliers and farmhands, which meant that the country banks had to have a lot of cash on hand—national bank notes, greenbacks, or gold or silver certificates. The country banks withdrew their bankers' balances from the regional banks, which withdrew their bankers' balances from banks in New York, which called in their loans to speculators in the stock market. In the winter and summer, deposits flowed into New York. In the spring and fall, they flowed back out.

In most years, this chain of relationships moved dollars back and forth as needed. But if there was a bad harvest on one end of the chain, or a drop in the stock market on the other, banks all over the country would be forced to suspend payments—shut their doors and bar access to deposits, until they could figure things out. Even if banks turned out to be ultimately healthy, a suspension would have real effects on the economy, as people waited to see whether their deposits had value.

It is easy to take the circulation of bank notes for granted now. The Federal Reserve keeps coins and paper dollars in twenty-eight secure warehouses around the country, delivering them to banks every day in armored trucks, as the banks request them. When you go to the ATM, you're converting a commercial bank deposit into a Federal Reserve note. Your confidence that the dollar will emerge from the machine rests on those warehouses, and the Fed's ability to physically move dollars around the country. In the early twentieth century, state banks could only get paper dollars from bigger, national banks, and the chains of relationships that provided them on demand stretched from places like Hawarden all the way to New York.

The bank panic of 1907 began in October, with runs on large banks in New York that had speculated in the copper market. By December the panic had moved west. The next summer, as the Hawarden State Bank was reorganizing to pull in more capital, Congress approved the National Monetary Commission, to look at ways to make American banks more stable. The commission, New York bankers, and some members of Congress looked to Britain and Europe for their solution: a central bank.

Over the nineteenth century the Bank of England had learned to take on a new role, what we now call the lender of last resort. In a crisis, banks all try to sell assets to each other so they can provide cash to their own depositors. All that frantic selling lowers the value of the assets—what economists now call a fire sale. The lender of last resort shows up during a panic as a buyer, taking assets and paying for them with its own bank notes or deposits, providing a reserve, an ultimate bankers' balance that can be transferred to pay other banks. Just as with banks and promissory notes in New Orleans in the 1830s, we call this discounting, since the lender of last resort buys assets from banks at a discount—at below face value, but above the collapsing fire-sale price.

In America, the tensions behind Andrew Jackson's Bank War had never really eased. There was still hostility to the idea of a central bank, particularly in rural areas. Imagine how it would have looked to depositors in Hawarden in the summer of 1908, walking up the steps and into the lobby of the granite building on the corner of Central and Ninth. They knew their own local state banks offered credit where no one else would, particularly against land. They also knew that big banks in New York already controlled the supply of cash all the way to Hawarden, and had consistently botched it, failing during panics to provide national bank notes all the way down the chain to their own state-chartered bank. Why would depositors in Hawarden expect that another big bank in Washington or New York would change anything?

The original design of the Federal Reserve—America's central bank—recognized this hostility. We still today refer to it as the Federal Reserve *System*. From the beginning, the Fed wasn't a single bank. It was a dozen banks, in cities around the country. They were designed to serve financial areas, not states. The New York Fed's district includes northern New Jersey, for example. The Philadelphia Fed serves southern New Jersey and eastern Pennsylvania, but western Pennsylvania is handled by Cleveland. All of Iowa is part of the district of the Federal Reserve Bank of Chicago. The Fed's reserve banks all act in concert now but were originally designed as a compromise. Each region got its own central bank.

Every bank with a national charter paid in capital to become a shareholder in one of the new reserve banks, the same way a few prominent citizens of Hawarden had contributed capital to the Hawarden State Bank. In return, the national banks kept mandatory minimum deposits at the reserve banks. Confusingly, we call these deposits "reserves," but there's a logic to it. For banks now, a deposit at one of the twelve reserve banks *is* a reserve, the same way silver was a reserve for New Orleans banks in the 1840s. From the perspective of the larger national banks, the new reserve banks functioned a little like the old bank clearinghouses in regional financial centers, where a few large banks helped each other out in a panic. What had been a voluntary form of cooperation for the clearinghouses became under the Federal Reserve mandatory for every national bank.

At the same time, Congress gave the Fed banks the right to print dollar notes. These are still the Federal Reserve notes you hold in your wallet—most of us call them dollar bills now. The Bureau of Engraving and Printing prints them. The secretary of the Treasury signs them. But it's the Federal Reserve that gives them value. Until the Depression, what backed Federal Reserve notes was a mix of discounts and government debt, similar to what was already on the balance sheets of the national banks, which made the new notes the same as the old national bank notes. And just like the national banks with their national bank notes, the new reserve banks had to hold enough gold to redeem each of their notes on demand. The Fed wasn't a radical departure from the nineteenth century, and it didn't fundamentally change the meaning of money. It was just recognizable pieces of the old system of big and little banks, reassembled in a slightly different way.

THE FEDERAL RESERVE DIDN'T MAKE THE STATE BANKS SAFE

The new system was designed explicitly to fix the problems of October 1907. When Fed member banks needed access to their bankers' balances or paper dollar cash in a hurry, they no longer had to rely on city clearinghouses or work their way up the chain of banks to New York. In a general panic, if their own loans were still decent, they could take one of their short-term loans and discount it at one of the twelve Federal Reserve banks. In return, the Fed bank would credit them with reserves, which could be transferred to other banks. Or it could hand them paper Federal Reserve notes.

There is some evidence that the Federal Reserve System smoothed out some of the seasonal variation in American bank dollars, making paper notes and short-term credit easier to come by in the fall and spring, when farmers needed both. And it eased some of the concentration of bankers' balances in New York as national banks developed stronger relationships with their own regional Fed banks. But a lot of problems from the old system remained in place. The state banks, which far outnumbered the national banks, did not have to join the Fed. Less than one in ten ever did. The logic of staying out of the Fed was simple: State banks could keep their state charters, which allowed them to hold lower reserves. The Hawarden State Bank was not a Fed member. Iowa overall had one of the lower percentages of Fed member banks. Its state charter was not the most lenient, but Iowa required only a 10 percent reserve on checking deposits. Most states required 15, and some required 20.

Small, local banks, then and now, are better at understanding the particular needs of local agriculture and local businesses, and in showing compassion when it comes to collecting on loans. But a small bank with only a single branch is also completely exposed to what happens in a single small community. And in September 1926, the Hawarden State Bank was exposed to the worst flood anyone in town could remember. More than seven inches of rain fell in five and a half hours. Dry Creek, a drainage canal dug by the railroad that flows into the Big Sioux River just south of town, hopped its banks near the ballpark and pushed across the train tracks and up Central Avenue.

Mary's grandmother called Mary's uncle at the Harker and Burket Drugstore to tell him the water was rising and he needed to open the doors to let it through. He didn't believe her, and the fire department had to cut the doors open. Mary's father later said that on Central Avenue a man trying to cross from city hall to Keehn's billiard parlor had been swept off his feet and drowned. The water ended up three to four feet deep all over the city. There was $50,000 in damage to the Chicago and North Western rail yards, and several rail bridges over the Big Sioux washed out. The *Hawarden Independent* estimated damage to downtown businesses at $75,000, and the Iowa Weather and Crop Bureau's annual report estimated damage to homes at several hundred thousand dollars.

You can see the flood in the Hawarden State Bank's loan portfolio. Sam Cooper, who ran the grain elevator by the railroad tracks, took out a total of $9,000 in loans in 1927 to rebuild after the flood. Ed Lynott, a farmer born near Sligo in Ireland, watched the water flow across his front porch, and took care of nine children who had gotten stranded on the way home from school. He lost all his chickens and many of his hogs and borrowed a total of $9,000 from the bank in 1927 to keep his farm going. Fred Vernon and Helmer Leafstedt signed together for $7,000 in loans to support the men's clothing store they had run together since 1911.

Helmer's brother, Fritz Leafstedt, was a director at the bank and part owner of the clothing store; both brothers were shareholders in the bank. It is bad practice for a bank to lend to its own officers and owners, and banks that did were more likely to fail, both in the 1920s and in the early years of the Depression. But the argument for a loan to keep a local business open after a flood is the same as the argument for helping out the Irish farmer and the owner of the grain elevator. Local banks know local borrowers better and might be willing to show compassion. The Hawarden State Bank made loans after the flood because it would have been apparent to everyone in town that no other lenders were coming to help.

Remember that a bank's assets are the loans it makes. Good loans bring in reliable payments every month. Bad loans don't. As depositors withdraw their dollars, if loans aren't bringing in cash payments, then the bank's cash on hand drops until it can no longer cover withdrawals, and the bank has to either sell some of its assets to raise cash quickly or close. Loans can go bad if there's bad banking: The bank lent to people who were never going to pay it back. Or loans can go bad if there's bad luck: Something happened, and everyone's good loans went bad at the same time. The books of the Hawarden State Bank show some of both.

A lot of bad luck—a flood and a drop in the price of corn—caused a little bit of bad banking.

There were two distinct episodes of bank suspensions around the Depression: one in the late 1920s and one in the early 1930s. During the 1920s, failures were concentrated in the country's agricultural regions, particularly in the upper western states of Minnesota, Iowa, Missouri, the Dakotas, Nebraska, and Kansas—which together accounted for almost half of the country's bank failures. And Iowa had more bank failures in the 1920s than any other state.

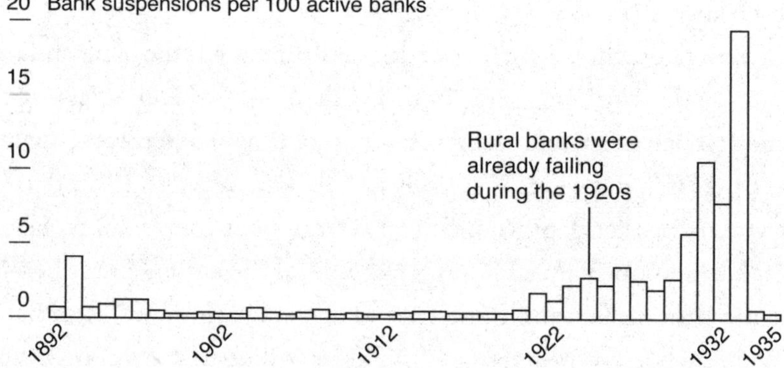

Graph by Evan Applegate. (Data from Federal Reserve Board of Governors, *Bank Suspensions, 1892–1935.*)

Overall, smaller banks that had less than $500,000 in assets were more likely to fail; the Hawarden State Bank had assets of just under $400,000. Banks in smaller communities, with fewer than twenty-five hundred residents, were likelier to fail; there were just under twenty-five hundred people living in Hawarden in the 1920s. Depositors in small towns were likely to recover less than those in bigger cities. And communities that, like Hawarden, had seen banks collapse in the 1920s were more likely to suffer bank failures in the early 1930s. The pain of the Great Depression had been long felt in small towns in rural America, well before it spread to the cities.

Economic historians looking at the nineteenth and twentieth centuries will sometimes refer to a core and a periphery. At the core were the manufacturing and financial centers, usually the U.K. and the United States. At the periphery were places like Argentina and West Africa, which provided commodities like cattle or wheat or rubber, but lacked big financial or manufacturing centers. The United States itself had a core and a periphery, too. At its periphery, farmers in Iowa raised hogs and grew corn, which meant that just like in Argentina they had no control over commodity prices that swung wildly in global markets. And in America's peculiar system, where small, single-branch state banks had to rely on loans from bigger banks in bigger cities, a financier in New York or even Chicago would have seen Iowa as a small, underdeveloped country, with small-country problems.

By the end of World War I, prices had shot up in America. During a war, a country's economy will shift radically toward making weapons and supplies for soldiers. Then after the war people begin buying things again, which can cause inflation as every manufacturer adjusts back to a peacetime economy. Even after a brief deflation in the early 1920s, prices were still so high that economists including Irving Fisher began thinking more seriously about what drove inflation and how to fix it. Inflation can be good in the periphery; if the price of corn is going up and you grow corn, you'll take on debt and grow as much as you can. But then global commodity prices dropped again toward the end of the 1920s, and there was a spike in bank suspensions in America, peaking in 1927. Out on the periphery, Iowa suffered something that looked like a depression earlier than most of the rest of the country. If you grow corn and the global price of corn drops, there's nothing you can do except suffer.

On the morning of Wednesday, September 14, 1927, the Hawarden State Bank did not open. Depositors arrived to find a note on the front door reporting that the bank's assets had been turned over to Iowa's State Banking Department. A representative from the department arrived from Sioux City later that morning and gave the usual reasons for a bank failure. The Hawarden State Bank had "steadily declining deposits": People had been pulling their dollars out of the bank, converting deposits to bank notes. There were also "frozen assets": Borrowers were delinquent on their loan payments and unlikely to pay at all.

One of the unfortunate truths about disasters is that they leave records. You can still read the bank examiner's report in a state archive in Des Moines, sixty carefully typed pages finished three days after the Hawarden State Bank failed to open. Banks in farm towns always had the same problem in late summer. Farmers took out loans in the spring to get the crops in but didn't have cash to make payments until the crops went to market in the early fall. The bank had last shared its balance sheet publicly in June 1927, when it had $332,000 in deposits. By September, that had already dropped to $278,000, and the state's bank examiner found only $7,788 in cash on hand. There had been a slow run on deposits all summer, and then the bank closed before anyone realized it was almost completely out of cash.

The old Hawarden State Bank building on the corner of Central and Ninth now holds two rental apartments, but the owner has trouble working around the one thing he can't remove: the vault. On the ground floor there's still a steel black plate with a handle and a combination lock, decorated with a small painting of an English farmhouse and the name "Hall's Safe & Lock Co., Cincinnati & Chicago." It's the entrance to a steel-plated room where the bank would have kept safe-deposit boxes, file cabinets for checks, and, according to the receiver's report, a manganese steel safe with the last cash the bank had on hand.

You can read in the receiver's report how the correspondent banking system broke down as the vault emptied out. In 1927, the Hawarden State Bank had correspondent relationships with two larger regional banks. To get more Federal Reserve notes in the vault that fall, the bank had borrowed $9,000 from the Security National Bank of Sioux City, Iowa. Security National must have been skeptical of Hawarden's loan book, because it asked for $18,700 worth of loans as collateral, including a $2,000 loan to the men's clothing store that had flooded. The Hawarden State Bank had also borrowed $50,000 from the Continental and Commercial Bank of Chicago, one of the region's biggest correspondent banks. Hawarden had pledged $98,525 in collateral to Chicago, including the $6,400 loan to Ed Lynott, the Irish farmer who had lost all his chickens in the flood.

On September 3, the bank's officers—including Fritz Leafstedt—had together paid in more than $10,000 of their own to keep cash in the vault. And on September 9, the Continental and Commercial Bank had transferred a final $1,000 to Hawarden; the transfer had not yet come through when the bank closed. Then it was over, clear to the correspondent banks in Sioux City and Chicago that there was neither purpose nor value in continuing to offer cash. The Hawarden State Bank closed its doors, and $280,000 in deposits suddenly became unavailable. Four years later, still only half had been paid back out.

Americans now don't have to think too hard about what their bank dollars are or how they work, because since the Great Depression almost every bank that takes consumer deposits pays for deposit insurance; if your bank collapses, a fund at the Federal Deposit Insurance Corporation guarantees every one of your dollars on deposit, up to $250,000. You will need a new bank, but your dollars will be safe. Like deposits, deposit insurance was not a new idea in the 1930s. Already in the first half of the nineteenth century, a few states had built up funds to make sure that if a bank failed, its dollar bank notes were still worth something.

Insurance on bank notes was no longer necessary after national banks started producing them in the 1860s; those dollars were already guaranteed by the U.S. Treasury. But as state banks began taking in deposits, the problem reappeared. The new deposit dollars at the state banks were fragile, in the exact same way the old bank notes had been. When a bank's loans failed, its deposits failed. By the 1920s, eight states had some kind of deposit insurance. Iowa was not one of them. State banks didn't want to pay for deposit insurance for the same reason no one wants to pay for any kind of insurance: Why lose money on something you don't think you're ever going to use?

The people like Mary's mother who held deposits at the Hawarden State Bank had two problems when it failed to open in 1927. First, they couldn't get at their own dollars. They immediately became what financiers call illiquid. If you're illiquid, you might have something of value, but it doesn't matter, because you can't turn it into cash on demand. Second, they didn't know how much cash they had, period. A bank could be suspended for just a week, with no permanent losses. Or the examiner could decide to liquidate it, slowly selling off the good assets to pay out the deposits, fractions at a time, until there was nothing left.

Elvina Harker—Mary Johnson's mother—sure enough had $184 in a savings account at the Hawarden State Bank. Hers is just one in the long list of accounts at the Hawarden State Bank, which runs to twelve pages, seventy lines a page—roughly one out of every three people in town. Mary has given me a book about Hawarden, nine hundred pages of oral histories the city published on its centennial; in the family stories and the examiner's report, you can start to see a picture of what was trapped in the bank's ledgers. Ralph Doty was holding $1,383 in a checking account. He ran a confectionary with his wife, Viola, who had $130 under her name in a savings account. Lewis Abbey, a farmer, had bought two certificates of deposit at 4 percent interest for a total of $2,103; he held $73 in checking, and his wife had $542. William Metcalf left England as a ten-year-old, worked as a cattle farmer, and remained a faithful member of the Men's Bible Class at the Presbyterian church all his life; he had $2,000 in deposits. John Harrison Huyck, who'd joined up to fight in the Civil War at fourteen and lived long enough to drive a Model T Ford, had $228 in checking. The Women's Society of the Baptist church had $119.

Between 1921 and 1930, before what we now think of as the Depression, Americans were shut out of $54 million in deposits in suspended banks. On average, if a state bank was liquidated, depositors could eventually expect to get about 58 cents on the dollar—a number that's a little misleading, since it includes banks in states that, unlike Iowa, had deposit guarantees. A week after the Hawarden State Bank failed to open, Iowa's superintendent of banking announced that the bank would close forever; the state was going to start the slow, uncertain process of liquidation. In Hawarden, the state receiver paid depositors back in staggered bits of 10 or 15 percent, over years, as it became clearer which of the bank's loans were still good and which had to be written off completely. By 1931, people in Hawarden had still received only half of what they'd held at the bank. To understand how they felt about bank dollars already several years before the Depression, imagine that you wake up one morning with all your money in limbo. You don't know whether you're going to get it back and, if so, how much of it. Then over four years you get back half of it, in tiny, irregular payouts.

Even with the Federal Reserve in place, all the Hawarden State Bank's correspondent relationships weren't enough to protect its deposits in 1927. The people in the Fed's reserve banks didn't believe deposits at a single country bank in Iowa were part of their job. The loss of a bank in a small community after a bad harvest and a fifty-year flood—that was just a thing that happened, a natural consequence of economic weakness. The Chicago Fed's annual report from 1927 is broadly positive about agricultural yields in the district that year and doesn't mention the local wave of bank failures in Iowa. It wasn't a national, seasonal bank panic. It just wasn't the Fed's job.

It is not completely a coincidence that of all places in America, Charles Zylstra was able to talk the city of Hawarden into an experiment in printing its own dollars. What seems like a quaint idea now was radical and urgent at the time, and it would have landed differently in a place that knew exactly how banks produced dollars, and exactly how banks could make dollars disappear. The whole state would have known.

THE MAYTAG SALESMAN'S DOLLAR SCRIP

Charles Zylstra grew up in Friesland, on the northwest coast of the Netherlands. He had a practical understanding of how money and credit worked; as a teenager, he had kept the books at his father's cooperative bank. He immigrated to Iowa as a young man, worked as a mail carrier, and in 1928 opened a shop selling Maytag washing machines. Most of what we know about him comes from a book published in 1933, *Men Without Money*. The two journalists who wrote it traveled across the country looking at experiments with money, spent some time in Hawarden with Zylstra, and were clearly taken with him. They describe Zylstra as "sturdy, bronzed and well over six feet in height," with friendly brown eyes and a "dignified and forceful style of speech." He must have been a charismatic man. He commanded respect.

He was also well read. He told the two journalists he was familiar with Silvio Gesell, a self-taught German economist who believed that money should be taxed to keep it in circulation. The problem with a depression, Gesell had argued, was hoarding; people hold on to cash, instead of spending it. The way to keep cash moving, then, was to assess a penalty for leaving it under the mattress. Gesell proposed stamp scrip; to keep a piece of paper scrip valuable, every week or month someone would have to buy a stamp and stick it to the back of the scrip. Anyone who spent the scrip quickly didn't have to buy the stamp. Anyone who waited too long paid a kind of tax. Gesell enjoyed a brief renaissance in the decade after the global financial crisis in 2008, when a few central banks pushed their policy interest rates below zero. Like Gesell's stamp scrip, negative interest is a tax on holding money.

In the 1920s, Charles Zylstra had tried to persuade the town of Hawarden to use scrip, but he couldn't sell the idea when times were good. In 1927, when the Hawarden State Bank had failed, there were three suspensions for every hundred active banks in America. By 1930, though, there were six. In 1931, there were eleven. By 1932, the bank suspensions in the agricultural areas of the country had spread to industrial areas and larger cities. Larger banks began to close their doors, and photos of bank runs in cities became part of popular culture. Zylstra had what he needed: an emergency.

At the time, the son of an Iowa blacksmith was in the White House: Herbert Hoover, the same man who with his wife had carefully translated and annotated *De re metallica,* the sixteenth-century mining reference researched and written at St. Joachimsthal. Hoover had first become famous running food distribution programs during World War I; he created, from scratch, a way to feed Europe. As commerce secretary during the flood year of 1927, he had assembled a navy of private yachts, river boats, and even bootlegger skiffs to rescue Americans trapped on rooftops after the Mississippi left its banks. The shorthand of history has recorded Hoover as the president who didn't care enough about bank failures to stop them, but he didn't lack compassion or attention to detail. Hoover was essentially a small-*c* conservative who believed in the power to motivate people to fix their own problems. That may seem naive now, but he had performed humanitarian miracles with volunteers. Hoover spent his last two years in office learning the painful limits of his ability to suggest.

In 1931, Hoover asked the Department of the Treasury to prepare data showing monthly bank failures of both national and state banks, along with estimates of national bank and Federal Reserve notes withdrawn from banks. He understood that America's bank dollars were frozen as deposits people couldn't get to, but also saw that people with notes already in their pockets weren't spending them. They were sitting on the notes, waiting. There are rational reasons to do this during a depression, but bank notes rolled up in coffee cans don't generate any new commerce, and they don't help banks make new loans. Hoover saw this as hoarding: an understandable human instinct with unfortunate economic consequences.

Something similar was going on in America's correspondent banking system. The big national banks in New York were reluctant to make loans to smaller state banks around the country. The smaller state banks, worried about producing cash on demand, were reluctant to make new loans to farmers and businesses. When a bank stops making new loans, it fails to produce any new dollars. So as some banks suspended and others stopped lending, the supply of dollars in America was both shrinking and failing to grow at the same time.

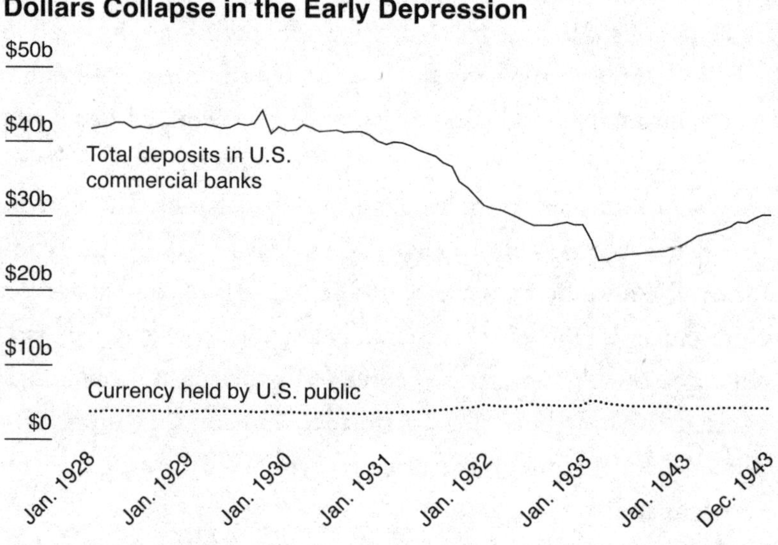

Graph by Evan Applegate. (Data from Milton Friedman and Anna Schwartz, *A Monetary History of the United States, 1857–1960.*)

Hoover's first plan, the National Credit Corporation, encouraged the large banks in New York to make a pool of cash available to lend to smaller banks to keep them afloat. A group of Iowa bankers happened to be meeting in Des Moines on October 7, 1931, the day the corporation was announced. They sent a telegram to the president that afternoon declaring themselves "delighted" and ready to help. The old problems of the American banking system hadn't changed, though. The banks in New York were unable to overcome their own instincts for self-preservation. The National Credit Corporation imposed high discounts on the financial assets it accepted in exchange for cash, and wouldn't accept real estate or farm loans as collateral at all—exactly the assets the smaller banks tended to hold.

Small banks continued to fail, and the banks that survived stopped lending. In December 1931, the governor of Iowa sent Hoover a telegram, explaining that "for the first time in a generation, it seems to be impossible for our farmers to obtain even the most conservative loans on their land." On December 7, Hoover announced his plan for the Reconstruction Finance Corporation, which would rest on some of the local administrative work that had already been set up for the first plan, but with $2 billion in capital from the federal government. The new corporation did help rescue some large banks, and the collapse in deposits slowed for a time. But banks still didn't start lending. We now call this problem pushing on a string; you can make it easier or cheaper for a banker to make a loan, but the loan itself is still the banker's decision.

Any aggressive rescue program to help banks has another inherent problem. If you rescue a bank, it looks like the bank needs to be rescued, which in turn makes the bank's depositors even more nervous. In August 1932, the Speaker of the House, who also happened to be the Democrats' nominee for vice president, asked the Reconstruction Finance Corporation to begin publishing the names of banks it had helped. Hoover's biographer has described this as a deliberate act of sabotage before the election. Either way, runs began on exactly those banks. As bank suspensions spread, they were still far worse in the small towns of the agricultural Midwest than anywhere else in America. In the 1920s, more banks closed their doors in Iowa than in any other state; between 1930 and 1933, bank suspensions in Iowa were second only to Illinois. On August 4, 1932, the Sioux County Fair announced that it would not charge admission "due to the existing conditions," the same day that Charles Zylstra published in the *Hawarden Independent* his plan for Hawarden stamp scrip.

Zylstra didn't believe people could be forced to spend their money, and so his plan did not require a new stamp every week to keep money in circulation. Instead, he proposed that anyone holding a scrip dollar should apply a stamp every time they chose to spend it. In Zylstra's plan, every scrip dollar would have thirty-six spaces for 3-cent stamps. The city sold the stamps, which created an individual sinking fund for each scrip dollar. By the time the last stamp was applied to the back of a dollar, the city would already have $1.08 on hand to sink the dollar. Anyone holding a full-stamped scrip dollar could swap it with the city for a Federal Reserve note, and the city would have 8 cents left over to pay for printing and administration.

Zylstra spent the next two months jawboning business owners to accept his plan to push dollars into Hawarden. Crucially, Sherman French, the president of the Chamber of Commerce, came on as head of a committee to promote the scrip. French, who had lost deposits in the Hawarden State Bank, was a former track star at Hawarden High with a gift for publicity; in the 1920s open houses at his lumberyard had featured raffles and food, and pulled in thousands of visitors. French talked fifty members of the chamber into signing a petition to the city in favor of the scrip, promising to accept the scrip in their own transactions. A staff writer for the *Des Moines Register* wrote later that year that the scrip was bottomed—the same word Horatio Sharpe had used to defend his Maryland dollars in the 1760s—on a commitment from the city's merchants that they would take it. On Thursday, October 6, 1932, the *Hawarden Independent* reported that the high school's football team had lost its season opener against Mapleton High; a grifter had cheated an attendant at the Standard Oil station out of $10; and the city had approved an issue of $300 in stamp scrip, "under the plan which Chas. J. Zylstra has been agitating during the past few months."

The city paid out the scrip dollars as a kind of stimulus. Starting with what is now Sixteenth Street, which runs from Central Avenue east to the cemetery, men graded and graveled dirt roads in Hawarden. Property holders along the street pitched in some of the cost; the city paid out each worker 60 cents in cash and $1 in scrip per day. The city kept

140 men in rotation on these jobs, to make sure each man got one day of work per week. Two weeks later, Irving Fisher showed up.

IRVING FISHER VERSUS CHARLES ZYLSTRA

Irving Fisher was what we would think of today as a public economist. He was anchored at Yale for his entire career, but was also restlessly entrepreneurial. He became wealthy in the 1920s after patenting and selling his filing system. He wrote books as quickly as he dreamed them up, and would print his opinions on almost anything. One of his biographers points out that Fisher took calls from journalists asking about the grammar of the title of the 1923 novelty song "Yes, We Have No Bananas," and that his best-selling book was a collection of advice titled *How to Live*. He was a quack on many subjects. But he was also among the early theorists on how to measure price changes. He worked out how to calculate the single-number inflation indexes we still use now, and created a company, the Index Number Institute, that supplied newspapers and the public with detailed price data. Working from his own numbers, Fisher was among the first to argue that high employment creates high inflation, a theory that is pocked with inconsistencies but is also still incredibly important for policymakers today.

When he gave that speech in Ames in 1932, Irving Fisher was fighting his way out of two related problems: He had lost his reputation, and he had lost his money. The stock market crash of October 1929 was just the last and most severe in a series of dips in the market over the course of a year. It is always tempting to read dips as a sign that the amateurs are scared, and that's exactly what Fisher did. Just before the crash he told newspapers that stock values had reached a "permanently higher plateau" and would be even higher in a few months. That is not what happened. But Irving Fisher believed his own predictions, was heavily invested in stocks, and lost most of his fortune. After the crash Fisher kept writing—*The Stock Market Crash and After, The Theory of Interest,* and then, in 1932, his attempt to explain the banking collapse, *Booms and Depressions.* Irving Fisher was in Iowa for the same two reasons he had done everything in his career. He wanted to explain what had happened. And he wanted to sell the explanation.

When Fisher spoke at Iowa State, he had only just heard about Hawarden. But the idea of scrip wasn't new to him. In July, Earl Barker, branch manager of the Barstone Oil Company in Chippewa Falls, Wisconsin, had sent Fisher a description of an article in the *Chicago Journal of Commerce,* describing in abstract a plan a lot like the one Hawarden would launch a couple of months later. This was the advantage of being Irving Fisher, famous economist. People from all over the country sent him mail, and some of it was useful. Within a week, Fisher and a rather flattered Barker had traded telegrams on the subject. Fisher also immediately added a brand-new chapter on scrip to the manuscript of *Booms and Depressions,* and sent the chapter to the head of the Senate's Banking and Currency Committee.

Ideas moved fast in the summer of 1932. In a crisis the blinds snap up, and people are suddenly willing to look outside. In a letter from Chippewa Falls, Irving Fisher saw a fairly radical idea—scrip money—and committed the next year of his life to it. After reading an article in *The New Republic* about experiments with scrip money in Austria and Germany, Fisher invited the author, a young German named Hans Cohrssen, to dinner at the Yale Club in New York. He asked Cohrssen to handle his correspondence about scrip money, without pay. Cohrssen was flattered, and accepted. Fisher had that effect on people. Much of what we know about the Hawarden scrip comes from Cohrssen's files, now kept at the New York Public Library.

Claude Million, a Swiss historian who wrote his dissertation on Irving Fisher and scrip dollars during the Depression, argues that there are two broad ways of thinking about scrip. It can serve a social goal, like encouraging people to spend money in locally owned stores. Or scrip can be a solution in a crisis, a replacement for some other kind of money that's either not working or has disappeared altogether. When we think about whether Hawarden's scrip worked, we should judge it by that second standard—whether it helped solve a problem in the winter of 1932. There's good evidence that it did.

In December of that year, the *Des Moines Register* sent a reporter out to Hawarden who estimated that the average scrip dollar had been stamped ten times, for ten transactions. No one had seen more than eighteen stamps on a scrip dollar—half of what was needed to hand it back in to the city for a Federal Reserve note. The reporter swapped a Federal Reserve note for a scrip dollar at Jack Boukans's clothing store, then traced it all the way back through the Kay Vee grocery and John Tilgner, who ran a filling station and had lost money in the Hawarden State Bank, to Frank Bryson, a navy veteran who'd gotten it as payment from the city for a day's work laying gravel. The reporter then bought a 3-cent stamp and spent the scrip at Field's, a drugstore. All these businesses willingly took payment in scrip.

The two authors of *Men Without Money,* traveling through Hawarden in early 1933, made a lot of the same observations. The owner of a filling station reported that he had no problem taking the scrip or passing it on. The scrip paid for groceries, clothing, meat, jewelry, even a premium on a life insurance policy—everything except products at national chain stores and produce from farmers, who wanted only hard cash for their vegetables and wouldn't have anything to do with the scrip. They talked to Merle Stone, the publisher of the *Hawarden Independent,* who had been writing cranky editorials about the scrip for several months. Stone pointed out that the scrip worked because Hawarden was a small town and the city owned its own utilities, which meant people could pay their light bill with the scrip. His only objection was that the scrip placed a burden on merchants, who had to accept the scrip for retail payments but buy their inventory from wholesalers outside the city, who, like the farmers, wouldn't take scrip and expected some kind of bank dollar.

The visit from Irving Fisher had made Hawarden famous. But it also started a race. Charles Zylstra wanted to teach other towns to make their own scrip dollars, and he wanted to sell them the plans to do it. Irving Fisher wanted to persuade the entire country to start printing scrip and, as was his habit, immediately began writing a book about it. The two men needed each other. And both men wanted the credit.

In Hawarden in 2021, only Mary Johnson knew about the scrip. Everyone else was surprised to hear the story about the newsreel, the national news, the famous economist. In desperation I asked Mary for the oldest business in town, and she pointed me two blocks off Central to Avenue E and Schoeneman's, a lumberyard and hardware store. William Schoeneman emigrated from Saxony in 1859, fought in the Civil War, and ended up in Hull, Iowa, where he farmed and opened a bank and then a lumberyard. The family expanded its yards to several towns in Iowa and South Dakota; in 1903, Frank Schoeneman, William's son, made Hawarden the seat of the family business, and put up a new building to house the bookkeepers for all his lumberyards.

The old bookkeeping office was still there, a squat block of tin siding surrounded by long sheds full of lumber. Inside the old office is now a hardware store, with supplies and professional tools packed in neat, tight rows for the kinds of people who already know what they're looking for. Next to the register sat a red baseball cap with the words "Make Plywood Cheap Again." I explained to the cashier that I had a long, complicated question, asked for a manager, and was pointed back to the office of Adam Hoogestraat. Hoogie, as his friends call him, used to work as a roofer and a general contractor. He is solid, in a way that suggests he knows how a hammer works.

I told Adam—I was never quite confident I could call him Hoogie—the whole story about the Depression and the scrip dollars, and he apologized, explaining that he had only moved his family to Hawarden recently, after losing his house to a tornado. He described the Schoenemans as "old blood and old money." Then, after thinking for a second, he said, "Hey. You want to see something?" There is only one correct answer to that question, and so he led me down a flight of concrete steps and through an open vault door to a room with a single bulb, stacked with document boxes and lined with wooden shelves of bound account books. The room contains just over forty years of the records of the Schoeneman family, from 1904 to 1945. Adam had been meaning to go through them but had never found the time. He asked whether I thought they'd be useful. I did not know how to express properly that they would.

Adam offered me a desk at Schoeneman's for as long as I needed it, and I sat down to figure out how Frank Schoeneman ran his business. I looked through the cash ledger, hoping to find a record of scrip payments in 1932. The ledger didn't distinguish between types of cash, but it did make clear that the Schoeneman family made profits on more than lumber. They owned several properties in Hawarden and took in rent every month. And the regular delivery and sale of lumber and coal meant that Schoeneman Bros. Co. had a reliable cash flow of paper Federal Reserve notes moving in and out every day, which meant that just like the Creole tailor in the French municipality in New Orleans, the Schoenemans could also make loans. What looked like a lumberyard on its face had also functioned as a small private lender. Adam had taken me to a complete financial record of the Depression.

In the winter of 1932, all kinds of Americans were coming up with ideas to solve what they called the money question. Pamphlets on money functioned as a kind of social media; people published them at their own expense and then sold them through the mail. Frank Grant Lewis of Canisteo, New York, sold a pamphlet on "scientific money" for 15 cents. C. H. White of Rainelle, West Virginia, promised "no more depressions through complete production and adequate purchasing power" for 50 cents. H. E. Dickinson of San Antonio offered "The Appeal Dedicated to the Intelligence of the People" on currency, gold, and government for free. But he did welcome subscriptions.

It wasn't at all odd that Irving Fisher, Yale economist, was writing to a Maytag dealer in Hawarden or the branch manager of the Barstone Oil Company in Chippewa Falls for details on a new idea about money.

Everyone was looking at the same problem: Deposit dollars were locked up and useless. And everyone had a bright idea on the best way to answer the money question. Fisher himself had started his tour in the fall of 1932 to promote his book *Booms and Depressions,* which laid out his debt-deflation theory of the crisis: As debts went bad and deposits dropped, the dollar deflated, making existing debts even more expensive for the borrowers, making even more debts go bad.

You can see pieces of Fisher's debt-deflation cycle happening in the Schoenemans' cash ledger. As more loans went into collections, monthly rents on the Schoenemans' property dropped, and without enough cash to go around, dollars became more valuable. C. L. Truthill negotiated his rent with the Schoenemans from $80 down to $60 in August 1932. The same month, Joe Kirby's rent dropped from $75 to $60. Deflation wasn't just an abstract thing happening to America. It was negotiated in Hawarden and recorded on the books in the accounting shed on Avenue E.

The way to stop a depression that followed a boom, Fisher argued, was to stop deflation by creating more dollars. The Federal Reserve had tried. In 1932 the Fed began buying Treasurys from its commercial member banks, crediting the banks with new deposits—reserves. We now call this quantitative easing. The Fed *eases* monetary policy by increasing the *quantity* of reserve dollars. People often describe quantitative easing as printing money, but it's just doing the same thing commercial banks have always done. The Fed issues the liabilities of new deposits—reserves—against the assets of federal debt. In the winter of 1932, people at the Fed banks were worried that Congress would steal the Fed's job by stepping in to print and spend its own greenbacks, as it had during the Civil War. But they also believed that by making reserves readily available, they were encouraging banks to make new loans, since there were more reserves in the banking system that could be swapped on demand for paper Federal Reserve notes. In practice the banks, as worried as everyone else in America, held on to the reserves and failed to make new loans. The Fed stopped the program before the end of the year.

The Fed's decision to stop pushing reserves into the system is often cited as one of the key policy failures of the Great Depression, one of the main arguments of a landmark book by Milton Friedman and Anna Schwartz, *A Monetary History of the United States.* But the problem with quantitative easing, as we discovered when the Federal Reserve fully committed to quantitative easing after 2008, is that not all dollars are the same. Putting a reserve dollar on a bank's balance sheet in New York doesn't mean that the bank will make any new loans, or that those loans will make it easier for a country bank in Iowa to make a new farm loan. Not all dollars are fungible. A new reserve at a bank in New York is not the same as a new deposit dollar for a farmer in Iowa.

Irving Fisher saw stamp scrip as the best way to get actual dollars into human hands. Like Silvio Gesell, though, Fisher was worried about hoarding—keeping dollars under a mattress or in a bank account. Both Fisher and his unpaid assistant, Hans Cohrssen, were convinced that each dollar needed to be stamped every week, not with every transaction. Fisher insisted on it in almost every letter and public statement. People holding a scrip dollar as a stamp deadline approached, he thought, would be more likely to spend it. Zylstra's response was simple: He had worked as a banker once, and no bank would ever take a paper dollar on deposit that would lose value every week without new stamps.

While I was looking through the Schoenemans' books, Adam Hoogestraat disappeared for about an hour and returned, grinning, holding a manila envelope. He had just bought a house in Hawarden and had spent months trying to clear the junk out of it. Adam had found something in a file cabinet that didn't make sense to him, but had seemed interesting, and this was what he pulled out of the envelope, triumphant. It was a clean run of 40 Hawarden scrip dollars, unstamped, still attached to a book, as if they'd come straight from the printer. He insisted that I take two of them, to have for myself. You can read at the bottom of Adam's scrip a message, printed in a separate font, like a footnote: "Copyrighted 1932 by C. J. Zylstra." Like Irving Fisher, Charles Zylstra didn't just have an idea about how to produce money. He was in the business of producing money.

By November, the *Hawarden Independent* described the city as a "mecca" for delegations from other towns, arriving almost every day to learn how to make dollars. South Dakotans came from Sioux Falls, Alcester, and Madison to learn from Hawarden. Iowans came from Lamoni, Belle Plaine, Rock Rapids, Spirit Lake, and Sioux City. Zylstra was ready for them. He had prepared packets of explicit instructions on how to make scrip dollars work. The instructions warned cities not to issue too much at first and offered to sell packets of printed scrip and stamp—for "cash on order," meaning Zylstra was asking for Federal Reserve notes up front. Fisher was promoting an idea to make dollars. Zylstra was selling dollar-making kits. In his packets, Zylstra included news releases to send to a local paper every week as a plan launched, signs for shopkeepers to put up in windows, and a letter for local business owners to sign declaring they'd accept the scrip. At the end of November, Hans Cohrssen wrote to Zylstra, telling him that Fisher had ordered a hundred copies of the news releases.

Back at Yale, Fisher wanted the City of New Haven to adopt a scrip plan. But he had also talked to other professors who informed him that what Hawarden had done couldn't possibly work in a city the size of New Haven, and so he wrote to both Sherman French and Charles Zylstra, asking them to help make his case. And, he emphasized, would they be honest about any shortcomings in their plan? When Fisher made his request, Zylstra had a packet ready to send. And just like the scrip Adam Hoogestraat found in his house, every page was copyrighted by Charles J. Zylstra.

In New York, Hans Cohrssen began responding to a staggering number of letters from people all over the country who had read about Dr. Fisher's idea and wanted to try it out. He put together a list of people in seventy-five American cities who wanted to issue their own stamp scrip and began sending—under Fisher's name—inquiry forms to places that had already begun producing their own dollars. Tenino, Washington, which had carved dollars, half-dollars, and quarters out of wood after a local bank failure. Merced County, California, where a group of merchants had agreed to pay their employees and each other in scrip. A catalog of Depression-era scrip shows about twelve hundred entries, in every state in America. Cities and boards of education paid employees with tax anticipation notes—paper dollars that would be sunk with future tax revenue. In Pismo Beach, California, merchants traded clamshells, actual clamshells, marked as dollars. The silver states of Nevada, Colorado, and Montana stamped tokens of pure silver to circulate as dollars. That is, they made joachimsthaler.

In late November 1932, Hans Cohrssen wrote to the American Bank Note Company in New York, asking for a quote on printing scrip notes—exactly the same product Zylstra was selling from Hawarden. At some point that fall, Fisher sat down at the Yale Club in New York with a pencil and wrote out a plan, which included recommendations similar to what Zylstra had shared from Hawarden—getting local merchants to commit, rolling out the idea to local newspapers, printing posters for shopwindows. By early January, Cohrssen was sending letters and full sets of instructions in Fisher's name to bigger cities and counties around the country. Spokane, Washington. Toledo, Ohio. Cook County, Illinois. In his letters, Cohrssen consistently instructed the cities to choose Professor Fisher's weekly plan over what he called the "Hawarden plan." Writing to a commissioner in Cook County, he pointed out that the mayor of St. Paul had visited Hawarden but, on the professor's advice, decided instead to choose the Fisher plan.

One of Cohrssen's form letters had gone to Hawarden, and at the end of December, Zylstra wrote an arch reply on the letterhead of "The Committee in Charge of 'Stamp-Money.'" Cohrssen's form letter had asked where the idea for stamp scrip came from. Zylstra responded that it was his idea. He had been thinking about it for years, and it worked in Hawarden because, by design, it traded one to one with bank dollars—a direct dig at Fisher's plan. He added a short list of towns using his kit. He said he was giving regular talks and was in contact with hundreds of other towns and a few large cities. In February 1933, Cohrssen followed up to ask for a full list of cities using Zylstra's kit. There was no response; it's the end of their correspondence. Fisher, Cohrssen, and Zylstra all reveal in their letters a kind of panic over who would be the man in America who solved the problem of making new dollars after deposit dollars failed.

In Iowa over the winter, banks had started coming to voluntary agreements with their customers to temporarily freeze deposits. On January 19, 1933, twenty-six more banks in Iowa suspended payments. The next day, the Iowa Senate turned those agreements into law, allowing banks to freeze deposits without going into receivership. Banks quickly began using the law in the northwest of the state around Hawarden, where farm loans were failing. Nebraska and Missouri copied the law as well. In Hawarden, the stamp scrip had worked well enough that in March 1933 the city approved a new issue of $1,000. This time, the city government used the scrip to pay salaries. The first issue had been an experiment, a way to move dollars into the hands of the unemployed and back into the town. By the second issue, the city had no choice; it couldn't get to its own deposit dollars to make payments. This is the scrip that ended up in an envelope in Adam Hoogestraat's house, and eventually in my hands. Unlike the first issue, the new scrip dollars used the Fisher plan; they required a new stamp every month, or else the scrip dropped in value. Charles Zylstra even lost the fight about money in his own town.

Adam Hoogestraat let me sit at the desk at Schoeneman's for two days, looking through the company's ledgers. It was well known among correspondent banks that country and private banks would accept collateral for mortgages that would be unimaginable anywhere else, and the Schoenemans' mortgage book shows the kind of flexibility that a farm community needed, particularly after a flood. In August 1928 the Schoenemans accepted an unharvested crop of corn and potatoes as collateral. In December they wrote a mortgage against five head of Hampshire brood sows.

It was in the Schoenemans' mortgage books, reading through ninety-five-year-old terms and payment schedules at the desk Adam gave me, that I found a mortgage for $800, written against a piece of property in downtown Hawarden in September 1928 for Charles and Sarah Zylstra. Pinned to the page was a note that the mortgage had finally been settled on April 19, 1939. It had gone to collections. Charles Zylstra, the entire time he was nationally famous for printing Hawarden scrip dollars, had been trapped in his own debt-deflation cycle, paying down and then renegotiating a mortgage written the year after the flood against what was likely his Maytag showroom. I shouted out my discovery to Adam, who joined me, standing over a yellowed ledger as if the two of us had found the Ark of the Covenant in the basement of Schoeneman's Building Materials Center.

Zylstra did make some profit off his scrip licensing kits. About a hundred communities used his plans, and in a catalog of Depression-era scrip you can see the dollars he designed in farm towns all over America. Haleyville and Opelika in Alabama. Grinnell, Iowa. Madelia, Minnesota. Lexington, Nebraska. Madison, South Dakota—which, Zylstra complained, had never asked about the copyright. He became a state senator in 1932, added to the ballot at the last minute, and passed a law in Iowa allowing counties to issue scrip. But he never made enough to clear his old debt with the Schoenemans. In September 1933, T. W. Searle, a farmer in Hawarden who lent money to people who couldn't get it from a bank, sued Charles and Sarah Zylstra for $3,700 they had owed him since 1924. They had given their property as collateral and likely lost it. The historian Sarah Elvins tracked Charles Zylstra down through news clippings to Chicago in 1941, where he worked for the Internal Revenue Service. He died in 1946, only fifty-five years old.

During the Depression, most scrip issues did not survive past 1933. Particularly in larger towns, it was difficult to get every store to agree to take scrip, hard to make sure everyone kept up with the stamps. In

Merced County, California, that year, the scrip tended to gather at just a few merchants, who had nowhere local to spend it. In Mason City, Iowa, an issue of $10,000 circulated successfully for three months, but then also started to pool at a few large stores. The city bought it back and distributed it to teachers, who returned it to the same stores. Polk County, the largest in the state of Iowa, issued $125,000 in scrip, but merchants tended to gather it in packs of $25 and deposit it at the banks, rather than returning it as change to customers.

Sarah Elvins points out, however, that the ultimate failure of stamp scrip doesn't mean it didn't work. It worked when it was needed. When it wasn't needed, it stopped working. In January 1934, when the Iowa legislature took up an ultimately successful bill to prevent counties from issuing any more scrip, Merle Stone, editor of the *Hawarden Independent,* crowed that no one even in Hawarden talked about scrip anymore. But on that same page there's an ad for the Farmers State Bank that suggests why the town had moved on. "DEPOSITS INSURED," the ad noted; anyone with money at the bank would be protected by the federal government's new deposit insurance program. The same ad also drew attention to corn loans; the bank would offer cash as part of a federal loan program for farmers, if their papers were in order.

Franklin Delano Roosevelt had been elected president in November 1932, but until his inauguration in March the United States didn't really have a president; Hoover had no power after his loss, and Roosevelt wasn't willing to commit to finishing anything Hoover might start. There were discussions within the Roosevelt White House about Fisher's scrip plan, but ultimately the administration was more interested in making the old deposit dollars work again, and within a year Roosevelt had taken four massive steps. Working with Democrats in Congress, the White House bailed out the banks with emergency loans, insured deposits, started handing out Federal Reserve notes to workers and farmers, and weakened the gold standard.

Roosevelt was inaugurated on March 4. By March 9, Congress had passed the Emergency Banking Act; the law was ready to go, because much of it had already been drafted during the last days of the Hoover administration. The Reconstruction Finance Corporation became a powerful, flexible tool. It made new loans against the assets of closed banks, to allow them to pay depositors quickly in cash. The Reconstruction Finance Corporation also started making capital investments in banks, becoming a partner and allowing them to open back up. The Federal Reserve was allowed to issue paper Federal Reserve notes against a wider range of bank assets, making currency more plentiful. It no longer mattered whether a bank had made good or bad choices. Preserving the value of a deposit dollar—the kinds of dollars most Americans used every day—became a federal priority. In 1934, the receiver managing the assets of the old Hawarden State Bank finally paid out the last of the bank's remaining deposits. The First National Bank of Hawarden reorganized and made all its old deposits available for withdrawal, and the Farmers State Bank in town was even strong enough to pay a dividend.

Within a hundred days, Congress had also created the Federal Deposit Insurance Corporation, to offer a national program for deposit insurance. Bankers in financial centers had been skeptical of deposit insurance, arguing that it was expensive for responsible banks and encouraged irresponsible banks to be reckless. Some states had run their own deposit insurance programs, but they tended to be underfunded, serving a pool of weaker country banks. But in the emergency of 1933 the objections no longer mattered. Even today, banks don't have to sign up for deposit insurance. But they do, and they put a plaque on the door that proves they do. Most depositors don't want to be credit analysts. They just want to know that a dollar is a dollar, without having to confirm what's on their bank's balance sheet. Deposit insurance is why banks don't advertise their reserves to consumers anymore. They don't have to. Deposit dollars in America have meaning now because they no longer suddenly become uncertain when a bank fails.

The Roosevelt administration also began immediately shoving

dollars directly into American pockets, any way it could. In Hawarden, work on flood control, street lighting, and graveling began as soon as December 1933—paid for by the Federal Emergency Relief Administration. Fisher had testified before Congress in favor of having the administration pay out its contracts in stamp scrip—the way Hawarden had—or help local organizations continue to print their own. Congress didn't listen. The Federal Reserve was also set against an idea that might erode its power to control dollars through banks. Even after a devastating national bank failure, America was already too committed to bank dollars to try anything else. And the idea of stamp scrip died.

A lot of ideas died in the first year of the Great Depression. For just over fifty years, the gold standard in America had offered a simple, brutal logic. If a bank could produce notes redeemable for gold on demand, its deposits had value. If it couldn't, they didn't. Economic historians sometimes refer to the gold standard as a commitment mechanism, a way to bind a country to a promise: If paper was always redeemable for gold, future politicians couldn't spend too much, creating inflation. It was supposed to keep base politics out of the market for money. You'll sometimes hear an echo of this today, when people argue that money has to be above politics, beyond the grubby fingers of the left or the right. But no matter how much we wish it weren't, money is always political. The economic historian Barry Eichengreen has argued that globally, the gold standard didn't survive democracy. As the franchise expanded in different countries and more people voted, it became clear that voters hated deflations and hated the gold standard.

When Roosevelt took office in 1933, he needed to create inflation on purpose, to raise the prices of farm products in places like Hawarden. In Iowa, the problem of low prices had become openly violent. Farmers near Hawarden had organized a farm strike in 1932, refusing to sell to the cities and organizing pickets to stop traffic; outside Sioux City there were gun battles as other farmers tried to run the pickets. As farm failures reached a peak in late 1932 and early 1933, farmers in northwestern Iowa began rioting at foreclosure auctions. They fought sheriff's deputies with bricks in Denison and almost hanged a judge in Le Mars, provoking the state to send in the National Guard. In May 1933, Congress passed the Agricultural Adjustment Act, which put a floor under the prices of cotton, wheat, tobacco, corn, and hogs, and even paid farmers to plow over crops to reduce production. But the act failed to push prices high enough to keep indebted farmers solvent through the winter. Deflation and the rolling financial collapse of farm after farm caught in debt traps weren't just an economic threat. They were a political threat.

In April 1933, an executive order directed anyone holding gold to sell it to a Federal Reserve bank, which meant that the Treasury Department couldn't guarantee the price of a dollar by continuing to take in dollar notes for gold. In May, Roosevelt secured permission from Congress to devalue the dollar against gold by as much as 50 percent. In June, Congress passed a law nullifying contract clauses that guaranteed payment in gold. And in October, Roosevelt instructed the Reconstruction Finance Corporation to start buying gold at higher and higher prices—that is, offering more and more dollars for the same amount of gold. Within three months, the price of an ounce of gold rose from $20.67—where it had been since 1879—to $30.

In a fireside chat announcing the policy, Roosevelt explained that farmers still weren't earning enough dollars to buy what the rest of the country was making in factories. Abandoning the gold standard, he argued, would make the dollar weaker against other commodities, like corn and cotton, funneling money back into farmers' hands. Roosevelt said he didn't yet know what the proper gold price of a dollar should be, and that he believed no one knew. He wanted the price of farm goods to recover, and he would continue to drive down the price of a dollar against gold until that happened. The old logic of the gold standard said that the United States had to go through a deflation until the Department of the Treasury could once again redeem all dollars for gold. Roosevelt wasn't willing to do that. What happened to the dollar at home, he said, was more important than the "accidents of international trade."

In our simplest stories, money comes from gold: Dollars represented gold in the bank, and then one day they didn't. But the actual sound-money gold standard in America lasted from 1879 to 1933, less than a single human lifetime. It didn't even outlive John Harrison Huyck, the Civil War veteran who had deposits at the Hawarden State Bank. The gold standard was just a voluntary constraint that had made it easier to make and take loans across borders, and guarded against the danger of inflation by ensuring periodic deflations. But in 1933, Roosevelt needed the dollar to help solve his biggest problem: Destitute and angry farmers weren't getting paid enough dollars for their crops. As the price of an ounce of gold continued to climb, eventually to $35, the dollar became both less valuable and more democratic. Americans have always had some power to decide what a dollar is worth, and how dollars should work. For a moment, in an emergency where Iowa farmers were literally up in arms, they took that power.

"I *AM* SQUEAKY CLEAN": CATHIE BROWN'S HAWARDEN SCRIP DOLLARS

There isn't a memory of the Depression scrip in Hawarden. But there's still a tradition. Every year the city participates in a monetary ritual it calls Christmas Scrip, an issue of paper dollars printed by the Chamber of Commerce that can only be spent in town. Cathie Brown, who was the head of the chamber when I visited, said she didn't know when the Christmas Scrip started. It was just something the city had always done.

There is only one place to have breakfast in Hawarden, and I became a curiosity at the Central Cafe: the guy who keeps talking about old money. Matt Hummel, Julie's son, took me on as a project, and put together a breakfast for me with business owners at the Central Cafe. None of them could remember how the Christmas Scrip started, either. But they did remember the winter raffles, when the city lured farmers downtown by giving out hams, steaks, blankets, televisions. Mary Johnson showed up at breakfast with a neat folder she had prepared, full of newspaper clippings from the raffles. Every year she had dug up—1986, 1974, 1967—showed that the city had also raffled off scrip, some years as much as $1,000 of it. The ads for the raffles never explained what scrip was, or how it would work; everyone in town already knew.

As head of the chamber, Cathie would begin the work of producing Hawarden Christmas Scrip every September. Sitting in her office in the old high school, she would call business owners in the city, making sure they were still willing to take the scrip like cash dollars. There are about fifty local businesses that do—the Central Cafe, Booth Pharmacy, Pizza Ranch, and Rooster's Midwest Steakhouse on Central, but also the regional hospital, the golf club, a family dentist, Eisma Trucking, Ericson Auto Body, H&R Block of Hawarden.

The calls are important. Mary Johnson used to make them, too, when she was head of the chamber. Over time, the chamber has figured out that if it wants to produce its own dollars, even just for the holidays, everyone in town needs to be reminded, every year, of what the Christmas Scrip is, how it works, and how it's always worked. We are often taught in textbooks that money is now a social convention, the product of a shared understanding within a group of people. In this book, I have tried to lay out how important the financial details of money are, but the details of a social convention are important, too. The Hawarden Christmas Scrip starts with a set of phone calls; without the calls it wouldn't work.

Under Cathie, the Hawarden Chamber of Commerce aimed to sell $20,000 of Christmas Scrip every year. Together, the city's business owners paid in advance to establish a fund of $3,000, 15 percent of the total scrip value. Cathie then literally printed out sheets of Christmas Scrip and sat down to cut out individual $10 bills. "Twenty-thousand dollars' worth," she told me. "That's a lot of cutting." In mid-November, residents would buy the scrip for 85 cents on the dollar, paying in cash or check but not credit cards, because credit card fees make the math more complicated. At that point, Cathie had a fully paid-up fund worth

$20,000—15 percent of it from local merchants and 85 percent from the people who line up outside her office to buy the scrip.

Then, Christmas Scrip in hand, the people of Hawarden could spend it at those fifty local businesses that had agreed to take the scrip as full-value dollars. The entire program is a 15 percent discount to buy local. The hospital buys packs of scrip to hand out to employees as bonuses. "All that money," said Cathie, "stays in Hawarden." Once a scrip dollar landed in a till, the business would hand it back to Cathie, who returned a full U.S. dollar out of the chamber's fund. Each scrip dollar is spent only once. Starting in January, Cathie checked off all the serial numbers of the scrip that had been paid in, then got on Facebook to track down the owners of the outstanding scrip, and tell them to spend it so she could close her books. Cathie Brown had to sink her scrip, just like a colonial official burning a bill of credit.

I pointed out to Cathie that she did some of the work of a central banker. Through regular communication, she maintained a social consensus around money. She handled the financing and distribution of cash. Then she went on a campaign to mop up any extra scrip sitting idle in desk drawers, making sure it got into the hands of local business owners so they could then present it back to Cathie for redemption in U.S. dollars. The Christmas Scrip could not exist without both the accounting and the phone calls, which together build trust in the chamber and its currency. "Squeaky clean" is how Matt Hummel described Cathie. "I *am* squeaky clean," she said.

The routines around scrip in Hawarden are strong enough that during the first few months of the pandemic in 2020, Cathie Brown was able to issue what she called stimulus scrip. Local businesses paid into a fund for scrip dollars, and the chamber gave them to citizens to spend at restaurants. The stimulus scrip worked because Cathie didn't have to explain anything. Julie Coyle now runs the chamber in Hawarden. The scrip dollars have turned into $10 checks, drawn on the chamber's account at the River's Edge Bank in town, but Julie still does all the central banking that Cathie Brown and Mary Johnson did before her.

On my last night in Hawarden, Matt Hummel took me to the Sportsman's Lanes, a bowling alley and bar on Avenue F, just around the corner from Schoeneman's. The bartender knew me as the guy who had been walking around asking about money, and he pulled from behind the bar a laminated sign that read, "We Accept Chamber Christmas Scrip Here"—exactly the sign that Charles Zylstra told merchants to put up in 1932. There is no actual memory of a connection between Depression scrip and chamber scrip in Hawarden. It's a cultural and financial habit the town never gave up.

Hawarden is like a village in the Alps where you can still occasionally see people in traditional dress. There was a way of making dollars once. It's gone now, except for an annual ritual. The Constitution prevented American states from printing their own bills of credit, and even after more than a century of failures and reforms of bank notes and then bank deposits, banks in the first year of the Great Depression were fragile enough that people in small towns had to reinvent the colonial practice of issuing and financing their own notes. The deposit insurance system that finally saved American banks during the Depression created a vast pool of safe dollars that would, within the next fifty years, become useful to the entire world as money. Deposit insurance also killed little experiments, all over the country, in making dollars work for everyone.

We left the Sportsman's Lanes and ended up at Matt Hummel's house, with Adam Hoogestraat. He had been telling people about the old Hawarden scrip dollars he found in his basement, and a friend had cautioned him to hold on to them in case they ended up being valuable. I offered to give mine back. "Nah," he told me. "I just had to share them. They're so cool."

6

The Dollar Becomes a Global Currency, Again

San Francisco, 1970

ANDREW BRIMMER WARNS ABOUT OFFSHORE DOLLARS

On April 1, 1970, Andrew Brimmer gave a lunch address to the San Francisco Bond Club at the Fairmont hotel. Brimmer, a governor at the Federal Reserve, arrived with a message carefully chosen for his hosts, a group of bankers and lawyers who sold the city's bonds. They called themselves "bondmen." It was both a description of what they did and a clubby identity, like Elks or Shriners. After the Depression, this is how Americans argued about the dollar: in genteel, coded talks in ballrooms over lunch. Instead of small merchants sacking bill brokers' offices for silver, or farmers fighting sheriff's deputies with bricks over mortgages, the fight over big money and little money got quieter and more technical. Economists and bankers get in rooms together and talk about intricate details with massive consequences. Andrew Brimmer went to San Francisco to tell the bondmen what they wanted to hear: The Fed was being unfair to the people who sold municipal bonds. Coded into that speech was a broader, more troubling argument: The Fed was being unfair to almost everyone.

At the time of Brimmer's speech, the Fed was tightening: making it more difficult on purpose for people to borrow money. More new loans in America means more new dollars, which can mean higher inflation.

When the Fed is worried about inflation, it tightens, by discouraging banks from making loans. The problem, Brimmer pointed out, was that the Fed hadn't tightened for everyone equally. It had become more expensive for cities to borrow, and more expensive for families to take out mortgages. But it hadn't become more expensive for corporations to borrow. The Fed had a single policy: tighten. And it *was* tightening—for some people, but not for others.

The large banks that made loans to large companies had figured out a way to get around the Fed. They were borrowing, in dollars, from banks in London. That is, banks outside America were producing what we could call offshore dollars. They were taking deposits and making loans denominated in dollars, but outside the reach of most American regulations on banking. They did this for the oldest and most obvious of reasons: It was more profitable that way. A pool of dollars had collected outside the borders of the United States. It was leaking back through the border, helping larger banks make loans for their customers.

The offshore dollars were called eurodollars—not because they had anything to do with the euro, a currency that didn't yet exist. Rather, they were dollars, produced by banks headquartered in Europe. If we think of dollars as created by fiat—by command of the federal government of the United States—then this doesn't make any sense. But if we let go of the idea of fiat money, then we can see that banks outside America were just doing exactly what banks in America had already been doing for a century and a half. They were issuing loans by marking up deposit accounts and calling those deposits dollars. Anyone, anywhere can make a dollar. They don't need the fiat of the United States.

In 1970, the market for eurodollars was already more than a decade old. Andrew Brimmer was one of the few people in the federal government with a grasp of the scale of eurodollar production, and the first to publicly identify the source of the dollars leaking back into America. Brimmer was a careful collector of data, and knew how to use Fed staff to help him make his arguments. He also understood how credit worked differently for different Americans. Brimmer was the first Black governor at the Federal Reserve. The son of sharecroppers, he had picked cotton as a teenager and worked in a shipyard during World War II. He spent his entire career as an economist as the only Black man in the room, an expert on international finance who was often asked to comment on race.

In his speech in San Francisco, Brimmer showed that as the Fed had tried to tighten in 1969, different kinds of banks had responded in different ways. Large multinational banks with access to offshore, lightly regulated eurodollars had made more loans than the year before. Smaller regional and local banks made fewer loans. For those smaller banks, the Fed had in fact tightened. This difference had also worked its way through to the banks' customers. Businesses, more likely to have relationships with larger and multinational banks, had been able to borrow more. Households and city governments, more likely to have relationships with smaller regional banks, had borrowed less. America was not sovereign over eurodollars, and as a consequence was losing sovereignty over bank dollars in the United States. Brimmer had made a detailed, technical argument explaining a problem as old as the dollar itself: The dollar wasn't working the same way for everyone.

At the Fairmont in San Francisco, Brimmer offered a solution. The Federal Reserve, he proposed, should have the power to encourage some kinds of loans and discourage others. In this case, the Fed would have been able to discourage loans to businesses in 1969, to make sure it tightened equally for every American. It's clear from the speech that Brimmer knew at the time how radical this suggestion was, describing it as a "thorough reexamination of the main tools and techniques of monetary control." If you are at all familiar with the Fed now, you're already reaching for a fire extinguisher as you read this. To treat different kinds of loans differently is what economists now call credit allocation. Policymakers at the Fed will often say they don't do credit allocation. They argue that it would be political, a choice to give loans to some people and not others.

As an institution, the Fed does not believe that it's political. We've seen throughout this book, though, that money is inherently political. Every choice about money helps some people and hurts others, which means everything the Fed does is political, whether they want it to be or not. The self-enforced ban on credit allocation is so clear to everyone at the Fed that the phrase "credit allocation" has itself become the boundary: To invoke it is to explain why it can't be crossed. The phrase has a history, though. It came out of a political response in the Fed and in Congress to Brimmer's speech at the Fairmont in 1970. It's not true that the Fed *can't* do credit allocation. Rather, the Fed *decided* not to do credit allocation and even adopted the phrase "credit allocation" as part of a programmatic rejection of Andrew Brimmer's argument.

The speech in 1970 provoked a reaction Brimmer later described as "vigorous"—from the banking lobby, from members of Congress, from within the Fed itself. The ideas he laid out were turned into legislation, which failed twice in Congress. Brimmer lost his fight, though he returned to the ideas he laid out at the Fairmont throughout his time at the Fed, and even afterward as an economic consultant. He had proposed a way to restrain the dollar, to make sure it worked equally well for everyone in America, to keep policy at the top from having different effects for different people at the bottom, the way we've seen so many times in the two-hundred-year history of the American bank dollar. The defiant rejection of Brimmer's proposals ultimately became an enduring principle for monetary policy at the Fed, keeping not only Andrew Brimmer's ideas but a wide range of tools and approaches off the table.

Even now, the Federal Reserve is wary of helping any specific group of people because it could then be accused of credit allocation—of helping a specific group of people. In 2019, when I worked as a journalist covering the Fed, I flew to Boston to cover a conference at the city's reserve bank. The conference focused on community development—

making investments in poorer areas. I wasn't yet familiar with Andrew Brimmer's work, but I raised my hand during a panel at the end of the conference and asked why, if this was a Federal Reserve conference, we weren't talking about Federal Reserve tools. Should Congress give the Fed the power to buy long-term state and municipal debt, to help cities and states finance community development, directing dollars into the underdeveloped communities we were talking about? On the panel was Larry Summers, a former secretary of the Treasury. He paused for a second and stared at me. Summers is famous for his outbursts, and I was briefly worried. Then he explained, carefully, that he would be surprised if the Fed got into deciding which places get credit.

The problems that Brimmer described in 1970 never went away. The way banks in America and offshore produce dollars still today works better for some people than others. The banks of the Federal Reserve System, now the world's most important financial institutions, built an approach in the 1970s that they still maintain today. They tacitly accept and even in some ways actively support the bankers and borrowers who use offshore eurodollars, which are useful for investors and traders making large, international transactions in dollars. But the Federal Reserve doesn't always make sure bank dollars work equally well for everyone in America, particularly the small-dollar borrowers who tend to run down their deposits every month.

Over the second half of the twentieth century, the American bank dollar began to serve as a global currency. But that old gap between big money and little money never went away. Smaller American banks and smaller American borrowers had trouble adjusting to the shift, a problem that's still with us today; the Fed is incredibly effective at using emergency loans to rescue foreign banks holding eurodollars, but less effective at figuring out how to get American banks to push loans out to Americans. There is no perfect dollar policy. As Andrew Brimmer pointed out in a hotel ballroom in 1970, every choice about the dollar is good for some people and bad for others.

DURING WORLD WAR II, THE FED HELPED THE WHITE HOUSE BORROW

Andrew Brimmer almost didn't survive to reach the age of one. After the 1926 flood that swept down Central Avenue in Hawarden, Iowa, heavy rain and snow continued through the winter across the Midwest. As snowmelt and even more rain pushed down the Mississippi in the spring of 1927, levees failed in Missouri and Mississippi. When the flood reached Newellton, Louisiana, the water stranded the Brimmer family on top of the levee: Andrew Sr., thirty; Rose, twenty-six; two toddler girls; and eight-month-old Andrew Jr. Hundreds of thousands of Americans were left on rooftops and high ground along the river that April. In Newellton, a commercial steamer found only Black sharecropper families on the levee, with the water still rising. The captain refused to let them board, so Andrew Sr. broke a railing and hustled his and several other families onto the deck, where after an hour of stalemate the captain agreed to take them. After that, Andrew Sr. was known in Newellton as "Big Brimmer."

Andrew Brimmer picked cotton as a child in the 1930s; the work was so important to the parish that the Black schools started later than the white schools to let students pick through the end of the harvest. The family also had other ways of getting by. Big Brimmer did jobs for Ed McDonald, one of the owners of the Newellton Elevator Company. The family kept chickens, hogs, and cattle, and Rose Brimmer had twenty rows of vegetables. Under the sharecropping system, tenants had been forced to buy staples on credit at a plantation commissary, often at inflated prices and punishing interest rates—exactly the same kind of truck system that Saxon miners at Joachimsthal had complained about in the sixteenth century. As prices dropped during the Depression, landlords in the parish had trouble making a profit on the commissaries, and agents from the Department of Agriculture gave talks in northeastern Louisiana, telling tenants that "'boss man' was broke, and if the negro didn't see about raising and storing his food he would starve." Rose knew how to preserve her vegetables, and taught other families in Newellton how to can in Ball Mason jars. She also knew how to read, and placed orders for other families in the Sears, Roebuck catalog. "We didn't prosper during the Depression," Brimmer would later say, "but we didn't suffer."

Prices for American commodities like cotton from Newellton rose fitfully during the 1930s, falling again in 1938, though not as severely as they had in 1933. What finally pulled prices back up to where they'd been in the 1920s was an emergency that generated even more consensus on the need to spend than the Depression: World War II. Already at the end of the 1930s, the promise of rearming at home and supplying allies in Europe had encouraged American factories to start producing again. After a short recession in 1937, factory output increased sharply beginning in 1938, pushing unemployment down from a high of 20 percent to 3.6 percent by December 1941. The sums of dollars the U.S. government spent once it entered the war, however, are staggering. In 1940, the War Department and the Department of the Navy together spent just under $2 trillion. By 1945, that had risen to $81 trillion. Over the same period, federal spending overall rose from $9 trillion to $100 trillion. The new spending moved farm wages up from $1.36 a day to $3.80, and it finally achieved Roosevelt's goal from 1933: It raised farm prices back to where they'd been in 1927. It moved men and women into factories, and it moved Andrew Brimmer out of Newellton.

In July 1944, at the age of seventeen, Brimmer left home with two suitcases, a graduation suit, and a copy of Booker T. Washington's autobiography, *Up from Slavery*. He was following his brother-in-law, who could pass as white and had left college in Baton Rouge in 1942 to work as an electrician at the Puget Sound Naval Shipyard. In Chicago, Brimmer missed his train, and a redcap took pity on him and helped him find a YMCA that would board Black men. The precision of Brimmer's recall, handwriting his memoirs almost seventy years later, is astonishing. He remembered prices, dates, even the name of the redcap: Emory Williams, a Black man who had migrated north from Mississippi a

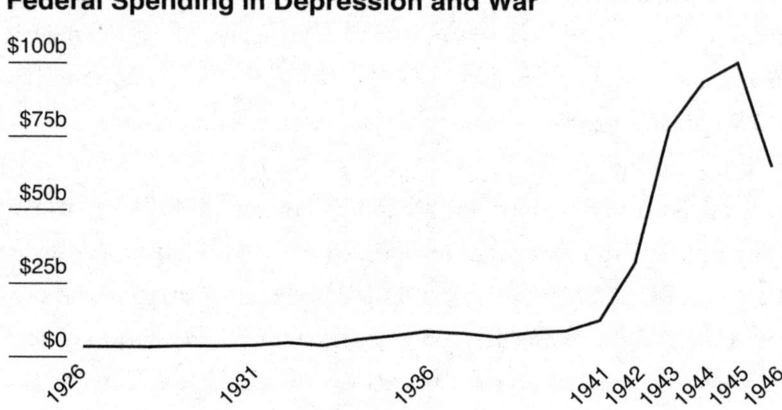

Graph by Evan Applegate. (Data from U.S. Department of Commerce, *Statistical Abstract of the United States,* 1947.)

generation earlier. Brimmer arrived in Bremerton, Washington, and started pulling cable at the shipyard as an electrician's helper.

Several things made it possible for the federal government to pay for Andrew Brimmer to work on battleships. Congress raised taxes, for the first time withholding income taxes in advance, rather than asking for them at the end of the year. In 1940, the federal government took in $2 billion in income taxes; five years later, that had risen to $35 billion. But taxes paid for only about half of what the federal government spent during the war. For the rest, the Treasury Department borrowed. In 1940, the public debt of the United States stood at $47 billion. By the end of the war in the Pacific, that had grown to $276 billion. Wars make things possible that seem outlandish in peacetime. Unlike during the Depression, the political will to borrow and spend was bottomless, and so the Treasury Department borrowed, and the War Department spent.

As it had during World War I, the Treasury sold war bonds directly to the public, running seven different bond drives during the war, with $48 billion in war bonds still outstanding in 1945. The war bond program was explicitly designed to keep inflation down by pulling dollars out of the consumer economy as the War Department was pushing dollars out into war production. There was a memory within the Treasury of how inflation during World War I had driven up the cost of the war by at least 50 percent; one of the war bond program's administrators later said that the "greatest single contribution the nation could make toward paying for the war was to avoid inflation."

To sell that much in bonds to that many people took a massive, brand-new logistical machine. The Division of Savings Bonds had to relocate to Chicago, near printing plants that could handle the volume of bonds and promotional materials that went out with each drive. Stars like Bing Crosby, Carole Lombard, Betty Grable, and Jimmy Cagney recorded newsreels and songs about buying war bonds. The Treasury enlisted retailers and banks in every city to sell and redeem the bonds, and the Boy Scouts hung more than a million posters urging Americans to buy. By the last drive, the Division of Savings Bonds employed eleven thousand people, took up a million square feet in floor space, and had the world's largest card file. We see fighting inflation as just the Fed's job now, but during World War II even Hollywood and the Boy Scouts helped.

Despite the spectacle of the war bond drives, it was financial institutions that did most of the lending. By the end of the war, commercial banks held $91 billion in federal debt. Mutual savings banks, insurance companies, and corporations held another $64 billion; local governments and federal agencies, $34 billion. By the 1940s, the United States already had close to a century of experience selling notes and bills for banks to use as safe assets, starting with experiments at the state level after the panic of 1837, and continuing with the new national bank charter during the Civil War that required banks to back their notes with federal debt.

By the time World War II started, the Federal Reserve had also gotten comfortable buying Treasurys. Before the Depression, the Fed's regional reserve banks had still operated like big commercial banks. Most of their portfolios consisted of rediscounts on commercial paper—discounts to banks that in turn had made discounts to manufacturers and wholesalers, who could prove they had sold something but were still waiting for payment. After the bank failures of the early 1930s, however, prices dropped, merchants stopped selling, and big regional merchants' banks stopped discounting, which meant they didn't need to rediscount anything at the Fed banks. So Congress let the Fed banks buy more Treasury bills to back new Federal Reserve notes. During the war, buying federal government debt on open markets would become the Fed's primary occupation. It still is today.

By the end of the war, the Fed held $24 billion in Treasurys. Economists tend to call this monetizing the debt; when the Fed bought a Treasury from a bank, it paid for it by marking up the bank's reserve account with new dollars. But this isn't any different from what a commercial bank does when it manufactures new deposits in return for the new asset of a mortgage loan. Again, the way the Fed produces dollars isn't fiat magic. It's just a really big bank.

The Fed didn't buy Treasurys so the War Department could have dollars. The commercial banks were already doing that, and the Fed's contribution by volume just wasn't proportionally that large. The Fed bought Treasurys to keep interest rates down. It was an explicit agreement between the Fed and the Treasury Department, as the chair put it, "a radical departure from all previous war-finance experience." When demand for a country's debt goes up, the interest rates on that debt go down; the country doesn't have to pay as much for the privilege of borrowing. The Fed didn't make dollars plentiful for the War Department. It guaranteed that it would buy Treasurys at fixed rates, which made dollars *cheap* for the War Department.

This agreement between the Fed and the White House didn't last much longer than World War II. In 1951, Harry Truman, expecting the same deference for his plans to spend on the war in Korea, summoned the Fed's policy committee to the White House to let them know he expected them to keep buying Treasurys. The fight that followed led to what we call the Fed-Treasury Accord, as if it were a peace treaty between two world powers. Congress and the White House would borrow and spend what they thought appropriate, and the Fed would respond on its own, encouraging banks to lend if it thought they should and discouraging them if not. This independence is foundational to how the Fed sees itself today, and the Fed's decision to defy Truman still serves as an origin story within the Fed. Policymakers at the Fed often talk as if the institution were born in 1951, the year they stopped helping the Treasury.

THE GLOBAL DOMINANCE OF THE AMERICAN BANK DOLLAR

In the summer of 1944 more than seven hundred economists, financiers, and bureaucrats traveled to the Mount Washington Hotel in Bretton Woods, New Hampshire, to negotiate a way to manage the world's money after the war. The challenge was to quickly reanimate a system of trade and lending across borders that had withered during the Depression and the war. But almost no one wanted the old system back exactly as it had been. Negotiators from the U.S. Department of the Treasury and the British Exchequer wanted to hold on to the control they had built over their national economies during the war. To do this, they would have to limit the ability of the wealthy to move their capital overseas in peacetime. American bankers wanted the gold standard back, and they wanted capital to move freely across borders, but with global trade and loans denominated in dollars and run out of New York. The agreements we now collectively refer to as Bretton Woods were supposed to be the product of negotiations among sovereign nations, but only one nation mattered. By the end of the summer negotiators had agreed on some of what the U.S. Treasury Department wanted, and much of what American bankers demanded.

The problem with the old gold standard was that too much gold was already in American hands. It's hard to pass gold around to settle debts among countries when more than half of it already belongs to one country. In 1935, after experimenting with the price of gold for a year, the U.S.

Treasury Department had committed to buying it at $35 an ounce. Then, before the war, frightened and wealthy Europeans had sold their own gold to the U.S. Treasury. During the war, foreign governments had shipped even more gold to the United States to pay for food and weapons. The Treasury Department continued to buy gold at $35 an ounce, adding to the stock in its new gold depository at Fort Knox in Kentucky. By the end of the war, the Treasury held 574 million fine ounces of gold, 60 percent of the total held by all the world's governments and central banks together. The gold standard is a promise to redeem notes and deposits for gold at a constant price; after the war the United States was the only government with enough gold to keep that promise.

As we have seen, though, redemption in gold had been only one part of what gave bank dollars their value. Wealthy Europeans didn't leave their gold in an American vault when they shipped it to the United States in the 1930s. They willingly traded it for deposits in American commercial banks; they kept a balance in bank dollars. Those bank dollars were backed by assets in the American economy on the balance sheets of American banks: some mortgages and a lot of agricultural and industrial loans. During the war, banks had also gotten comfortable holding portfolios of Treasurys, backed by the federal government's ability to demand bank dollars for taxes and pay them back out as interest and principal on its loans. And deposits at those banks were guaranteed not just by the quality of their loans but also by a national deposit insurance program that covered even the smallest banks in every state of the union, a responsibility the countries of the European Union don't share even today.

By the 1940s, the United States had spent more than a century and a half figuring out how to regulate bank dollars. The system it had ended up with wasn't fair: A lot of Americans—in particular, Black Americans—didn't have access to banks or deposit dollars in the first place. But it was vast, stable, and without comparison anywhere else in the world. Many domestic banking systems barely worked after the war; debts denominated in pounds sterling had meaning only within the countries of Britain's Commonwealth, and then only because of quiet, frantic arm-twisting by the British government. Before the war, the Federal Reserve had already begun supporting a global market for bills of exchange denominated in dollars; when global trade began to move again after the war, exporters anywhere in the world could invoice in dollars, knowing they would ultimately have access to deposits at a bank in the United States. The American bank dollar was a domestic currency that had become valuable for other countries. After the war, American bank dollars became a reserve for the rest of the world.

What counts as a reserve changes slowly over time, as new financial instruments become more plentiful and reliable. In the early nineteenth century, American commercial bankers had to hold some silver Mexican dollars as a reserve so they could convert their bank notes into silver on demand. After the gold strike in California and then the Civil War, banks with the new national charter held some gold as a reserve against their deposits, but also had to hold federal debt as a reserve for their bank notes. At the end of the nineteenth century, state banks held their reserves as banker's balances—deposits at large national banks that could be converted to national bank notes on demand. Under the Federal Reserve System, all banks still today have to hold some reserves as deposits at the Fed, which can be converted to Federal Reserve notes on demand. There is no magic in any of this, no fiat, just a slow accumulation of habits and laws over time.

Before the Depression and World War II, most trading countries had operated on a gold exchange standard. For central banks, both gold and foreign exchange counted as a reserve. Countries pegged their currencies, keeping their values stable against gold. That's the gold part of the gold exchange standard. But central banks also held foreign exchange as a reserve, mostly in the currencies of a few stable countries with large markets like Great Britain, the United States, France, or the Netherlands. Most of us encounter foreign exchange now as central bank notes in another currency; when we exchange, we trade in a stack of dollars for euros, for example, on arrival in Frankfurt. But to the bankers at

How Reserves Changed over Time

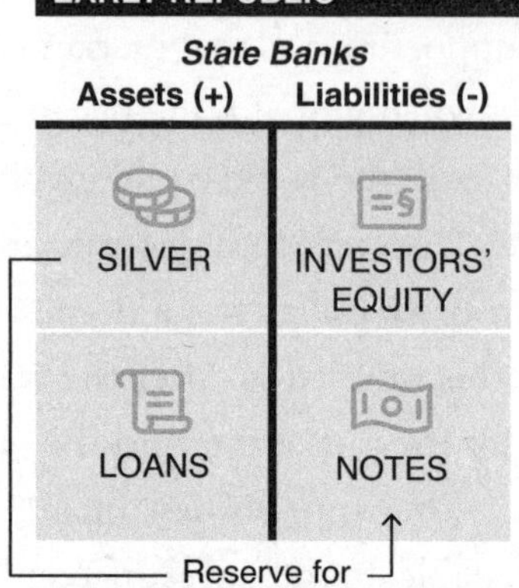

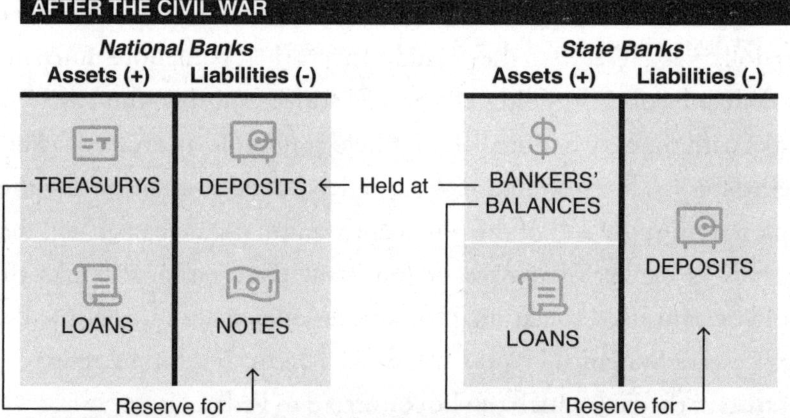

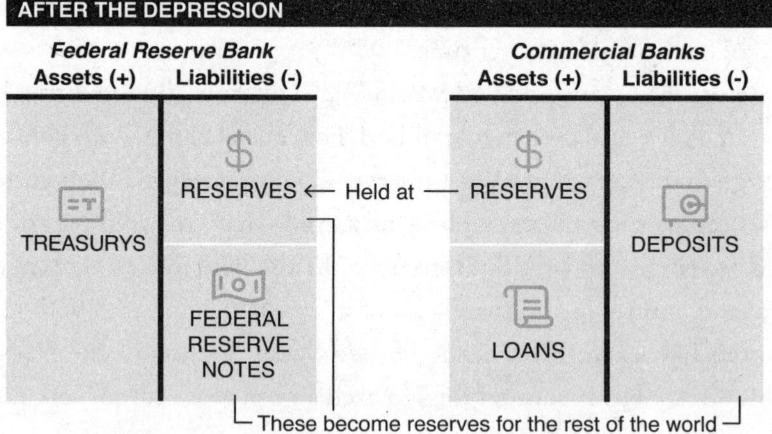

Illustration by Evan Applegate.

Bretton Woods, foreign exchange was a claim on bank deposits in another country, similar to the way a merchant in antebellum New Orleans would have seen a bill of exchange payable in London as a claim on currency in London. Central banks held foreign exchange as a reserve. They could sell it to their own domestic commercial banks, which could in turn sell it to customers to pay for things in other countries. But a central bank could also sell foreign exchange for another reason: to raise the value of its own currency. That's the exchange part of the gold exchange standard. Still today, most central banks hold reserves as foreign exchange—portfolios of bank deposits and the government debt of other countries.

In 1944, the compromise that emerged from the Mount Washington Hotel was a modified gold exchange standard. Countries could still peg their currencies to a specific weight of gold. Or they could peg them directly to a specific value in foreign exchange. The only foreign exchange that mattered was dollars: deposits in American banks to pay for American food and machinery after the war. The U.S. Department of the Treasury continued maintaining the dollar's peg at $35 to an ounce of gold after the war, and everyone else pegged their currencies to the dollar. People traveled to New Hampshire in 1944 to negotiate on the margins of what was already clear: They would have to rely on American dollars, and they would have to take America's terms. The Bretton Woods agreements did create the International Monetary Fund, which was supposed to help countries out with loans to cover temporary shortages of foreign exchange—dollars. But after the war countries in Europe continued to suffer from what came to be called the dollar gap. There weren't enough dollars available to buy things from America.

The gap would get worse. During the Depression and the war, both Allied and Axis countries had put up capital controls; they had prevented their citizens from making loans to other countries and moving assets across borders. This was good for war planners, who wanted to make sure that people with capital kept it at home, where they couldn't evade taxes or inflation and had no choice but to invest in war production. It was bad for the bankers in financial centers who moved money back and forth across the Atlantic. Within the United States, during the war, financial power moved away from the bankers in New York, who had decided where loans would go, and toward politicians in Washington, who decided what to buy.

As the Treasury Department wound down the war effort, however, it found that it liked the control and stability of a closed economy. So did other governments. The Bretton Woods agreements aimed to get to full convertibility: Every currency could be exchanged for any other currency, on demand, for any reason. But the agreements also recognized that this would take some time, and so allowed countries to stop their own wealth from leaving for a while so it could be invested at home, in new buildings and machinery. Early drafts of what would become the Bretton Woods agreements would have forced countries to cooperate with each other to prevent wealth from moving from one country across a border to another. Bankers in New York hated the drafts; it had been good business to take in European wealth before the war, and they wanted that business back. So the drafts changed. Countries would not have to help each other keep wealth at home. In theory, the United States agreed to a set of rules and institutions at Bretton Woods that would give other countries the freedom to manage their own domestic currencies. In practice, a gaping hole opened after the war, for anyone in the world to send their wealth to a bank in New York and convert it into dollars.

In a series of essays and testimony to Congress in 1943 and 1944, John Williams, professor at Harvard and head of research at the New York Fed, argued that early drafts of the Bretton Woods agreements were trying to meet two completely different needs at the same time. One was to rebuild after the war; farms and factories in Europe needed time and capital to start producing again. The other was to fulfill the U.S. Treasury Department's long-term hope for a mechanism that would give countries more control over their domestic economies.

The destruction from the war, Williams pointed out, was too massive to take on with the new International Monetary Fund; it could only be fixed with direct loans or grants from the United States. He was right. Between 1948 and 1951, the United States sent almost $12 billion to Europe through the Marshall Plan. Americans see the plan now as an example of their country's generosity, and as a canny way to create friends in the early years of the Cold War. It *was* generous and canny, but the Marshall Plan was also a way to fix a financial problem. In a closed economy, the wealthy have no choice but to invest their capital in the businesses and government debt of their own country. After the war, however, wealthy Europeans took advantage of the porous terms of the Bretton Woods agreements and returned to their old habit of sending their wealth to New York, where it could become dollars and earn a safe profit.

It's difficult to come up with exact numbers, since this capital flight was often disguised as trade in goods, but estimates of the wealth that shifted from Europe to New York range between $4.3 billion and more than the full $12 billion sum of the Marshall Plan grants. American bankers, just as they had promised, declined to help stop the inflows. They argued that European countries, instead of stopping wealth at the border, could just choose to go through a deflation—as they would have under the gold standard—and make investment more attractive at home. It was a well-identified problem at the time, discussed in Congress. We could see the Marshall Plan simply as a way to send dollars back to Europe to make up for the wealth that had left after the war to become dollars in New York.

The problem with Bretton Woods as a long-term plan, Williams argued, was that it was hard to believe that countries that had pegged their currencies to the dollar would always continue to volunteer for the pain of deflation, or that America would always act with generosity to produce just the right amount of reliable dollars for the world. Williams proposed instead a much simpler arrangement: to accept over the longer term that certain key currencies, in particular the dollar, would come to dominate international trade. That would happen with or without any of the institutions created at Bretton Woods. It was better to address it openly than to pretend it away by assuming politicians would decline to act in their own interests. Williams's essays, written before V-E Day, make for interesting reading now: He more or less described what ended up happening. The economic historian Harold James has suggested that we think of Bretton Woods as just a vision, conceived in New Hampshire and imperfectly executed ever since. No amount of hope or negotiation could disguise the plain fact that the dollar was already the world's key currency.

AMERICAN GOLD AND EURODOLLARS

Andrew Brimmer tried to join the Tuskegee Airmen during the war, but the Army Air Corps had stopped taking pilots for the unit without a college degree. So he volunteered for the army, entered basic training with Black soldiers from all over the country, and, as he later remembered, met his first Black Marxist. He trained as an infantryman and was given classes in Japanese politics and culture, but never made it farther than Hawaii. After the war Brimmer returned to Bremerton, where his brother-in-law showed him a newspaper article about the GI Bill. He arrived an hour late for his entrance exam for the University of Washington after his ferry was delayed, begged the registrar to let him see how much of the exam he could finish in the remaining time, passed it, and started school in January 1947.

Brimmer finished his undergraduate degree in economics at the University of Washington in three years, then spent a summer in Washington, D.C., as an intern working on development in Southeast Asia for the Economic Cooperation Administration, the office that had managed the Marshall Plan grants. He was the only person at the ECA who had spent time on a farm, and said it sounded like rice farmers working in the upland could use posthole diggers, a proposal the office later adopted and introduced to Vietnam. His professors in Seattle had planned to send him to Berkeley for a PhD, but his boss in Washington, D.C., told him to think about Harvard instead.

Andrew Brimmer often referred to himself as a country boy, but it's striking how unafraid he was of important people. At a reception in Cambridge for new grad students, he approached Wassily Leontief, who later won a Nobel Prize, and admitted he hadn't understood something Leontief had written. At the end of the conversation, Leontief called across the room to a colleague and said, "Andy's going to come work with us." Under Leontief at Harvard, Brimmer assembled data sets from boxes of bills of lading on flows of commodities within the American economy—wheat, and the cotton he had picked as a boy.

Brimmer had intended to study international development for his PhD but was captured—his word—by John Williams and Alvin Hansen, an economic adviser to the Fed. They taught a subject we now call monetary economics but then still had a name in plain English: money and banking. After his dissertation, Brimmer followed a trail of other Harvard graduates to a job as an economist working for Williams at the New York Fed. By 1958, the end of his time in New York, he had moved to the Balance of Payments Division, studying the massive and growing amounts of foreign wealth moving through New York and the New York Fed to become dollars.

Andrew Brimmer had a way of dismissing his own talent, choosing words that made him sound passive: He was "captured," or "identified." But within ten years, a Black electrician's assistant and infantryman from rural Louisiana had become one of a small group of elite economists, working on global capital flows at the New York Fed, the center of global capital flows. Brimmer was perhaps a little lucky, but mostly he seems to have been universally recognized as very, very good. Either way, he had become a recognized expert just in time to work on a new problem. After the war, foreigners hadn't held enough dollar deposits to buy American goods. By the end of the 1950s, they were starting to hold too many. There was no longer a dollar gap. There was a dollar glut.

In 1957, Fred Klopstock, Andrew Brimmer's boss at the New York Fed, published a paper puzzling over what he'd noticed in some data sets he'd assembled with Marie Collins in the Balance of Payments Division. Foreigners and foreign central banks had accumulated dollar deposits in American banks. Theory predicted that central banks would hand these deposits over to the Treasury Department in return for gold from Fort Knox, to hold as a reserve. They did, but not as much as Klopstock expected. "Numerous central banks," he wrote, "are finding dollar assets increasingly attractive relative to gold as an *international store of value.*" The italics are his, not mine. Klopstock seems to have been genuinely astonished. It wasn't just deposits. Foreign central banks were also holding Treasurys. Both kinds of dollars were preferable to gold, and Klopstock was beginning to see that they were useful to foreigners for more than just buying things in America.

It wasn't just central banks holding dollars. After the war, foreign governments had required domestic commercial banks to sell any dollar holdings to their own central banks, either to hold as reserves or to convert to gold with the U.S. Treasury Department. But those rules had been relaxed, and foreign commercial banks were holding more dollars, too. Klopstock suggested this increase in dollar holdings, both from foreign central banks and from foreign commercial banks, could indicate "the increasing use of the dollar as a *means of international settlement.*" Again, the shocked italics are his. People outside the United States were using American deposit dollars to pay each other, rather than to pay Americans. Klopstock had come to believe that the gold exchange standard had become what he called a *dollar* exchange standard. American Treasurys and bank deposits had started to function as a universal reserve.

Klopstock saw some potential problems with the dollar exchange standard. It was good business for New York banks to manage and invest all those dollars held by foreigners. It was convenient for the federal government that the market for its Treasurys was so broad and deep. But researchers at the Fed were just catching up to something that had been quietly happening to the dollar beyond the border: All that demand abroad could subject the United States to forces it couldn't control. The tools the Fed had for discounting commercial loans or buying Treasurys were inherently national; they only worked where U.S. law worked. It is difficult to corral a domestic currency when some of its participants are on another continent. And while it was curious that foreign central banks hadn't shown up at the Treasury Department to ask for gold, they still could. Klopstock did not see any of this as an urgent problem. But he had already seen what was coming.

In October 1959, Robert Triffin showed Congress a scary chart. Triffin, a Belgian-born economist at Yale, had ascended the same ladder as Brimmer: PhD at Harvard, mentored by Leontief and Hansen, time as an economist at the Fed. His testimony does not seem to have attracted any notice from newspapers at the time, but it has since become enshrined as the basic description of the weakness of the Bretton Woods system. His chart, later reproduced as the cover to a book, *Gold and the Dollar Crisis,* told a simple story. The amount of dollars held as deposits in America by foreign central banks had doubled, from $8.4 billion in 1950 to $16.8 billion nine years later. But foreign central banks did trade some of those dollars for gold, and the stock of gold at Fort Knox had declined over the same period, from $22.9 billion to $19.7 billion, with a pronounced drop over the previous two years. The lines were converging: Foreign central banks held almost as many dollars as the Treasury Department had gold at Fort Knox to redeem them.

Gold was leaving America, creating what we now call the Triffin dilemma. As Europe and the rest of the world rebuilt and flourished after the war, central banks would need to hold even more dollar foreign exchange as a reserve, which meant that the Treasury Department was potentially obliged to redeem even more of those dollars with gold. But the gold at Fort Knox was finite and dwindling. At some point, just like a run on a bank with low reserves, there could be a run on America

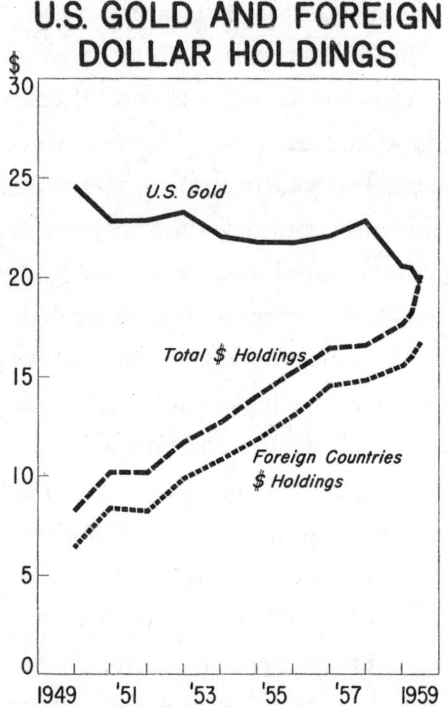

Graph from Robert Triffin's presentation to Congress in 1959 (figures in billions).

for its gold. By the end of the 1950s, America was no longer the only functioning industrial economy. This put U.S. policymakers in direct conflict with U.S. bankers. America's domestic financial system continued to provide both reserves and banking services to the entire world. That was great for Wall Street, but it was storing up the risk of a run on Fort Knox.

Eventually, one of two things would have to happen. Either the Department of the Treasury would have to stop redeeming dollars for gold, or companies in other countries would have to stop accumulating dollar deposits in American banks as a way to pay each other. Triffin's solution was to strengthen the International Monetary Fund to create a global central bank, which would hold reserves of every country and allow central banks to trade with each other directly on the balance sheet of the IMF—relieving the dollar of its obligations. That was exactly what American bankers had fought so hard in 1944 to prevent. Triffin also suggested internal adjustments in the United States. He wanted America to lower its defense spending abroad, keeping more dollars at home. Triffin also wanted to force a deflation at home and have the Fed raise interest rates. This would encourage foreigners to buy and hold more dollar assets, buying more for their dollars in America and earning more interest. Economists frequently recommend internal adjustments the way Triffin did, and politicians almost always ignore them. Internal adjustments are painful, and there's no political reward for pain.

Klopstock and Triffin were both hacking at the same problem. Assumptions about what *should* have happened under the Bretton Woods system were banging up against the practice of what *was* happening. After other economies began to recover from the war, demand for their products should have created demand for their currencies. Central banks abroad should have been more eager to off-load their dollar deposits in America for gold, to help encourage growth at home. Commercial banks abroad should have wanted currencies other than dollars, to buy things in countries other than America. Had any of these things happened in the late 1950s, it would have forced the United States into an internal adjustment. The Federal Reserve might have had to find a way to raise interest rates and encourage more investment in America. Investors might have had to charge higher interest rates on Treasurys, discouraging the U.S. government from spending. Either of these might have forced a deflation in America, making its products more attractive to foreign buyers. But none of that happened.

THE LONDON TRADE IN DOLLAR DEPOSITS

Already at the end of the 1950s, banks in London were actively buying and selling claims on dollar deposits held in American banks. If a German company sold something in America, for example, the American buyer would pay in American bank deposits. Instead of going through the complex and expensive process of cashing those deposits and converting them to *deutschmarks,* the German company could just leave its new dollar deposits in the American bank, then sell its claim on them to a bank in London. It was a quiet practice that the journalist Paul Einzig later called a "remarkable conspiracy of silence." Einzig knew so much about the foreign exchange market that he had written a book on the subject, but the dollar trade in Europe was so new to him that he had to start asking around the City of London about it in October 1959, right as Triffin was testifying to Congress. Bankers in London begged Einzig not to write about what they were doing; someone important might notice and stop them. By early 1960, the Fed's Board of Governors, alarmed about a practice they couldn't control and didn't even completely understand, had approved money for Fred Klopstock to travel to Europe, talk to bankers, and figure out what dollars were actually doing on the other side of the Atlantic.

As is the case for the early decades of American bank notes, we don't have great data on the first couple of years of the U.K. trade in dollar deposits; you have to know something exists before you start tracking it. This also makes it difficult to figure out how exactly they started. In the late 1990s, the historian Catherine Schenk offered the simplest explanation: Holding and trading dollar deposits was a profitable business for banks in Britain, and authorities in London didn't care to stop them.

In 1955, the Bank of England had noticed that Midland Bank in Manchester was asking around for claims on dollar deposits in American banks, far more than what Midland needed to pay for U.S. products for its customers. Midland had hit on a complex trade. The bank took in those claims as deposits on its own balance sheet, paying higher interest than the Fed allowed in the United States. Then Midland swapped those dollars; it traded them temporarily for sterling deposits, to buy British government debt at an attractive return. Even after it had paid for the swap, it was still cheaper to pay interest on dollar deposits than it would have been to borrow at the domestic sterling rates the Bank of England had set. When the swap expired, Midland could unwind the whole deal and walk away with a profit. The Bank of England raised an eyebrow, then decided to allow it. It had set a precedent. It was okay to play with dollars in London.

By 1956, Midland had half of the foreign currency deposits in Britain. Then merchant banks in the City of London and U.S. and Japanese banks with branches in the U.K. all began competing to take in claims on dollar deposits. Schenk argues that as this market developed, it was important that the Bank of England decided not to see what was happening. Switzerland, France, Germany, and Italy all within a few years found ways of preventing their own banks from evading domestic central bank policy by actively seeking and trading claims on dollar deposits held in the United States. In November 1960, a parliamentary question tried to clarify whether Britain would follow. The answer was no: What was good for profits in the City of London was good for the rest of the country.

That same month, Klopstock returned to the Fed from his summer trip across the Atlantic and described a deep global market in claims on dollar deposits, based primarily at branches in London. Banks with headquarters all over the world would take deposits in a foreign currency, then temporarily swap them with a claim on dollars held on deposit at a bank in the United States. Banks in London also freely traded claims on dollar deposits in American banks. Dutch, Swiss, Scandinavian, and German banks were the most active sellers of those claims, but European companies, foreign subsidiaries of American companies, and even oil suppliers from the Middle East were selling them as well. Central banks, which tended to hold their reserves in dollars, were always willing to buy or sell claims on American bank dollars, keeping the market liquid. Italian, French, British, Canadian, German, and Japanese banks all bought dollars, as did foreign branches of American banks. The market for dollar deposits, Klopstock discovered, had become "less and less a strictly European affair and had assumed world-wide proportions and ramifications." Klopstock called all these claims on dollar deposits trading among European banks continental dollars, but noted that some people in the City of London used another name, the one we still use today: eurodollars.

THE CREAM GOES TO LONDON

The Kennedy administration wanted economists in every department, and what Andrew Brimmer described as a "Harvard mafia" began spreading across the federal government. A made Harvard man, Brimmer took a job with the Commerce Department in 1963, working on the economic and legal case to desegregate hotels and restaurants for what would become the Civil Rights Act of 1964. Presenting to Congress, Brimmer briefly got into a dustup with Senator Strom Thurmond over whether a hotel in Aiken, South Carolina, was segregated. Brimmer asked the department to call its field office in the state, which interviewed the hotel's owner and confirmed forty minutes later that the senator had in fact seen Black people at the hotel—working there. Brimmer's daughter, Esther, says that of his life's work, Brimmer was proudest of what he did for the Civil Rights Act.

In 1965, with Lyndon Johnson as president, Brimmer was put in charge of a program to address a problem that had been consuming the White House: The Triffin dilemma had not resolved itself. The United States still exported more goods than it imported, but that surplus had declined as other economies recovered and began selling things back to America. The Department of Defense continued to spend dollars on bases abroad, and even after the Marshall Plan the federal government continued to provide foreign aid. American companies borrowed dollars at home, then moved them out of the country to build new plants overseas. Japanese and European companies were eager to raise dollars in America as well, issuing dollar-denominated bonds in New York markets. In 1963, Congress levied what it called an interest equalization tax on bonds held by foreigners. In response, New York banks just made direct loans to foreign companies instead. All of this added up to what we call a balance of payments deficit; every year foreigners continued to accumulate more dollar deposits and assets in the United States than Americans did of other currencies, raising the risk that a foreign government or central bank would hand over a lot of dollars and ask for a lot of gold. In the early 1950s, the balance of payments deficit had stayed below $1 billion. In 1956, it jumped to $2 billion. And by 1965, it had grown to $4.6 billion.

The White House tried a new approach: It asked nicely. The Johnson administration had the Federal Reserve and the Commerce Department begin a program it called Voluntary Foreign Credit Restraint. Through the program, the president was asking American businesses to focus on exporting goods to earn back dollars, and to hold off spending dollars on investments in new plants overseas. Johnson was also asking American banks to halt the growth in new domestic dollar loans to foreigners. On the Commerce side, Andrew Brimmer essentially ran the program, traveling around the country to make speeches and talk to trade groups. In April 1965 he met with the Illinois Manufacturers' Association in Chicago and gave a press conference with the president of the Chicago Fed. He reassured reporters that a fifth of the companies he had heard from in his survey had agreed that if they were going to spend abroad, they would borrow abroad, too.

Brimmer had made brief mention of a very big deal, a fundamental shift in the eurodollar market: American companies could borrow dollars abroad. In London, after almost a decade of trading claims on dollar deposits, bankers felt comfortable enough with that market that they had added another layer to it. They began helping companies issue brand-new dollar-denominated bonds. When companies issued bonds in the United States, they raised money as American bank deposits. When companies started issuing bonds in dollars in London, they raised money as *claims* on American bank deposits—eurodollars.

Companies often sell bonds through a syndicate. A lead manager, usually an investment bank, structures the deal and takes a cut; then more banks in the syndicate agree to buy the bonds so they can sell them to their own clients. In the 1950s and early 1960s, European banks would participate in syndicates to help European companies list dollar-denominated bonds in New York, before turning around and selling those bonds to European investors. But since the deals took place in New York, the lead manager was always an American bank. Julius Strauss, a bond broker in London, complained that the Americans "got all the cream but did none of the work"; bankers in London found the clients, sold the bonds, then watched, helpless, as American banks took the biggest share of the commissions. But there was already expertise right there in London with dollar bonds, familiarity with the trade in claims on American deposits. So Europeans cut the Americans out of the deal altogether and began helping companies sell what Strauss called eurobonds—dollar-denominated bonds, structured and sold completely in London.

In July 1963, S. G. Warburg & Company of London took the lead and got all the cream on a $15 million bond listing for Autostrade, a shell company that paid for public works in Italy. The bonds paid 5.5 percent and were guaranteed—in dollars—by the Italian Republic. Autostrade got claims on dollar deposits in American banks, and in return the London banks sold dollar-denominated bearer bonds to their own European customers. The Banque de Bruxelles in Belgium participated in the syndicate, as did Germany's Deutsche Bank and the Rotterdamsche Bank in the Netherlands. Julius Strauss's firm was one of the brokers. There is still some disagreement over whether the Autostrade listing was the first eurobond, but it was the first to be listed publicly, which made it hard to hide. The market for eurodollars had added a brand-new financial instrument: the eurobond, a dollar-denominated piece of paper you could hold in your hand and, as the bearer, give to someone else as payment. The eurobonds from Autostrade paid interest in dollars, and were guaranteed by a European state. And the entire transaction had closed outside American borders, without American banks or regulators.

London banks were already eager to take American business. The United States, desperate to make sure the Europeans kept trading those claims on dollar deposits abroad instead of sending them to Fort Knox for gold, didn't do anything to try to stop the eurobond market from growing. In 1963, there was a total of $143 million in eurobonds. The next year it grew to $620 million, then $777 million in 1965. The U.S. interest equalization tax, expressly designed to push European and Japanese bond borrowers out of New York markets, sent them to London for eurobonds. Then Andrew Brimmer's Voluntary Foreign Credit Restraint program discouraged American bank loans to foreigners—which again sent foreign borrowers to London for dollar loans. The program worked. By 1965, just as they had promised Andrew Brimmer, American companies were borrowing dollars in London instead of New York. In September of that year, American Cyanamid, a chemical manufacturer, floated $20 million in eurobonds. Monsanto borrowed $25 million in October, followed by General Electric, Bristol Myers, and Federated Department Stores by the end of the year.

The whole eurodollar system—dollar claims held in London on dollar deposits in America, eurobonds denominated in dollars and sold for those claims—was a triumph of practice over theory. It wasn't until the late 1960s that there was even reliable data about eurodollars, and policymakers struggled to comprehend how, after a century and a half of American attempts to regulate dollars from American banks, European banks had simply started trading dollars in London. Andrew Brimmer, through his work at the Commerce Department and under Fred Klopstock at the New York Fed, was one of the few government economists in America who even understood what was happening. In the summer of 1965, he flew to London for a meeting between British and American economists. According to Brimmer's account, Harold Wilson, the prime minister, said that "since Dr. Brimmer is doing such a good job in the Commerce Department managing that capital flow program and the Federal Reserve was doing such a poor job, maybe Dr. Brimmer ought to be sent to the Federal Reserve." When the Americans got home, that is exactly what Gardner Ackley, chair of the Council of Economic Advisers, told the president.

There was some conflict over Brimmer's appointment to the Fed. He was sanguine about it when it came up, but his archives show that years later he was still trying to figure out who had proposed other candidates. Lyndon Johnson knew Brimmer well from his work on the balance of payments problem, but had a journalist ask around quietly about Brimmer's reputation. The answer, recorded on White House tape and eventually also filed away as a transcript in Brimmer's papers, was that he was bright, ambitious, and not radical. A few financiers were worried about three things. He had been part of the attempt to restrain American banks from lending to foreign companies; he might have a chip on his shoulder because he was Black; and he was an economist, when the Fed needed more bankers. The concern at the time was that bankers looked out for banks, and businessmen looked out for businesses, but economists were unpredictable.

In February 1966, returning from a day in Colonial Williamsburg with his wife and daughter, Brimmer was summoned to the White House. Characteristically, Johnson received Brimmer while lying in bed. "If I send you over to the Board," the president said, "I would not expect you to be my man! I would not expect you to be an easy money man nor a hard money man, but a right money man!" Brimmer was thirty-nine years old when Johnson announced his appointment, and "Right Money Man" became the title of the memoir he never published. The dollar had two roles in 1966: the old domestic one in American banks and a new international one in London banks. Brimmer was one of the few people who could see both roles clearly—and how American banks in London had started to interfere with his new job of managing domestic bank dollars back home.

HERBIE FROM BOOT HILL: AMERICAN BANKS START BORROWING EURODOLLARS IN LONDON

In the summer of 1969, *Euromoney* published its first issue. It was a magazine dedicated exclusively to the foreign currencies and bonds being traded in the City of London. The editor was a page short of copy when he arrived at the printer on the coast of Sussex, so on the spot he wrote a back-page satire in the voice of a letter home from Herbie, an American sent to London to open an office for the Last National Bank of Boot Hill. In his letter, Herbie is pleased by the small office near Moorgate, a prestigious address for bankers. He is bothered by warm gin and letters from Boot Hill in America demanding eurodollars. "Why come to London to look for dollars, you might as well go to Boot Hill to look for tea and muffins," he wrote. Herbie was a joke, because the Americans in London were real. Banks from the United States had in fact come to London to borrow eurodollars.

There was an argument among economists in the late 1960s over what, exactly, eurodollars were. Policymakers and economists knew that banks in London were trading claims on dollar deposits held in America, and swapping some of those claims for eurobonds. They suspected that this activity was just moving around existing American bank dollars—keeping them abroad, instead of sending them to Fort Knox for gold. But in 1969, Milton Friedman published some basic arithmetic showing that estimates coming in from London on the size of the market were too vast. There couldn't just be claims on existing American bank dollars in London. There had to be *new* dollars as well.

Friedman argued that a lot of eurodollars had come from a "bookkeeper's pen"—a bookkeeper in London. Banks in America had always manufactured brand-new dollars when they made a loan and marked up a borrower's account with new deposits. Banks in London were doing the exact same thing: making loans and marking up deposit accounts with new eurodollars. Since the founding of the United States, American banks had made loans by handing out new dollar notes, or marking up their ledgers with new dollar deposits. In London in the 1960s, even though the pound sterling was still the domestic currency, banks were making loans by marking up their own balance sheets with brand-new eurodollars. Banks in London still traded claims on bank deposits in America. But these claims functioned as a kind of reserve, the safest dollars in a market where foreign banks were also making their own dollars, an ocean away from the Federal Reserve. Just as Spain's silver reales de a ocho were more or less faithful copies of the original silver joachimsthaler, eurodollars had become more or less faithful copies of American bank dollars. The new American empire had not exported its dollars on purpose, though it did benefit when they stayed abroad, instead of coming home to be redeemed for gold. Bankers in London had simply started trading dollars, then making more of their own. The bankers didn't ask for permission. They just did it.

A memo from 1971, meant at the time to be shared only among central bankers, made it clear that that's exactly what was going on. The memo estimated that there had been $9 billion in total new eurodollar loans in 1964, and that had grown to $41.5 billion by 1970. Half of that growth had taken place in 1968 and 1969; most of it, the memo explained, came from brand-new dollar loans. Banks in London discounted trade bills denominated in dollars, handing over new deposit dollars to pay for them. Banks opened lines of corporate credit in new eurodollars. All the things we've learned so far that banks do, they were doing in London, in eurodollars. Central bankers in Europe and the United States were sending memos back and forth because they were worried no one had any real regulatory control over what the British were allowing. American bankers came to London in late 1960 not to lend dollars but to *borrow* them.

There were nine American bank branches in the City at the end of 1963. In 1969, there were thirty-two: large New York investment banks like Morgan Stanley and Lehman Brothers, but also smaller regional banks. The Girard Trust Bank from Philadelphia had opened a branch on Queen Street. The City National Bank of Detroit was on Cornhill. Both the Texas Commerce Bank and the First National Bank of Boston had landed offices right on Moorgate, which Londoners renamed "Avenue of the Americas." In 1964, American bank subsidiaries in London had borrowed a total of $1.1 billion in claims on deposits held in America. By the end of 1969, that had grown to $12.7 billion.

Anything that seems crazy in finance rests on the reality that bankers are both creative and profit seeking. American banks borrowed claims on American deposits, in London, to get around rules that prevented them from doing the exact same thing back home. Since the Depression, the Fed had set a ceiling on how much interest banks could pay on deposits; in the 1960s that ceiling was set at 4 percent. The original idea was to encourage state banks to lend locally, rather than lock up their capital by keeping balances on deposit with larger commercial banks paying high interest rates. The consequence, though, was that American banks couldn't compete with each other to pull in more deposits by raising interest rates—in America. In London, any American bank with a local branch could borrow eurodollars by paying between 8 and 12 percent.

Those eurodollars, in turn, made what came to be known as the round trip. American banks borrowed eurodollars in London, then turned right around and made loans back to their head offices in America. The London branch of the Girard Trust Bank on Queen Street would borrow eurodollars, then rebook them as an asset called "due from head office." Then the head office in Philadelphia would book a liability titled "due to foreign branches." Perversely, the head office didn't even have to hold any kind of reserve against the new deposits; since they were technically a loan from its London branch, Girard Trust could describe them to the Fed as "other liabilities." If this all sounds like financial engineering, it was. But it allowed the Girard Trust Bank to borrow as many dollars as it wanted from Queen Street in London, which meant it could then increase its loans in Pennsylvania and its profits at the head office in Philadelphia. In 1964, head offices in the United States owed their London branches $1 billion. By 1969, that had risen to $12 billion.

That year the Federal Reserve System, worried about a full percentage-point increase in inflation over the previous year, had taken several steps to tighten monetary policy—to discourage banks from borrowing at the Fed or making new loans. In 1969, the Fed's reserve banks raised discount rates, increasing the interest that commercial banks would have to pay to take out short-term loans. Then the Fed increased the required reserves on deposits; for each dollar in a checking account, commercial banks would have to keep a higher percentage sitting idle as reserves at the Fed. But all the Americans in the eurodollar market meant that as the Fed tried to restrain American banks at home, the banks had just moved all their activity across the Atlantic. *Euromoney* magazine introduced the fictional character of Herbie the confused American because at the end of the 1960s a lot of confused Americans were wandering around Moorgate in London, trying to figure out how to send dollars home.

Herbie was not the only American to arrive in July 1969. After meetings in Paris and Rome, the very real Andrew Brimmer, governor at the Federal Reserve, stopped in London to ask about eurodollars. Officials at the Bank of England told Brimmer the Fed should have one policy on reserves and interest rates for bank headquarters in the United States *and* their branches in London; they were desperate for the Fed to treat all dollars at home and abroad the same way for American banks, to get the Americans out of the eurodollar markets—the competition for eurodollar deposits had started to drive up interest rates in London. British commercial bankers told Brimmer that the new Americans didn't know what they were doing. And the American bankers around Moorgate seemed worried the fun wasn't going to last forever.

ANDREW BRIMMER NOTICES THAT EURODOLLARS ARE CAUSING PROBLEMS BACK HOME

As the markets for eurodollars grew in London, the United States was confronting the problem of sovereignty over the dollar. It did not have meaningful control over foreign banks making dollar loans, or even American banks in London taking on dollar debt. At Brimmer's urging in 1969, the Fed made American banks hold a reserve against loans from their branches in London, but left the ceiling on interest rates on deposits intact. What eventually slowed the flow of loans back to head offices was the Fed's domestic policy: It stopped tightening, and American banks could borrow more cheaply at home again.

Eric Helleiner, a political scientist at the University of Waterloo in Canada, has argued that the market for eurodollars grew not despite the efforts of the United States and the U.K. but *because* both countries needed the eurodollar markets to succeed. It was good for banks in the City of London, which collected fees on eurobond issues and interest on eurodollar loans. It was good for American banks, which had found a way around even the modest restrictions of the New Deal and Bretton Woods. It was good for the U.S. federal government, too. Claims that foreigners had on American commercial banks could stay in London, instead of returning to Fort Knox for gold. And so long as eurodollars stayed in London, the United States would not have to go through a painful internal adjustment. America didn't have to stop spending on its military, or lower prices to make its exports more competitive, or raise interest rates punitively to reduce credit and attract more investors from overseas. Eurodollars came out of private creativity in London, but the federal government began to accept them, tacitly, as useful for policy in America.

In 1969, Andrew Brimmer began building a public case for how the round-trip trade in eurodollars, even if it was good for lots of other people, was making the Fed's job harder. The Fed had tightened, but bigger

American banks with branches in London hadn't felt the same restraint as the rest of the country's smaller, regional banks. Then, in April 1970, armed with even more data, he flew out to San Francisco to give his speech to the bondmen at the Fairmont hotel. He had sharpened his argument to make the problem clear. For the bigger banks with eurodollars and their industrial customers, there had been no tightening. Regional and local banks, however, had been forced to tighten, as had their customers: cities and households.

Brimmer's speech put data and an explanation under an anecdotal problem that Congress had already noticed. Loans to households, and in particular mortgages, had dropped in 1969. In response, Congress had passed the Credit Control Act, which allowed the administration to direct the Fed to impose selective credit controls that would encourage banks to make more mortgage loans. But the Nixon administration declined to use the power. Arthur Burns, an adviser to Nixon, left the White House to become chair of the Fed's Board of Governors in January 1970 and made it clear in his nomination hearings that he did not approve of deciding which kinds of loans were more important.

In March 1970, just before Brimmer's San Francisco speech, Democrats on the Joint Economic Committee asked Nixon to instruct the Fed to exercise its power to direct credit anyway. The Republican minority on the committee proposed instead that the president establish a "National Voluntary Credit Allocation Committee," modeled on Brimmer's old Voluntary Federal Credit Restraint program, in which banks would promise to provide more mortgages. *The Wall Street Journal*'s editorial board immediately hated the idea. "Lenders are already allocating credit," they wrote, "as they must do when demand exceeds supply."

At the Fairmont, Brimmer laid out a different solution. Rather than ask the banks to help, he wanted to make the banks help. Banks already held reserves against some of their *liabilities*—domestic deposits. Brimmer wanted the Fed to have the power to make banks hold reserves against their *assets*—loans. Further, the Fed might make banks hold higher reserves against specific kinds of loans, such as industrial loans or business lines of credit, which would discourage banks from lending to businesses. The opposite could be true as well; lower reserves against mortgages or local government debt would encourage banks to make those loans. Remember, bankers hated holding reserves, because they made dollars safe but didn't make a profit.

Brimmer knew at the time the speech was a big deal. Major newspapers and wire services led with the "sweeping change" he had suggested. Regional newspapers, recognizing the importance of the speech, pulled the article from the wires for their own pages. Arthur Burns, still only months into his term as chair of the Fed, definitely read the speech, marking the policy proposals in pencil on his own copy. Brimmer's speech at the Fairmont had presented an idea: Build policy tools that can distinguish among types of loans. He wanted the Fed to have the sovereign power to make American bank dollars work equally for everyone. The speech also started a fight in which commercial bankers clarified their objections to Brimmer's attempt to exercise sovereignty. In 1970, they were not going to allow anyone to tell them which kinds of loans they were supposed to make.

THE FEDERAL RESERVE SYSTEM SHUT BRIMMER DOWN

William Proxmire, a powerful member of the Senate's Banking, Housing, and Urban Affairs Committee, received Brimmer's speech with gratitude. Proxmire had already been frustrated. Military spending and business investment—fueled in part by the eurodollar round trip—had raised inflation. But the Nixon administration was refusing to use its brand-new power to instruct the Federal Reserve to impose selective credit controls—to encourage mortgages, for example, or discourage business loans. After reading Brimmer's speech, Proxmire decided it might be possible to get a bill through his committee that would give the Fed its own power to impose selective credit controls on banks—without having to wait for the White House's permission. An intellectual argument at the Fed over how to protect American bank dollars from eurodollars reanimated an older fight in Congress over whom dollars were supposed to work for in the first place.

Brimmer would later say that the Federal Reserve System "split wide open" over the bill. The presidents of the regional Fed banks tended to be more directly responsive to the commercial bankers who had hired them, and Darryl Francis, president of the Federal Reserve Bank of St. Louis, began to speak regularly on the topic. "Social priorities," he argued, should not interfere with the "market allocation of credit." David Eastburn, president of the Philadelphia Fed, pointed out in a speech in Manhattan that the Fed had tried to direct credit flows before—the cap on deposit interest, for example. "The task is distasteful," he said, "and results have not been outstandingly successful." Any decision on *who* got credit was inherently political, he concluded, and would likely be a "difficult and thankless" compromise of the Fed's independence. Francis and Eastburn didn't just reject Brimmer's solution. They weren't even interested in thinking about the problem.

Brimmer found some support at the board. Sherman Maisel, one of those unpredictable economists, voted with Brimmer to support the bill. So did James Robertson, a former lawyer at the Department of the Treasury. The other four members of the board opposed the idea, none so vehemently as Arthur Burns; Brimmer described it as the "most intense" disagreement he had had with the chair. Burns initially didn't want Brimmer to testify on the bill at all, then suggested that Congress could invite Brimmer to speak on his own behalf, on a separate day. Burns went first. He killed the bill before it ever had a chance to live.

Proxmire opened the hearings for the bill on March 31, 1971, by framing a broader argument. He made it clear that the hearings were not about his bill but about a problem: When the Fed tightened, it hit housing and state and local governments the hardest. Dollars were working differently for different people, and the Fed was the only major central bank that did not take on some responsibility for "allocating credit to socially important sectors." Anyone who testified against Brimmer's plan still had an obligation to come up with an alternative. To Proxmire, it was clear that even an independent Fed had its own political ideas on how to do its job.

Burns responded with a tight argument, focusing only on technical aspects of why the bill's section on credit controls couldn't work. It applied only to commercial banks that were members of the Federal Reserve and would drive them out of the system. It would introduce uncertainty into the Fed's main job of expanding or contracting overall bank credit. Then he broadened out. "Our free credit markets have served our nation well over the years," he said, "by channeling financial resources to productive and socially beneficial uses."

Fed policy had a disproportionate effect on mortgages, Burns conceded, but it was Congress's job to provide its own solutions, through the federal home loan banks or the Department of Housing and Urban Development. The board, he said, had "grave doubts" about the bill but understood how important it was to prevent monetary policy from hitting some industries harder than others. Burns could see the problem: The Fed couldn't restrain the big banks with London branches the way it restrained local banks. He just wanted nothing to do with fixing it. Memos from around the same time show that Burns was looking over his shoulder at the banking lobby; the American Bankers Association had made clear it would not accept any new restraints under a bill it said could "result in virtual dictation of the loan policies of banks." Banks were set against the bill and using apocalyptic language. Burns wasn't going to upset them.

In the hearing, Burns pulled what looks like a sleight of hand. The Fed governors at the board, he said, were unanimously against the bill. This was narrowly true. Brimmer thought the bill was too specific about the types of credit named, and wanted to extend the new requirements to all banks, not just Fed member banks. Pressed on whether there was any disagreement *in general* at the board on the subject of variable reserves, Burns repeated, simply, that the board was unanimously opposed to the bill, and that he didn't care to speculate on the opinions of any other board members. According to Brimmer, the board had been split, 4–3, on the idea. Burns had converted an internal vote against one specific bill into a unanimous vote against ever having the Fed favor certain kinds of loans at all.

Andrew Brimmer didn't testify until April 7, almost a week after the hearings began. It was too late. After Burns's testimony, the financial papers and the banking trade press had already decided what they had learned. "The Fed Says 'No'" was the headline in *The Economist,* preserved in a pile of clippings in Brimmer's folders. The reporter from *The Washington Post* came to the same conclusion. "The Federal Reserve Board unanimously opposes legislation," he wrote, "that would give it wide discretionary powers to channel money into what it considers socially desirable areas." *The Wall Street Journal* went with the headline "Federal Reserve Opposes Move to Bolster Its Credit-Control Power." The decision, the *Journal* clarified, had been unanimous. "Mr. Burns Buys Some Time" was what an editorial in *American Banker* concluded.

In October, Brimmer appeared at the annual meeting of a trade group for bankers, cast as the heel. It was in this appearance that he referred to the response to his San Francisco speech as "vigorous," slyly noting the role that his audience had played in organizing an opposition to his own proposal. Brimmer pointed out what his research showed. Eurodollar loans were making the round trip for big companies with access to international banks. By declining to restrain those loans, he argued, the Fed was already allocating credit, whether it wanted to or not. He also began to talk about *why* banks preferred business loans: Dollar for dollar, they were more profitable, supported by the need to maintain longer-term relationships with large business lenders. The banks with London branches and corporate clients were dealing in big money. Just like a late medieval mint banging out silver coins on a stump, bank profits were higher for a few big loans than they were on a lot of little ones. Brimmer saw a new version of the old problem. Dollars were working one way for merchants, another for everyone else.

Proxmire's bill made it through committee, but it did not pass in the full Senate. In the fight over the bill, arguments and language about credit controls at the Fed, still open the previous year, had already been set. In early 1970, Brimmer had presented data to describe a problem and offered what he believed was the best solution. By the end of 1971, that solution had moved through bankers, the Fed, and Congress, and emerged as a broad ideological question. Someone had to allocate credit, directing bank dollars one way or another. Should it be the state, as it often is after panics or during wars? Or should it be the markets? The phrase "credit allocation" was just a description of that problem. But within the Fed and on the pages of *The Wall Street Journal,* the phrase itself was also starting to become a slur, a simple way to say "never the state."

NIXON TAKES THE DOLLAR OFF GOLD AND THE DOLLAR DOESN'T COLLAPSE

On Friday, August 13, 1971, Arthur Burns was summoned to the White House. He got into a helicopter with the president, the secretary of the Treasury, and several of the administration's economic advisers, then flew to Camp David, where the president said that phone calls were prohibited and "any leak would be treason." They met for four hours with the president on Friday, then again on Saturday, after which Nixon spent some time with his speechwriter, watched the Washington Redskins beat the Denver Broncos on television, and was in bed by 11:15. On Sunday morning they all flew back to the White House, and at 9:00 p.m. Nixon announced to the nation on television that he had instructed his Treasury secretary to temporarily close the gold window. Foreign central banks could no longer trade dollar deposits for gold from Fort Knox at $35 an ounce—or at all, for any price.

We often treat that weekend at Camp David as a crucial human decision in the long history of money, when the United States and by extension the world abandoned the tradition of gold convertibility and ascended into fiat. If that's true—if gold was what had always been holding money aloft—then something truly magical happened in 1971. Richard Nixon closed the gold window, and the value of the dollar and all the rest of the world's currencies didn't evaporate. That takes a healthy belief in magic. But as we've seen over the last three chapters, gold and silver had never been the *source* of the value of the American bank dollar. Gold was just a way of controlling the dollar. When Nixon took the gold away, he didn't take away banks, with their matched liabilities and assets. He didn't take away the accumulated experience of regulators in America, or centuries of human habit. The gold was gone. The dollar remained.

Nixon was trying to get free from the Triffin dilemma; if foreigners can always convert their American bank dollars to gold, then eventually either there won't be enough dollars for everyone to use, or the gold will run out. The balance of payments—the difference between what other countries owed the United States and what the United States owed in return—had begun to drop precipitously. And as the rest of the world lost interest in ever buying American products, the pressure to redeem some of those American bank deposits for gold had grown, too. In 1965, when Andrew Brimmer had asked banks and companies to volunteer to shave down the balance of payments, it ran at minus $1.8 billion; these were all American deposit dollars and dollar assets, held by foreigners who had sold things to Americans. By 1970, it was minus $3.8 billion. In 1971, minus $10.6 billion. And even as that negative balance grew, and claims on American bank dollars continued to circulate in the eurodollar market, foreign central banks began to arrive at the Treasury Department for gold. The eurodollar market kept dollars offshore and away from the gold window—just not enough of them. In 1965, Federal Reserve banks and Fort Knox held 394 million fine ounces of gold. By 1971, that had dropped to 292 million.

In America in the twentieth century, every president after Kennedy

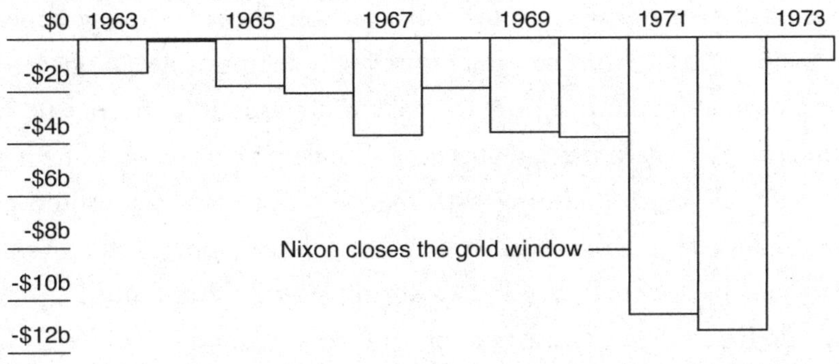

Graph by Evan Applegate. (Data from U.S. Senate, *Tables and Statistical Material on U.S. Balance of Trade and Balance of Payments,* 1974.)

faced the same choice: either run up the balance of payments abroad or make serious adjustments at home—raise interest rates, force a deflation, lower the budget deficit. Each president had always chosen to let the balance of payments slide. There were half measures, like the interest equalization tax or Andrew Brimmer's Voluntary Foreign Credit Restraint program, but overall Americans approached the prospect of foreigners holding dollar balances on American banks with what Secretary of the Treasury John Connally called "benign neglect." People abroad wanted dollars. The easiest political option for any American politician was to just keep making dollars and hope enough of them stayed abroad, sloshing around as eurodollars in London.

The language of finance is so alienating that it's hard to see the balance of payments as a product, but that's what it was. American banks manufactured deposit dollars. The federal government manufactured Treasurys. Foreigners wanted to hold both, because they had become useful as money, particularly within the eurodollar market. The dollars held abroad as the balance of payments became America's cheap *mita* silver dollars and, like the silver moving through Castile in the seventeenth century, began to warp the place that manufactured them. Easy choices about the dollar in America became enduring policy. Congress and the White House had less and less reason to restrain the American banks making profits in the eurodollar markets, because it kept American bank deposits from coming home for redemption. Manufacturers didn't have to figure out how to make their products cheaper to sell them abroad, to earn foreign currency. The Federal Reserve didn't have to destroy American lending with high interest rates that would encourage more foreigners to invest in the United States, swinging the balance of payments back. Unlike during World Wars I and II, presidents no longer had to raise taxes or run massive bond drives to pay for the war in Vietnam. They just kept borrowing, and it was fine.

Monetary economists can sometimes make a fetish of discomfort. Deflations and high interest rates seem like elegant solutions to a balance of payments deficit, but they cause real pain to actual human beings. There is no such thing as an easy internal adjustment. If you produce the world's money, though, all those hard choices become easy. You simply don't make them. You let foreigners accumulate more bank dollars, because that's what they want. The federal government issues Treasurys in dollars, and foreigners want those, too. It was already becoming clear by the end of the 1960s that there was infinite demand for any kind of financial instrument denominated in dollars.

At the same time, inflation in the United States had swung up sharply, from a low of about 1 percent in 1965 to a high of just above 6 percent in 1970. There are several different explanations for this, and the simplest answer is that all of them were true. Manufacturing in America was as close to capacity as it has been since. Of what Americans *could* produce, they were producing a lot of it. The federal government ran a deficit that was modest by today's standards but contributed to growth through direct spending on social programs and the war in Vietnam. And in 1970, the Fed under Arthur Burns had begun to ease policy, making it cheaper to borrow. Michael Bordo, an economic historian, has written that inflation was the "elephant in the room" at Camp David: the problem that had to be solved.

Under the rules of the Bretton Woods system, currencies were still pegged. They were fixed in value against the dollar, which was fixed in value against gold. One challenge of a pegged system is that if investors *think* you're going to adjust your peg, they may force you to do it, regardless. No one wants to hold on to a dollar that's about to get less valuable, which was likely the reason for the telephone restrictions at Camp David. It's possible the Nixon administration's final decision about the gold window had been forced by a report published on August 6 by a subcommittee of the powerful Joint Economic Committee in Congress. The report concluded that the dollar was too strong; it was overvalued against other currencies. That spooked investors, who began trading their dollars for European currencies and Japanese yen, and bid up the price of gold. In late 1970, an ounce of gold had traded in London at about $37, just above the price at Fort Knox. But as London traders began to sell eurodollars and buy gold, demand had pushed that price up to $43 on August 13, the day Burns got in the helicopter with the president.

The subcommittee offered a familiar list of unappetizing solutions to prevent the drain of gold from Fort Knox. The Fed and the Treasury Department could work with other countries to regulate the eurodollar markets, which would disappoint American banks. The administration could force its allies to pay for defense in Europe and cut back military expenditures in Southeast Asia. Congress could enact wage and price controls at home to reduce inflation. The dollar could leave its Bretton Woods peg and become cheaper against other major currencies. Or the United States could finally give the International Monetary Fund the authority to become a true international central bank, replacing American bank dollars with something else, held on the balance sheet of a big institution being controlled by a bunch of other countries.

Faced with all these options, Nixon chose two. In his speech that Sunday night in 1971, he announced wage and price controls. He added a 10 percent tariff on imported manufactures. And then he solved the balance of payments problem in the simplest way possible: He decided it didn't exist. The Triffin dilemma argued that as the dollar became valuable, generating a balance of payments deficit, there would eventually be a run on America's gold. But there can't be a run if foreigners can't have the gold. So Nixon closed the gold window, and his dilemma disappeared. Burns, who had vehemently opposed the move, noted in his diary that the president didn't want to announce a new gold price for the dollar, since it might be the wrong price and blow up before the 1972 election. "The President explained that he had a way of dealing with crises, as in the case of Laos," wrote Burns. "That is, taking a tough decision, accepting immediate criticism, but reaping the harvest of approval later on. So it would be also with the gold matter under discussion."

There had been talk among policymakers for years about revaluing all the world's major trading currencies, to let the mark and yen and pound strengthen against the dollar. Milton Friedman had pushed hard to let all the currencies simply float, to reach a price on their own that reflected demand from currency traders, without any management or intervention from the world's central banks. By declining to name a new dollar price for gold, Nixon had decided that the United States would just float the dollar against gold, alone. There were no immediate, spectacular shifts in price. The Friday after Nixon's speech an ounce of gold was $43.30 in London, barely higher than it had been before the speech. By the first week of September, it had fallen back to $41.70. The dollar's exchange rate against other currencies basically held steady as well. Already in May of that year the German and Dutch governments had allowed the mark and the guilder to float. After Nixon's speech, currency markets closed for a week. When they reopened on August 23, other major trading countries had allowed their currencies to float as well—pounds sterling, yen, lira, kroner. Most had appreciated some against the dollar, the yen a little more so, but these were all steps and not leaps. Without the fixed peg to gold, the value of the dollar didn't collapse.

After Nixon's speech, everything else about the dollar had stayed the same. The FDIC and the Federal Reserve still made sure that American banks held good assets, making their deposits reliable. The United

States was still the largest single currency market in the world. All those American bank deposits continued to serve as reserves in the offshore eurodollar markets in London. Congress and the White House continued to indulge American banks, encouraging them to hold dollars for foreigners in New York and play in an unregulated market for dollars in London. In an article in *Euromoney* right after Nixon's speech, Evan Galbraith of Bankers Trust International made the traditional banker's argument against oversight of eurodollar loans: They were working fine already. "I feel that my competitors at, say, Bank of America, Citibank, Morgan Guaranty, *et al.,* can pretty well look after themselves," he wrote. "To replace the credit judgement of a eurodollar bank with guidelines set by some central bank or, worse still, committee would tangle the market with red tape." When fixed exchange rates and gold convertibility evaporated, they weren't replaced by another system. Rather, they revealed a system already in place: dollar deposits in American banks and Galbraith's sophisticated, liquid, deep, flexible—and unregulated—eurodollar market.

When I began research for this book, I thought I might start it right here in 1971, at the definitive end of the gold standard. Under the economists' view of money, this was the moment when the dollar became purely a social convention—a habit that remained when the gold went away. Surely the dollar *is* a social convention. But naming it doesn't explain it. The reluctance among economists to describe exactly how that convention works is what drove me all the way back to 1520, for a view of money where a big silver coin sat on the edges of different local systems of private and public credit. Gold replaced silver; then gold became a constraint under the gold standard, limiting the amount of dollars in the world.

When Nixon closed the gold window, it revealed what had already been there the whole time: different local systems of private and public credit. The second half of this book has been an attempt to describe where those systems came from and how they worked, so that the continued value of the dollar in 1972 and 1973 and still today doesn't come as a surprise. I have tried not to burden you with too much theory, but we have arrived at what the economist Perry Mehrling calls the money view. American bank deposits, Treasurys, London claims on American bank deposits, eurobonds, and eurodollar loans—these are all overlapping claims of assets and liabilities on different balance sheets. The liabilities have value when the assets have value.

The U.S. federal government has some control over these balance sheets, through the FDIC and the banks of the Federal Reserve. But that control is limited, and it was already clear in 1971 that it was useful for the federal government to have the eurodollar markets as a release valve for surplus American dollars. It was also clear that the eurodollar markets had a power of their own, luring American banks to London and disrupting the way the dollar worked in America. The United States did not push its dollar into Europe. The dollar got pulled, with policymakers making regular trips to London in the 1960s to figure out who, exactly, was doing the pulling.

Recently a group of political economists has argued that both Europe and the United States worked actively to support and protect the eurodollar markets in the 1970s, and that those markets wouldn't have been able to keep growing if central bankers from different countries hadn't met regularly to figure out ways to make sure they continued to function. Early in the history of the eurodollar market, commercial banks had traded in swaps, selling a eurodollar for a deposit in another currency, always with an agreement to buy it back. Central banks began to offer swaps to their own commercial banks as well, and these swaps ultimately turned central banks into a lender of last resort for banks holding eurodollars: Central banks would temporarily lend some of their own dollar reserves to commercial banks, to protect eurodollar deposits that were in theory unregulated. Eurodollars became so important that they became, in a way, official.

That system of swaps is still very much alive today. It is the mechanism through which the Federal Reserve, working through connections and trust confirmed every year among the central bankers at Jackson

Hole, bails out foreign central banks with temporary dollar loans in a panic. When necessary, the Fed's reserve banks swap some of their reserves with other central banks for their own currencies. Those central banks can in turn lend those dollars to their own commercial banks, whose unregulated, offshore eurodollars have become questionable. The eurodollar markets were and still are an ad hoc, private system that became important enough that from time to time central banks get together to provide official support. This is exactly the system John Williams had predicted in 1944, where a few key currencies and in particular the dollar serve as global trade money. The U.S. federal government did not create the eurodollar system on purpose. It was a surprise, and then it became policy.

WHAT WILL THE ARABS DO WITH THEIR MONEY?

There's another popular explanation for the continued value of the dollar: The gold was replaced by oil, and gold dollars became petrodollars. In this argument, the dollar floats with the U.S. Navy: The Saudis agreed to price their oil in dollars, and the Americans agreed to send a carrier group to the Persian Gulf when necessary. That makes the dollar system a fragile, political system, likely to collapse if that single deal does. Before the 1970s, though, eurodollars in London were already a robust, established system for international transfers, investments, and trade loans. The Saudis didn't create that system. They used it.

In the summer of 1973, a new question began to appear in *Euromoney:* What to do with all the oil profits? Oil wealth had always had a presence in the eurodollar markets, but in the early 1970s it became clear in London how much more was on its way. In 1960, Saudi Arabia had \$190 million in monetary reserves, meaning dollar deposits and assets from selling oil. By 1970, that had grown to \$1.6 billion. By 1972, \$2.9 billion. Oil producers were pulling in more reserves each year than they needed to pay for imports, and it was just piling up. The next month, an article in *Euromoney* abandoned all subtlety, asking in a headline, "What Will the Arabs Do with Their Money?"

In the early 1970s politicians and central bankers continued to meet, trying to resurrect some kind of planned global financial system, anything other than floating currencies and the haphazard dominance of the dollar. The price of gold in London had risen to about $120 an ounce by 1973; the dollar had continued to decline against other currencies, though not dramatically. Several rounds of discussions at the IMF returned to the possibility of creating some kind of new, jointly managed composite currency to replace the job the dollar was doing in London. But that doesn't seem to be what anyone with power actually wanted.

The arrival of oil surpluses added urgency to the question of whether dollars would continue to dominate London markets and trade invoicing. The United States was actively hostile to even the hypothetical suggestion that oil profits might move through the IMF, and so those profits began to move through the existing eurodollar markets in London, instead. In the back pages of *Euromoney,* fictional Herbie from the Last National Bank of Boot Hill spent 1973 frantically talking to his bond broker, who in turn spent the year flying to Kuwait with briefcases full of eurodollar bearer bonds, to sell them to Kuwaitis looking for some kind of return on their brand-new oil wealth.

David Spiro, a political scientist, has collected data on where that oil wealth went. In 1974 the single largest chunk, a little over half, went into the eurodollar markets in London. That flow continued, with some declines, into the next decade. In 1980, though, there was a sudden leap in purchases of a different asset, a different way to save: loans to the U.S. federal government. Spiro argues that the single most effective thing the United States did to support global dollar markets was to offer the Saudis a special facility to buy Treasurys cheaply. At first, oil wealth had been funneled into eurodollar markets in London. Then, as it increased, it started moving into American dollars: Treasurys. By 1982, just under a sixth of that extra oil wealth was held in Treasurys—$57 billion worth.

The Saudis didn't just decide to price their oil in dollars. They were already using the eurodollar banks in London, so they decided to buy dollar assets. A Treasury was the single safest, most liquid financial asset anyone could buy in an existing global system that already rested on American bank dollars. Those Treasurys, in turn, added to the U.S. balance of payments as they became even more valuable in a developed Atlantic dollar market, tacitly supported by the federal government, the Federal Reserve, and several other governments and central banks. Dollars and eurodollars became what countries did with extra wealth they didn't want to bring home to their domestic economies, a pattern that continues today.

Nixon closed the gold window in 1971 to solve a balance of payments crisis. What was left was a system already in place: the global dollar we have today. By the early 1980s it was clear that America's balance of payments could continue to slosh around in London in the eurodollar markets, and America's budget deficits simply created Treasurys, the world's most valuable asset. Central banks had agreed on a program of swaps—temporary loans of one currency for another—to rescue any commercial banks that got in trouble in the eurodollar market. And for Americans, the balance of payments and the budget deficit didn't ever have to be a problem again.

"A FIRM NO TO CREDIT ALLOCATION": THE END OF ANDREW BRIMMER'S IDEA

Andrew Brimmer had seen and measured how offshore eurodollars were dribbling as loans back into America and causing problems for domestic bank dollars. He had suggested that the Fed take on the job of treating different loans in different ways, to try to restrain the bigger banks that had access to eurodollars. He lost that fight in 1970 at the Fed and in Congress, then slowly lost allies at the Board of Governors, as his proposals became known among bankers as the bugbear of "credit allocation." In 1974, Henry Reuss, about to become the chairman of the House Committee on Banking, Currency, and Housing, introduced the Credit Allocation Incentive Act, again modeled on Brimmer's idea of requiring reserves against some kinds of loans. Again, Brimmer lost an internal vote on Reuss's bill, this time 5–1. Again, Burns testified first for the board, then allowed Brimmer to testify on his own behalf. As a governor, Brimmer had to suffer the indignity of reading a report to the governors from the board's research staff, describing the "conceptual, technical and administrative problems" behind a bill Brimmer himself had inspired. He underlined his copy of the report with annoyed comments in red pen.

In his folder on the bill, Brimmer preserved a piece of forensic evidence, proof that the Fed and indeed Arthur Burns already believed in quiet, ad hoc credit allocation—when it suited them. It's a copy of a letter from Burns to the president of the Federal Reserve Bank of Chicago. A group of cattlemen from the Midwest had visited Burns that same month, telling him the price of beef had dropped and that they were worried about access to bank credit. Would it be possible, Burns asked, for the Chicago Fed to lean on the banks to help?

Burns pointed out in his letter that even though small banks preferred to make safer loans to other, larger banks, sometimes it was important to extend credit to the community to keep some industries productive over the long run, which was after all the first obligation of a banker. In public, Burns was adamant that it was unacceptable for the Fed to allocate credit. In private, he believed that bankers seeking returns still had social obligations. The mimeographed copy of the letter, tucked away in Brimmer's files, is a record of animosity between the two men, a weapon laid ready but never discharged.

By 1974, the arguments against Brimmer and the new bill had already been rehearsed and given a clear name. In an economic letter that September, the Research Department of the Federal Reserve Bank of San Francisco repeated the arguments in the board's staff report under the simple headline "Allocating Credit." In November, Jeffrey Bucher, a new banker on the Board of Governors, gave an address to a banking trade group under the unambiguous title "A Firm No to Credit Allocation." The bill did not pass. "If central bankers could earn Bronze Stars for valorous combat Arthur Burns should get one," the editorial board for *The Wall Street Journal* wrote, "for straight-arming Rep. Reuss . . . and others who would put the Federal Reserve into the business of allocating credit."

Burns didn't just kill both of Brimmer's bills. He likely pushed Brimmer out of the Federal Reserve as well. An entry in his diary in January 1972 refers to a discussion about Brimmer's "inadequacy," after which Nixon offered to "do what he could to rid me of Brimmer." A month later, Nixon confirmed that he had considered ambassadorships for Brimmer, possibly in Sweden or Austria. Burns told the president it was unlikely Brimmer would accept a position in Africa. In an interview decades later, Brimmer waved this story off.

Brimmer left the Fed in 1974. The next year Reuss introduced his bill again. Burns testified. Brimmer testified. That bill did not pass, either. Brimmer had tried for five years to get the Fed to take on the responsibility of making sure its policies affected all banks—and all borrowers, big and small—the same way. As an institution, the Fed had refused.

Brimmer continued working on the problem of credit allocation after he left the Fed. In December 1974, he gave a speech at the University of Texas at Austin, "Central Banking and Credit Allocation," summarizing the "considerable amount of time" he had spent documenting the problems he'd identified while on the board. In 1980, Brimmer & Company, an economic and financial consultancy he'd founded, produced a report on how to allocate credit to small businesses for the Small Business Administration. Brimmer lingered on history, showing how the Fed had always favored some loans over others and arguing that to direct credit away from industrial loans and toward mortgages was not a departure from practice. History was important to Brimmer;

it was a way to nudge the Fed toward paying closer attention to what it had always done by accident.

It is possible now to see the influence of Brimmer's work in the Fed's mandate—its legal purpose. In 1975, Proxmire and Reuss helped push through Resolution 133. It wasn't a law, just a set of instructions, but it contained language similar to what had been in Reuss's credit allocation bill that year. The Federal Reserve, the resolution read, should "maintain long run growth of the monetary and credit aggregates commensurate with the economy's long run potential to increase production, so as to promote effectively the goals of maximum employment, stable prices and moderate long term interest rates." In English: The resolution gave the Fed a new way to measure success. Monetary aggregates were sums of different kinds of notes and deposits. Credit aggregates were sums of different kinds of loans. With Resolution 133, Congress had instructed the Fed to make sure that different kinds of money and loans were growing in a way that, overall, made the United States more productive. The Fed was supposed to direct new loans—new dollars—in a way that created economic growth, exactly what the board's staff report the year before had claimed would be impossible.

Milton Friedman thought the resolution was a "major breakthrough." Friedman, a committed free-market conservative, seems an odd bedfellow for Brimmer. But both agreed that it was important to measure and understand movements in deposits and loans. Banks make dollars, so it matters how many dollars banks make, and where those dollars go. As Friedman pointed out, though, the Fed began to undermine its instructions "so subtly and effectively that the resolution has proved to be a noteworthy minor step." The Fed and, in particular, Burns had fought the resolution and didn't want to be constrained by it. The Board of Governors responded to the resolution by confusing Congress, offering a shifting menu of different monetary and credit aggregates—different ways to sum up deposits and loans. All the new definitions of new aggregates made any single target difficult to agree on.

In 1978, that text from Resolution 133 became law. The instructions became a "shall," a statutory obligation for the Fed. That language is still part of the Federal Reserve Act today. The Fed will always remind Congress that it has a dual mandate of stable prices and maximum employment. But it treats the rest of the text like something left by accident on the books, archaic instructions to keep sheep off the village green on the Sabbath. The Fed does not have a way to measure which loans are productive. It does not have meaningful monetary or credit aggregates, or a way to decide which ones are important. The Federal Reserve decided in response to Andrew Brimmer that it would not do credit allocation; it would not have an opinion on who should get new loans and new dollars. A political decision from the early 1970s has left the Fed without theories or even benchmarks, nothing that might help it carry out its "shall" from Congress. The Fed doesn't want to distinguish among the kinds of dollars that banks make. It's supposed to, but it just doesn't.

By the end of the Great Depression, it had become clear that only banks would make dollars in America. Since then, there have been no large-scale experiments in other ways of making dollars, like the Hawarden scrip, or the hard-times municipal notes in New Orleans, or the Maryland bills of credit. Questions about money and whom it's made for have become arcane and technical, discussed in a language—Fedspeak—you have to be trained to understand. The basic reliability of deposit dollars under the FDIC has robbed this argument of its public drama.

Andrew Brimmer was looking for a way to recognize that money *is* political, whether we want it to be or not. The tools he wanted the Fed to have would have given the United States a way, as a democracy, to have frank conversations about who, in America, gets which kinds of loans. Instead, we have allowed ourselves to believe that there is no conflict, because money is not political. But as Brimmer realized when he slyly tucked away that letter from Arthur Burns about loans to ranchers, the politics of the dollar are happening all around us, all the time.

I started writing this book because I was curious about where the global dollar had come from, but I ended up finding a history of the dollar I'd never gotten, even as a close observer of economists and the Fed. That history is intensely political, a fight between big and little dollars that goes all the way back to Saxon miners, striking for good pennies. I had to figure out that different dollars work differently for different people. But that wouldn't have come as a surprise to any of the people in this book. The story of Andrew Brimmer is the story of how we forgot.

Epilogue

Naples, Doral, and Grand Forks, 2020

AMANDA DOLLARS AFTER A HURRICANE

Amanda Burke is a manager for Sunshine Ace, a chain of hardware stores around Naples, Florida. When Hurricane Irma passed right over Naples on the night of September 10, 2017, winds at 142 miles per hour ripped the roof clean off one of Sunshine's stores, but Amanda was relatively lucky. She had only lost a window at home, and the store she ran at Bonita Springs had only lost power. National hardware chains wouldn't open for another several days, but on the morning of September 11, Amanda opened her doors with twelve employees and a line of customers that snaked around the parking lot.

It wasn't safe to walk around the store with the lights out, so Amanda ran it like a warehouse. She stationed a runner at every cash register to pick up orders, handed out bottles of water to the customers lined up out front, and started selling hardware. Florida's guidelines for hurricane prep instruct citizens to take out extra cash before a storm, but Amanda says people held on to their own cash after Irma, in case they had to use it for food. So she took checks. She took the little cash that people were willing to part with. She took combinations of whatever people had.

Her registers had a backup system for credit cards, but after the storm the internet would be down for minutes at a time, and so Amanda took a calculated risk. She started making loans. "If it's, say, a regular customer and they're short a couple of bucks or their card won't go through, I'll pay for it," she told me, "and tell them, you know, to catch me the next time you're in and we'll square up." She wouldn't do it for more than $20. She didn't want it to get messy.

Amanda was taking book credits, granting small loans that sat directly on the books of the Bonita Springs Sunshine Ace hardware store, calling them out publicly without signing a note. She was manufacturing dollars, in a way that would have been immediately familiar to Anne Catharine Green and Robert Henwood in eighteenth-century provincial Maryland. People are inventive. They will find ways under any circumstances to produce something that functions like money, so that transactions clear and commerce moves on.

I met Amanda in late January 2020 when I was writing about cash. I had wanted to know how Sunshine Ace had handled cash in an emergency, and then Amanda told me her story about the book credits she offered after the hurricane. I didn't understand why that story was important until several years later, when I started to catalog all the forms the dollar can take. I think of what she produced after the hurricane as Amanda dollars, backed by the asset of the relationships she had with longtime customers and the likelihood that they would return to the store and clear their debts with either Federal Reserve notes or FDIC-insured bank deposits.

Amanda dollars may seem like exotic little instruments, but historically they're quite common. When we tell ourselves for simplicity's sake that the United States of America issues fiat dollars and backs them with full faith and credit, we miss everything. We fail to see the dollar production going on everywhere around us, in small and big banks, in tills and trading floors, onshore and offshore. I have attempted several times to come up with a list of all the different kinds of dollars I could think of. I have never completed it. I keep adding to it.

The same week I met Amanda, I visited the Miami branch of the Federal Reserve Bank of Atlanta. It sits west of the airport, across the street from the four golf courses of the Trump National Doral. To even get into the parking lot of the Fed branch, I had to follow a procedure similar to what it takes to enter a U.S. embassy in a hostile country.

When you're a Fed reporter, most of what you cover is theoretical and public. The Federal Open Market Committee meets for two days and gives you a decision about where they think interest rates should be; then in a press conference you get to ask them what they were thinking. But a lot of what the Fed does is practical and quiet. Andrew Brimmer had a lot of little jobs at the Fed. One of them was to set up the cash depot at the Miami branch, and that's exactly what I went to see.

Once I got inside the branch, I had to leave my bag behind as an employee badged me through two sealed doors. There, behind a vault door and another stainless-steel grating with two padlocks, was a warehouse full of dollars. Shrink-wrapped cash packs, each with 16,000 brand-new bills, were stacked on one side of the warehouse. On the other sat rows of wheeled Plexiglas containers of older bills, 400,000 per container. There were too many of both to quickly count. I asked how much money was in the warehouse, and a Fed employee told me, "I would go with 'a lot.' We don't talk about specifics."

In the United States, the Treasury Department prints cash in Washington, D.C., and Fort Worth, Texas, but it's basically just selling a product. The Treasury is fulfilling an order from the Fed for fancy green pieces of cloth. In turn, the Fed is responding to orders from commercial banks. All that paper has to move, securely, on armored trucks, from Treasury's printers to one of twenty-seven other depots like the one in Miami. To get cash, a commercial bank somewhere in South Florida sends an armored truck to a bay in the warehouse near the airport. The Federal Reserve Bank of Atlanta deducts the value of the cash from the commercial bank's reserves, then passes the cash packs through a cabinet with doors on each side. No one from the truck enters the building.

If a bank has too much cash, it can make a deposit at the Fed, running the same operation in reverse. An armored truck parks in the bay at the warehouse with cash to hand back through the cabinet. Workers at a table inside the warehouse get a rough count from the bags and credit the value of the cash back to the bank's reserves. Then, for a final count, the bills get wheeled into rooms with massive machines from the German firm Giesecke+Devrient—founded in Leipzig, where Saxon investors traded silver joachimsthaler five hundred years ago. The machines confirm the count and examine the bills, forty per second, then immediately shred any old bills and shoot them through a pipe in the ceiling.

The depot in Miami doesn't look like a bank. It looks like a factory. The bills collected at the Sunshine Ace hardware stores on the other side of the state come from here, then return here. And there are twenty-eight of these depots around the country, moving thirty-three billion bills a year. A Federal Reserve note is still exactly what it was in the 1930s: an entry on the Fed's balance sheet, a liability paired on the asset side with a Treasury. But part of its value is also ensured by the industrial process inside this building. When you go to the ATM, dollars come out. This is not money creation. It's money production.

You probably don't use cash as much as you used to. In 2016, Americans handed over cash for 31 percent of what they bought. By 2024, that had dropped to 14 percent. But even if the percentage of cash use continues to drop, the overall size of the economy continues to grow, so the absolute demand for bills continues to grow, too, with the rest of the economy. In 2014, there was $1.3 trillion in physical dollars in the world. By 2024, that amount had grown to $2.3 trillion. But this number is a little misleading. If you break down the number of bills, rather than the amount, and look at them by denomination, you can see that most of the denominations—$1s, $10s, $20s—are growing evenly, at the same proportion to each other. This stands to reason. As the economy expands, there's no reason why anyone would use proportionally more $20s from one year to the next.

Not the $100 bill, though. It's growing wildly out of proportion with everything else. In 2004, there were about the same number of $100s in circulation as there were $20s. In 2024 there were nineteen billion $100 bills out in the world, and only eleven billion $20s. The Fed doesn't always know where cash goes after it leaves a bank, but in 2022 a Fed researcher estimated that about 60 percent of all U.S. physical currency is held abroad, most of it as $100 bills.

The $1s, $5s, $10s, and $20s are a product the Federal Reserve provides to commercial banks so the public can take out enough cash to pay for things without having to think too hard about how. Think of them as a public service, like traffic signals or the water supply, or what Amanda Burke did on a tiny scale in Bonita Springs. The United States is perfectly competent at manufacturing this kind of money, no better or worse than any other developed economy. The $100s are a product, too—one that only America can provide. If you're a bank or a foreign government, you can keep a balance in reserves at the Fed. If you're anyone else, the only way you can have anything close to dollars that reliable is a stack of $100 bills. Money is a product, and different people need different kinds of money. Hundred-dollar bills have become an export product, useful for the rest of the world just like the silver joachimsthaler and reales de a ocho. America is the Saudi Arabia of money.

The changes that have happened to the dollar since the early 1980s are more in scale than in kind. Foreign central banks still hold claims on other currencies as their reserves—either deposits in banks in those countries or assets like government debt. The single reserve currency that matters the most is still the dollar. In 2000, foreign central banks held 71 percent of their foreign exchange reserves as some kind of dollar. By 2024, that had dropped, but only to 58 percent. That's still wildly out of proportion with any other currency. Central banks hold just under 20 percent of their reserves as euros, and just over 2 percent as Chinese renminbi. In the last several years there's been a slight movement away from dollar claims to a group of less traditional reserve currencies—the Australian, Canadian, and Singaporean dollars, South Korea's won, and the krone and krona of the Nordic countries. Part of this is that it's become easier to trade into the currencies of smaller countries, and they offer a higher return. Renminbi growth has plateaued, despite aggressive moves by the Chinese government to encourage international use.

When I tell people I'm writing a book about the dollar, I usually get two questions. First, why isn't the dollar backed by gold? I hope I've answered that one. Second, with Donald Trump elephanting around, how much longer will the dollar be the world's most powerful currency? Here I give an unsatisfying answer: for a while, probably. Robert Mundell's theory of dominant currencies argued that currencies for international trade are stable in value over the long term, and come from strong internal markets and countries that allow for the free movement of capital across borders. I can see this, but at the risk of being churlish—Robert Mundell has a Nobel Prize and I do not—I don't completely agree.

A couple of things are true of both the silver joachimsthaler and the American bank dollar. Both freely allowed what Carlo Cipolla called more or less faithful copies. The taler was copied all over the Baltic and by a brand-new Spanish empire, whose coins eventually moved around in the brand-new United States. Economic historians have tended to assume that the rules of money are different for coins and credit, but it does seem that one feature of the American bank dollar is just how many faithful copies there are. American presidents, Congresses, and Federal Reserve Boards since Kennedy have been willing to tacitly and sometimes even openly support the offshore eurodollar markets. In 2020, according to an analysis by the Bank for International Settlements, foreign commercial banks held $13 trillion in dollar deposits on their books. Of that, only $3 trillion was held in branches and subsidiaries physically in America. The rest—$10 trillion—was held on the balance sheets of banks outside the United States. They're dollars, but they aren't regulated or even explicitly guaranteed by the FDIC, the Federal Reserve, or the U.S. government. There are Amandas everywhere in the world, making their own dollars for their own reasons.

When countries began floating their currencies in the 1970s—letting them rise and fall against each other with demand—most economists believed in a model where a country's currency would rise in value as foreign demand rose for the country's products. That's not what happened, though. Work by the economist Gita Gopinath shows that even though the United States accounts for only 9 percent of the world's exports and 14 percent of its imports, about 40 percent of international trade bills are denominated in dollars. Even as other economies expanded and America's share of global trade dropped, people continued to invoice in dollars. Trading dollars for dollars is more stable and predictable than trading two currencies for each other. And all those offshore eurodollars make it easy to get instant dollar deposits by discounting an invoice denominated in dollars at commercial banks all over the world.

As I write, there's alarm in financial markets over the erratic shifts of the second Trump administration, and the value of the dollar against other currencies has been dropping, slowly but perceptibly. This could become a real change over time, but the dollar isn't a global currency just because people are in awe of the United States. All those foreign commercial banks marking up dollar deposit accounts and discounting dollar-denominated invoices aren't doing it out of respect. They're doing it as part of a series of habits built over the last fifty years, a constant expansion of the offshore eurodollar markets invented in the 1960s in London.

People manufacture their own dollars all the time, for their own reasons, and most of them have nothing to do with America. On the other side of all those foreign banks' balance sheets are dollar-denominated loans and dollar-denominated bonds. Of all the bonds issued in international markets, $14 trillion of them—just under half—are denominated in dollars. For people worried that the renminbi will replace dollars, I have only more questions. Which dollars? Where? Will all these banks convert all those dollar liabilities into renminbi liabilities? Will they sell all their dollar assets and buy renminbi assets? Where are the renminbi assets? Among all those offshore dollar liabilities are $1 trillion held by Chinese banks outside America. After more than fifty years of letting the rest of the world create dollars, America has allowed what historians and political scientists call institutions to grow—established markets, banks, knowledge, everything that builds on half a century of habit. Let Amanda dollars go on long enough, and eventually you get Amanda Inc.

And the United States does, in fact, tacitly support a lot of those dollars. You don't have the time and I don't have the sanity to explain the global financial crisis of 2008, but one part of it is that a lot of offshore dollar deposits failed, and the Federal Reserve stepped in with swaps—emergency temporary dollar loans—to bail them out. Ever since central banks developed the swap lines that allowed them to temporarily trade currencies in a crisis, the Fed had always kept swap lines open for a few trusted central banks, just as an option in an emergency. By the end of the global financial crisis, the Federal Reserve had opened swap lines with the central banks of the eurozone, Switzerland, Australia, Brazil, Canada, Denmark, the U.K., Japan, South Korea, Mexico, New Zealand, Norway, Singapore, and Sweden. Those central banks had the right to temporarily swap their currencies for dollars held by the Fed, which they in turn lent to their own commercial banks, which had gotten in trouble for the exact same reason the Hawarden State Bank had in 1927. Commercial banks all over the world held questionable dollar assets, which meant their dollar liabilities suddenly became questionable, too.

At the height of the crisis in December 2008, the Fed held $583 billion in outstanding currency swaps from other central banks—it had temporarily bought euros, pounds, Swiss francs, Australian dollars, Brazilian reals—as a courtesy to other central banks, in the interest of keeping the global offshore eurodollar system stable. When things calmed down, the value of all those assets became clearer, allowing foreign commercial banks to pay back their own central banks, which in turn closed out the swaps with the Fed.

No other country provides unlimited emergency swaps of its own currency to trusted partners. China has opened swap lines, but they've never been tested. Again it's not even clear who would need renminbi swaps. Not only does the United States accept the production of offshore dollars; it protects them in a crisis. It is easier and safer to create more or less faithful copies of dollars than it is of any other currency, by far. Amanda dollars become Amanda Inc., and then if the Fed steps in, maybe it's possible to think of all those Amanda dollars as just dollars. There is no hard definition of what a dollar is. If you make a dollar and it works, then congratulations: It's a dollar.

I also don't think Robert Mundell was quite right when he said that a global currency has to come from a country with a large internal market. That definitely helps. If you hold a currency, you want to know that it's good in a country with a lot of banks, a lot of businesses, a lot of assets, and prospects of solid growth. But it doesn't really explain the joachimsthaler, which wasn't even supposed to be a domestic currency. It was just a dividend for mine investors. The same was true of the real de a ocho, which wasn't even really part of Castile's domestic currency system, and only over time came to define trade in Latin America. What both of those coins had in common was *volume.* The mines at Joachimsthal didn't have to deal with small coins for domestic use, and instead pumped an unprecedented volume of big silver coins up into the Baltic. The pieces of eight weren't for the Castilian market, either, and didn't tend to end up there. Like the taler, they were mined and minted for export. They were useful all over the world because there were a lot of them out in the world.

Presidents used to fret when the U.S. current account balance—what Americans sell to the world, minus what they buy from the world—dipped negative. In 1971, when Nixon closed the gold window, the current account balance was minus $1.4 billion. By 2024 it had reached minus $1.2 trillion. America makes up the difference by borrowing, producing what the rest of the world considers dollar-denominated assets. The offshore eurodollar market relies on safe American dollar bank deposits and assets as a reserve, and the United States is willing to provide them, in staggering volume. American dollar-denominated assets are useful and valuable because there are a lot of them, and there are a lot of them because even as I write in the late summer of 2025, they're still useful and valuable. All of this sounds a little triumphal: Ha ha, dollars rule! But sometimes when I tell people the dollar probably won't stop being the world's reserve or trade currency anytime soon, I'll add a kicker that usually makes them uncomfortable: Would it be so bad, though? When we say the dollar is powerful, whom is it powerful for?

When American presidents and legislators finally threw up their hands and accepted their current account overhang in the 1970s, they decided they kind of liked it. Different administrations have embraced it different ways. The political sociologist Greta Krippner has pointed out that the Reagan administration quietly realized that there wasn't really a practical limit to the amount of Treasurys they could sell. The Clinton administration closed up deficits, but encouraged a strong-dollar policy that brought foreign banks onshore to hold American assets. My first job out of college in 1997 was as a temp at a subsidiary of a German bank in New York that was buying dollar assets—mortgage-backed securities that would collapse in value in 2008. Adam Tooze, a financial historian at Columbia, has pointed out another explanation for the global financial crisis: Foreigners were so desperate for onshore dollar assets that Americans started putting together really crummy ones.

George W. Bush paid for tax cuts by selling Treasurys, then paid for two wars by selling Treasurys. Just like Lyndon Johnson, Bush didn't have to run a war bond drive or raise taxes. The funding was available and he took it. Barack Obama financed a stimulus program with Treasurys, and made some of Bush's tax cuts permanent. Donald Trump added more tax cuts and then funded another stimulus. Joe Biden funded yet another stimulus and an infrastructure bill. Donald Trump added another tax cut. Investors in America and abroad want dollar assets. A Treasury is the safest dollar asset there is. We have yet to see the limits of how many Treasurys an American president can issue.

I am not a current account fetishist or a federal deficit fetishist. It's reasonable to think that a country for a time might import more than it exports, or that it might borrow for war or infrastructure spending.

It does seem that the United States, with its massive internal market and functional bank regulation, might be able to run deficits indefinitely. But as an American myself, it's frustrating that politicians never have to be openly aware of how any of it works. In Norway, after the government realized it had a gusher of oil offshore, it created a sovereign wealth fund, a big pool of investments from saved oil profits that pays for health insurance and a lot of other nice things. The United States has a gusher of dollars, but we don't openly talk about it. What should it pay for? Do we use it for ongoing spending on tax cuts? Or for health care? I think it's important to buy long-term infrastructure like fiber-optic internet, local transit, and distributed power. I think it's important to pay for public education. These things make an economy more resilient and productive, meaning that people in the future will continue to pay their taxes in bank dollars. Then the federal government can clear its Treasurys in bank dollars as they come due. And I like aggressive, intrusive financial regulation, to keep all those dollar deposits and assets safe and useful to the rest of the world. But I can't really make those suggestions as a journalist or a historian, just as a guy in a democracy.

When I read about imperial Madrid, it sounded a lot like the Washington, D.C., I had reported from off and on for twenty years. All of Castile's economic activity began to move toward the capital, as the most important industrial skill in Castile became begging money from the Habsburg kings. What is Washington, D.C., now, if not a place to beg for tax cuts or subsidies? Donald Trump has suggested a sovereign wealth fund for America, a way to save dollars and invest them in something—it's not clear what. I read through his proposals with sadness. America could have invested in anything with all the Treasurys it sold over the last twenty-five years. Instead, America just avoided hard decisions about *why* it was borrowing, and what it was getting when it did.

I blame the dollar. It's too useful, too easy for America to produce, too easy to copy; there are too many of them out in the world. The temptation to produce more dollars is too exciting for any American politician to resist. I don't think the global dollar is going to collapse. I do wish Americans had held a more honest conversation about how it's worked for the last generation, and what we wanted to do with it.

After I met Amanda Burke in January 2020, I had to drive back across the state of Florida to Miami, to catch a flight home. In the car I finally got in touch with someone I had been playing phone tag with, a virologist I knew from reporting I had done years earlier on Ebola. I had wanted to ask what he thought about the rumors coming out of China.

DARRYL DOLLARS DURING A PANDEMIC

The Federal Reserve and the Treasury Department did an extraordinary job protecting global and American dollar markets during the pandemic. Together they started so many emergency loan programs that in the early weeks of the pandemic I never felt comfortable being more than a few steps away from my desk as the Fed continued to announce with very little notice each new market it was going to step into. The dollar swap lines with foreign central banks, already tested during the global financial crisis, worked again as designed: They protected offshore eurodollars in commercial banks based in other countries. By April 2020 the Fed held $450 billion in outstanding swaps, including $145 billion to the European Central Bank and $223 billion to the Bank of Japan. People abroad use dollars and make their own because the Fed makes sure offshore dollars are safe for an expanding circle of economies. The political scientist Eric Helleiner calls this the status quo crisis: Every time something goes wrong in financial markets, leaders get together to talk through multilateral solutions, but in the end the Fed just protects all the dollars.

What the Fed and the Treasury protected without question or failure, though, were what we still might call *moneta grossa*—big-money dollars, the ones that move in financial markets and overseas. Their record during the pandemic on little-money dollars for families and businesses was less impressive. After the Federal Reserve decided in the 1970s that it wasn't even going to develop theories about credit allocation, the macroeconomists who move in and out of the Fed and write college textbooks stopped thinking about aggregates—the way different kinds of money and credit all add up. And so both in practice and in theory all the different kinds of dollars became fungible. It was all the same water. Pour it somewhere into the system and it will come out everywhere.

It's not just economists, though, who've made it difficult to think about different kinds of dollars. Anthropologists tend to rely on a framework inherited from the economic historian Karl Polanyi, who in 1957 argued that newer economies used *general-purpose* money for all payments. Older societies used *special-purpose* moneys—each for a specific market and social purpose. This is a transformation story just like the fiat one economists use, where there used to be many moneys and now there is one. The economists approve of the transformation. The anthropologists regret it. Both believe it happened.

This left me as a Fed reporter without any theories to understand something that kept showing up in my notes: Different kinds of dollars behaved in different ways. Little money, petty money, payment money, what we might call low finance just isn't that important to the Fed. The Fed has a research section that focuses on community development, but they're separate from the macroeconomic forecasters. Policymakers at the Fed and the macroeconomists who prepare research briefs for decisions as part of the Federal Open Market Committee just don't spend that much time thinking about what drives car loans or small-business loans or pawnshop loans or even credit card loans. People at the Fed will mention Americans without bank accounts who end up using high-fee check cashers and payday lenders. But it's never a policy priority to force banks to offer low-fee services to customers with low balances.

It is profoundly more expensive in the United States than it is in other places to transfer small amounts of money from one bank account to another. The Fed has begun to address this, but is far behind other developed countries. It just wasn't a priority. During the pandemic, when Congress approved direct transfers of dollars from the Treasury Department's account at the Fed to bank accounts of actual Americans, it became clear that the Treasury didn't even have a lot of Americans' bank account information. Some didn't have bank accounts. Some had used tax preparation services that veiled their customers' bank account information. The department had the ability to sell Treasurys into financial markets in return for bank dollars, but it couldn't transfer those bank dollars to actual people.

I don't think money now is all that different from the way it used to be. The problem that the Treasury and the Fed have getting banks to focus on small-dollar transfers and loans is the exact same problem that early modern princes had in getting mints to focus on petty coins: The brassage costs are higher. It is more expensive, per dollar, to make small-dollar loans than big ones. It is more expensive, per dollar, to transfer small amounts than big ones. Normal people and poor people just don't provide profits for banks, the way they didn't provide profits for mints, and so banks, like mints, avoid them if they can. I don't think there ever *was* a transformation in money. The same problem has been with us since the miners walked off the job at the St. Joachimsthal mines in 1517. It was true in Annapolis in 1764 and New Orleans in 1837 and Hawarden in 1932. It's still true today. Small-money coins, transfers, and loans are terrible business.

In the last few years when I tell people what I do, I've been getting a new question: What do I think of crypto? I'm not inherently hostile to crypto; I just don't think it's all that different from the banking system we already have. Coins that are created by communities of miners, like bitcoin and ethereum, are just assets. Assets are useful, but they've always been just one part of systems of credit and assets working together. If we wanted to build a system on bitcoin, we'd have to think about what banking looks like with bitcoin as the asset, and then we'd have to think about bank regulation, and eventually you get the same set of challenges we already have. People like credit, and just as provincial

Marylanders did in 1767, they will create little local credit systems to solve their own problems, no matter what you tell them.

As I write, Congress has just passed legislation that will give special status to stable coins, a kind of crypto produced by companies that's supposed to stay on par with the dollar. But stable coins don't need a special status. They're just banks. The stable coin itself is a dollar deposit. The company holds assets to give it value. The value of the assets is the value of the coin. There's nothing about a stable coin that would have been out of place among the commercial banks on the American side of Canal Street in New Orleans in the early 1830s, and in fact the new legislation has given stable coin regulation back to the states, a solution that did not produce reliable money before the panic of 1837 or during the bank failures at the beginning of the Great Depression. The bill sending stable coins to the states for regulation confirmed my biggest worry about the dollar: that America's bank regulations, hard-won through more than two centuries of financial crises, will decay. And as they do, so will the certainty that American bank dollars will always have value.

Where I do see the appeal of crypto, though, is in its promise to make low finance cheaper and more accessible. I just don't think it will succeed. As has been clear in almost every chapter of this book, low finance is not great business. To make low finance possible, you either bring in help from the state or charge exorbitant fees. It's not an accident that much of the innovation in crypto took place in America, where it's expensive to make small transfers. The cost of transferring money in America is a problem that needs to be solved. You solve it, unfortunately, by doing all the unprofitable and often tedious work of caring about low finance.

In 2021, I flew to Fargo, North Dakota, then drove north to Grand Forks to meet Darryl Jorgenson, a Coast Guard veteran who had moved back to his hometown to work as the business banker at the Grand Forks branch of the Gate City Bank. It's a community bank, which is difficult to define precisely, but a community bank generally holds less than $10 billion in assets, takes deposits, and holds a traditional portfolio of mortgages and business loans.

A year earlier, in March 2020, Congress had authorized the first round of the Paycheck Protection Program, $350 billion in loans to small businesses, to keep workers on payrolls during shutdowns. The loans were refundable, and guaranteed by the Federal Reserve. But the applications had to go through a bank. A month into the program, researchers at the Federal Reserve Bank of New York noticed something peculiar. Density of paycheck loan approvals was higher in some states, but didn't seem to have an obvious relationship with either COVID case count or unemployment. They did find, however, that states with a higher share of business deposits at community banks were more likely to have more approved paycheck loans per business.

In the first round of the program demand for the loans was dramatically higher than supply, which meant that a relationship with a bank and access to an office made a bigger difference. Community banks hold 15 percent of the total loans in the banking system, but in the first round of paycheck loans they processed 60 percent of the total funding for the program. Even after the second round closed at the end of that summer and larger banks began to participate, community banks still accounted for 45 percent of funding.

North Dakota had one of the highest shares of community bank business deposits, and the highest density of approved paycheck loans in the country. No bank in the state processed more loans than Gate City. And so in 2021, Darryl Jorgenson and I got into his cherry-red Ford pickup to talk to one of his customers. Darryl apologized for the glitter in the back seat left over from his son's trip to prom, and we drove to Rumors, a hockey bar at the Grand Cities Mall. It is one of the many small businesses he helped keep alive during the pandemic.

Smaller banks still tend to have lower overall returns, because they don't trade assets or tend to offer wealth management services, which are profitable lines of business. They require more bodies, too. Community banks hold $7 million in assets for every employee. Larger banks hold $12 million, a gap that has been growing since the financial crisis. Community banks tend to have more branches, which are expensive, and take more consumer deposits—though their share of both has dropped over the last two decades. And even though people talk to a teller less often than they used to, the share of families that still visit a branch at least once a year has barely budged. Sometimes, people still really need to talk to a banker.

The day after the paycheck program started, Darryl Jorgenson came into his office to seventy-three voicemails asking about the loans, and emails arriving at 100–150 an hour. "It was customers, neighbors," he said, "people who weren't even a customer of mine, who knew I was a banker." He deputized the branch's deposits manager as a small business banker, and together they began returning calls.

At its headquarters in Fargo, the bank had made three decisions. It would process all applications by order of arrival, not account size. It would take all applications from any kind of existing customer—not just business customers, but anyone with deposits or a mortgage. Calls had been coming from as far away as California, so Gate City also decided it would take applications from anyone in North Dakota, so long as they showed a driver's license and went through the normal process to open a checking account. The bank used its drive-through teller stations for in-person meetings, and came up with ways to reopen lobbies quickly. In Grand Forks, Jorgenson collected proof of payroll at restaurant take-out windows, met hairdressers outside their homes, and drove documents to car-repair-shop owners who didn't have email addresses. The paycheck program was a stress test for financial relationships: If you could find a human being at a bank to talk to, you could get a loan.

At Rumors, Darryl introduced me to Bill Tyrrell, one of the bar's owners. When Bill goes to the branch at Grand Forks, the tellers let his Maltese Shih Tzu puppy run around behind the counter. He heard about the paycheck program on the news; the next day, as the rules for the loans changed by the hour and bigger banks still weren't sure they'd participate, he got an email from Darryl, explaining how to apply. By April 8—five days into the program—the loan had been approved, and Bill walked a rent check through the mall to the Hope Church, his landlord.

Andrew Brimmer was right in 1970. Not all dollars are the same, and different banks respond to the same stimulus by sending dollars in different directions. Community banks tend to be stronger in rural areas, which means they're stronger in whiter areas, which meant that because of a quirk in the American banking system there were racial differences in who got money, when. To fix this problem, the Federal Reserve would have to start thinking about who gets credit, and how, and for what, and whether those loans are productive—the way the Fed's statute says they need to be. And the Fed would need to reexamine its preference for buying large amounts of Treasurys, which make existing assets more valuable, which favor people with houses and stock portfolios.

Once you do that, you're starting to think about credit allocation. As Brimmer pointed out, credit allocation happens already. The only choice is whether we do it on purpose or let it happen by accident. It's still true now. If you wanted Darryl dollars in 2020, you had to get lucky and know someone like Darryl. Banks in the United States produce American bank dollars, still in the uncertain summer of 2025 the most useful, coveted financial asset in the world. That gives America the grace to make bad decisions and then keep borrowing. I guess that's a privilege. But often Americans still have to be lucky enough to know someone like Darryl to solve their problems in a crisis. The almighty dollar didn't fix that for America. It never did anywhere else, either.

Acknowledgments

This book was Kevin Doughten's idea. In 2017 he emailed me to ask whether there was "anything interesting in a book-length history of the dollar." It is a journalist's job to say yes to an editor and then figure it out later, so that's what I did, offering a brief description of a book I might write that in no way resembles this one. "Cool," he wrote back. "But can it be done through a compelling, character-driven narrative?" That was a more difficult question, one it has taken me nine years to answer.

I am told editors like Kevin no longer exist. I don't know; I've only written one book. But I can tell you he carefully drew this book out of me year by year, quietly shelving it when it took me longer than agreed, then longer, then longer again. And I can tell you every paragraph is in some way the product of his ruthless determination to tell a complex story simply, through human characters, for humans to read. If editors like Kevin no longer exist, we are the poorer for it, and I am grateful to him for the partnership that became this book.

While I am thanking people for their patience, allow me to add Liz Parker, my agent at Verve, now at Parker Projects, who had absolutely no reason to believe this book would ever get done and yet continued to negotiate for time, initially out of conviction and eventually, I can only assume, out of curiosity. In the depths of this project she finally said, "Look: either you'll write this book, or you won't." She was right.

I am grateful for the many people who spent most of a decade listening to half-formed ideas over the phone. Mark Blyth did far more of this than could have been reasonably expected. So did Tanner Colby,

Lane Greene, Chris Suellentrop, Colin Baker, and Justin Mikolay, who all assured me it was possible to both start and finish a book. Rob Greeley, Lowry Greeley, Eric Van Gieson, and Julie Baron aren't writers or academics, and yet I made them listen anyway.

And then there is Sean Trask, who shepherded me through the hardest parts of this book, reading daily pages as I finished them and encouraging me to keep going. In Chapter 5, all the footprints except Sean's disappear, as he carried me fireman-style over his shoulder into Chapter 6.

To all of them I say thank you and also: I'm sorry I'm not the strong, silent type.

Several people read this book in its shaggy, ungainly first draft. Harold James, my advisor, read individual chapters and then went back and read the whole thing with such care that he has been able to pull off his party trick of recalling and responding to individual passages at will. Rebecca Spang is not my advisor and yet acted like one anyway, offering detailed notes that are now part of every page. Jess Scott at Crown recently pointed out that she was 14 when I started work on this book, and she is somehow already one of the finest editors I've ever worked with.

Sharon Murphy made careful corrections on most of this book. Ann Daly did the same for the first half, as did Sean Vanatta for the second half. I had so many conversations with Sean about the New Deal that eventually his wife suggested I not call during dinner time in Scotland. Steffen Murau read most of the book, then went back and read the eurodollar chapter again. Iñaki Aldasoro read the eurodollar chapter, too. And if I got eurodollars wrong, at the very least it's not Ben Braun's fault. He tried. Chris Hughes was the only person I could talk to about Andrew Brimmer. To all of them: I promise to pay this favor forward. Or back, if I ever have the chance.

Evan Applegate did all the illustrations for this book. I don't know whether it's possible for everyone to find an illustrator who's a dear friend who will catch up with you on what are supposed to be work calls, but I recommend it.

I did some of the reporting for this book while I was still at the *Fi-*

nancial Times, under the patient care of Gillian Tett and Demetri Sevastopulo, and with Colby Smith and the delightful savages of *FT Alphaville*. I am grateful to that paper and in particular Tony Tassell for holding the door open to let me keep writing columns after I decided I'd rather be a historian than a journalist.

Against advice and reason I began a PhD at Princeton in the middle of writing this book. It is hard to describe how much of these pages I owe to the Department of History, but I am again grateful to Harold James, whose office in Dickinson Hall is so full of books that there is just enough room for one person to sit and talk for hours about money. Michael Blaakman volunteered as guide through both the literature of early America and the steep ascent into academia. I am grateful that Isadora Moura Mota took me on as a project, and for her help thinking about New Orleans as part of the Caribbean economy.

I am grateful to Seth Rockman, who invited me to a conference where I learned for the first time that there are historians who write about money. Hannah Farber read an early draft of the Maryland chapter and then asked me question I hadn't yet considered: What is this book about? Alan Stahl showed me how coins are made, then let me spend way too much time with an astonishing collection of coins and bank notes in a tiny room near his office.

Kristy Novak and Beth Lew-Williams made it possible, in dozens of tiny ways, to be a student in New Jersey while remaining a father and a husband in Maryland. I don't know whether I thanked them enough at the time. Allow me to do it here.

All the twentysomething PhD students of what came to be known as the Camper Cohort took me in, an old guy with a family, as one of their own. Charlie Argon and Albert Kohn helped me hash this book out over regular lunchtime tacos. Santiago Conti and Laura Nelson did the same over regular roommate bourbons. And I remain indebted to Friedrich Asschenfeldt, who ran the Economic History Workshop with me and taught me how to crack the Enigma Code of the intradepartmental email.

Several chapters of this book were also helped greatly by thoughtful responses at conference presentations—Early American Money at Brown in 2020, Money as A Democratic Medium in Cambridge in 2023, and the US Political Economy Lab in 2025.

One of the great pleasures of this book has been discovering how many dear friends and complete strangers will help you, if only you tell them you are on a quest. I have tried to mention them where I could in the book proper and I am certain several names are still missing, but some help is bigger than a footnote.

In Czechia, Jan Nedvěd hosted me for two weeks at the regional museum in Karlovy Vary, organized a trip down the mine at Jáchymov, and had me over for meals and pub nights. This book would not have been possible without Jan's enthusiastic early help. Markus Denzel at the University of Leipzig drew out for me on a legal pad the two-millennium history of Europe's pennies, shillings, and pounds. Christian and Petra Wagenlechner took me in on weekends between trips to the Ore Mountains. Christian picked me up every time Lufthansa left me stranded in Frankfurt. Christian accepted my deliveries of German books. Christian did too much.

In Toledo I would have been lost without Simeon Simeonov, who translated passages of Sancho de Moncada for me and did research for me in Spanish-language documents. Simeon's time was made possible with a grant from the William R. Rhodes Center for International Economics & Finance at Brown University. María Victoria Guadamillas Gómez translated for me in town and refused any offer of pay, for which I can only thank her again. Mauricio Drelichman read an early outline and assured me I was on the right track. And close to publishing time, Larissa Jimenez Gratereaux jumped in with even more translations of work on Sancho de Moncada.

In Annapolis I was researching my own hometown but started with a long conversation with Farley Grubb, who has spent a career taking the financial backing of colonial money seriously, and whose work pointed me toward Horatio Sharpe, the hapless and possibly heartbroken colonial governor of Maryland. If you are a screenwriter and have read this far, please get in touch; I have a pitch for a prestige historical comedy called *Baltimore and Sharpe*.

In New Orleans I have to thank first Jeff Clary and Victoria Lintott, who kept finding places for me to sleep. Vic got me ready for the archives every morning with extraordinary coffee from what I am told is a very expensive and delicate machine. Jeff helped me wind down from the archives with whiskey at St. Joe's. Neely Whites offered her spare apartment for a week. Jay and Megan Forman hosted me for another week in the middle of Mardi Gras, when Jay was getting up in the dark every morning to drive king cakes to Baton Rouge. Manuel Bautista-González pointed me toward the view of American financial history up from New Orleans. And Erin Greenwald met me for a long conversation about money and introduced me to Randy Haynie, whose collection made the whole chapter come together.

In Hawarden, Matt Hummel took a cold call and hosted me for an entire week, introducing me around town, letting me interview his own mother, and taking me out for what remains the best steak I've ever eaten. And Adam Hoogestraat not only led me to an archive in a basement but let me fly home with a box of documents. Adam: I still have it all. It's coming home to Iowa, I promise.

I am grateful to Esther Brimmer for a long and open conversation about her father. And it would not have been possible to spend as much time as I did in Andrew Brimmer's papers at the Baker Library at Harvard Business School without the spare bedroom of Katie and Kevin Phillips, inarguably and empirically the world's greatest in-laws.

This book would not exist without a community in Annapolis for which I am grateful every day. Tom Sfakiyanudis and the five a.m. masochists kept me healthy and sane, often against my will. The Admiral Heights neighborhood cabal threw a party the day I finished a first draft. Maybe they love me. Maybe they just love parties. I thank them for either and both. Brian Ray, while on vacation, wrote a program that reformatted my footnotes, saving me a week of work. If you don't have a Brian Ray of your own, you should get one.

Let me attempt, finally, to thank the people for whom my thanks can only be inadequate. Jane and Luke Terry responded only with curiosity and enthusiasm when their son-in-law told them he was leaving his steady job as a journalist for the reliable and lucrative profession of historical nonfiction. Knut and Frieda Zimmermann offered love and support in the way they always have: without question. Okay: with some questions. Even though she never knew about this book, Inge Zimmermann is in it, and wherever she is she just heard her name and smiled.

My father, Mac Greeley, who kept horses at Horatio Sharpe's barn, taught me through example how to treat books as companions and strangers as friends. My mother, Nancy Greeley, who found me a real colonial Maryland dollar, filled our house with love and structure. I don't think I ever properly thanked her for letting me sneak back to Tulane for the rest of a history degree when I lost my scholarship in 1993 but nobody at the dean's office noticed. Mom: It worked!

Phebe, Delphia, Clyde, and Luke: I'm sorry. This book was supposed to take a year, and it took most of your childhood. I have been so relieved every day to leave my office and see your little faces, even during Covid, when your little faces were everywhere. Thank you for letting me play my sad dad country music in the car. You make me the happiest dad in the world.

And Beth. None of this work would be possible without you. None of it would have any meaning without you. In the last decade we spent two years running a small elementary school in a rental. We went through a catastrophic renovation. A house fire. A house fire! And every morning I when I drove to school or the airport, you got up with me, poured me coffee, and reminded me that it always gets done. You I cannot thank. It's not enough. But I can tell you I love you more than I have ever learned how to express with words, and that I will never, ever write a book again.

I promise?

Notes

INTRODUCTION TO PART I

1 **But when Robert Henwood died:** " 'News' from the 'Maryland Gazette,' " *Maryland Historical Magazine* 18, no. 3 (1923): 279.

1 **His most valuable possessions:** Alice Hanson Jones, *American Colonial Wealth: Documents and Methods* (Arno Press, 1977), 2:1261.

2 **Histories of the dollar tend to start:** See, for example, Paul Blustein, *King Dollar: The Past and Future of the World's Dominant Currency* (Yale University Press, 2025); and Kenneth S. Rogoff, *Our Dollar, Your Problem: An Insider's View of Seven Turbulent Decades of Global Finance, and the Road Ahead* (Yale University Press, 2025). Both books focus on the dominance of the dollar in the twentieth and twenty-first centuries. In the trade press, H. W. Brands's *Greenback Planet* (University of Texas Press, 2011) and Jason Goodwin's *Greenback: The Almighty Dollar and the Invention of America* (Henry Holt, 2003) begin before the American Revolution but focus on the dollar as an American currency. The canonical twentieth-century history of the dollar, Arthur Nussbaum's *A History of the Dollar* (Columbia University Press, 1957), takes a similar approach.

4 **Money started as a commodity:** Economists generally credit this story to Karl Menger, "On the Origin of Money," *Economic Journal* 2, no. 6 (1892): 239–55; and William Stanley Jevons, *Money and the Mechanism of Exchange* (D. Appleton, 1875). For an account of how economists embraced this story and the way it endures among other central banks, see Nigel Dodd, *The Social Life of Money* (Princeton University Press, 2014), 17–22; Geoffrey Ingham, *The Nature of Money* (Polity Press, 2004), 15–33; or Joseph Schumpeter and Elizabeth Boody Schumpeter, *History of Economic Analysis* (Oxford University Press, 1954), 277–300. You can read this story in one of the more dominant college macroeconomics textbooks, Gregory Mankiw, *Macroeconomics,* 8th ed. (Worth Publishers, 2013), 81–87. It shows up as well in Federal Reserve speeches and research—for example Alan Greenspan, "The History of Money" (speech, Opening of the American Numismatic Society

Exhibition, Federal Reserve Bank of New York, Jan. 16, 2002); Laurence Meyer, "The Future of Money and Monetary Policy" (speech, Distinguished Lecture Program, Swarthmore College, Dec. 5, 2001); and François Velde, "Lessons from the History of Money," *Economic Perspectives* 22, no. 1 (1998).

4 **Anthropologists, sociologists, and historians:** The most recent and prominent example comes from David Graeber, *Debt: The First 5,000 Years* (Melville House, 2011), but Graeber built on a longer tradition. Scholars who see money as purely a creation of the state often start with Georg Friedrich Knapp, *The State Theory of Money,* trans. H. M. Lucas and James Bonar (published on behalf of the Royal Economic Society by Macmillan, 1924). There's also a complementary tradition from A. Mitchell Innes that sees the origin of money as either private or state credit; Innes's work was recently collected in L. Randall Wray, ed., *Credit and State Theories of Money: The Contributions of A. Mitchell Innes* (Edward Elgar, 2004). As with the metallists, there are summaries of chartalist theory in Dodd, *Social Life of Money,* 23–46; and Ingham, *Nature of Money,* 38–56.

5 **What matters is how different kinds:** Here, again, Schumpeter in *History of Economic Analysis,* part 3, chap. 7, offers a useful framework for thinking of payments as systems of private credit, with the money of coins as a "special case," 717.

5 **Money is manufactured:** Ann Pettifor makes this point about how banks manufacture money in *The Production of Money: How to Break the Power of Bankers* (Verso, 2017).

5 **Or perhaps people made:** Bill Maurer makes this point about anthropologists in particular in "The Anthropology of Money," *Annual Review of Anthropology* 35 (2006): 15–36.

6 **At a conference someone urged me:** See, for example, Akinobu Kuroda, "Concurrent but Non-Integrable Currency Circuits: Complementary Relationships Among Monies in Modern China and Other Regions," *Financial History Review* 15, no. 1 (2008): 17–36; and Akinobu Kuroda, *A Global History of Money* (Routledge, 2020). The author thanks Andrew Edwards at the University of St. Andrews for recommending Kuroda.

6 **Perry Mehrling at Boston University:** See, for example, Perry Mehrling, "Where's My Swap Line," *Jahrbuch für Wirtschaftsgeschichte* 63, no. 2 (2022): 1–16; or Perry Mehrling, *The New Lombard Street: How the Fed Became the Dealer of Last Resort* (Princeton University Press, 2010).

6 **And I read Rebecca Spang's:** Rebecca Spang, *Stuff and Money in the Time of the French Revolution* (Harvard University Press, 2015), 3.

7 **Before about a hundred years ago:** John Mack Faragher, *Sugar Creek: Life on the Illinois Prairie* (Yale University Press, 1986), 46; Spang, *Stuff and Money,* 49; Jan De Vries and A. M. van der Woude, *The First Modern Economy: Success, Failure, and Perseverance of the Dutch Economy, 1500–1815* (Cambridge University Press, 1997), 83.

8 **In this book you will read:** Joshua Greenberg refers to this understanding of how people used to think about money as "monetary knowledge" in *Bank Notes and Shinplasters: The Rage for Paper Money in the Early Republic* (University of Pennsylvania Press, 2020), 191–98.

8 **In eighteenth-century Annapolis:** John J. McCusker, *Money and Exchange in Europe and America, 1600–1775: A Handbook* (University of North Carolina Press, 1978), 3. You can also see the distinction between real and imaginary money in contemporary accounting handbooks—for example John Mair, *Book-Keeping Methodised; or, A Methodical Treatise of Merchant-Accompts, According to the Italian Form,* 9th ed. (H. Saunders, at the Salmon in Castle-Street, 1772), 188–93; Alexander Justice, *A General Treatise of Monies and Exchanges; in Which Those of All Trading Nations Are Particularly Describ'd and Consider'd* (S. and J. Sprint, and J. Nicholson; and R. Smith, 1707), 1–3; or Jean Boizard, *Traité des monoyes, de leurs circonstances & dépendances* (N. le Clerc, 1696), 6–9.

9 **Anne Catharine threatened to publish:** "Anne Catharine Hoof Green (c. 1720–1775), MSA SC 3520-14736," Archives of Maryland (Biographical Series), accessed Sept. 2, 2025, msa.maryland.gov/megafile/msa/speccol/sc3500/sc3520/014700/014736/html/14736bio.html.

10 **In the late 1960s, Alice Hanson Jones:** Alice Hanson Jones, *Wealth of a Nation to Be: The American Colonies on the Eve of the Revolution* (Columbia University Press, 1980).

11 **Alexander Hamilton:** Alexander Hamilton, "Final Version of the Report on the Establishment of a Mint," Jan. 28, 1791, Founders Online, National Archives, founders.archives.gov/documents/Hamilton/01-07-02-0334-0004. Originally *The Papers of Alexander Hamilton,* vol. 7, *September 1790–January 1791,* ed. Harold C. Syrett (Columbia University Press, 1963), 570–607.

12 **The Japanese yen and the Chinese yuan:** *Oxford English Dictionary,* "yen (n.[1])," Sept. 2024, doi.org/10.1093/OED/3841597407; *Oxford English Dictionary,* "yuan (n.[2])," July 2023, doi.org/10.1093/OED/6459703753; and *Oxford English Dictionary,* "ringgit (n.)," Sept. 2024, doi.org/10.1093/OED/7762184597.

15 **Money is still today a frantic:** See, for example, Steffen Murau and Jens van 't Klooster, "Rethinking Monetary Sovereignty: The Global Credit Money System and the State," *Perspectives on Politics* 21, no. 4 (2023): 1319–36.

15 **His theory rests on sovereignty:** See, for example, Robert Mundell, "The Euro and the Stability of the International Monetary System," in *The Euro as a Stabilizer in the International Economic System* (Kluwer Academic, 2000), 57–84, in which he argued that "strong international currencies have always been linked to strong central states in the period of their ascendancy"; or Robert Mundell, "Currency Areas, Exchange Rate Systems, and International Monetary Reform," *Journal of Applied Economics* 3, no. 2 (2000): 217–56, in which he wrote that "strong currencies are the children of empires and great powers."

15 **Even the silver mines at Potosí:** John TePaske and Herbert Klein, *The Royal Treasuries of the Spanish Empire in America,* vol. 2, *Upper Peru (Bolivia)* (Duke University Press, 1982), xvi–xvii.

CHAPTER 1: A BIG SILVER COIN FROM BOHEMIA

21 **By the end of the night:** Karl Knopf, *Die Wunderstadt St. Joachimsthal* (Leipzig, n.d.), 22.

22 **I have found two mentions:** Erich Matthes, *Das erste Bergbuch, 1518–1520, von St. Joachimsthal* (Korb'sches Sippenarchiv, 1965), 11.

23 **In the sixteenth century, St. Joachimsthal:** John Munro, "The Monetary Origins of the 'Price Revolution': South German Silver Mining, Merchant-Banking, and Venetian Commerce, 1470–1540," in *Global Connections and Monetary History, 1470–1800,* ed. Dennis Flynn, Arturo Giraldez, and Richard von Glahn (Ashgate, 2003), 1–34.

24 **That year two men walked up:** Details of the story from Heribert Sturm, *Abriss der geschichtlichen Entwicklung von Stadt und Bezirk St. Joachimsthal: Ein Behelf für den heimatkundlichen Schulunterricht* (Rudolf Weis, 1932), 93; points on mining law from Ingrid Mittenzwei, *Der Joachimsthaler Aufstand 1525: Seine Ursachen und Folgen* (Akademie-Verlag, 1968), 7.

25 **By the last two quarters of 1516:** Hans Lorenz, *Bilder aus Alt-Joachimsthal* (Verlag der Stadtgemeinde, 1925), 4.

26 **Medieval and early modern European kings:** Account of Bohemian silver and the Schlick family from Petr Vorel, *From the Silver Czech Tolar to a Worldwide Dollar: The Birth of the Dollar and Its Journey of Monetary Circulation in Europe and the World from the 16th to the 20th Century* (Columbia University Press, 2013), 29–43.

27 **As self-declared lord:** Petr Vorel (University of Pardubice), conversation with the author in Pardubice, July 12, 2019.

27 **Just like the king of Bohemia:** Details of the loan from Mittenzwei, *Der Joachimsthaler Aufstand,* 11.

28 **From the ninth to the twelfth:** Account of medieval penny from Peter Spufford, *Money and Its Use in Medieval Europe* (Cambridge University Press, 1988), 109–11. Overviews on early modern European money in Niklot Klüßendorf, *Numismatik und Geldgeschichte: Basiswissen für Mittelalter und Neuzeit* (Verlag Hahnsche Buchhandlung, 2015), 77–90; Markus Denzel (Universität Leipzig), in conversation with the author, July 15, 2019; Uwe Schirmer (Friedrich-Schiller Universität Jena), correspondence with the author, July 22, 2019; and Philipp Robinson Rössner, "From the Black Death to the New World (c. 1350–1500)," in *Money and Coinage in the Middle Ages,* ed. Rory Naismith (Brill, 2019), 156–57.

29 **Around the same time, merchants:** Spufford, *Money and Its Use,* 163–86.

29 **The Rhine florin was a copy:** Spufford, *Money and Its Use,* 278–80, 310–20, 408; and Oliver Volckart, "Technologies of Money in the Middle Ages: The 'Principles of Minting,'" London School of Economics and Political Science, Economic History Working Papers No. 275, Feb. 2018. I have adopted the translation "Rhine florin" for the German *Rheingulden* to stress the connection to florins, since florins were called *Gulden* in German-speaking areas.

29 **Just 1 Rhine florin could buy:** Uwe Schirmer, *Das Amt Grimma 1485 bis 1548: Demographische, wirtschaftliche und soziale Verhältnisse in einem kursächsischem Amt am Ende des Mittelalters und zu Beginn der Neuzeit* (Sax-Verlag, 1996), 347, 353.

29 **Stephan Schlick started his lordship:** Purchase of the castle from Sturm, *Abriss,* 42. Details on the loan from Mittenzwei, *Der Joachimsthaler Aufstand,* 11.

30 **They were likely investors:** A *Gewerk* was a particular kind of joint-stock company, with unique characteristics that are laid out in the text. But to avoid confusion for the English-language reader, I've chosen to refer to the *Gewerke* in Leipzig and Joachimsthal as "joint-stock companies." Details on the *Gewerke* in Saxony from Paul Arnold and Werner Qellmalz, *Sächsisch-Thüringische Bergbaugepräge* (VEB Deutscher Verlag für Grunstoffindustrie, 1978), 15–21, 42; on the market for shares in Leipzig, see Uwe Schirmer, *Der Finanz- und Messeplatz Leipzig vom 13. bis zur Mitte des 17. Jahrhunderts: Geldwesen—Waren- und Zalungsverkehr—Rentengeschäfte* (Sächsische Akademie der Wissenschaften zu Leipzig, 2021).

31 **All he got was a slim profit:** Petr Vorel (University of Pardubice), conversation with the author in Pardubice, July 12, 2019.

31 **Schlick must have known:** Wilhelm Weizsäcker, *Sächsisches Bergrecht in Böhmen: Das Joachimsthaler Bergrecht des 16. Jahrhunderts* (Reichenberg Stiepel, 1929), 250; Mittenzwei, *Der Joachimsthaler Aufstand,* 23.

32 **Von Könneritz arrived in person:** Mittenzwei, *Der Joachimsthaler Aufstand,* 8; Lorenz, *Bilder aus Alt-Joachimsthal,* 1; Matthes, *Das erste Bergbuch,* 12.

33 **The Saxon miners could increase:** Matthes, *Das erste Bergbuch,* 8.

34 **Some sold their claims:** Mittenzwei, *Der Joachimsthaler Aufstand,* 20.

34 **In 1516 there were:** Lorenz, *Bilder aus Alt-Joachimsthal,* 35.

34 **On July 13, 1517, the miners:** Matthes, *Das erste Bergbuch,* 10.

36 **It was an odd decision:** Lorenz, *Bilder aus Alt-Joachimsthal,* 6.

36 **As with the rest of the changes:** Matthes, *Das erste Bergbuch,* 11.

36 **The miners were also worried:** Mittenzwei, *Der Joachimsthaler Aufstand,* 69. Rebecca Spang has also talked about the historical distinction between quantities and qualities of money in *Stuff and Money,* 8.

37 **In 1953, Carlo Cipolla gave:** Cipolla's explanation of big money and petty coins is in two chapters of *Money, Prices, and Civilization in the Mediterranean World* (Princeton University Press, 1956), "The Dollars of the Middle Ages" and "The Big Problem of the Petty Coins." His argument is well known to economic historians;

see, for example, Thomas Sargent and François Velde, *The Big Problem of Small Change* (Princeton University Press, 2001); or Oliver Volckart, "'The Big Problem of the Petty Coins,' and How It Could Be Solved in the Late Middle Ages," London School of Economics, Department of Economic History, Working Papers No. 107, Feb. 2008.

37 **This caused what Cipolla called:** Philip Grierson, *Numismatics* (Oxford University Press, 1975), 97.

38 **A merchant paying:** Volckart, "Technologies of Money in the Middle Ages."

38 **The demand for coins in the valley:** Matthes, *Das erste Bergbuch,* 10.

39 **The lack of regular payment:** Philipp Robinson Rössner, "Contextualizing Luther: The Powers of Time and Space," in Martin Luther, *On Commerce and Usury (1524),* ed. Philipp Robinson Rössner (Anthem Press, 2015), 68.

39 **Hans Dickmichel from Annaberg:** Matthes, *Das erste Bergbuch,* 7.

40 **"gathering of honorable men":** Weizsäcker, *Sächsisches Bergrecht,* 29; Lorenz, *Bilder aus Alt-Joachimsthal,* 5.

40 **By the end of 1518:** Mittenzwei, *Der Joachimsthaler Aufstand,* 15.

40 **The next year, 395 more single holders:** Matthes, *Das erste Bergbuch,* 8–9.

40 **By 1520, there were almost five thousand:** Lorenz, *Bilder aus Alt-Joachimsthal,* 35.

40 **That year Schlick's uncles:** Weizsäcker, *Sächsisches Bergrecht,* 29; Mittenzwei, *Der Joachimsthaler Aufstand,* 37, 41. The author decided not to attempt to explain to the lay reader the distinctions at the time between the two dukes and the two Saxon states.

41 **But there's only one record:** Mittenzwei, *Der Joachimsthaler Aufstand,* 9–12.

41 **The king approved the Saxon mining law:** Weizsäcker, *Sächsisches Bergrecht,* 31.

42 **That year, a little over 136,600:** Petr Vorel, "European Merchant Trading Firms and the Export of the Precious Metals from the Kingdom of Bohemia During the Sixteenth Century," in *Mercantilism, Account Keeping, and the Periphery-Core Relationship,* ed. Cheryl S. McWatters (Routledge, 2019), 54.

42 **The coin itself is:** Much of this passage comes from the author's conversation with Petr Vorel on July 12, 2019.

45 **In 1521, Stephan Schlick:** Sturm, *Abriss,* 95.

45 **Schlick and von Könneritz ordered new robes:** Details of the shooting festival from Lorenz, *Bilder aus Alt-Joachimsthal,* 65–66.

45 **Philip Robinson Rössner, a monetary historian:** From "Contextualizing Luther: The Powers of Time and Space," 50.

46 **This part of Svornost:** "Jachymov Uranium Mines," Central Intelligence Agency Information Report, Supplement to Report No. 50X1-HUM, Central Intelligence Agency, Aug. 30, 1943.

47 **He spent all his free time:** Georgius Agricola, *De Re Metallica,* trans. Herbert Hoover and Lou Henry Hoover (Dover Publications, 1950), vii.

47 **The Hoovers worked nights:** George Nash, *The Life of Herbert Hoover: The Engineer, 1874–1914* (W. W. Norton, 1983), 493.

47 **By the early 1520s, joint-stock companies:** Jiří Majer, "Der Bergbau im Joachimsthaler Revier des 16. Jahrhunderts—seine Bedeutung und sein Widerhall," in *Sächsisch-Böhmische Beziehungen im 16. Jahrhundert,* ed. Friedrich Naumann (Chemnitz, 2001), 31.

49 **Agricola recommended that miners:** Agricola, *De Re Metallica,* 214–17.

49 **Sometimes during the second shift:** Mittenzwei, *Der Joachimsthaler Aufstand,* 69.

49 **In 1521, the same year:** Mittenzwei, *Der Joachimsthaler Aufstand,* 68; Lorenz, *Bilder aus Alt-Joachimsthal,* 8.

50 **The next year they stayed:** Vorel, "European Merchant Trading Firms," 54.

50 **It could have been an infectious disease:** Mittenzwei, *Der Joachimsthaler Aufstand,* 84.

50 **Ultimately the family was so burdened:** Mittenzwei, *Der Joachimsthaler Aufstand,* 25.

51 **On May 20, 1525, three thousand miners:** Mittenzwei, *Der Joachimsthaler Aufstand,* 91.

51 **Von Könneritz and the Schlicks fled:** Mittenzwei, *Der Joachimsthaler Aufstand,* 91; Lorenz, *Bilder aus Alt-Joachimsthal,* 9.

51 **There has been some argument:** Susan Karant-Nunn, "Between Two Worlds: The Social Position of the Silver Miners of the Erzgebirge, c. 1460–1575," *Social History* 14, no. 3 (1989): 308, 320.

51 **The smaller shareholders:** Mittenzwei, *Der Joachimsthaler Aufstand,* 107.

52 **And Schlick had still never fixed:** George H. Waring, "The Silver Miners of the Erzgebirge and the Peasants' War of 1525 in the Light of Recent Research," *The Sixteenth Century Journal* 18, no. 2 (1987): 256; Mittenzwei, *Der Joachimsthaler Aufstand,* 111.

52 **By July 7, Schlick had agreed:** Lorenz, *Bilder aus Alt-Joachimsthal,* 10.

52 **After that, half:** Mittenzwei, *Der Joachimsthaler Aufstand,* 117.

53 **Georgius Agricola, the scholar:** Georgius Agricola, *Bermannus oder über den Bergbau,* trans. Helmut Wilsdorf, vol. 2 of *Ausgewählte Werke* (Deutsche Verlag der Wissenschaften, 1955).

54 **And they remember Stephan Schlick:** Norbert Pap and Máté Kitanics, "The Battle and Its Aftermath," in *The Battle of Mohács, 1526,* ed. Norbert Pap (Brill, 2024), 171–213.

55 **Ferdinand had the power:** Vorel, "European Merchant Trading Firms," 57; Ekkehard Westermann and Markus Denzel, *Das Kaufmannsnotizbuch des Matthäus Schwarz aus Augsburg von 1548* (Franz Steiner Verlag, 2011), 148.

55 **Between 1520 and 1528, according to records:** Wolfgang Heß and Dietrich Klose, *Vom Taler zum Dollar 1486–1986* (Staatliche Münzsammlung München, 1986), 30.

57 **In August 1963, Christian Kasbohm:** Annemarie Radoměrský and Bernhard Blaschke, "Der Talerfund von Glave / Kreis Güstrow," *Forschungen und Berichte* 19 (1979): 161–87.

59 **In 1486, for example, Sigismund:** Heß and Klose, *Vom Taler zum Dollar,* 7–9.

60 **In 1471, only about three merchants:** Heike Fischer, *Märkte, Muster, Menschen: 850 Jahre Leipziger Messen* (Leipziger Medien Service, 2014), 19.

60 **The Dukes of Saxony used:** Schirmer, *Der Finanz- und Messeplatz Leipzig.*

60 **All this meant that:** Explanation of the significance of the trade routes from conversation with Vorel, July 12, 2019.

60 **An English traveler who passed through:** Artur Attman, *The Bullion Flow Between Europe and the East, 1000–1750,* trans. Eva Green and Allan Green (Kungl. Vetenskaps- och Vitterhets-Samhället, 1981), 35–45, 61–67, 109.

61 **A list compiled by Bavaria's:** Heß and Klose, *Vom Taler zum Dollar,* 30.

61 **In the pile, van Reymerswaele placed:** Heß and Klose, *Vom Taler zum Dollar,* 57.

61 **By the end of the 1540s:** Westermann and Denzel, *Matthäus Schwarz,* 271; Vorel, *From the Silver Czech Tolar,* 50.

62 **Münster, a German city:** Heß and Klose, *Vom Taler zum Dollar,* 50; Petr Vorel, "How the Word 'Tolar' Became a General Term for European Silver Coins in the 16th Century," *Comenius: Journal of Euro-American Civilization* 7, no. 2 (2020): 178.

63 **Of 130 different silver coins:** Oliver Volckart, "Power Politics and Princely Debts: Why Germany's Common Currency Failed, 1549–1556," London School of Economics and Political Science, Economic History Working Papers, No. 223, Sept. 2015, 33–40.

CHAPTER 2: THE SPANISH DOLLAR AND THE COLLAPSE OF TOLEDO

65 **Approach Toledo on the highway:** Jesús Álvarez-Sanchís, "Ciudades vettonas," *Complutum* 22, no. 2 (2011): 147–83.

66 **Charles V, Philip II, and Philip III:** In Castile, Charles was known as Charles I, but I have chosen here to use his Holy Roman Empire title of Charles V, used elsewhere in Europe at the time and more generally among historians now.

66 **At their peak in the 1530s:** Munro, "Monetary Origins," 41.

67 **By law, the kings had:** J. H. Elliott, *Imperial Spain, 1469–1716* (1963; Penguin, 2002), 183.

67 **In 1581 we get the first:** *Oxford English Dictionary,* "dollar (*n.*)," March 2025, doi .org/10.1093/OED/7936244852.

68 **It was silver Spanish dollars:** See Earl Rosenthal, "*Plus Ultra, Non Plus Ultra,* and the Columnar Device of Emperor Charles V," *Journal of the Warburg and Courtauld*

Institutes 34 (1971): 204–28. The two columns and the ribbon are often said to be the origin of the dollar sign, but a summary of the arguments in Eric Newman, "The Dollar $ign: Its Written and Printed Origins," in *America's Silver Dollars* (American Numismatic Society, 1995), has convinced me that the pillars and ribbon as the origin of $ are a just-so story.

68 **In the sixteenth and seventeenth centuries:** Mauricio Drelichman and Hans-Joachim Voth, "The Sustainable Debts of Philip II: A Reconstruction of Castile's Fiscal Position, 1566–1596," *Journal of Economic History* 70, no. 4 (2010): 827.

68 **Silver made the Spanish Empire possible:** For a short overview of Spain's silver system, see Stanley Stein and Barbara Stein, *Silver, Trade, and War: Spain and America in the Making of Early Modern Europe* (Johns Hopkins University Press, 2000), 1–39.

68 **By the beginning of the seventeenth century:** For discussions on Castilian and Spanish identity, see John Elliott, *Spain, Europe, and the Wider World, 1500–1800* (Yale University Press, 2009), 138; I. A. A. Thompson, "Castile, Spain, and the Monarchy: The Political Community from Patria Natural to Patria Nacional," in *Spain, Europe, and the Atlantic: Essays in Honour of John H. Elliott,* ed. Geoffrey Parker and Richard Kagan (Cambridge University Press, 1995), 125–59.

68 **In 1500, per capita GDP:** Carlos Álvarez-Nogal and Leandro Prados de la Escosura, "The Decline of Spain (1500–1850): Conjectural Estimates," *European Review of Economic History* 11, no. 3 (2007): 324.

69 **But Toledo isn't laid out:** Jonathan Brown and Richard Kagan, "View of Toledo," *Studies in the History of Art* 11 (1982): 22.

69 **By 1622, that had dropped:** Linda Martz, *Poverty and Welfare in Habsburg Spain* (Cambridge University Press, 1983), 97.

69 **Toledo had a strong intellectual community:** Linda Martz, *A Network of Converso Families in Early Modern Toledo: Assimilating a Minority* (University of Michigan Press, 2003), 358–70. See also Francisco José Aranda Pérez, "La preocupación 'arbitrista' en el seno del Ayuntamiento de Toledo por la dec linación de la ciudad en un período crítico: 1618–1621," *Toletum: Boletín de la Real Academia de Bellas Artes y Ciencias Historicas de Toledo* 29 (1993): 215–18.

70 **The church is just a short walk:** Mariano García Ruipérez, "Plaza de Zocodover," Ayuntamiento de Toledo, accessed June 28, 2025, www.toledo.es/toledo-siempre/exposiciones-virtuales/plaza-de-zocodover/.

71 **Moncada wanted the kingdom's universities:** See also Cosimo Perrotta, "Early Spanish Mercantilism: The First Analysis of Underdevelopment," in *Mercantilist Economics,* ed. Lars Magnusson (Springer Netherlands, 1993), 39.

71 **"orgy of national introspection":** Elliott, *Imperial Spain,* 300.

71 **Men called *arbitristas* recorded their suggestions:** Elliott, *Imperial Spain,* 300; Henry Kamen, "The Decline of Spain: A Historical Myth?," *Past & Present,* no. 81 (1978): 24–50.

71 **Miguel de Cervantes, who was injured:** Michael Gordon, "Morality and Politics in Seventeenth Century Spain: The Arbitrista Pedro Fernandez Navarrete" (PhD diss., University of Chicago, 1972), 6–10; Marjorie Grice-Hutchinson, *Early Economic Thought in Spain, 1177–1740* (George Allen & Unwin, 1978; repr., Liberty Fund, 2015), 154–55.

72 **One is institutional:** See, for example, Paul M. Kennedy, *The Rise and Fall of the Great Powers: Economic Change and Military Conflict from 1500 to 2000* (Vintage Books, 1989); or Daron Acemoglu and James A. Robinson, *Why Nations Fail: The Origins of Power, Prosperity, and Poverty* (Crown, 2012).

72 **The other explanation is monetary:** Most famously Earl Hamilton, *American Treasure and the Price Revolution in Spain, 1501–1650* (Harvard University Press, 1934).

72 **It was written with only one audience in mind:** Martz, *Converso Families,* 365.

72 **I found him through a single quotation:** J. H. Elliott, "Self-Perception and Decline in Early Seventeenth-Century Spain," *Past & Present* 74, no. 1 (1977): 56–57.

72 **The poverty of Spain, Moncada wrote:** Sancho de Moncada, *Restauración política de España,* discourse 3, chap. 2, translated for the author by Simeon Simeonov, Biblioteca Virtual Miguel de Cervantes, www.cervantesvirtual.com/obra-visor/restauracion-politica-de-espana--0/html/.

72 **"It is well known":** Moncada, *Restauración política de España,* discourse 3, chap. 3.

73 **"The prosperity that is usually":** Moncada, *Restauración política de España,* discourse 1, chaps. 5, 7.

73 **Foreigners ran the silver trade:** Moncada, *Restauración política de España,* discourse 1, chap. 12.

73 **Cloth merchants like the Moncada family:** See also Michael Weisser, "The Decline of Castile Revisited: The Case of Toledo," *Journal of European Economic History* 2, no. 3 (1973): 619.

74 **It held a lot of capital:** See also Cyril Milhaud, "Interregional Flows of Capital and Information in Spain: A Case Study of the Theresian Carmelite Order," *Revista de Historia Económica—Journal of Iberian and Latin American Economic History* 37, no. 1 (2019): 81–110.

74 **Sancho de Moncada grew up inside:** Linda Martz, "La familia y hacienda del doctor Sancho de Moncada," *Anales toledanos* 24 (1987): 55, 61.

74 **In his *arbitrio,* Moncada pointed out:** Moncada, *Restauración política de España,* discourse 1, chap. 17.

75 **Moncada understood the details:** Moncada, *Restauración política de España,* discourse 3, chap. 5.

76 **Over the last two decades:** See Dennis Flynn, "A New Perspective on the Spanish Price Revolution: The Monetary Approach to the Balance of Payments," *Explorations in Economic History* 15, no. 4 (1978): 388–406; Dennis Flynn and Arturo

Giráldez, "Arbitrage, China, and World Trade in the Early Modern Period," *Journal of the Economic and Social History of the Orient* 38, no. 4 (1995): 429–48; Dennis Flynn and Arturo Giráldez, "Born with a 'Silver Spoon': The Origin of World Trade in 1571," *Journal of World History* 6, no. 2 (1995): 201–21; Dennis Flynn, "Silver, Globalization, and Capitalism," in *Capitalisms,* ed. Kaveh Yazdani and Dilip Menon (Oxford University Press, 2020), 35–70. The author is also grateful for a conversation with Dennis Flynn on March 22, 2021.

76 **In the sixteenth century, silver:** Richard von Glahn, *Fountain of Fortune: Money and Monetary Policy in China, 1000–1700* (University of California Press, 1996), 127.

76 **Demand for silver in China:** Von Glahn, *Fountain of Fortune,* chaps. 2–4; and Richard von Glahn, "The Changing Significance of Latin American Silver in the Chinese Economy, 16th–19th Centuries," *Revista de Historia Económica—Journal of Iberian and Latin American Economic History* 38, no. 3 (2020): 553–85.

77 **Smugglers brought silver in:** Harriet Zurndorfer, "Silver, Piracy, Conspicuous Consumption, and the Transformation of Ming China in the 16th Century," *Oxford Research Encyclopedia of Asian History,* April 26, 2021; William Atwell, "Time, Money, and the Weather: Ming China and the 'Great Depression' of the Mid-Fifteenth Century," *Journal of Asian Studies* 61, no. 1 (2002): 83–113.

77 **This encouraged a cycle:** Dennis Owen Flynn and Arturo Giraldez, "Cycles of Silver: Global Economic Unity Through the Mid-Eighteenth Century," *Journal of World History* 13, no. 2 (2002): 391–427.

77 **"wanders throughout all the world":** Quoted in Von Glahn, *Fountain of Fortune,* 129.

77 **Already in the 1490s:** Philipp Robinson Rössner, *Deflation—Devaluation—Rebellion: Geld im Zeitalter der Reformation* (Franz Steiner Verlag, 2013), 273, 277, 281–84, 286.

77 **The Portuguese had connected:** Rössner, *Deflation—Devaluation—Rebellion,* 251–54, 258–62.

78 **Martin Luther, who grew up:** Luther, *On Commerce and Usury (1524),* 174.

78 **All the other routes out of Europe:** See Attman, *Bullion Flow.*

78 **In 2011 a group of chemists:** Anne-Marie Desaulty et al., "Isotopic Ag—Cu—Pb Record of Silver Circulation Through 16th–18th Century Spain," *Proceedings of the National Academy of Sciences of the United States of America* 108, no. 22 (2011): 9002–7.

79 **In 1521, immediately after the fall:** John TePaske and Kendall Brown, *A New World of Gold and Silver* (Brill, 2010), 85.

79 **Over the same period, Joachimsthal:** Munro, "Monetary Origins," 41.

79 **By the early 1530s Charles:** Hamilton, *American Treasure,* 26.

80 **In 1501 in Toledo, you could buy:** Hamilton, *American Treasure,* 172, 175–77, 316, 320, author's conversion; Albert Frey, "A Dictionary of Numismatic Names:

Their Official and Popular Designations," *American Journal of Numismatics (1897–1924)* 50 (1916): 143.

80 **But anything a normal person:** Frey, "Dictionary of Numismatic Names," 198.

80 **Just as with the Italian:** Frey, "Dictionary of Numismatic Names," 80; Hamilton, *American Treasure,* 51–54.

80 **They were different currencies:** Akinobu Kuroda described a comparable system in early twentieth-century China as "concurrent, but non-integrable currency circuits." Kuroda, "Concurrent but Non-Integrable Currency Circuits."

81 **The first mention of the piece of eight:** TePaske and Brown, *New World of Gold and Silver,* 214; José Maria Pérez García (Museo Casa de la Moneda, Madrid), email to the author, Aug. 4, 2020.

82 **Markets in the Holy Roman Empire:** Oliver Volckart, *The Silver Empire: How Germany Created Its First Common Currency* (Oxford University Press, 2024), 185, 65.

82 **Charles was never able:** Volckart, *Silver Empire,* 77–79, 140–42; Volckart, "Power Politics and Princely Debts"; Oliver Volckart, "Bimetallism and Its Discontents: Cooperation and Coordination Failure in the Empire's Monetary Politics, 1549–59," *VSWG: Vierteljahrschrift für Sozial- und Wirtschaftsgeschichte* 105, no. 2 (2018): 201–20. See also Petr Vorel, *Monetary Circulation in Central Europe at the Beginning of the Early Modern Age: Attempts to Establish a Shared Currency as an Aspect of the Political Culture of the 16th Century (1524–1573)* (Pardubice, 2006).

83 **In the 1540s, silver finds:** Adolf Soetbeer, *Edelmetall-Produktion und Werthverhältniss Zwischen Gold und Silber seit der Entdeckung Amerika's bis zur Gegenwart* (Justus Perthes, 1879), 107.

84 **In Zacatecas, the mining technology:** Robert C. West, "Early Silver Mining in New Spain, 1531–1555," in *Mines of Silver and Gold in the Americas,* ed. Peter Bakewell (Routledge, 1997), 64; D. A. Brading and Harry Cross, "Colonial Silver Mining: Mexico and Peru," *Hispanic American Historical Review* 52, no. 4 (1972): 552.

84 **It's possible this became a place:** Brading and Cross, "Colonial Silver Mining," 549; Peter Bakewell, *Silver Mining and Society in Colonial Mexico: Zacatecas, 1546–1700* (Cambridge University Press, 1971), 133.

84 **In the early 1550s, local officials:** West, "Early Silver Mining," 72.

85 **At Potosí the challenge was even more difficult:** Kris Lane, *Potosí: The Silver City That Changed the World* (University of California Press, 2019), 25; Peter Bakewell, *Miners of the Red Mountain: Indian Labor in Potosí, 1545–1650* (University of New Mexico Press, 1984), 8. The author is also grateful for several conversations with Kris Lane.

85 **Under the growing empire of the Habsburgs:** Jeffrey Cole, *The Potosí Mita, 1573–1700: Compulsory Indian Labor in the Andes* (Stanford University Press, 1985), 4; Brading and Cross, "Colonial Silver Mining," 554; Bakewell, *Miners of the Red Mountain,* 49–51.

85 **In the early 1550s, Bartolomé de Medina:** Alan Probert, "Bartolome de Medina:

The Patio Process and the Sixteenth Century Silver Crisis," *Journal of the West* 8, no. 1 (1969): 90–124.

86 **The clay stoves disappeared:** Rossana Barragán, "Extractive Economy and Institutions? Technology, Labour, and Land in Potosí, the Sixteenth to the Eighteenth Century," in *Colonialism, Institutional Change, and Shifts in Global Labour Relations,* ed. Karin Hofmeester and Pim de Zwart (Amsterdam University Press, 2018), 218.

86 **Skilled local workers earned a wage:** Brading and Cross, "Colonial Silver Mining," 558–59.

87 **"This fierce beast," wrote Capoche:** Quoted in Lane, *Potosí,* 74.

87 **At its peak, from 1591 to 1595:** Munro, "Monetary Origins," 43.

87 **The Saxons lost, but the dollar won:** Details of the reichstaler agreement of 1566 from Vorel, *From the Silver Czech Tolar to a Worldwide Dollar,* 66–70; and Volckart, *Silver Empire,* 204–9.

88 **Thomas Gresham, an English merchant:** Carlos Marichal, "The Spanish-American Silver Peso: Export Commodity and Global Money of the Ancien Regime, 1550–1800," in *From Silver to Cocaine: Latin American Commodity Chains and the Building of the World Economy, 1500–2000,* ed. Steven Topik, Carlos Marichal, and Zephyr Frank (Duke University Press, 2006), 36.

88 **Then they added an apple:** Lubomír Nemeškal, *Jáchymovská mincovna v první polovině 16. století (1519/20–1561): Význam ražby tolaru* (Nakladatelství Československé Academie Věd, 1964), no page numbers.

89 **Thousands of pieces of eight:** John M. Kleeberg, *Numismatic Finds of the Americas: An Inventory of American Coin Hoards, Shipwrecks, Single Finds, and Finds in Excavations* (American Numismatic Society, 2009), 270.

89 **In 1589, Genoa banned foreign coins:** Carlo M. Cipolla, *Conquistadores, piratas, mercaderes: La saga de la plata española* (Fondo de Cultura Económica, 1999), 59.

89 **By the 1590s, more than half of the silver:** Hamilton, *American Treasure,* 30.

89 **That decade Dutch merchants:** Michel Morineau, *Ces incroyables gazettes et fabuleux métaux: Les retours des trésors américains d'après les gazettes hollandaises (XVI–XVIIIe siècles)* (Maison des Sciences de l'Homme and Cambridge University Press, 1985), 51.

89 **Over the next two decades:** Kleeberg, *Numismatic Finds of the Americas,* 273.

89 **In 1614 the Dutch exported:** Artur Attman, *Dutch Enterprise in the World Bullion Trade, 1550–1800* (Kungl. Vetenskaps- och Vitterhets-Samhället, 1983), 8, 92.

89 **Ottoman sources started to distinguish:** Attman, *Bullion Flow,* 101–2.

89 **Thousands of pieces of eight:** Kleeberg, *Numismatic Finds of the Americas,* 277–78.

89 **Galleons carried silver from Acapulco:** Flynn and Giráldez, "Born with a 'Silver Spoon'"; Anne-Marie Desaulty and Francis Albarede, "Copper, Lead, and Silver Isotopes Solve a Major Economic Conundrum of Tudor and Early Stuart Europe," *Geology* 41, no. 2 (2013): 135–38.

90 **It's possible that's what Chinese merchants:** Kendall Brown (Brigham Young University), interview by the author, March 16, 2021.

90 **At each step, someone had to get paid:** Kris Lane (Tulane University), interview by the author, March 16, 2021.

90 **By the 1640s we can find:** Kleeberg, *Numismatic Finds of the Americas,* 279–80.

91 **In the spring of 1577:** Katharine Baetjer, "El Greco," *Metropolitan Museum of Art Bulletin* 39, no. 1 (1981): 1–48; "El Greco (Domenikos Theotokopoulos)," Museo Nacional del Prado, accessed July 7, 2025, www.museodelprado.es/en/the-collection/artist/el-greco-domenikos-theotokopoulos/b031da57-6a7e-43f2-a855-293275efc340.

92 **The best-known scholar of Sancho de Moncada's work:** Jean Vilar, introduction to *Restauration política de España,* by Sancho de Moncada (Institutos de Estudios Fiscales, Ministerio de Hacienda, 1974), 8.

92 **But he was also part of their community:** Richard Kagan, "El Greco and the Law," *Studies in the History of Art* 11 (1982): 78–90.

92 **The way we interpret that painting now:** Alicia Faxon, "Painter and Patron: Collaboration of Mary Cassatt and Louisine Havemeyer," *Woman's Art Journal* 3, no. 2 (1982): 15; El Greco (Domenikos Theotokopoulos), *View of Toledo,* Metropolitan Museum of Art, accessed Aug. 5, 2020, www.metmuseum.org/art/collection/search/436575.

92 **Brown and Kagan think the painting:** Brown and Kagan, "View of Toledo."

94 **There was no manufacturing:** Elliott, *Imperial Spain,* 185.

94 **In 1528 there were:** Martz, *Poverty and Welfare in Habsburg Spain,* 95.

94 **The city's cloth merchants:** Michael Weisser, "Les marchands de Tolède dans l'économie castillane, 1565–1635," *Mélanges de la Casa de Velázquez* 7, no. 1 (1971): 223–36.

94 **Already at a *Cortes* in 1548:** Elliott, *Imperial Spain,* 190; Grice-Hutchinson, *Early Economic Thought in Spain,* 136.

94 **What we know about prices:** This work is usually credited to Earl Hamilton alone, but Gladys was so crucial to the data collection that I have added her name, distinguishing between the archival work they did together and the book that Earl published under just his name.

94 **In 1552 the Hospital de Tavera:** Hamilton, *American Treasure,* 97, 340–46.

95 **Even though he read Castilian writers:** Hamilton, *American Treasure,* 290.

95 **It was clear to the Castilian writers:** Elliott also makes this point in *Imperial Spain,* 193.

95 **There were constant complaints:** Marjorie Grice-Hutchinson, *The School of Salamanca: Readings in Spanish Monetary Theory, 1544–1605* (Clarendon Press, 1952), 3.

95 **Tomás de Mercado, a Dominican friar:** Grice-Hutchinson, *School of Salamanca,* 8; Grice-Hutchinson, *Early Economic Thought in Spain,* 135–36; Louis Baeck, *The Mediterranean Tradition in Economic Thought* (Routledge, 2012), 12–14.

97 **The city's population peaked in 1597:** Carlos Álvarez-Nogal and Leandro Prados

de la Escosura, "The Decline of Spain (1500–1850): Conjectural Estimates," *European Review of Economic History* 11, no. 3 (2007): 319–66.

97 **Contracts at the Zocodover market:** Weisser, "Decline of Castile Revisited," 634–36.

97 **Looking back from 1620:** Moncada, *Restauración política de España,* discourse 1, chap. 2.

98 **The chapel had been funded:** "El Greco and the Oballe Chapel, Madrid 6/15/2004–9/19/2004," Museo del Prado, accessed July 9, 2025, www.museodelprado.es/en/whats-on/exhibition/el-greco-and-the-oballe-chapel/e50d40b5-f983-4481-9e7f-094d9b51801d.

98 **Greco painted it in 1613:** "Jerónimo de Cevallos—The Collection—Museo Nacional del Prado." Museo del Prado, accessed March 15, 2021, www.museodelprado.es/en/the-collection/art-work/jeronimo-de-cevallos/e3c594b5-e334-45f7-9550-ea0665be3f30.

98 **"streets of Toledo were deserted":** As paraphrased in Weisser, "Decline of Castile Revisited," 617.

98 **Sancho de Moncada probably handed:** Jean Vilar Berrogain, "Conciencia Nacional y Conciencia Economica," in Sancho de Moncada, *Restauracion Politica de España* (La Fabrica Nacional de Moneda y Timbre, 1974), 21–23.

98 **In the first discourse:** Moncada, *Restauración política de España,* discourse 1, chap. 12.

99 **The kingdom imported books:** Moncada, *Restauración política de España,* discourse 1, chap. 13.

99 **"a bad religion":** Quoted in Kamen, "Decline of Spain," 26.

99 **Castile's kings spent too much:** See Kennedy, *Rise and Fall of the Great Powers.*

99 **Or they had too much power:** See Acemoglu and Robinson, *Why Nations Fail.*

99 **In 1983, two economists from Australia:** P. J. Forsyth and St. J. Nicholas, "The Decline of Spanish Industry and the Price Revolution: A Neoclassical Analysis," *Journal of European Economic History* 12, no. 3 (1983): 601–10.

100 **In 1977, *The Economist* named this paradox:** Michael Ellman, "Report from Holland: The Economics of North Sea Hydrocarbons," *Cambridge Journal of Economics* 1, no. 3 (1977): 281–90; W. M. Corden, "Booming Sector and Dutch Disease Economics: Survey and Consolidation," *Oxford Economic Papers* 36, no. 3 (1984): 359–80.

100 **Once industrial skills are lost:** Aaron Tornell and Philip R. Lane, "The Voracity Effect," *American Economic Review* 89, no. 1 (1999): 22–46; Patrick K. Asea and Amartya Lahiri, "The Precious Bane," *Journal of Economic Dynamics and Control* 23, no. 5 (1999): 823–49; Paul Krugman, "The Narrow Moving Band, the Dutch Disease, and the Competitive Consequences of Mrs. Thatcher: Notes on Trade in the Presence of Dynamic Scale Economies," *Journal of Development Economics* 27, no. 1 (1987): 41–55.

101 **"the curse of Moctezuma":** Mauricio Drelichman, "The Curse of Moctezuma: American Silver and the Dutch Disease," *Explorations in Economic History* 42, no. 3 (2005): 349–80.

101 **Sudden wealth can make governments *worse:*** Mauricio Drelichman and Hans-Joachim Voth, "Institutions and the Resource Curse in Early Modern Spain," in *Institutions and Economic Performance,* ed. Elhanan Helpman (Harvard University Press, 2008), 120–47; Carlos J. Charotti, Nuno Palma, and João Pereira Dos Santos, "American Treasure and the Decline of Spain," University of Manchester Economics Discussion Paper Series, EDP-2201, University of Manchester School of Social Sciences, Jan. 2022.

102 **The *asientos* were short-term contracts:** Carlos Álvarez-Nogal and Christophe Chamley, "Debt Policy Under Constraints: Philip II, the Cortes, and Genoese Bankers," *Economic History Review* 67, no. 1 (2014): 192–213.

102 **About 40 percent of these payments:** Mauricio Drelichman and Hans-Joachim Voth, *Lending to the Borrower from Hell: Debt, Taxes, and Default in the Age of Philip II* (Princeton University Press, 2014), 148.

102 **Median interest on the asientos:** Sydney Homer and Richard Sylla, *A History of Interest Rates,* 4th ed. (John Wiley & Sons, 2005), 119.

102 **Philip paid the bankers back:** Cipolla, *Conquistadores, piratas, mercaderes,* 60.

102 **Philip stopped payment on the asientos:** Mauricio Drelichman and Hans-Joachim Voth, "The Sustainable Debts of Philip II: A Reconstruction of Castile's Fiscal Position, 1566–1596," *Journal of Economic History* 70, no. 4 (2010): 813–42.

102 **A *juro* is an annuity:** Drelichman and Voth, *Lending to the Borrower from Hell,* 91.

103 **By the 1590s, that had grown:** Drelichman and Voth, *Lending to the Borrower from Hell,* 91–99; Drelichman and Voth, "Sustainable Debts of Philip II."

104 **Sancho de Moncada is often dismissed:** Perrotta, "Early Spanish Mercantilism."

104 **But the people with wealth:** Moncada, *Restauración política de España,* discourse 1, chap. 4.

104 **Sancho de Moncada spent the rest of his life:** Martz, "La familia y hacienda del doctor Sancho de Moncada."

104 **In 1585, he donated 3,400 maravedis:** Mario Arellano García, "Iglesia de San Nicolás de Bari," *Toletum,* ser. 2, vol. 24 (1990): 111–54.

CHAPTER 3: THE FIRST AMERICAN DOLLAR

107 **In the last week of August 1764:** Sharpe to Lord Baltimore, Annapolis, Aug. 22, 1764, in *Correspondence of Governor Horatio Sharpe,* vol. 3, *1761–1771* (Maryland Historical Society, 1895), 171; Sharpe to Cecilius Calvert, Annapolis, Aug. 24, 1764, 172–77. The letter to Calvert is cited in James Celia and Farley Grubb, "Non-

Legal-Tender Paper Money: The Structure and Performance of Maryland's Bills of Credit, 1767–75," *Economic History Review* 69, no. 4 (2016): 1132–56.

107 **The other letter went:** To avoid confusion, I have adopted the convention of "Calvert" for Cecilius Calvert and will refer to his nephew Frederick Calvert as Lord Baltimore.

107 **He had already been governor:** Paul Giddens, "Governor Horatio Sharpe and His Maryland Government," *Maryland Historical Magazine* 32 (1937): 157.

107 **He didn't need to create wealth:** Lois Green Carr and Lorena Walsh, "Inventories and the Analysis of Wealth and Consumption Patterns in St. Mary's County, Maryland, 1658–1777," *Historical Methods* 13, no. 2 (1980): 81–104; Paul Clemens, "The Operation of an Eighteenth-Century Chesapeake Tobacco Plantation," *Agricultural History* 49, no. 3 (1975): 517–31.

108 **There just weren't enough physical coins:** See, for example, Curtis Nettels, "British Policy and Colonial Money Supply," *Economic History Review* 3, no. 2 (1931): 227; E. James Ferguson, "Currency Finance: An Interpretation of Colonial Monetary Practices," *William and Mary Quarterly* 10, no. 2 (1953): 168; John J. McCusker and Russell R. Menard, *The Economy of British America, 1607–1789* (University of North Carolina Press, 1991), 339; and more recently Mark Peterson, *The City-State of Boston: The Rise and Fall of an Atlantic Power, 1630–1865* (Princeton University Press, 2019), 96–104.

108 **But they all knew to the penny:** Leslie Brock, *The Currency of the American Colonies, 1700–1764: A Study in Colonial Finance and Imperial Relations* (Arno Press, 1975), 8; Curtis Nettels, *The Money Supply of the American Colonies Before 1720* (1934; Augustus M. Kelley, 1973), 204; McCusker and Menard, *Economy of British America,* 338–39; Farley Grubb (University of Delaware), conversation with the author, June 16, 2019.

109 **In Maryland, the few coins:** Clarence Gould, *Money and Transportation in Maryland, 1720–1765* (Johns Hopkins Press, 1915), 12–14.

109 **Read through the August 1764 issues:** *Maryland Gazette* (Annapolis), Aug. 2, 1764; Aug. 9, 1764; Aug. 16, 1764; and Aug. 23, 1764, Maryland Gazette Collection, MSA SC 2731, Archives of Maryland Online.

109 **Wilmot thought Taney might be waiting:** In this chapter I have used the word "dollar," rather than $, to denominate amounts in dollars. The dollar sign would not have been in use at the time, and it's important to distinguish between the silver Spanish dollars circulating in the colonies and the American bank dollars, marked with $, that followed in the early American republic.

110 **The practice was particularly common:** Gould, *Money and Transportation in Maryland,* 27–28.

110 **There's an old argument:** For a summary of these arguments, see Mara Caden, "'One Certain Standard': Colonial Currencies and the Politics of Economic Knowledge in Late Stuart Britain," *Journal of British Studies* 63, no. 4 (2024): 836–62.

110 **In April 1761, Stephen West:** *Maryland Gazette,* April 9, 1761, mentioned in Kathryn Behrens, "Paper Money in Maryland, 1727–1789" (Johns Hopkins University Press, 1923), 46.

111 **In September 1763, the Greens:** *Maryland Gazette,* Sept. 15, 1763.

111 **Even when there had been gold:** See also Gould, *Money and Transportation in Maryland,* 15–17.

111 **We don't think of paper money:** Ferguson, "Currency Finance," 163–64; McCusker and Menard, *Economy of British America,* 337.

111 **In the summer of 1764, Lord Baltimore:** Lord Baltimore, *Tour to the East in the Years 1763 and 1764 with Remarks on the City of Constantinople and the Turks Also Select Pieces of Oriental Wit, Poetry, and Wisdom* (W. Richardson and S. Clark, 1767), 72, 78.

113 **Until the early eighteenth century:** Behrens, *Paper Money,* 9; Nettels, *Money Supply,* 49–50, 65.

113 **The money of the early tobacco economy:** Brock, *Currency of the American Colonies,* 2.

114 **Maryland planters also sold some of their bills:** Gould, *Money and Transportation in Maryland,* 14; see also chapter on bills of exchange in Gould, 38–47.

114 **Tavern keepers and tradespeople offered:** For the origins of book credit in England, see Christine Desan, *Making Money: Coin, Currency, and the Coming of Capitalism* (Oxford University Press, 2015), 207–14; and Dror Goldberg, *Easy Money: American Puritans and the Invention of Modern Currency* (University of Chicago Press, 2023), 31–34, 87–88. For general treatments of book credits in the colonies, see William T. Baxter, "Observations on Money, Barter, and Bookkeeping," *Accounting Historians Journal* 31, no. 1 (2004): 129–39; and Ellen Hartigan-O'Connor, *The Ties That Buy: Women and Commerce in Revolutionary America* (University of Pennsylvania Press, 2009). For book credits in seaports, see Gary B. Nash, *The Urban Crucible: Social Change, Political Consciousness, and the Origins of the American Revolution* (Harvard University Press, 1979); and Thomas M. Doerflinger, *A Vigorous Spirit of Enterprise: Merchants and Economic Development in Revolutionary Philadelphia* (University of North Carolina Press, 1986). For the practice in Connecticut, see Richard L. Bushman, *From Puritan to Yankee: Character and the Social Order in Connecticut, 1690–1765* (Harvard University Press, 1967), 112. In New England more broadly, see David T. Flynn, "The Duration of Book Credit in Colonial New England," *Historical Methods* 38, no. 4 (2005): 168–77.

115 **By the seventeenth century, it was common:** Raymond De Roover, "New Interpretations of the History of Banking," *Journal of World History* 2, no. 1 (1954): 59.

115 **A law in Maryland in 1642:** Jacob J. Rabinowitz, "Origin of the Negotiable Promissory Note," *University of Pennsylvania Law Review* 104, no. 7 (1956): 927; Frederick K. Beutel, "The Development of Negotiable Instruments in Early English Law,"

Harvard Law Review 51, no. 5 (1938): 830, 842–43; Frederick K. Beutel, "Colonial Sources of the Negotiable Instruments Law of the United States," *Illinois Law Review* 34, no. 2 (1939–40): 141–42.

115 **In Maryland's early tobacco economy:** Louis Jordan, "Lord Baltimore Coinage and Daily Exchange in Early Maryland," *Colonial Newsletter,* Aug.–Dec. 2004, 2663; Gould, *Money and Transportation in Maryland,* 19.

116 **In September 1657:** Judicial and Testamentary Business of the Provincial Court, 1649/50–1657, *Archives of Maryland,* ed. William Hand Browne (Maryland Historical Society, 1891), 10:542–46.

117 **Planters eventually figured out:** Gould, *Money and Transportation in Maryland,* 57–58.

117 **Tobacco notes worked as a currency:** Gould, *Money and Transportation in Maryland,* 51.

117 **Maryland had what one historian called:** Brock, *Currency of the American Colonies,* 2–4.

118 **Boston had briefly had a mint:** For an account of the Royal Mint's antipathy toward American mints, see Caden, " 'One Certain Standard.' "

118 **Mather and Phips also complained:** "America and West Indies: November 1691," in *Calendar of State Papers Colonial, America and West Indies: Volume 13, 1689–1692,* ed. J. W. Fortescue (London, 1901), British History Online, accessed July 18, 2025, www.british-history.ac.uk/cal-state-papers/colonial/america-west-indies/vol13/pp563-572, mentioned in Nettels, *Money Supply,* 204.

118 **In 1699, Richard Coote:** Nettels, *Money Supply,* 204.

118 **In 1701, Nathaniel Blakiston:** "America and West Indies: May 1701, 21–25," in *Calendar of State Papers Colonial, America and West Indies: Volume 19, 1701,* ed. Cecil Headlam (His Majesty's Stationery Office, 1910), 256–62, British History Online, accessed July 11, 2021, www.british-history.ac.uk/cal-state-papers/colonial/america-west-indies/vol19/pp256-262, mentioned in Brock, *Currency of the American Colonies.*

119 **The colonies were competing:** Nettels, *Money Supply,* 232.

119 **In New Jersey and Pennsylvania:** Brock, *Currency of the American Colonies,* 8.

119 **You can see why Maryland's Blakiston:** Accounts of the colonial dollar exchange rates in Brock, *Currency of the American Colonies,* 130–51; Nettels, *Money Supply,* 233–47; and Caden, " 'One Certain Standard,' " 852–59.

120 **In 1704, a crown proclamation:** Brock, *Currency of the American Colonies,* 135.

121 ***Sotweed Redivivus* is twenty-eight pages:** Ebenezer Cooke, *Sotweed Redivivus; or, The Planters Looking-Glass* (William Parks, 1730), in the Evans Early American Imprint Collection, University of Michigan Library Digital Collections, name.umdl.umich.edu/N02746.0001.001.

121 **He was likely educated in England:** Lawrence Wroth, "The Maryland Muse by Ebenezer Cooke," *Proceedings of the American Antiquarian Society* 44 (1934): 267.

121 **In 1690, Massachusetts issued £7,000:** Account of the Massachusetts bills of credit in Brock, *Currency of the American Colonies,* 17–64; Dror Goldberg, "The Massachusetts Paper Money of 1690," *Journal of Economic History* 69, no. 4 (2009): 1092–106; and Goldberg, *Easy Money.*

124 **When a tradesman in colonial America:** Ann Pettifor uses a similar formulation in *The Production of Money.*

124 **After the bank failures:** Curtis Nettels and Leslie Brock published their monographs on colonial currency, both extensively referenced in this book, in the early years of the Great Depression.

124 **More recently, Farley Grubb:** See, for example, Farley Grubb, "Is Paper Money Just Paper Money? Experimentation and Variation in the Paper Monies Issued by the American Colonies from 1690 to 1775," *Research in Economic History* 32 (2016): 147–224; and Celia and Grubb, "Non-Legal-Tender Paper Money."

124 **Christine Desan, a legal historian:** See, for example, Christine Desan, "From Blood to Profit: Making Money in the Practice and Imagery of Early America," *Journal of Policy History* 20, no. 1 (2008): 26–46; and Christine Desan, "The Market as a Matter of Money: Denaturalizing Economic Currency in American Constitutional History," *Law & Social Inquiry* 30, no. 1 (2005): 1–60.

124 **Within New England:** This account comes from Brock, *Currency of the American Colonies,* 52–64.

125 **William Douglass, a physician in Boston:** Maxine Van De Wetering, "A Reconsideration of the Inoculation Controversy," *New England Quarterly* 58, no. 1 (1985): 46–67; Douglass is quoted in Jeffrey Sklansky, *Sovereign of the Market: The Money Question in Early America* (University of Chicago Press, 2017), 79.

125 **As Douglass was writing:** Extensive discussion of the bills of credit from New York, Pennsylvania, and New Jersey in Brock, *Currency of the American Colonies,* 65–96.

125 **The fund was a way:** *The Colonial Laws of New York* (James B. Lyon, state printer, 1894), vol. 1, chaps. 190, 227, 231, and 280, vol. 3, chaps. 280 and 437.

126 **In 1722, Pennsylvania issued bills:** Katie A. Moore, "America's First Economic Stimulus Package: Paper Money and the Body Politic in Colonial Pennsylvania, 1715–1730," *Pennsylvania History: A Journal of Mid-Atlantic Studies* 83, no. 4 (2016): 529–57.

126 **First, the assembly paid out bills:** James Tyndale Mitchell and Henry Flanders, *The Statutes at Large of Pennsylvania from 1682 to 1801,* vol. 3 (Clarence M. Busch, state printer of Pennsylvania, 1896), chap. 261, pp. 270, 276, 327, 332–33; Brock, *Currency of the American Colonies,* 87.

128 **And tobacco production had become:** Carr, "Diversification in the Colonial Chesapeake," 355.

129 **Tools for crafts started to show up:** Carr, "Diversification in the Colonial Chesapeake," 359.

129 **So did the kinds of basic:** T. H. Breen has argued that the demand for consumer luxuries and the supply of bills of credit reinforced each other in *The Marketplace of Revolution* (Oxford University Press, 2004), 187–90.

129 **The new shillings were legal tender–ish:** Behrens, "Paper Money in Maryland," 19–22.

129 **"helicopter money":** Milton Friedman, *The Optimum Quantity of Money and Other Essays* (Aldine, 1969).

130 **The province held the bills:** Gould, *Money and Transportation in Maryland,* 84.

131 **When the province first started handing:** Exchange rates from John McCusker, *Money and Exchange in Europe and America, 1600–1775: A Handbook* (University of North Carolina Press for the Institute of Early American History and Culture, 1978), 203. The author is also grateful for a conversation with John McCusker on July 28, 2020, that helped clear up some of the details behind Maryland's bills of credit.

132 **In March 1764, Cecilius Calvert:** Calvert to Sharpe, Feb. 29, 1764, in *Correspondence.*

132 **The commissioners then immediately began:** Brock, *Currency of the American Colonies,* 418.

132 **Over the next decade, twenty-two ships:** Voyage itinerary: imputed principal port of slave disembarkation is Maryland, 1754–1764, Transatlantic Slave Trade Database, accessed July 25, 2025, slavevoyages.org.

133 **In 1985, Bruce Smith, an economist:** Bruce Smith, "Some Colonial Evidence on Two Theories of Money: Maryland and the Carolinas," *Journal of Political Economy* 93, no. 6 (1985): 1178–211, doi.org/10.1086/261355.

133 **Marylanders continued to sell:** Joseph Albert Ernst, *Money and Politics in America, 1755–1775: A Study in the Currency Act of 1764 and the Political Economy of Revolution* (Published for the Institute of Early American History and Culture by the University of North Carolina Press, 1973), 139, 141.

133 **More tools for making carts:** Carr, "Diversification in the Colonial Chesapeake," 352.

134 **"Jobber" was almost always an insult:** OED Online, "jobber, n.[2]," March 2022.

134 **"Little currency has circulation":** Also quoted in Gould, *Money and Transportation in Maryland,* 106–7.

134 **Grenville was following:** Andrew David Edwards, "Grenville's Silver Hammer: The Problem of Money in the Stamp Act Crisis," *Journal of American History* 104, no. 2 (2017): 337–62.

134 **David Hume had articulated:** Margaret Schabas, "'Let Your Science Be Human': David Hume and the Honourable Merchant," *European Journal of the History of Economic Thought* 21, no. 6 (2014): 977–90; David Hume, *Political Discourses* (printed by R. Fleming, for A. Kincaid and A. Donaldson, 1752), 41–45, Eighteenth Century Collections Online, accessed May 7, 2023.

135 **In May 1764, England's Board of Trade:** Board of Trade to Sharpe, May 11, 1764, 162.

135 **In July he reported back to London:** Sharpe to Board of Trade, July 17, 1764, 169.

135 **Merchants in Maryland were so desperate:** Ernst, *Money and Politics in America,* 154.

135 **Henry Callister, a planter and slave trader:** Quoted in Ernst, *Money and Politics in America,* 143–45.

136 **They were deflating by the month:** Lois Green Carr, "NEH Urbanization Effect Grant—Currency & Tobacco Conversion Rates" (n.d.), MSA SC 5906-5-845, Dr. Lois Green Carr Research Collection, Maryland State Archives Special Collections.

137 **In the late summer of 1764:** Charles Scarlett, "Governor Horatio Sharpe's Whitehall," *Maryland Historical Magazine* 46, no. 1 (1951): 19.

137 **Eight enslaved men rowed:** Scarlett, "Sharpe's Whitehall," 22.

137 **He was fascinated with the possibility:** Matilda Ridout Edgar, *A Colonial Governor in Maryland: Horatio Sharpe and His Times, 1753–1773* (Longmans, Green, 1912), 188.

138 **There's a clear picture of money:** *Gazette,* Aug. 1, 1765, Supplement edition.

139 **He left behind a record:** See James Boswell, *Boswell on the Grand Tour: Germany and Switzerland, 1764,* ed. Frederick Pottle (McGraw-Hill, 1953), 48–49, including lengthy footnotes on the number of people who had unpleasant encounters with Lord Baltimore.

139 **In January 1765, Baltimore wrote:** Baltimore to Sharpe, Jan. 16, 1765, 192.

140 **In October, Sharpe finally wrote:** Sharpe to Baltimore, Oct. 3, 1765, in *Correspondence.*

140 **The assembly also had to close:** "Report . . . at a Committee of Both Houses of Assembly Appointed to Inspect the Office and Proceedings of the Commissioners for Emitting Bills of Credit Established by Act of Assembly," Nov. 29, 1765, in *Proceedings and Acts of the General Assembly, 1764–1765,* Archives of Maryland, vol. 59, ed. J. Hall Pleasants (Maryland Historical Society, 1942), 63–68.

141 **On November 28, they proposed:** "Report . . . of What Will Be the Best Way of Disposing of the Public Money in the Treasury & Paper Currency Office," Nov. 28, 1765, in *Proceeding and Acts of the General Assembly, 1764–1765,* 183–84.

141 **Sharpe explained in a letter:** Sharpe to Calvert, Nov. 21, 1765, 250–53.

143 **The last son of a large family:** Scarlett, "Sharpe's Whitehall"; *Horatio Sharpe (1718–1790),* Archives of Maryland (Biographical Series) MSA SC 3520-1113, Maryland State Archives, accessed July 25, 2025, msa.maryland.gov/megafile/msa/speccol/sc3500/sc3520/001100/001113/html/01113bio.html.

144 **Hamersley himself couldn't find:** Hamersley to Sharpe, likely March 1766, in *Correspondence.*

145 **Maryland exports of grain, staves, and shingles:** Vaughan W. Brown, *Shipping in the Port of Annapolis, 1748–1775* (U.S. Naval Institute Press, 1965), 29–30.

145 **Pennsylvania and New York had the same problem:** Ernst, *Money and Politics in America,* 163.

145 **As of May of that year:** "Report from the Committee Appointed to Inspect the Office and Proceedings of the Late Commissioners or Trustees for Emitting Bills of Credit Established by Act of Assembly," Nov. 26, 1766, in *Proceeding and Acts of the General Assembly, 1766–1768,* ed. J. Hall Pleasants (Maryland Historical Society, 1944), 115.

145 **In December 1766, both houses:** "An Act for the Payment of the Publick Claims for Emitting Bills of Credit and for Other Purposes Therein Mentioned," Dec. 6, 1766, in *Proceedings and Acts of the General Assembly, 1766–1768,* 264–77.

147 **Sharpe seems to have been worried:** Sharpe to Baltimore, Dec. 7, 1766, 351; Sharpe to Hamersley, Dec. 8, 1766, 355.

147 **He was also annoyed:** Baltimore to Sharpe, Feb. 16, 1767, 370.

147 **Sharpe's letters begging for approval:** Sharpe to Hamersley, June 9, 1767, 389; Sharpe to Baltimore, June 11, 1767, 396; Hamersley to Sharpe, Aug. 13, 1767, 415.

147 **But already on January 1:** *Gazette,* Jan. 1, 1767.

148 **Horatio Sharpe did not remain governor:** Paul Giddens, "Governor Horatio Sharpe Retires," *Maryland Historical Magazine* 31, no. 3 (1936): 215–24.

149 **He was acquitted:** See, for example, *The Trial of Frederick Calvert, Esq.; Baron of Baltimore, in the Kingdom of Ireland, for a Rape on the Body of Sarah Woodcock* (printed for William Owen, in Fleet-Street; and Joseph Gurney, at No. 39, in Bread-Street, 1768), HeinOnline World Trials Library, heinonline.org/HOL/P?h=hein.trials/lbeaakj0001&i=1.

149 **That year, a woman claiming:** Sophia Watson, *Memoirs of the Seraglio of the Bashaw of Merryland, by a Discarded Sultana* (printed for S. Bladon, in Paternoster-Row, 1768), Gale Primary Sources, Eighteenth Century Collections Online, link.gale.com/apps/doc/CW0116396183/ECCO?u=prin77918&sid=bookmark-ECCO&xid=f99dde59&pg=1.

149 **Letters from Hamersley show Baltimore:** Hamersley to Sharpe, May 27, 1769, 562; Nov. 30, 1769, 565; July 13, 1770, 566.

149 **His last letter to Horatio Sharpe:** Baltimore to Sharpe, likely June 22, 1770, 567.

150 **Horatio Sharpe stayed in Maryland:** *Horatio Sharpe (1718–1790);* Giddens, "Sharpe Retires."

150 **Farley Grubb has argued:** Celia and Grubb, "Non-Legal-Tender Paper Money."

150 **Ronald Michener:** Ronald Michener, "Reconsidering Colonial Maryland's Bills of Credit, 1767–1775," SSRN Scholarly Paper ID 3103312 (Social Science Research Network, 2018).

INTRODUCTION TO PART II

156 **In 2011 researchers at the Bank of England:** The Bank of England did not come up with this theory all on its own. There is a long history of credit theories of money, laid out in Schumpeter's *History of Economic Analysis,* chap. 7, parts 3–4, in which he argues for a credit theory of money, where any loan used as payment is money. Schumpeter credits Henry Thornton, a nineteenth-century British banker, with articulating the way bank loans produce new money, a view that was subsequently ignored by the classical economists. This view is also sometimes referred to as the Banking School or endogenous money; see Ingham, *Nature of Money,* 52–54.

160 **After lunch at the lodge:** Mark Carney, "The Growing Challenges for Monetary Policy in the Current International Monetary and Financial System" (speech, Challenges for Monetary Policy, Jackson Lake Lodge, Jackson Hole, Wyo., Aug. 23, 2019), online with transcript of responses at www.kansascityfed.org/research/jackson-hole-economic-symposium/challenges-for-monetary-policy/.

161 **Currency theory in the late twentieth century:** Economists often refer to this as the Mundell-Fleming model, after papers published by Robert Mundell and J. Marcus Fleming in the early 1960s. It was named by Rudiger Dornbusch in several papers, including Rudiger Dornbusch, "Exchange Rate Expectations and Monetary Policy," *Journal of International Economics* 6, no. 3 (1976): 231–44; and Rudiger Dornbusch et al., "Flexible Exchange Rates in the Short Run," *Brookings Papers on Economic Activity* 1976, no. 3 (1976): 537–84. There's an overview of the history of the model and its adoption in James Boughton, "On the Origins of the Fleming-Mundell Model," *IMF Working Paper* 02, no. 107 (2002).

161 **When a company in Brazil imports:** Gita Gopinath et al., "Dominant Currency Paradigm," *American Economic Review* 110, no. 3 (2020): 677–719.

162 **Economists now refer to:** For a summary of recent work on the dominant currency paradigm, see Gita Gopinath and Oleg Itskhoki, "Dominant Currency Paradigm: A Review," Working Paper 29556, Working Paper Series, National Bureau of Economic Research, Dec. 2021, doi.org/10.3386/w29556.

CHAPTER 4: SILVER DOLLARS BECOME BANK DOLLARS

167 **On the morning of May 20, 1842:** Account of the May 20, 1842, riot from "Municipality Notes," *Daily Picayune,* May 21, 1842, 2, Newspapers.com. Some details of the Place d'Armes, Denis Prieur, and the covered markets from Henry Castellanos, *New Orleans as It Was: Episodes of Louisiana Life,* 2nd ed. (L. Graham & Son, 1905), 135, 143, 146.

168 **The Frenchmen had seen the value:** "New Orleans Money Market," *Picayune,* May 13, 1842, 4; May 19, 1842; and May 20, 1842.

168 **A refugee from the Haitian Revolution:** "Denis Prieur," in *A Dictionary of Louisiana Biography,* Louisiana Historical Association, accessed July 31, 2025, www.lahistory.org/resources/dictionary-louisiana-biography/.

168 **Running north from the river, Canal:** Richard Campanella, *Cityscapes of New Orleans* (Louisiana State University Press, 2017), 14; Eliza Ripley, *Social Life in Old New Orleans, Being Recollections of My Girlhood* (D. Appleton, 1912), 3.

169 **The Americans had arrived:** "Commerce, Navigation, and Tonnage of the United States, 1835," Treasury Department, May 18, 1836, 166, 212, 219, 281; Thomas E. Redard, "The Port of New Orleans: An Economic History, 1821–1860" (PhD diss., Louisiana State University, 1985), 324.

169 **In 1789 there were 2 banks:** Bank numbers from J. Van Fenstermaker, *The Development of American Commercial Banking, 1782–1837* (Kent State University, 1965), 111, 201.

169 **Banks tended to print their notes:** See Howard Bodenhorn, "Small-Denomination Banknotes in Antebellum America," *Journal of Money, Credit, and Banking* 25, no. 4 (1993): 812–27.

169 **In the blocks around the parade ground:** For example, Felix Lacroix, tailor and lender, mentioned later. See Andrew N. Wegmann, *An American Color: Race and Identity in New Orleans and the Atlantic World* (University of Georgia Press, 2022), 88–90.

170 **The *True American,* a newspaper:** "Shin Plasters," *True American* (New Orleans), Dec. 7, 1839, 2, Newspapers.com.

172 **And states can't force anyone:** U.S. Constitution, Article I, Section 10, Clause 1: "No State shall enter into any Treaty, Alliance, or Confederation; grant Letters of Marque and Reprisal; coin Money; emit Bills of Credit; make any Thing but gold and silver Coin a Tender in Payment of Debts; pass any Bill of Attainder, ex post facto Law, or Law impairing the Obligation of Contracts, or grant any Title of Nobility."

172 **Economic historians often present:** See, for example, among contemporary economic historians, Richard Sylla, "Public Credit, the National Bank, and Securities Markets," in *Founding Choices: American Economic Policy in the 1790s,* ed. Douglas A. Irwin and Richard Sylla (University of Chicago Press, 2011). In the same volume, Peter Rousseau treats the colonial bills of credit seriously in "Monetary Policy and the Dollar," 121–50, but ultimately concludes that the ban on state bills of credit enabled a currency union, a key condition for economic growth. James Ferguson, Curtis Nettels, Leslie Brock, and Bray Hammond, all working in the mid-twentieth century, drew clear distinctions among the more and less reliable bills of credit, and their work is cited heavily in this book. A generation of nineteenth-century financial historians was universally scathing on what they saw as the inflationary chaos of the colonial bills of credit. See, for example, William Graham Sumner's *History of American Currency* (1874), William Gouge's *Short History of*

Paper Money and Banking in the United States (1833), and Stanley Jevons's *Money and the Mechanism of Exchange* (1875).

172 **The Continental Congress began issuing:** Eric P. Newman, *The Early Paper Money of America,* Bicentennial ed. (Western Publishing Company, 1976), 13, 415–16. See also Farley Grubb, *The Continental Dollar: How the American Revolution Was Financed with Paper Money* (University of Chicago Press, 2023), esp. chap. 13, "1779: The Turning Point."

173 **By the mid-1780s the state exchange rates:** Newman, *Early Paper Money,* 14, 414.

173 **America's first chartered bank:** Description of the chartering of and initial subscriptions to the bank in Bray Hammond, *Banks and Politics in America: From the Revolution to the Civil War* (Princeton University Press, 1957), 48–51.

174 **The Bank of North America made:** George David Rappaport, "The First Description of the Bank of North America," *William and Mary Quarterly* 33, no. 4 (1976): 661–67. Descriptions of discounting from Sharon Murphy, *Other People's Money: How Banking Worked in the Early American Republic* (Johns Hopkins University Press, 2017), 47–49; and Fenstermaker, *Development of American Commercial Banking,* 45–49.

176 **In 1785, still under the Articles:** E. James Ferguson, *The Power of the Purse: A History of American Public Finance, 1776–1790* (University of North Carolina Press, 1961), 228; James T. Mitchell and Henry Flanders, eds., *The Statutes at Large of Pennsylvania from 1682 to 1801* (Harrisburg Publishing Co., State Printer, 1906), 11:480–86.

177 **The bills traded below par:** Ronald W. Michener and Robert E. Wright, "State 'Currencies' and the Transition to the U.S. Dollar: Clarifying Some Confusions," *American Economic Review* 95, no. 3 (2005): 688.

177 **Farmers in Pennsylvania argued:** Hammond, *Banks and Politics in America,* 53–56; Janet Wilson, "The Bank of North America and Pennsylvania Politics: 1781–1787," *Pennsylvania Magazine of History and Biography* 66, no. 1 (1942): 7–8, 19.

177 **This argument between bank notes:** Wilson, "Bank of North America and Pennsylvania Politics," 13, 28.

177 **Correspondence among the framers:** See Terry Bouton, *Taming Democracy: The People, the Founders, and the Troubled Ending of the American Revolution* (Oxford University Press, 2007), 61–82, 170–80; see also Pauline Maier, *Ratification: The People Debate the Constitution, 1787–1788* (Simon & Schuster, 2010).

178 **"indulgence to debtors":** Quoted in Farley Grubb, "The US Constitution and Monetary Powers: An Analysis of the 1787 Constitutional Convention and the Constitutional Transformation of the US Monetary System," *Financial History Review* 13, no. 1 (2006): 48.

178 **Economic historians have described:** Peter L. Rousseau, "A Common Currency: Early US Monetary Policy and the Transition to the Dollar," *Financial History Review* 13, no. 1 (2006): 97–122.

179 **It's likely the dollar sign:** See Newman, "Dollar $ign."

180 **Until the arrival of regular steamboat traffic:** William F. Switzler, "Special Report on the Commerce of the Mississippi, Ohio, and Other Rivers, and of the Bridges Which Cross Them," in *Report on the Internal Commerce of the United States: Commerce and Navigation* (Government Printing Office, 1888), 186.

180 **In the 1820s steamboats:** Redard, "Port of New Orleans," 258; *Special Report on the Commerce of the Mississippi, Ohio, and Other Rivers, and of the Bridges Which Cross Them,* II, William F. Switzler, ed., Report on the Internal Commerce of the United States: Commerce and Navigation (Government Printing Office, 1888), 190–92, 199, online at the Hathi Historical Trust, catalog.hathitrust.org/Record/008391406.

181 **By 1830, banks in Louisiana:** Fenstermaker, *American Commercial Banking,* 128, 201, 219, 225; author's calculations.

182 **Investors also often had to promise:** Murphy, *Other People's Money,* 49–55; Fenstermaker, *American Commercial Banking,* 21–27.

182 **In the early 1830s, Louisiana chartered:** Stephen Caldwell, "A Banking History of Louisiana" (PhD diss., University of Texas, 1933), 50–53; Samuel Trufant, "Review of Banking in New Orleans, 1830–1840: History of the Panic of 1837," Louisiana Historical Society, New Orleans, 1918, 5, 8, Hathi Trust, catalog.hathitrust.org/Record/008892355; George Green, *Finance and Economic Development in the Old South: Louisiana Banking, 1804–1861* (Stanford University Press, 1972), 33; Joe Regan, "Irish Canallers and the Second Slavery in the Lower Mississippi Valley," *Agricultural History* 96, no. 3 (2022): 317–41.

183 **In northern merchant cities:** See, for example, *Sylvester's Bank Note and Exchange Manual* (S. J. Sylvester, 1833), 8.

183 **Traveling paper money men did move:** For a thorough account of paper money men and note circulation, see Greenberg, *Bank Notes and Shinplasters.*

184 **Cecee Macarty, a free Black woman:** Robert C. Reinders, "The Free Negro in the New Orleans Economy, 1850–1860," *Louisiana History* 6, no. 3 (1965): 278; "The World of François Lacroix" (2002), online exhibit from the New Orleans Public Library. The link is no longer active, and the relevant file on Lacroix has disappeared from the City Archives & Special Collections at the New Orleans Public Library.

184 **This kind of private banking:** Greenberg, *Bank Notes and Shinplasters,* 24–25; for an example of a free Black private lender in Natchez, Mississippi, see Kimberly Welch, "William Johnson's Hypothesis: A Free Black Man and the Problem of Legal Knowledge in the Antebellum United States South," *Law and History Review* 37, no. 1 (2019): 89–124; and Kimberly Welch, "Arteries of Capital: William Johnson and the Practice of Black Moneylending in the Antebellum U.S. South," *Slavery & Abolition* 41, no. 2 (2020): 304–26.

184 **The word "picayune":** Charles White, "The Archaic Monetary Terms of the United States," *Smithsonian Miscellaneous Collections* 50 (June 1907): 98–102.

184 **A picayune was a little coin:** *Oxford English Dictionary,* "picayune (n. & adj.)," Sept. 2024, doi.org/10.1093/OED/6756188220.

184 **Picayunes rang in the offering box:** Ripley, *Social Life in Old New Orleans,* 4, 24–27.

184 **The history of all this silver:** *Picayune,* Jan. 25, 1837, 2.

185 **"of the value of the Spanish milled dollar":** An Act Establishing a Mint, and Regulating the Coins of the United States, Stat. 1, Chap. 16 (1792).

185 **It is difficult to pass a law:** Jesse C. Kraft, "The Circulation of Foreign Coinage: An American Response, ca. 1750–1857" (PhD diss., University of Delaware, 2019), 39–78.

185 **And so Congress kept allowing:** See Neil Carothers, *Fractional Money: A History of the Small Coins and Fractional Paper Currency of the United States* (John Wiley & Sons, 1930), chaps. 6–10.

186 **In the first few decades:** Richard von Glahn, "The Changing Significance of Latin American Silver in the Chinese Economy, 16th–19th Centuries," *Revista de Historia Economica—Journal of Iberian and Latin American Economic History* 38, no. 3 (2020): 568.

186 **Or they bought silver dollars:** Green, *Finance and Economic Development in the Old South,* 79.

186 **Politicians in the early American republic:** Dael A. Norwood, "Trading in Liberty: The Politics of the American China Trade, c. 1784–1862" (PhD diss., Princeton University, 2012), 98, 113–18.

186 **The coins that did pass:** Kraft, "Circulation of Foreign Coinage," 100–108.

186 **Between 1806 and 1835:** Carothers, *Fractional Money,* 76.

187 **It was clear to them:** *The Report of the Director of the Mint, of the Operations of That Institution, During the Last Year* (A. & G. Way, printers, 1806), 6; J. L. Riddell, *A Monograph of the Silver Dollar, Good and Bad* (Norman, 1845), 18.

187 **The few silver dollars minted:** Carothers, *Fractional Money,* 75.

188 **The sugarcane fields that ran:** Sharon Murphy in *Banking on Slavery* also points out that sugar production required far more up-front capital than cotton.

188 **The sugar machine was expensive:** Edmond J. Forstall, *Agricultural Productions of Louisiana, Embracing Valuable Information Relative to the Cotton, Sugar, and Molasses Interests, and the Effects upon the Same of the Tariff of 1842* (Tropic Print, 1845), 5, Gale Primary Sources, Making of the Modern World, link.gale.com/apps/doc/U0106468874/.

188 **By 1841 there were fifty-one thousand slaves:** Emile Philippe Grenier, "Property Banks in Louisiana" (PhD diss., Louisiana State University, 1942), 42; Forstall, *Agricultural Productions.*

188 **Sugar planters needed longer loan terms:** Property banks were complex, and this description of how they worked is summarized from several different sources: Green, *Finance and Development in the Old South;* Grenier, "Property Banks"; Mur-

phy, *Banking on Slavery;* and Calvin Schermerhorn, "Bank Bonds and Bondspersons," in *The Business of Slavery and the Rise of American Capitalism, 1815–1860* (Yale University Press, 2015).

189 **At first, agents for the Consolidated:** Considerable detail on the initial bond sale in Grenier, "Property Banks," 45–65; and Schermerhorn, "Bank Bonds and Bondspersons."

190 **Planters in Louisiana shipped:** Green, *Finance and Economic Development in the Old South,* 196.

190 **Edmond Forstall, a merchant:** Historians and contemporary documents have spelled his name both "Edmund" and "Edmond," and in one case, even "Edward." I have chosen "Edmond."

190 **Forstall drafted a charter:** Irene D. Neu, "Edmond Jean Forstall and Louisiana Banking," in "Economy, Society, and Government in Medieval Italy," special issue, *Explorations in Economic History* 7, no. 1 (1969): 383–98.

190 **"been the means of saving":** Forstall, *Agricultural Productions,* 7.

190 **"a sweeping mutation":** Forstall, *Agricultural Productions,* 7.

191 **"equal to any ever tendered":** Edmond J. Forstall, "Baring Papers: Letters Received—1418," April 30, 1835, Library and Archives Canada, heritage.canadiana.ca/view/oocihm.lac_reel_c1418, 057225.

191 **Sharon Murphy, a historian:** Murphy, *Banking on Slavery,* 14.

192 **David Morgan fought:** David B. Morgan Papers, Manuscripts Collection 624, Louisiana Research Collection, Howard-Tilton Memorial Library, Tulane University, New Orleans, box 1, folder 4.

192 **In January 1838, Edmond Forstall:** Louisiana Banking Collection, LaRC-539, Tulane University Special Collections, box 13, folder 2.

194 **In 1835, Andrew Crane:** Andrew E. Crane Papers, MSS 89, 1361, Louisiana and Lower Mississippi Valley Collections, LSU Libraries, Baton Rouge, La., item F16 ledger, page titled "Walton"; and U47, box 1a, folder 2a.

194 **Crane occasionally took in cash:** Crane Papers, from a survey of item F16 journal.

195 **In 1838, for example, George Bostwick:** *Picayune,* Dec. 9, 1838, 4; Crane Papers, U45, box 1a, folder 1a.

196 **In 1830 there were 330 banks:** "Condition of the State Banks," Doc. No. 111, 26th Cong., 2nd Sess. (U.S. House of Representatives, March 3, 1841), 1455–56; Green, *Finance and Economic Development in the Old South,* 202–4.

196 **The bank took in dollar bank notes:** The best technical description of how the Second Bank worked comes from Jane Knodell, *The Second Bank of the United States: "Central" Banker in an Era of Nation-Building, 1816–1836* (Routledge, 2017).

196 **Money and banking didn't map:** On the politics of the Bank War, see Sean Wilentz, *The Rise of American Democracy: Jefferson to Lincoln* (W. W. Norton, 2005), esp. chap. 11, "Radical Democracies," and chap. 13, "Banks, Abolitionists, and the Equal Rights Democracy"; and Daniel Walker Howe, *What Hath God Wrought:*

The Transformation of America, 1815–1848 (Oxford University Press, 2007), esp. chap. 10, "Battles over Sovereignty."

197 **One story of the panic of 1837:** See, for example, Hammond, *Banks and Politics in America,* 326–499; Richard H. Timberlake, "The Specie Circular and Distribution of the Surplus," *Journal of Political Economy* 68, no. 2 (1960): 109–17; Peter L. Rousseau, "Jacksonian Monetary Policy, Specie Flows, and the Panic of 1837," *Journal of Economic History* 62, no. 2 (2002): 457–88; and Jane Knodell, "Rethinking the Jacksonian Economy: The Impact of the 1832 Bank Veto on Commercial Banking," *Journal of Economic History* 66, no. 3 (2006): 541–74.

197 **The financial relationships that bound merchants:** The canonical description of these relationships and the way panic spread comes from Jessica Lepler, *The Many Panics of 1837: People, Politics, and the Creation of a Transatlantic Crisis* (Cambridge University Press, 2013).

197 **"is in a most strange situation":** *New-Orleans Price-Current and Commercial Intelligencer,* April 15, 1837, 3; and April 22, 1837, 3, Newspapers.com.

198 **Andrew Crane's journal for Thursday:** Crane Papers, F16 ledger, 188.

198 **"was there so much liquor drank":** *Picayune,* May 14, 1837, 2, 4.

198 **"We know not which way to turn":** *Price-Current,* May 20, 1837, 3.

199 **"The whole machinery of our commerce":** *Price-Current,* May 27, 1837, 3.

199 **There were fewer of them:** "Condition of the State Banks," Doc. No. 111, 26th Cong., 2nd Sess. (U.S. House of Representatives, March 3, 1841), 1455–56; Green, *Finance and Economic Development in the Old South,* 202–4.

200 **A merchant in the city reported:** *Picayune,* May 18, 24, 27, 30, 31, June 6, 9, 11, Aug. 5, Oct. 14, 1837; April 27, 1838.

200 **When the city passed a law:** Conseil de Ville de la Nouvelle-Orleans, *Digeste des ordonnances, resolutions et reglemens de la corporation de la Nouvelle-Orleans, et recueil des lois de la legislature relatives a la dite ville* (Gaston Brusle, 1836), 335.

201 **Businesses and cities all over the country:** Greenberg, *Bank Notes and Shinplasters,* 35–36, 51–52, 123–24.

202 **The Deer Creek Iron Works:** Lot 29229, "4 1837–1845 Hard Times–Era Six-Subject Horizontal Format Scrip Note Remainder," in National Numismatic Portal, Washington University in St. Louis, accessed Aug. 10, 2025, nnp.wustl.edu/library/ImageDetail/561430.

202 **In December 1839, the American municipality:** "Second Municipality Council Journal of Minutes and Proceedings, Vol. 1, 1836–1839" (n.d.), AB 300 Vol. 1, New Orleans City Archives & Special Collections, 604.

202 **The next day the American municipality:** New Orleans Second Municipality Comptroller's Office, "Register of Municipal Notes Delivered to the Treasurer" (1842 1839), New Orleans City Archives & Special Collections, 2; *Picayune,* March 1, 1840, 1.

203 **After reforms in the middle:** Alejandra Irigoin, "A Trojan Horse in Daoguang

China? Explaining the Flows of Silver in and out of China," London School of Economics, Working Papers, no. 173, Jan. 2013, 16, quoting M. Kishimoto, "'The Seventy-Percent Cash (Ch'i-che Ch'ien)' Custom of the Mid-ching Period," *Memoirs of the Toyo Bunko* 49 (1991): 18; Von Glahn, "Changing Significance of Latin American Silver in the Chinese Economy," 573.

203 **Traders in China developed a language:** Hsin-wei P'eng, *A Monetary History of China,* trans. Edward H. Kaplan (Center for East Asian Studies, Western Washington University, 1994), 671–72; Von Glahn, "Changing Significance of Latin American Silver in the Chinese Economy," 572–73.

204 **Already by 1800, almost half:** Hosea Ballou Morse, *The Chronicles of the East India Company Trading to China, 1635–1834* (Oxford University Press, 1926), 2:279, quoted in Irigoin, "Trojan Horse in Daoguang China?," 14.

204 **In the second half of the 1820s:** Von Glahn, "Changing Significance of Latin American Silver in the Chinese Economy," 576.

204 **More recently, however, Alejandra Irigoin:** Irigoin, "Trojan Horse in Daoguang China?"; Alejandra Irigoin, "The End of a Silver Era: The Consequences of the Breakdown of the Spanish Peso Standard in China and the United States, 1780s–1850s," *Journal of World History* 20, no. 2 (2009): 207–44.

204 **In 1823, for example, the mint:** P'eng, *Monetary History,* 672.

205 **"the Chinese having hitherto obstinately refused":** Morse, *Chronicles of the East India Company,* 4:259.

205 **Then, during the boom years:** *Merchant's Magazine, and Commercial Review* 10, no. 4 (April 1844): 376.

205 **They got stranded in the United States:** This is the essential argument in Peter Temin, *The Jacksonian Economy* (W. W. Norton, 1969).

206 **Starting in the mid-1830s:** Hugh Rockoff, "Stock of Money and Its Components: 1820–1858 [Temin]," table Cj22-25, in *Historical Statistics of the United States, Earliest Times to the Present: Millennial Edition,* ed. Susan B. Carter et al. (Cambridge University Press, 2006); and Hugh Rockoff, "Stock of Money and Its Components: 1790–1859 [Friedman and Schwartz]," table Cj7-21, in *Historical Statistics of the United States.*

207 **In most years of the 1820s and 1830s:** *American Commerce: Commerce of South America, Central America, Mexico, and West Indies, with Share of the United States and Other Leading Nations Therein, 1821–1898* (U.S. Bureau of Statistics, 1899), 3323; calculated using *Merchant's Magazine, and Commercial Review* 10, no. 4 (April 1844): 376.

207 **New Orleans sat on the old silver routes:** Green, *Finance and Economic Development in the Old South,* 79.

207 **It took trust to move:** Linda K. Salvucci and Richard J. Salvucci, "The Lizardi Brothers: A Mexican Family Business and the Expansion of New Orleans, 1825–1846," *Journal of Southern History* 82, no. 4 (2016): 759–88.

207 **Forstall had his hands on:** The author thanks Manuel Bautista-González for multiple conversations on silver and gold in New Orleans, and for sharing drafts of a dissertation pointing out how important Edmond Forstall was to the specie trade in the city in the era that followed the panic of 1837: "Gold and Silver Chains: The New Orleans Specie Market Under International Bimetallism, 1839–1861" (PhD diss., Columbia University, 2023).

207 **Just before the panic of 1837:** Grenier, "Property Banks," 248–51; George D. Green, "The Citizens Bank of Louisiana: Property Banking in Troubled Times, 1833–1842," *Papers of the Annual Meeting of the Business History Conference* 15 (Feb. 1968): 62; Salvucci and Salvucci, "Lizardi Brothers," 781–82.

208 **The banks didn't all collapse:** For more details on how the property banks stayed open, see also Murphy, *Banking on Slavery,* part 2, "The Collateral Damage of the Panics of 1837 and 1839."

208 **The bank presidents of New Orleans:** Neu, "Edmond Jean Forstall and Louisiana Banking," 389; Green, "Citizens Bank of Louisiana," 64; Grenier, "Property Banks," 254.

209 **New York's free banking law:** Arthur J. Rolnick and Warren E. Weber, "New Evidence on the Free Banking Era," *American Economic Review* 73, no. 5 (1983): 1080–91.

210 **Chartered bankers in Louisiana proved:** Caldwell, *Banking History,* 63–64; Branch W. Miller and Thomas Curry, *Reports of Cases Argued and Determined in the Supreme Court of the State of Louisiana* (J. B. Steel, 1854); Benjamin Levy; E. Johns, 497–511.

210 **Anyone who's worked as a banking reporter:** The author is grateful to have learned this maxim in a newsroom from Greg Ip, now a columnist for *The Wall Street Journal.*

210 **Prices for cotton and sugar fell again:** Peter H. Lindert and Richard Sutch, "Consumer Price Indexes, for All Items: 1774–2003," table Cc1-2, in Carter et al., *Historical Statistics of the United States;* Christopher Hanes, "Wholesale Price Indexes for New Orleans—Louisiana and Other Domestic Products, and Foreign Imports: 1800–1861," table Cc176-187, in *Historical Statistics of the United States;* useful analysis of available indices in Green, *Finance and Economic Development in the Old South,* 191–99.

211 **"the Banks were prostrated":** Quoted in Neu, "Edmond Jean Forstall and Louisiana Banking," 394–95.

211 **Other states had borrowed money:** Grenier, "Property Banks," 303.

212 **Praise for Forstall's bill:** Green, *Finance and Economic Development in the Old South,* 118; Fritz Redlich, *The Molding of American Banking: Men and Ideas,* Part 2, *1840–1910,* vol. 2 of *History of American Business Leaders* (Edwards Brothers, 1951), 36; Hammond, *Banks and Politics in America,* 682.

212 **Before that law, Hammond argued:** Hammond, *Banks and Politics in America,* 690.

212 **"We have fallen on evil times":** Quoted in Green, *Finance and Economic Development in the Old South,* 127.

212 **Louisiana bank notes in circulation:** "Condition of the State Banks," Exec. Doc. No. 111, 26th Cong., 2nd Sess. (U.S. House of Representatives, 1841), 392–93.

212 **Notes from the Citizens' Bank:** *Thompson's Bank Note Reporter,* July 15, 1843, archive.org/details/thompsonsbanknot0743jtho.

213 **There was a run on those banks:** *Picayune,* May 17, 1842, 2.

214 **The day before the currency riot:** New Orleans Second Municipality Comptroller's Office, Ordinances and Resolutions Passed by the Council of the Second Municipality, 1840–1846 (New Orleans, 1846), No. 388, p. 69; "Second Municipality Council Journal of Minutes and Proceedings, Vol. 2, 1839–1846" (n.d.), AB 300 Vol. 1, New Orleans City Archives & Special Collections, May 20, 1842; *Picayune,* May 21, 1842, 2.

214 **The discounts indicate that the notes:** *Thompson's Bank Note Reporter,* July 15, 1843.

214 **The finance committee:** "Second Municipality Council Journal of Minutes and Proceedings, Vol. 2, 1839–1846," Dec. 20, 1842, and June 17, 1845, plus observations from consistent weekly entries of the Finance Committee.

215 **Andrew Crane, the carriage dealer:** *Picayune,* March 13, 1845, Feb. 16, 1848.

215 **The St. Charles also held regular slave auctions:** Maurie D. McInnis, "Mapping the Slave Trade in Richmond and New Orleans," *Buildings & Landscapes* 20, no. 2 (2013): 113; Campanella, *Cityscapes of New Orleans,* 138–39.

215 **Crane auctioned off:** Crane Papers, U47, box 3b.

216 **On January 11, he paid:** Crane Papers, U45, box 1a, folder 3a.

216 **In February, Crane opened:** Crane Papers, U45, box 1a, folder 3a.

216 **In April he bought land:** Crane Papers, U45, box 1a, folder 3b.

216 **John Sutter, a serial debtor:** Albert L. Hurtado, "Empires, Frontiers, Filibusters, and Pioneers: The Transnational World of John Sutter," *Pacific Historical Review* 77, no. 1 (2008): 25.

216 **That year the territory of California:** U.S. Bureau of Statistics, *Statistical Abstract of the United States: 1887* (Washington, D.C., 1888), 35.

217 **The United States had already been:** The best account of this first gold rush is in Ann Marsh Daly, "Minting America: The Politics, Technology, and Culture of Money in the Early United States" (PhD diss., Brown University, 2021).

217 **Congress recognized that:** Carothers, *Fractional Money,* 94–99; see also David A. Martin, "1853: The End of Bimetallism in the United States," *Journal of Economic History* 33, no. 4 (1973): 825–44.

217 **This steady increase in small change:** Martin, "1853," 829.

217 **California was wildly out of scale:** U.S. Bureau of Statistics, *Statistical Abstract of the United States: 1887,* 41.

217 **New Orleans was one of the first ports:** "Report of the Director of the Mint for the Year 1849," Ex. Doc. No. 21, 31st Cong., 1st Sess. (U.S. Senate, 1850), 21.

217 **By 1850, the *Picayune* reported:** *Picayune,* July 3, 1850, 2, mentioned in Carothers, *Fractional Money,* 101.

217 **Gold coins were suddenly:** Richard G. Kelly and Nancy Y. Oliver, *Treatise of the Early Era of the New Orleans Mint, 1837–1861* (self-published, 2023), 61.

217 **In 1851, the director:** "Report of the Director of the Mint for the Year 1850," Ex. Doc. No. 21, 31st Cong., 2nd Sess. (U.S. Senate, 1851), 2, 6, 9.

218 **Bank notes in circulation made the same climb:** "Report of the Comptroller of the Currency to the Second Session of the Fifty-Fourth Congress of the United States" (Government Printing Office, 1896), 544.

218 **He opened an account:** Crane Papers, U45, box 1a, folders 3c and 4d.

218 **Crane negotiated a mortgage:** Crane Papers, U45, box 1b, folder 7b.

219 **The Citizens' Bank did not pay out:** Crane Papers, box 1b, folder 7c.

219 **Crane hired enslaved workers:** Crane Papers, box 1b, folder 7e; letter also mentioned in Richard J. Follett, *The Sugar Masters: Planters and Slaves in Louisiana's Cane World, 1820–1860* (Louisiana State University Press, 2005), 83.

219 **A year later Crane gave Hebert:** Crane Papers, box 1b, folder 8a.

CHAPTER 5: BANK NOTES BECOME BANK DEPOSITS

221 **He met with students:** We don't have a transcript of the speech, but can get a sense of it from a newspaper report: "Dr. Irving Fisher Finds Nation Suffering from Dollar Disease," *Ames Daily Tribune-Times,* Oct. 19, 1932.

221 **After Fisher's broadcast in Iowa:** Cards from listeners in Irving Fisher Papers, New York Public Library Archives & Manuscripts, vol. 33, reel 2.

223 **He stayed only a couple:** Ruth Schiefen, *Hawarden Centennial, 1887–1987: One Hundred Years on the Right Track* (self-published, 1987), 612–13; "Praises Scrip Plan Highly," *Hawarden Independent,* Oct. 20, 1932, 1; Fisher to French, Nov. 4, 1932, Fisher Papers, vol. 33, reel 1.

223 **A correspondent:** See, for example, Associated Press, "Yale Economist Approves Hawarden Scrip Currency," *Iowa City Press-Citizen,* Oct. 20, 1932, 1, www.newspapers.com/image/363030891/.

224 **Abraham Lincoln had always been critical:** Emir Phillips, "How Lincoln's Revolutionary Monetary Policies Tipped the Scales in the Civil War," *Cambridge Journal of Economics* 48, no. 6 (2024): 1005–26.

225 **Greenbacks were structured like:** Ariel Ron and Sofia Valeonti, "The Money War:

Democracy, Taxes, and Inflation in the U.S. Civil War," *Cambridge Journal of Economics* 47, no. 2 (2023): 263–88, doi.org/10.1093/cje/bead006.

225 **Just as with the colonial bills:** See text of Legal Tender Act, Pub. L. No. at 345, 12 Stat. 345, chap. 33 (1862).

225 **During the war, the private markets:** Kristen L. Willard, Timothy W. Guinnane, and Harvey S. Rosen, "Turning Points in the Civil War: Views from the Greenback Market," *American Economic Review* 86, no. 4 (1996): 1001–18; Gregor W. Smith and R. Todd Smith, "Greenback-Gold Returns and Expectations of Resumption, 1862–1879," *Journal of Economic History* 57, no. 3 (1997): 697–717; Charles W. Calomiris, "Price and Exchange Rate Determination During the Greenback Suspension," *Oxford Economic Papers* 40, no. 4 (1988): 719–50.

225 **The new federal charter created:** More detail on national banks in Hugh Rockoff, "Banking and Finance, 1789–1914," in *The Long Nineteenth Century,* ed. Robert E. Gallman and Stanley L. Engerman (Cambridge University Press, 2000), 651; and Hammond, *Banks and Politics in America,* 718–27.

226 **If a national bank failed:** The author thanks Sean Vanatta of the University of Glasgow for explaining the mechanics of the redemption guarantee contained in the national bank charter.

226 **But during the war, banks began:** David F. Weiman and John A. James, "The Political Economy of the US Monetary Union: The Civil War Era as a Watershed," *American Economic Review* 97, no. 2 (2007): 271–75; and John A. James, *Money and Capital Markets in Postbellum America* (Princeton University Press, 1978), 75.

226 **Both national banks and state banks:** The shift from notes to deposits is a prominent theme in chapters 2, 3, and 4 in Milton Friedman and Anna Schwartz, *A Monetary History of the United States, 1867–1960* (Princeton University Press, 1971).

228 **Deposits are an old idea:** Peter Spufford, Wendy Wilkinson, and Sarah Tolley, *Handbook of Medieval Exchange* (Offices of the Royal Historical Society, 1986), xxvii–xxviii; Reinhold Mueller, *The Venetian Money Market Banks, Panics, and the Public Debt, 1200–1500* (Johns Hopkins University Press, 1997); Raymond De Roover, *Money, Banking, and Credit in Mediaeval Bruges: Italian Merchant-Bankers, Lombards, and Money-Changers: A Study in the Origins of Banking* (Mediaeval Academy of America, 1948).

228 **Just after the Civil War:** Cash and deposit data from Friedman and Schwartz, *Monetary History,* 302, and app. A, table A-1.

229 **There had been about five hundred:** *Bank Suspensions, 1892–1935* (Federal Reserve Board of Governors, 1936), 7, 22.

231 **What would become the Hawarden:** Schiefen, *Hawarden Centennial,* 174.

232 **The Department of the Treasury sold bonds:** Mention of the bond financing in an article on redemption in *The New York Sun,* Dec. 3, 1878, 1.

232 **By the end of the nineteenth:** Friedman and Schwartz refer to this list as "an assemblage of assorted relics from earlier monetary episodes" in *A Monetary History,* 189.

232 **Fights over money:** There's a good summary of the politics behind different kinds of cash in the late nineteenth century in Gretchen Ritter, *Goldbugs and Greenbacks: The Antimonopoly Tradition and the Politics of Finance in America, 1865–1896* (Cambridge University Press, 1997).

233 **In July 1908:** Schiefen, *Hawarden Centennial,* 174.

234 **These big regional correspondent banks:** Descriptions of the correspondent banking system in John A. James, *Money and Capital Markets in Postbellum America* (Princeton University Press, 1978), 111, 118–19, 127; Jeffrey A. Miron, "Financial Panics, the Seasonality of the Nominal Interest Rate, and the Founding of the Fed," *American Economic Review* 76, no. 1 (1986): 125–40; and Charles W. Calomiris, "Volatile Times and Conceptual Errors: U.S. Monetary Policy, 1914–1951," in *The Origins, History, and Future of the Federal Reserve: A Return to Jekyll Island,* ed. Michael D. Bordo and William Roberds (Cambridge University Press, 2013).

235 **Even if banks turned out:** John A. James, James McAndrews, and David F. Weiman, "Wall Street and Main Street: The Macroeconomic Consequences of New York Bank Suspensions, 1866–1914," *Cliometrica* 7, no. 2 (2013): 99–130.

235 **The bank panic of 1907:** Elmus Wicker, *Banking Panics of the Gilded Age* (Cambridge University Press, 2000), 86, 95.

237 **There is some evidence:** Michael Bordo and David Wheelock, "The Promise and Performance of the Federal Reserve as a Lender of Last Resort, 1914–1933," in Bordo and Roberds, *Origins, History, and Future of the Federal Reserve,* 77; and Miron, "Financial Panics, the Seasonality of the Nominal Interest Rate, and the Founding of the Fed."

238 **And it eased some of the concentration:** Matthew Jaremski and David Wheelock, "The Founding of the Federal Reserve, the Great Depression, and the Evolution of the U.S. Interbank Network," *Journal of Economic History* 80, no. 1 (2020): 69–99.

238 **The logic of staying out of the Fed:** Charles W. Calomiris and Matthew Jaremski, "Why Join the Fed?," *Journal of Economic History,* June 14, 2022, 1–36.

238 **The *Hawarden Independent* estimated:** "Iowa Weather and Crop Bureau Annual Report for 1926" (State of Iowa, 1927), 65.

239 **You can see the flood:** "Hawarden State Bank," Sept. 16, 1927, RG 10 Banking, Bank Inventories, State Historical Society of Iowa, State Archives; biographical details from Schiefen, *Hawarden Centennial.*

239 **It is bad practice for a bank:** *Bank Suspensions, 1892–1935,* 8.

240 **Overall, smaller banks:** *Bank Suspensions, 1892–1935,* 3–9, 14, 16–17.

241 **But then global commodity prices:** "Bank Suspensions in the United States, 1892–1931," Committee on Branch, Group, and Chain Banking (Federal Reserve System, 1932), 8.

241 **Depositors arrived to find a note:** "Two Hawarden Banks Close," *Hawarden Independent,* Sept. 15, 1927.

242 **The bank had last shared:** "Hawarden State Bank."

243 **Insurance on bank notes:** Early history of deposit and note guarantees in *The First Fifty Years: A History of the FDIC, 1933–1983* (Federal Deposit Insurance Corporation, 1984), chap. 2, "Antecedents of the FDIC."

244 **Mary has given me a book:** Biographical details from Schiefen, *Hawarden Centennial.*

244 **Between 1921 and 1930:** *Bank Suspensions, 1892–1935,* 79–82.

245 **A week after the Hawarden State Bank:** "Receivership Is Permanent," *Hawarden Independent,* Sept. 22, 1927, 1.

245 **The Chicago Fed's annual report:** *Operation of Federal Reserve Bank of Chicago, 1927,* Thirteenth Annual Report to the Federal Reserve Board, fraser.stlouisfed.org/title/annual-report-federal-reserve-bank-chicago-472/operation-federal-reserve-bank-chicago-1927-18222.

246 **He immigrated to Iowa as a young man:** "Zylstra, Former Sioux County Representative, Dies in Chicago," *Sioux Center News,* Dec. 12, 1946, 1.

246 **"sturdy, bronzed and well over six feet in height":** Quoted in Sarah Elvins, "Scrip Money and Slump Cures: Iowa's Experiments with Alternative Currency During the Great Depression," *Annals of Iowa* 64, no. 3 (2005): 226. The author also thanks Sarah Elvins for an incredibly helpful conversation about Zylstra.

246 **Gesell proposed stamp scrip:** Rosario Patalano, "The Gesell Connection During the Great Depression," *Journal of the History of Economic Thought* 39, no. 3 (2017): 349–79; Werner Onken, "The Political Economy of Silvio Gesell: A Century of Activism," *American Journal of Economics and Sociology* 59, no. 4 (2000): 609–22.

246 **In 1927, when:** *Bank Suspensions, 1892–1935,* 22.

247 **Herbert Hoover, the same man:** Nash, *Life of Herbert Hoover,* 492–93.

247 **Hoover had first become famous:** Details of Hoover's humanitarian work from Glen Jeansonne, *Herbert Hoover: A Life,* with David Luhrssen (New American Library, 2016), 122–33, 181–83.

247 **In 1931, Hoover asked the Department:** Calvin W. Coquillette, "A Failure or 'a Very Great Public Service'? Herbert Hoover, Iowa Banks, and the National Credit Corporation," *Annals of Iowa* 58, no. 4 (1999): 391.

248 **A group of Iowa bankers:** Coquillette, "A Failure or 'a Very Great Public Service'?," 394.

248 **The National Credit Corporation imposed:** Glen Jeansonne, *The Life of Herbert Hoover: Fighting Quaker, 1928–1933* (Palgrave Macmillan, 2012), 270.

249 **In December 1931, the governor of Iowa:** Coquillette, "A Failure or 'a Very Great Public Service'?," 405, 411.

249 **We now call this problem:** Ben Bernanke also won a Nobel Prize in part for describing this in Ben S. Bernanke, "Nonmonetary Effects of the Financial Crisis in the

Propagation of the Great Depression," *American Economic Review* 73, no. 3 (1983): 257–76.

249 **In August 1932:** Friedman and Schwartz, *Monetary History,* 325; Jeansonne, *Life of Herbert Hoover: Fighting Quaker,* 276.

249 **On August 4, 1932, the Sioux County Fair:** Chas. J. Zylstra, "Offers Plan to Issue Scrip," *Hawarden Independent,* Aug. 4, 1932, 2.

250 **Instead, he proposed that anyone:** Zylstra to Fisher, Oct. 28, 1932, Fisher Papers, vol. 33, reel 1.

250 **French talked fifty members of the chamber:** Chamber of Commerce to City of Hawarden, n.d., Fisher Papers, reel 1, "Script Money [*sic*], Clippings & Correspondence," n.p.

250 **A staff writer for the *Des Moines Register:*** C. C. Clifton, "Nation Eyes Hawarden's Experiment in Scrip Money," *Des Moines Register,* Dec. 4, 1932, 1.

250 **"under the plan which Chas. J. Zylstra":** "Lost Opening Football Game," "Clever Short Change Game," "City to Issue $300 in Scrip," *Hawarden Independent,* Oct. 6, 1932, 1.

250 **The city paid out the scrip:** Clifton, "Nation Eyes Hawarden's Experiment in Scrip Money," 1, 6.

251 **One of his biographers points out:** Robert W. Dimand, *Irving Fisher* (Palgrave Macmillan, 2019), 5.

251 **"permanently higher plateau":** Quoted in Dimand, *Irving Fisher,* 157.

251 **But Irving Fisher believed his own predictions:** For an explanation of Fisher's business as a predictor, see Walter A. Friedman, *Fortune Tellers: The Story of America's First Economic Forecasters* (Princeton University Press, 2014), 68–83.

252 **In July, Earl Barker, branch manager:** Barker to Fisher, Chippewa Falls, Wis., July 7, 1932, Fisher Papers, vol. 33, reel 2.

252 **Cohrssen was flattered, and accepted:** Hans Cohrssen, *Einer der auszog die Welt zu verändern* (Josef Knecht, 1996), 65.

252 **Claude Million, a Swiss historian:** Claude Million, *Stamp Your Scrip—Stamp Out Depression: Irving Fisher's Advocacy of Stamped Money, 1932–1934* (Stämpfli Publishers, 2019), 14.

253 **All these businesses willingly took:** Clifton, "Nation Eyes Hawarden's Experiment in Scrip Money," 1, 6.

254 **William Schoeneman emigrated from Saxony:** Schiefen, *Hawarden Centennial,* 158.

255 **Pamphlets on money functioned:** Pamphlets on U.S. Money During the Depression, bound collection held at the Princeton University Library.

256 **As debts went bad and deposits dropped:** See also Irving Fisher, "The Debt-Deflation Theory of Great Depressions: Introductory," *Econometrica (Pre-1986),* vol. 1 (1933): 337.

256 **The Federal Reserve had tried:** Allan H. Meltzer, *A History of the Federal Reserve,*

vol. 1, *1913–1951* (University of Chicago Press, 2003), 357–67; Friedman and Schwartz, *Monetary History,* 384–89.

257 **The Fed's decision to stop pushing:** Friedman and Schwartz, *Monetary History,* 407–19.

257 **Irving Fisher saw stamp scrip:** See also Elvins, "Scrip Money and Slump Cures."

257 **Zylstra's response was simple:** Zylstra to John Murphy, Nov. 18, 1932, Fisher Papers, vol. 33, reel 1.

258 **By November, the *Hawarden Independent*:** "Wide Interest in Scrip Plan," *Hawarden Independent,* Nov. 17, 1932, 1; Fred Gefke to Fisher, Nov. 10, 1932, Fisher Papers, vol. 33, reel 1.

258 **At the end of November:** Cohrssen to Zylstra, Nov. 25, 1932, Fisher Papers, vol. 33, reel 2.

258 **Back at Yale, Fisher wanted:** Fisher to French, Nov. 4, 1932, Zylstra to Fisher, Nov. 18, 1932, Fisher Papers, vol. 33, reel 1.

258 **He put together a list:** C.S. Argo to Cohrssen, Jan. 2, 1933; T. W. Fowler to Cohrssen, Nov. 8, 1932, Fisher Papers, vol. 33, reel 1.

259 **In late November 1932, Hans Cohrssen:** American Bank Note Company to Cohrssen, Dec. 2, 1932, Fisher Papers, vol. 33, reel 2.

259 **Fisher sat down at the Yale Club:** N.d., Fisher Papers, vol. 33, reel 1.

259 **By early January, Cohrssen:** Cohrssen to Warren Lathame, Jan. 1, 1933; Fisher to Burman Curry, January 9, 1933; Cohrssen to Amelia Sears, Jan. 7, 1933, Fisher Papers, vol. 33, reel 3.

259 **One of Cohrssen's form letters:** Cohrssen to Zylstra, Feb. 9, 1933, Fisher Papers, vol. 33, reel 1.

260 **In Iowa over the winter:** Calvin W. Coquillette, "The Struggle to Preserve Iowa's State Banking System, 1920–1933," *Annals of Iowa* 60, no. 1 (2001): 53.

261 **About a hundred communities used his plans:** Mitchell and Shafer, *Standard Catalog of Depression Scrip of the United States in the 1930s,* 29, 30, 86, 136, 144, 237.

261 **a catalog of Depression-era scrip:** Ralph Mitchell and Neil Shafer, *Standard Catalog of Depression Scrip of the United States in the 1930s Including Canada and Mexico* (Krause, 1984).

261 **Madison, South Dakota:** Zylstra to Fisher, Dec. 31, 1932, Fisher Papers, vol. 33, reel 1.

261 **Searle, a farmer in Hawarden:** *Hawarden Independent,* Sept. 28, 1933, 7.

261 **He died in 1946:** Elvins, "Scrip Money and Slump Cures."

261 **During the Depression, most scrip:** Mitchell and Shafer, *Standard Catalog of Depression Scrip of the United States in the 1930s,* 312.

261 **Particularly in larger towns:** Jonathan Warner, "Iowa Stamp Scrip: Economic Experimentation in Iowa Communities During the Great Depression," *Annals of Iowa* 71, no. 1 (2012): 26.

262 **When it wasn't needed, it stopped working:** Elvins, "Scrip Money and Slump Cures."

262 **In January 1934:** *Hawarden Independent,* Jan. 4, 1934, 8.

262 **There were discussions within the Roosevelt White House:** See, for example, Million, *Stamp Your Scrip,* 123.

263 **The Reconstruction Finance Corporation became:** James Stuart Olson, *Saving Capitalism: The Reconstruction Finance Corporation and the New Deal, 1933–1940* (Princeton University Press, 1988), 35–41.

263 **But in the emergency of 1933:** Peter Conti-Brown and Sean Vanatta, *Private Finance, Public Power: A History of Bank Supervision in America* (Princeton University Press, 2025), chap. 6, "Supervision's New Deal."

264 **In Hawarden, work on flood control:** Schiefen, *Hawarden Centennial,* 467–68.

264 **Fisher had testified before Congress:** Million, *Stamp Your Scrip,* 149–52.

264 **It was supposed to keep base politics out:** See, for example, Michael D. Bordo and Finn E. Kydland, "The Gold Standard as a Commitment Mechanism," in *Modern Perspectives on the Gold Standard,* ed. Barry Eichengreen, Mark P. Taylor, and Tamim Bayoumi (Cambridge University Press, 1997), 55–100.

264 **The economic historian Barry Eichengreen:** See Barry J. Eichengreen, *Golden Fetters: The Gold Standard and the Great Depression, 1919–1939* (Oxford University Press, 1992).

264 **In Iowa, the problem of low prices:** Mentioned in Eric Rauchway, *The Money Makers: How Roosevelt and Keynes Ended the Depression, Defeated Fascism, and Secured a Prosperous Peace* (Basic Books, 2015), 55–56. Details in F. D. Dileva, "Iowa Farm Price Revolt," *Annals of Iowa* 32, no. 3 (1954): 190–92; P. B. Bauer, "Farm Mortgagor Relief Legislation in Iowa During the Great Depression," *Annals of Iowa* 50, no. 1 (1989): 24; F. D. DiLeva, "Attempt to Hang an Iowa Judge," *Annals of Iowa* 32, no. 5 (1954): 339–42.

265 **In May 1933, Congress passed:** Rauchway, *Money Makers,* 80; see also Kenneth Finegold, "From Agrarianism to Adjustment: The Political Origins of the New Deal Agricultural Policy," *Politics & Society* 11, no. 1 (1982): 25–26; Wayne D. Rasmussen, "The New Deal Farm Programs: What They Were and Why They Survived," *American Journal of Agricultural Economics* 65, no. 5 (1983): 1159; and Theodore Saloutos, "New Deal Agricultural Policy: An Evaluation," *Journal of American History* 61, no. 2 (1974): 403.

265 **In April 1933, an executive order:** For details on the mechanics of loosening the gold standard, see Friedman and Schwartz, *Monetary History,* 462–70.

265 **"accidents of international trade":** Franklin Delano Roosevelt, "Fireside Chat," Oct. 22, 1933, online at American Presidency Project, UC Santa Barbara, www.presidency.ucsb.edu/documents/fireside-chat-22.

266 **But the actual sound-money gold standard:** The author is grateful to Rebecca Spang, who pointed out that the gold standard lasted less than the span of a human life.

CHAPTER 6:
THE DOLLAR BECOMES A GLOBAL CURRENCY, AGAIN

271 **They called themselves "bondmen":** Details on the makeup of the San Francisco Bond Club are in Destin Jenkins, *The Bonds of Inequality: Debt and the Making of the American City* (University of Chicago Press, 2021), 45–67.

272 **Rather, they were dollars:** The origins of the word "eurodollar" are even more complicated than this, but if the author had chased every interesting question into the hills, he would have never finished this book, and you would not now be reading it. He barely finished as it is.

272 **Anyone, anywhere can make:** Hyman Minsky wrote, similarly, that "everyone can create money; the problem is to get it accepted," but the author despaired of cramming yet another unorthodox economist with fascinating ideas into this book and in particular into this chapter. Hyman Minsky, *Stabilizing an Unstable Economy* (Yale University Press, 1986), 228.

273 **In his speech in San Francisco:** Andrew F. Brimmer, "The Banking Structure and Monetary Management" (remarks before the San Francisco Bond Club, Fairmont Hotel, San Francisco, April 1, 1970), 1, fraser.stlouisfed.org/title/statements-speeches-andrew-f-brimmer-463/banking-structure-monetary-management-10376.

273 **The Federal Reserve, he proposed:** This chapter began as a column by the author, "The Contentious Idea That Still Challenges the Fed," *Financial Times,* April 2, 2023, and was developed as a conference paper, "Burns Against Brimmer: A Missed Chance for Small-Money Policy at the Fed," for "Money as a Democratic Medium 2.0," held at Harvard Law School on June 15–17, 2023. Another author working along similar lines is Chris Hughes in *Marketcrafters: The 100-Year Struggle to Shape the American Economy* (Simon & Schuster, 2025), 91–110.

274 **The speech in 1970 provoked:** Andrew F. Brimmer, "Commercial Bank Lending and Monetary Management" (57th Annual Fall Conference of the Robert Morris Associates, Century Plaza Hotel, Los Angeles, Oct. 25, 1971), 22, fraser.stlouisfed.org/title/statements-speeches-andrew-f-brimmer-463/commercial-bank-lending-monetary-management-10401.

274 **In 2019, when I worked as a journalist:** "Has the Time for Place-Based Policies Finally Arrived? A Panel Discussion," in "A House Divided: Geographic Disparities in Twenty-First Century America," Federal Reserve Bank of Boston, Oct. 5, 2019, question at 3:21:04 in video archived at https://www.bostonfed.org/housedivided2019/agenda/.

276 **When the flood reached Newellton:** Andrew F. Brimmer, "The House in Which We Lived (Typewritten Draft)" (n.d.), 19–20, box 424, folder 18, Andrew Brimmer Papers, Baker Library Special Collections, Harvard Business School.

276 **"Big Brimmer":** Brimmer, "House in Which We Lived," 13–14.

276 **Andrew Brimmer picked cotton:** Andrew Brimmer, interview by David Small et al., July 13, July 27, and Aug. 1, 2007, 5–7, Federal Reserve Oral History Project, www.federalreserve.gov/aboutthefed/centennial/federal-reserve-oral-history-interviews.htm.

276 **Under the sharecropping system:** William Thomas Okie, "Agriculture and Rural Life in the South, 1900–1945," in *Oxford Research Encyclopedia of American History,* Nov. 19, 2020.

276 **As prices dropped during the Depression:** James Reonas, "Once Proud Princes: Planters and Plantation Culture in Louisiana's Northeast Delta, from the First World War Through the Great Depression" (PhD diss., Louisiana State University, 2006), 164–66, repository.lsu.edu/gradschool_dissertations/579.

276 **"'boss man' was broke":** Reonas, "Once Proud Princes," 165.

277 **"We didn't prosper during the Depression":** Brimmer, interview by David Small et al., 10.

277 **Prices for American commodities:** Hugh Rockoff, *America's Economic Way of War* (Cambridge University Press, 2012), 163; Board of Governors of the Federal Reserve System (US), Industrial Production: Total Index [INDPRO], retrieved from FRED, Federal Reserve Bank of St. Louis, accessed April 19, 2024, fred.stlouisfed.org/series/INDPRO; National Bureau of Economic Research Public Use Data Archive, Macrohistory: VIII. Income and Employment, m08292a, U.S. Unemployment Rate, Seasonally Adjusted 04/1929–06/1942.

277 **The sums of dollars:** Morris H. Hansen, *Statistical Abstract of the United States, 1947* (U.S. Department of Commerce, 1947), 316.

277 **The new spending moved farm wages:** Hansen, *Statistical Abstract of the United States, 1947,* 190, 199.

277 **In July 1944:** Andrew Brimmer, "The Way West" (handwritten draft), Andrew Brimmer Papers, Box 424, Folder 2, 1–13; Brimmer, interview by David Small et al., 20–22.

278 **In 1940, the federal government:** Hansen, *Statistical Abstract of the United States, 1947,* 322.

278 **But taxes paid for only about half:** Hansen, *Statistical Abstract of the United States, 1947,* 320; see also Rockoff, *America's Economic Way of War,* 171.

278 **the Treasury Department borrowed:** Hansen, *Statistical Abstract of the United States, 1947,* 364.

278 **As it had during World War I:** Hansen, *Statistical Abstract of the United States, 1947,* 364.

278 **The war bond program was explicitly designed:** Lawrence M. Olney, *The War Bond Story* (U.S. Department of the Treasury, 1971), 4–5, 10, 25, 39, 55, 83.

279 **it was financial institutions:** Hansen, *Statistical Abstract of the United States, 1947,* 364.

279 **Most of their portfolios:** Meltzer, *History of the Federal Reserve,* vol. 1, *1913–1951,* 417.

280 **"a radical departure":** Marriner Eccles, *Beckoning Frontiers* (Alfred A. Knopf, 1951), 350.

281 **In the summer of 1944:** Summaries of the conference are in Michael Bordo, "The Bretton Woods International Monetary System: A Historical Overview," in *A Retrospective on the Bretton Woods System: Lesson for International Monetary Reform,* Michael Bordo and Barry Eichengreen, eds. (University of Chicago Press, 1993); and Benn Steil, *The Battle of Bretton Woods: John Maynard Keynes, Harry Dexter White, and the Making of a New World Order* (Princeton University Press, 2013).

282 **frightened and wealthy Europeans:** Eric Helleiner, *States and the Reemergence of Global Finance* (Cornell University Press, 1994), 29–31.

282 **By the end of the war:** Donald T. Regan, "Report to the Congress," Commission on the Role of Gold in the Domestic and International Monetary Systems, March 1982, 195–205.

282 **And deposits at those banks were guaranteed:** The author is aware that not all of the countries in the European Union have adopted the euro, but used "European Union" here to avoid confusion with the eurodollars in this chapter, which will be new to most readers.

282 **The system it had ended up with:** See, for example, Mehrsa Baradaran, *The Color of Money: Black Banks and the Racial Wealth Gap* (Harvard University Press, 2017).

283 **Before the war, the Federal Reserve:** J. Lawrence Broz, *The International Origins of the Federal Reserve System* (Cornell University Press, 1997), 17–55.

286 **Within the United States, during the war:** Helleiner, *States and the Reemergence of Global Finance,* 30–33.

286 **Bankers in New York hated:** Helleiner, *States and the Reemergence of Global Finance,* 52–58.

287 **It's difficult to come up with:** Helleiner, *States and the Reemergence of Global Finance,* 55; and Harold James, "The IMF and the Creation of the Bretton Woods System, 1944–58," in *Europe's Postwar Recovery,* ed. Barry Eichengreen (Cambridge University Press, 1995), 106.

287 **They argued that European countries:** Helleiner, *States and the Reemergence of Global Finance,* 57–59. Eccles quoted in Helleiner, 59.

287 **The problem with Bretton Woods:** See John H. Williams, "Currency Stabilization: The Keynes and White Plans," *Foreign Affairs* 21, no. 4 (1943): 645; John H. Williams, "Currency Stabilization: American and British Attitudes," *Foreign Affairs* 22, no. 2 (1944): 233; and John H. Williams, "The Postwar Monetary Plans," *American Economic Review* 34, no. 1 (1944): 372–84, mentioned in Harold James, *International Monetary Cooperation Since Bretton Woods* (International Monetary Fund, 1996), 64.

288 **Harold James has suggested:** Harold James, "The IMF and the Creation of the Bretton Woods System, 1944–58," in *Europe's Post-War Recovery* (Cambridge University Press, 1995), 96.

288 **Andrew Brimmer tried to join:** Brimmer, "House in Which We Lived," 22.

290 **In 1957, Fred Klopstock:** Fred H. Klopstock, "The International Status of the Dollar," *Essays in International Finance,* no. 28 (May 1957).

291 **Triffin, a Belgian-born economist at Yale:** Ivo Maes and Ilaria Pasotti, *Robert Triffin: A Life* (Oxford University Press, 2021).

291 **The amount of dollars held as deposits:** Robert Triffin, *Gold and the Dollar Crisis: The Future of Convertibility* (Yale University Press, 1960), 4–5.

293 **Already at the end of the 1950s:** Stefano Battilossi provides an indispensable summary of both the history and historiography of eurodollars in "International Money Markets: Eurocurrencies," in Stefano Battilossi et al., eds., *Handbook of the History of Money and Currency* (Springer Singapore, 2020), 269–314.

294 **It was a quiet practice:** Paul Einzig, *Foreign Dollar Loans in Europe* (Macmillan, 1965), vi–viii.

294 **By early 1960, the Fed's Board of Governors:** "Meeting Minutes, Volume 47, Part 5," Minutes of the Board of Governors of the Federal Reserve System, May 4, 1960, 3–5, fraser.stlouisfed.org/title/821/item/515514.

294 **Holding and trading dollar deposits:** Catherine R. Schenk, "The Origins of the Eurodollar Market in London, 1955–1963," *Explorations in Economic History* 35, no. 2 (1998): 221–38; Gary Burn, "The State, the City, and the Euromarkets," *Review of International Political Economy* 6, no. 2 (1999): 225–61, doi.org/10.1080/096922999347290.

295 **That same month, Klopstock returned:** Alan R. Holmes and Fred H. Klopstock, "The Market for Dollar Deposits in Europe," *Federal Reserve Bank of New York Monthly Review* 42, no. 11 (1960): 197–202.

296 **"Harvard mafia":** Brimmer, interview by David Small et al., 90.

296 **Brimmer briefly got into a dustup:** Brimmer, interview by David Small et al., 96; "Civil Rights: Public Accommodations," Committee on Commerce, U.S. Senate, 88th Cong., 1st Sess. (U.S. Government Printing Office, 1963), 693.

296 **Brimmer's daughter, Esther, says:** Esther Brimmer, interview by the author, March 3, 2023.

297 **In response, New York banks:** "Bank Credit to Foreigners," *Federal Reserve Bulletin* 51, no. 3 (1965): 361–63.

297 **In the early 1950s:** "Tables and Statistical Material on U.S. Balance of Trade and Balance of Payments," Committee on Finance, U.S. Senate, Dec. 1974, 27.

297 **In April 1965:** "Investments Abroad Reduced, Commerce Aid [*sic*] Asserts," *Chicago Tribune,* April 21, 1965, sec. 3, p. 5.

298 **"got all the cream but did none of the work":** Quoted in Ian M. Kerr, *A History of the Eurobond Market: The First 21 Years* (Euromoney Publications, 1984), 17. Kerr's book has also been an incredibly useful summary of the early years of the eurobond markets.

298 **So Europeans cut the Americans out:** Stanislas M. Yassukovich, *Two Lives: A Social and Financial Memoir* (Austin Macauley, 2016), 201.

298 **In July 1963, S. G. Warburg & Company:** Kerr, *Eurobond Market,* 11.

299 **In 1963, there was a total:** Kerr, *Eurobond Market,* 30–31.

299 **American Cyanamid, a chemical manufacturer:** Kerr, *Eurobond Market,* 22.

299 **According to Brimmer's account:** Brimmer, interview by David Small et al., 122.

300 **The concern at the time:** Telephone Conversation 9609, Sound Recording, LBJ and SYLVIA PORTER, 12/2/1966, 12:29 PM, LBJ Presidential Library, www.discoverlbj.org/item/tel-09609.

300 **"If I send you over to the Board":** Andrew Brimmer, "Politics and Monetary Policy: My Appointment as Member Board of Governs [*sic*] of the Federal Reserve" (handwritten draft), Dec. 2009, Andrew Brimmer Papers, box 426, folder 13.

301 **The editor was a page short:** "The Editors: Christopher Fildes, 1969 to 1972," *Euromoney,* Jan. 4, 2019, www.euromoney.com/article/b1cjr33lj5p890/the-editors-christopher-fildes-1969-to-1972.

301 **"Why come to London to look":** "The Moorgate Saga," *Euromoney* 1, no. 1 (1969): 34.

301 **But in 1969, Milton Friedman published:** Milton Friedman, "The Euro-Dollar Market: Some First Principles," *Federal Reserve Bank of St. Louis Review* 53, no. 7 (1971): 16–24.

302 **A memo from 1971:** Milton Gilbert, *Joint Supervision of the Euro-Currency Market* (Bank for International Settlements, 1970), Arthur F. Burns Papers, box B34, folder "Eurodollars, 1970–73 (3)," Gerald R. Ford Library, 2, www.fordlibrarymuseum.gov/library/document/0001/324359065.pdf.

302 **There were nine American bank branches:** Kerr, *History of the Eurobond Market,* 29.

303 **In 1964, American bank subsidiaries:** John M. Lee, "London's City: It's Not the Same," *New York Times,* May 23, 1971, sec. F, p. 1; Gilbert, *Joint Supervision of the Euro-Currency Market,* 4.

303 **Since the Depression, the Fed had set:** "Requiem for Regulation Q: What It Did and Why It Passed Away," *Federal Reserve Bank of St. Louis Review* 68, no. 2 (1986): 22–37.

303 **American banks borrowed eurodollars in London:** Andrew F. Brimmer, "Euro-Dollar Flows and the Efficiency of U.S. Monetary Policy" (speech, Conference on Wall Street and the Economy '69, New School for Social Research, New York, March 8, 1969), 2, fraser.stlouisfed.org/title/statements-speeches-andrew-f-brimmer-463/euro-dollar-flows-efficiency-us-monetary-policy-10359.

304 **In 1964, head offices:** Andrew F. Brimmer and Frederick R. Dahl, "Growth of American International Banking: Implications for Public Policy," *Journal of Finance* 30, no. 2 (1975): 345; the numbers are slightly different but show a comparable

growth and magnitude in Gilbert, *Joint Supervision of the Euro-Currency Market,* table, "Estimated Net Amount of Euro-Dollar Credit Outstanding Through Banks in Eight European Countries, 1964–70," n.p.

304 **Then the Fed increased:** Raymond E. Owens and Stacey L. Schreft, "Identifying Credit Crunches," *Contemporary Economic Policy* 13, no. 2 (1995): 63.

304 **Herbie was not the only American:** United States Federal Open Market Committee, "Memorandum of Discussion," Minutes, Federal Open Market Committee, July 15, 1969, 20–22, fraser.stlouisfed.org/title/federal-open-market-committee-meeting-minutes-transcripts-documents-677/meeting-july-15-1969-22954/content/pdf/fomcmod19690715.

305 **What eventually slowed the flow:** Allan H. Meltzer, *A History of the Federal Reserve,* vol. 2, book 1, *1951–1969* (University of Chicago Press, 2009), 568; vol. 2, book 2, *1970–1986* (University of Chicago Press, 2009), 740–41.

305 **Eric Helleiner, a political scientist:** Helleiner, *States and the Reemergence of Global Finance,* 81–82.

305 **In 1969, Andrew Brimmer began building:** Andrew F. Brimmer, "The Tasks of Monetary Management," *Euromoney* 2, no. 2 (1970): 21–25; Brimmer, "Euro-Dollar Flows and the Efficiency of U.S. Monetary Policy."

306 **Arthur Burns, an adviser to Nixon:** "Nomination of Arthur F. Burns: Hearing Before the Committee on Banking and Currency, United States Senate, Ninety-First Congress, First Session, Dec. 18, 1969" (Washington, D.C.: U.S. Government Printing Office, 1969).

306 **"Lenders are already allocating credit":** "Credit in the 'Right' Places," *Wall Street Journal,* March 31, 1970, 20.

307 **Brimmer knew at the time:** See Andrew F. Brimmer, "Central Banking and Credit Allocation" (speech, W. H. Irons Memorial Lecture Series, Bureau of Business Research, Graduate School of Business, University of Texas at Austin, April 4, 1975), The author has only been able to find the speech in hard copy saved with the Andrew Brimmer Papers, box 286, folder 8.

307 **Major newspapers and wire services:** See, for example, Lindsay Arthur, "Production Dip Fails to Hold Down Prices," *San Francisco Examiner,* April 1, 1970, 66; "Reserve Plan to Channel Money," *Oakland Tribune,* April 1, 1970, 13; UPI, "Fed Member Would Divert Loan Money," *Modesto Bee,* April 1, 1970, 48; "Sweeping Change Suggested in Federal Monetary Policy," *Lincoln Star,* April 2, 1970, 36; Hobart Rowan for *The Washington Post,* "Fed's Brimmer Proposes Bank Loan End-Use Control," *Boston Globe,* April 2, 1970, 35; Edwin Dale for *The New York Times,* "Money Policy Change Asked," *Atlanta Constitution,* April 2, 1970, 61.

307 **But the Nixon administration was refusing:** Senator William Proxmire Collection, Wisconsin Historical Society, Press Releases, File 1, 1970, content.wisconsinhistory.org/digital/collection/proxmire/id/9474/rec/18; Proxmire Collection, U.S. Sena-

tor William Proxmire reports to you from Washington, 1964–1977, Jan. 1970, content.wisconsinhistory.org/digital/collection/proxmire/id/4833/rec/28.

307 **After reading Brimmer's speech:** *The President's New Economic Program: Hearings Before the Joint Economic Committee*, Part 1, Aug. 19, 20, and 23, 1971 (U.S. Government Printing Office, 1971), 469.

308 **"split wide open":** Brimmer, interview by David Small et al., 205; Meltzer, *History of the Federal Reserve,* vol. 2, 568.

308 **Darryl Francis, president of the Federal Reserve Bank:** Darryl R. Francis, "Social Priorities and the Market Allocation of Credit" (speech, 13th Commercial Bank Management Program Sponsored by the Graduate School of Business, Columbia University, New York, Nov. 8, 1970), fraser.stlouisfed.org/title/statements-speeches-darryl-r-francis-481/social-priorities-market-allocation-credit-18606; Darryl R. Francis, "Social Priorities and the Market Allocation of Credit" (speech, College of Business and Industry, Mississippi State University, State College, Feb. 23, 1971), fraser.stlouisfed.org/title/statements-speeches-darryl-r-francis-481/social-priorities-market-allocation-credit-18609. Francis's arguments also offer a frame-for-frame version of what Albert O. Hirschman would later call the arguments of perversity, futility, and jeopardy in *The Rhetoric of Reaction* (Harvard University Press, 1991).

308 **David Eastburn, president of the Philadelphia Fed:** David P. Eastburn, "Federal Reserve Policy & Social Priorities" (speech, Money Marketers of New York University, Bankers Club, New York City, Oct. 8, 1970), fraser.stlouisfed.org/title/statements-speeches-david-p-eastburn-4125/federal-reserve-policy-social-priorities-495579.

308 **"most intense":** Brimmer, interview by David Small et al., 205; Meltzer, *History of the Federal Reserve,* vol. 2, 568.

308 **Proxmire opened the hearings:** "Selective Credit Policies and Wage-Price Stabilization: Hearings on S. 1201 and H.R. 4246" (U.S. Government Printing Office, 1971), 1–3.

309 **Memos from around the same time:** See Robert Holland to Burns, Memorandum, Oct. 5, 1971, Burns Papers, box B14, fraser.stlouisfed.org/archival-collection/papers-arthur-burns-1193/memorandum-robert-holland-arthur-burns-3544, in which Holland warns Burns that any attempts at selective credit controls "could prove highly upsetting to the financial community." American Bankers Association quotation in "Selective Credit Policies," 151–52.

309 **Burns pulled what looks like a sleight of hand:** "Selective Credit Policies," 35.

310 **After Burns's testimony, the financial papers:** Burns likely also knew that the papers would run with his first statement on the subject, since journalists often begin writing as they are handed hard copies of prepared remarks. His first statement on Brimmer's proposal was that the board was unanimously against it.

310 **"Mr. Burns Buys Some Time":** All newspaper quotations from clippings preserved in Brimmer Papers, box 244, folder 7.

310 **He also began to talk:** Brimmer, "Commercial Bank Lending and Monetary Management."

311 **In the fight over the bill:** See, for example, Francis, "Social Priorities and the Market Allocation of Credit," Feb. 23, 1971; "Social Priorities for Loans," *Wall Street Journal,* April 28, 1971, 20; Holland to Burns, Oct. 5, 1971.

311 **On Friday, August 13, 1971:** Arthur Burns, *Transcript of Arthur F. Burns' Handwritten Journals January 20, 1969–July 25, 1974,* Journal II (Blue Notebook), 1, accession 2006-NLF-057, Gerald R. Ford Presidential Library & Museum, online at https://www.fordlibrarymuseum.gov/sites/default/files/pdf_documents/library/document/0428/burnstranscript2.pdf; Folder "President Richard Nixon's Daily Diary August 1–15, 1971," box RC-8, Office of Presidential Papers and Archives, Richard Nixon Presidential Library, www.nixonlibrary.gov/sites/default/files/virtuallibrary/documents/PDD/1971/057%20August%201-15%201971.pdf.

312 **The balance of payments:** *Tables and Statistical Material on U.S. Balance of Trade and Balance of Payments, Committee on Finance, United States Senate* (Government Printing Office, 1974), 1.

312 **In 1965, Federal Reserve banks:** Regan, "Report to the Congress," 205.

313 **"benign neglect":** Quoted in James, *International Monetary Cooperation,* 212.

314 **At the same time, inflation:** U.S. Bureau of Labor Statistics, Consumer Price Index for All Urban Consumers: All Items in U.S. City Average [CPIAUCNS], retrieved from FRED, Federal Reserve Bank of St. Louis, accessed June 16, 2024, fred.stlouisfed.org/series/CPIAUCNS; Board of Governors of the Federal Reserve System (US), Capacity Utilization: Total Index [TCU], retrieved from FRED, Federal Reserve Bank of St. Louis, accessed June 16, 2024, fred.stlouisfed.org/series/TCU; U.S. Bureau of Economic Analysis, Contributions to percent change in real gross domestic product: Government consumption expenditures and gross investment: Federal: National defense [A824RY2Q224SBEA], retrieved from FRED, Federal Reserve Bank of St. Louis, accessed June 16, 2024, fred.stlouisfed.org/series/A824RY2Q224SBEA; U.S. Bureau of Economic Analysis, Contributions to percent change in real gross domestic product: Government consumption expenditures and gross investment: Federal: Nondefense [A825RY2Q224SBEA], retrieved from FRED, Federal Reserve Bank of St. Louis, accessed June 16, 2024, fred.stlouisfed.org/series/A825RY2Q224SBEA; Board of Governors of the Federal Reserve System (US), Federal Funds Effective Rate [DFF], retrieved from FRED, Federal Reserve Bank of St. Louis, accessed June 16, 2024, fred.stlouisfed.org/series/DFF.

314 **"elephant in the room":** Michael Bordo, "The Imbalances of the Bretton Woods System from 1965 to 1973: U.S. Inflation, the Elephant in the Room," NBER Working Paper Series, Dec. 2018.

315 **It's possible the Nixon administration's:** James, *International Monetary Cooperation,* 218.

315 **But as London traders began to sell:** Samuel Montagu and Co., "Bullion," *Euromoney* 3, no. 5 (1971): 59.

315 **The subcommittee offered a familiar list:** *Action Now to Strengthen the Dollar: Report, Together with Minority Views* (U.S. Government Printing Office, 1971), www.jec.senate.gov/reports/92nd%20Congress/Action%20Now%20to%20Strengthen%20the%20US%20Dollar%20(517).pdf.

315 **"The President explained that he had":** "Transcript of Arthur F. Burns' Handwritten Journals, January 20, 1969–July 25, 1974," 5, Ford Library, www.fordlibrarymuseum.gov/library/document/0428/burnstranscript2.pdf.

317 **"I feel that my competitors":** Evan G. Galbraith, "Alternatives to Euromarket Controls," *Euromoney* 3, no. 5 (1971): 30. The author feels compelled to mention that he once worked as a crew member on a boat where Evan Galbraith was a frequent guest, but didn't understand what Galbraith actually did for a living until decades later, when the name popped up in research for this book.

318 **Perry Mehrling calls the money view:** See Mehrling, *New Lombard Street;* and Perry Mehrling, "'Where's My Swap Line?': A Money View of International Lender of Last Resort," *Jahrbuch für Wirtschaftsgeschichte,* vol. 62, no. 2 (2022): 559–74.

318 **Recently a group of political economists:** Benjamin Braun, Arie Krampf, and Steffen Murau, "Financial Globalization as Positive Integration: Monetary Technocrats and the Eurodollar Market in the 1970s," *Review of International Political Economy* 28, no. 4 (2021): 794–819, doi.org/10.1080/09692290.2020.1740291.

319 **In the summer of 1973:** M. S. Mendelsohn, "Oil, Payments, and the Exchanges," *Euromoney* 5, no. 7 (1973): 29–31.

320 **The United States was actively hostile:** Helleiner, *States and the Reemergence of Global Finance,* 111–12.

320 **David Spiro, a political scientist:** David Spiro, *The Hidden Hand of American Hegemony: Petrodollar Recycling and International Markets* (Cornell University Press, 1999), 59.

322 **In his folder on the bill:** Brimmer Papers, box 244, folder 7.

322 **In an economic letter that September:** Verle B. Johnston, "Allocating Credit," *Economic Letter* (Federal Reserve Bank of San Francisco), Sept. 6, 1974, fraser.stlouisfed.org/title/economic-letter-federal-reserve-bank-san-francisco-4960/allocating-credit-527163; Jeffrey M. Bucher, "A Firm No to Credit Allocation" (speech, Fall Conference of the Robert Morris Associates, Atlanta, Nov. 12, 1974), fraser.stlouisfed.org/title/statements-speeches-jeffrey-m-bucher-931/a-firm-credit-allocation-36193.

323 **"If central bankers could earn":** "Bucking the Credit Managers," *Wall Street Journal,* Aug. 19, 1974, sec. 1.

323 **In an interview decades later:** Burns, *Transcript of Arthur F. Burns' Handwritten Journals,* 41–44; Brimmer, interview by David Small et al., 195.

323 **In December 1974, he gave a speech:** Andrew F. Brimmer, "Central Banking and Credit Allocation."

323 **In 1980, Brimmer & Company:** Brimmer & Company, "Monetary Policy, Interest Rates, and Credit Allocation for Small Business," for the U.S. Small Business Administration, Aug. 29, 1980. Located in hard copy in the Brimmer Papers, box 308, folder 11.

324 **Milton Friedman thought the resolution:** Milton Friedman, "Monetary Policy: Theory and Practice," *Journal of Money, Credit, and Banking* 14, no. 1 (1982): 98–118, doi.org/10.2307/1991496.

324 **All the new definitions of new aggregates:** James L. Pierce, "The Myth of Congressional Supervision of Monetary Policy," *Journal of Monetary Economics* 4, no. 2 (1978): 363–70, doi.org/10.1016/0304-3932(78)90014-4.

EPILOGUE

330 **In 2016, Americans handed over cash:** Berhan Bayeh et al., *2025 Findings from the Diary of Consumer Payment Choice* (Federal Reserve Financial Services, 2025).

330 **In 2014, there was $1.3 trillion:** "Currency in Circulation: Value," Board of Governors of the Federal Reserve System, accessed Sept. 3, 2025, www.federalreserve.gov/paymentsystems/coin_currcircvalue.htm.

331 **60 percent of all U.S. currency:** Ruth Judson, "Demand for U.S. Banknotes at Home and Abroad: A Post-Covid Update," *Board of Governors of the Federal Reserve System International Finance Discussion Papers,* no. 1387 (March 2024): 1–42, doi.org/10.17016/ifdp.2024.1387.

331 **Hundred-dollar bills have become an export:** Binyamin Appelbaum made the same argument in "America's Most Profitable Export: Money," *New York Times,* March 9, 2019.

331 **Renminbi growth has plateaued:** Serkan Arslanalp et al., "The Stealth Erosion of Dollar Dominance: Active Diversifiers and the Rise of Nontraditional Reserve Currencies," *IMF Working Papers* 2022, no. 058 (2022).

332 **foreign commercial banks held $13 trillion:** Iñaki Aldasoro et al., "Global Banks' Dollar Funding Needs and Central Bank Swap Lines," *BIS Bulletin,* no. 27 (July 2020).

333 **Work by the economist Gita Gopinath:** "World Trade Statistics 2024," World Trade Organization, accessed Sept. 3, 2025, www.wto.org/english/res_e/statis_e/world_trade_statistics_e.htm; Gopinath et al., "Dominant Currency Paradigm."

333 **Of all the bonds issued:** "Amounts Outstanding of Debt Securities Issued in International Markets by Residents of All Countries Excluding Residents of All Issuers,"

Bank for International Settlements, International Debt Securities (BIS-Compiled), accessed Sept. 4, 2025, data.bis.org/topics/IDS.

334 **By the end of the global financial crisis:** "Central Bank Liquidity Swaps," Board of Governors of the Federal Reserve System, accessed Sept. 4, 2025, www.federalreserve.gov/monetarypolicy/bst_liquidityswaps.htm.

334 **When things calmed down:** Board of Governors of the Federal Reserve System (US), Assets: Central Bank Liquidity Swaps: Central Bank Liquidity Swaps: Wednesday Level [SWPT], retrieved from FRED, Federal Reserve Bank of St. Louis, accessed June 19, 2024, fred.stlouisfed.org/series/SWPT.

335 **If you make a dollar:** Again here we've arrived at Hyman Minsky's rule, "Everyone can create money; the problem is to get it accepted," in *Stabilizing an Unstable Economy,* 228. The author agonized over whether to explain Minsky's work in the main text of this book, and eventually decided it was one theorist too many for the trade press.

336 **The political sociologist Greta Krippner:** Greta Krippner, *Capitalizing on Crisis* (Harvard University Press, 2011).

336 **My first job out of college:** "Bayerische Landesbank to Cut One-Third of Work Force," *New York Times,* Dec. 1, 2008.

336 **Adam Tooze, a financial historian:** Adam Tooze, *Crashed: How a Decade of Financial Crises Changed the World* (Viking, 2018).

338 **By April 2020 the Fed held:** "Swap Lines Curbed Global Dollar Shortages, Appreciation During COVID-19 Crisis," accessed June 19, 2024, www.dallasfed.org/research/economics/2024/0521.

338 **The political scientist Eric Helleiner:** Eric Helleiner, *The Status Quo Crisis* (Oxford University Press, 2014).

339 **Anthropologists tend to rely:** Karl Polanyi, "The Economy as Instituted Process," in *Trade and Market in the Early Empires,* ed. Karl Polanyi, Conrad M. Arensberg, and Harry W. Pearson (Free Press, 1957), 243–69.

340 **During the pandemic, when Congress:** Brendan Greeley, "Millions of Americans Face Crisis Payment Delays," *Financial Times,* April 11, 2020.

342 **They did find, however, that states:** Lei Li and Philip Strahan, "Who Supplies PPP Loans (and Does It Matter): Banks, Relationships, and the Covid Crisis," NBER Working Paper Series no. 28286, Dec. 2020.

342 **Even after the second round closed:** *FDIC Community Banking Study* (Federal Deposit Insurance Corporation, 2020), vii.

342 **It is one of the many small businesses:** Much of the reporting in this section is adapted from Brendan Greeley, "How US Community Banks Became 'Irreplaceable' in the Pandemic," *Financial Times,* Aug. 29, 2021.

Index

About the Author

BRENDAN GREELEY has spent twenty years as a journalist, covering economic and monetary policy. He was the U.S. economics editor at the *Financial Times,* where he is still a regular contributor. Before that, he was a staff writer for *Bloomberg Businessweek* and *The Economist,* as well as an anchor and correspondent for Bloomberg TV. He has written for *The New York Times, The New York Times Magazine, The Washington Post, Los Angeles Times,* and *The Wall Street Journal Europe.* He is currently completing a PhD in financial history at Princeton University and lives in Annapolis, Maryland, with his family.